RE-PRESENTING DISABILITY

What part might museums play in reframing the ways in which society perceives and understands disability? What ethical, interpretive and pragmatic challenges are generated by museums' attempts to redress the invisibility of disabled people in their narratives and how might these be overcome? How are increasing interactions between museums and disability constituencies (activists, community groups, disability studies scholars) generating both new opportunities to engage visitors and new insights into collections and, at the same time, demanding and creating new forms of museum practice?

This volume brings together an international group of academics and professionals whose recent scholarship and practice addresses these under-researched but increasingly pressing questions. It addresses gaps in both the museum studies and disability studies fields. While a growing body of literature in museum studies has explored issues of representation pertaining to groups whose histories have been excluded or marginalized, this is the first comprehensive international analysis and exploration of the treatment of disability-related narratives in museums and galleries. Similarly, while the burgeoning field of disability studies includes investigations of representational practices within film, television, journalism, literature, and charity advertising, the museum as both a site of exclusion and a site for the staging of interventions intended to elicit support for disability rights has been largely overlooked. *Re-Presenting Disability: Activism and Agency in the Museum* is an invaluable volume for researchers, practitioners and students interested in the social role of museums; disability; and representation and identity.

Richard Sandell is Director and Head of the School of Museum Studies at the University of Leicester.

Jocelyn Dodd is Director of the Research Centre for Museums and Galleries (RCMG) in the School of Museum Studies at the University of Leicester.

Rosemarie Garland-Thomson is Professor of Women's Studies at Emory University in Atlanta, Georgia.

D1355181

(Photo: Julian Anderson)

RE-PRESENTING DISABILITY

Activism and agency in the museum

Edited by
Richard Sandell, Jocelyn Dodd,
Rosemarie Garland-Thomson

Routledge
Taylor & Francis Group

LONDON AND NEW YORK

TO NICKI, JONATHAN AND THE ARTISTS AND SUBJECTS OF DISABILITY ART

First published 2010
by Routledge
2 Park Square, Milton Park, Abingdon, OX14 4RN

Simultaneously published in the USA and Canada
by Routledge
270 Madison Ave, New York, NY 10016

Routledge is an imprint of the Taylor & Francis Group, an informa business

© 2010 Richard Sandell, Jocelyn Dodd, Rosemarie Garland-Thomson,
editorial and selection matter; individual chapters, the contributors

Typeset in Garamond by Taylor & Francis Books
Printed and bound in Great Britain by TJ International Ltd, Padstow,
Cornwall

British Library Cataloguing in Publication Data
A catalogue record for this book is available from the British Library

Library of Congress Cataloging in Publication Data
Re-presenting disability : activism and agency in the museum / edited by
Richard Sandell, Jocelyn Dodd, Rosemarie Garland-Thomson. -- 1st ed.
p. cm.
Includes bibliographical references and index.
1. Museums--Social aspects. 2. Museum techniques--Social aspects.
3. Museum exhibits. 4. Museum visitors. 5. Disability studies.
6. People with disabilities--History. 7. People with disabilities--Public
opinion. 8. People with disabilities–Political activity. 9. Agent
(Philosophy) 10. People with disabilities--Civil rights. I. Sandell,
Richard, 1967- II. Dodd, Jocelyn. III. Garland-Thomson, Rosemarie.
IV. Title: Representing disability.
AM7.R395 2010
069--dc22
2009028480

ISBN10: 0-415-49471-0 (hbk)
ISBN10: 0-415-49473-7 (pbk)

ISBN13: 978-0-415-49471-7 (hbk)
ISBN13: 978-0-415-49473-1 (pbk)

CONTENTS

LIST OF ILLUSTRATIONS

Figures

Colour Plates

Colour Plates can be found between pages 76 and 77

NOTES ON CONTRIBUTORS

Julie Anderson is a Research Associate at the Centre for the History of Science, Technology and Medicine and Wellcome Unit at the University of Manchester. She has written a number of articles on the history of disability and war, blindness, medical technologies and orthopaedics. She has published an edited collection (with Carsten Timmermann) on medical technologies in 2006 and her book (with John Pickstone), *Surgeons, Manufacturers and Patients: A Transatlantic History of Hip Replacement* was published in 2007. Her book, *The Soul of a Nation: Rehabilitation, Disability and the Second World War* will be published by Manchester University Press in 2010.

Joanna Besley is Senior Curator at the Museum of Brisbane in Queensland, Australia. She trained as an architect and is working on a PhD about the history of suburban home improvement and do-it-yourself activities. She publishes in both academic and popular publications. Her publications include (with Lisanne Gibson) *Monumental Queensland: Signposts on a Cultural Landscape* (University of Queensland Press, 2004), a book that explores the monuments and public artworks of Queensland and 'Hayes and Scott and the modest house' in *Hayes and Scott: post-war houses* (University of Queensland Press, 2005). Jo is interested in collaborative practice and working with the community to present exhibitions.

Ana Carden-Coyne is co-Director of the Centre for the Cultural History of War, University of Manchester, and co-founder of the Disability History Group, UK/Europe. She has published widely in books and journals on the cultural history of the body, war and sexuality, gender and commemoration. She co-edited *Cultures of the Abdomen: A History of Diet, Digestion and Fat in the Modern World* (with Christopher E. Forth, Palgrave, 2005), and a special edition of the *European Review of History* entitled 'Enabling the past: new perspectives in the history of disability' with Julie Anderson (2007). She is the author of *Reconstructing the Body: Classicism, Modernism and the First World War* (Oxford University Press, 2009).

Emma Chambers is a curator at University College London Art Collections, which holds the collections of the Slade School of Fine Art. Her research interests include art and medicine, art education, early twentieth-century British art and nineteenth-century print culture. Recent articles include 'Fragmented identities: reading subjectivity in Henry Tonks' surgical portraits', *Art History* (2009), and 'Redefining history painting in the academy', *Visual Culture in Britain* (2005). Catalogues include a history and collections guide to UCL Art Collections (2008), a complete catalogue of the Slade painting collection (2005), and exhibition catalogues of the work of Augustus John and William Orpen (2004) and Henry Tonks (2002).

Chia-Li Chen is an assistant professor at the Graduate Institute of Museum Studies, Taipei National University of the Arts, Taiwan. She is the author of *Wound on Exhibition: Notes on Memory and Trauma* and co-editor of *Collecting: Nostalgia and Popular* (Artco Publisher, Taiwan). Her research interests focus on three main areas: museums and contemporary social issues, visitor studies and the history of community museums.

Geraldine Chimirri-Russell is an associate curator at The Nickle Arts Museum, University of Calgary and curates exhibitions on numismatics, art and ethnographic material. Her main focus of research and publication is in the examination of visuality in the ancient world using coinage, particularly those produced by Iron Age Celtic societies. By extension of this work she is also examining issues of interpretation of visual elements within the museum environment. Working with the museum's mandate she is broadening her research to include museum studies and is teaching courses on museum and heritage studies at the University of Calgary.

Kathryn Church is Associate Professor in the School of Disability Studies at Ryerson University, Toronto. Her research practice is an experiment in fusing ethnographic studies of ruling with arts-informed methods of representation. Kathryn is among a handful of academics who have documented the activist work of the Canadian psychiatric survivor movement. She consulted to the documentary film titled *Working Like Crazy* and has curated two exhibits, the more recent being *Out from Under: Disability, History and Things to Remember* (with Catherine Frazee and Melanie Panitch). Kathryn is author of *Forbidden Narratives: Critical Autobiography as Social Science* and co-editor of *Learning through Community*.

Jocelyn Dodd is Director of the Research Centre for Museums and Galleries (RCMG) in the School of Museum Studies at the University of Leicester. She has co-directed a number of research projects focused on disability issues including *Buried in the Footnotes: the representation of disabled people in museum and gallery collections* (2004) which was funded through an Innovation Award from the Arts and Humanities Research Board and the action research project which followed this, *Rethinking Disability*

Representation in Museum and Galleries (2006–9) which was funded by the Heritage Lottery Fund and National Endowment for Science, Technology and the Ats. Her research interests focus on the social role and agency of museums, museums and galleries as learning environments and, in particular, the impact museum experiences have on visitors and project participants.

Catherine Frazee is a Professor of Distinction in the School of Disability Studies at Ryerson University and Co-director of the Ryerson-RBC Institute for Disability Studies Research and Education. As a writer, educator and activist with particular interest in disability culture and resistance, her work is informed by life experience as a disabled woman and by varied and long-standing involvements in the equality struggles of marginalized groups in Canada.

Rosemarie Garland-Thomson is Professor of Women's Studies at Emory University in Atlanta, Georgia. Her fields of study are feminist theory, American literature, and disability studies. She is the author of *Staring: How We Look* (Oxford University Press, 2009) and *Extraordinary Bodies: Figuring Physical Disability in American Literature and Culture* (Columbia University Press, 1997), editor of *Freakery: Cultural Spectacles of the Extraordinary Body* (NYU Press, 1996), and co-editor of *Disability Studies: Enabling the Humanities* (MLA Press, 2002). She is currently writing a book called *Cure or Kill: The Cultural Logic of Euthanasia*, which traces eugenic thought through American literature.

Helen Graham is currently a Research Associate at the International Centre for Cultural and Heritage Studies (ICCHS) at Newcastle University and also holds a Visiting Research Fellowship in the Faculty of Health and Social Care at The Open University. Before joining ICCHS, Helen co-ordinated the Croydon-based 'History of Day Centres for People with Learning Disabilities' project and has also worked in learning and access roles at Museums Sheffield, Glasgow Museums and the National Maritime Museum, Greenwich. Her current research focuses on the intersection between social policy and museums and on theories and practices of participative curation and research.

Lain Hart received a Master of Arts in Museum Anthropology from Columbia University, and a Diploma in Asian Art History from the British Museum. He has conducted fieldwork in Thailand and Cambodia and now lives in San Francisco.

Tari Hartman Squire's EIN SOF Communications is a strategic marketing, PR and accessible event production firm specializing in disability, diversity and public policy, working with arts and disability organizations, corporations, foundations, and the media.   Her award-winning MY LEFT FOOT promotion launched disability niche marketing as a genre. Clients include AT&T; U.S. Holocaust Memorial Museum; Smithsonian Institution's Accessibility Program; Kennedy Center's Leadership Exchange in Arts & Disability; McDonald's; HSC Foundation; UCLA Leadership Institute for Managers with Disabilities. With strategic partner Nielsen NRGi, they created 'Disability Community Market Research Initiatives' to build disability community business cases for employment and marketing.

David Hevey is an award-winning director, screenwriter and photographer. He directs innovative and critically acclaimed films and television and has shot photographic portraits for LA Movieline and Timelife. He has written and directed eleven films for BBC2, on landmark series like *Modern Times* and *The Disabled Century*. He is the author of *The Creatures Time Forgot: Photography and Disability Imagery* (Routledge 1992). He is currently concentrating on directing and screenwriting.

Heather Hollins is the Learning and Access Manager for Museums Luton and is currently studying for a PhD, which focuses on creating a dialogue with young disabled people to challenge access issues. Her research draws on emancipatory research methodologies from the field of disability studies to enable an analysis of the institutional power structures that contribute to disabled people's exclusion from museums. She is also an Associate Tutor with the School of Museum Studies at the University of Leicester.

Sarah Jacobs is the Curator of the Museum of Sex in New York and, during her tenure, has worked over twelve exhibitions and online installations. She has been featured in the *New York Times, New York Post, El Diario, Time Out New York, Art Daily, I-D, Sculpture*, and *New Scientist* and has spoken about sex and sexuality for a wide range of conferences, documentaries and television programming. She holds a MA in Anthropology from the New School University and a BA in Anthropology from Connecticut College. Her research has focused on gender issues in Latin America, primarily in Mexico and Venezuela.

Debbie Jolly is a freelance disabled researcher and activist. She has written and presented widely on disability issues, has worked with government and non-governmental organizations, within universities, and with organizations of disabled people in both the UK and Europe to further the disability rights agenda. Advocacy and project areas have included de-institutionalization, health services, transport, employment, discriminatory attitudes and the Disability Equality Duty. Debbie has contributed to a number of international research projects and authored key papers on the right of disabled people to independent living. She is on the editorial board of the international journal *Disability and Society*.

Ceri Jones is a Research Associate with the Research Centre for Museums and Galleries (RCMG), based in the School of Museum Studies,

University of Leicester. Since joining RCMG in 2002 she has been involved in a number of projects around learning and the social role of museums, including *Rethinking Disability Representation* where she was primarily involved in the analysis and interpretation of visitor responses. She is also currently studying for a PhD in Museum Studies.

Phaedra Livingstone is Assistant Professor of Museum Studies in the Arts and Administration graduate program at the University of Oregon. Her research interests include museum interpretation and representation practices, museum management and social inclusion, critical museology and visitor studies. Before joining the University of Oregon, she was Research Coordinator at the Centre for Voluntary Sector Studies, Ryerson University. Her training includes a PhD in Curriculum Studies (Museum Learning), a Master of Museum Studies, a BA in Anthropology from the University of Toronto, and a post-doctoral research fellowship with the University of British Columbia. She has worked in the museum field since 1990.

Carol Low comes to the museum field with a community work and education background. Through her community consultations she became further committed to bringing forward stories of those not generally represented in museums. Carol's core interest is in the potential for reconciliation and healing via museums and other public memory sites. Her Masters studies addressed meaning-making amongst South Africans visiting Holocaust memorial sites. Pertinent publications include 'Taking to the Streets – review of Museum of Brisbane exhibition' for *Queensland Review* (2007) and 'Lwandle Migrant Labour Museum South Africa: Just how responsible is a museum to its local community?' for *Museums Australia* (May 2007).

Hanna Mellemsether is research coordinator at Trøndelag Folkemuseum in Trondheim, Norway, and is responsible for establishing and developing the new Norwegian Museum of Deaf History and Culture. She has a PhD in history from The Norwegian University of Technology and Science (NTNU) and has published research on women's history and African history. She has also been a lecturer in museology at NTNU.

Elizabeth Mariko Murray is the Collections Manager at the Museum of Sex in New York. She has completed graduate coursework in Museum Anthropology at Columbia University and holds a BA in Anthropology from the University at Albany, with a double minor in Psychology and Women's Studies. Originally trained as an archaeologist, she continues to explore material culture through museum collections and has worked on projects at the American Museum of Natural History, the Kalaupapa National Historic Park Museum, and the Museum of Television and Radio. Her current research interests include the role of museums in public health and advocacy.

Lisa O'Sullivan is Senior Curator of Medicine at the Science Museum, London, and works with the Wellcome Collection held at the Museum. She was Head of Research for the *Brought to Life* project (www.science-museum.org.uk/broughttolife), an educational website which traces the history of medicine with a focus on its material culture, personal stories and broader social context. Her research interests include the material cultures of anatomical and anthropological research in the British and French empires; representations of the body within medicine; medical responses to homesickness and the transformation of clinical, particularly psychiatric, categories in different socio-political contexts.

Katherine Ott is a curator at the Smithsonian's National Museum of American History, in the Division of Medicine and Society where she works on the history of medicine, the body, disability and bodily differ-ence, among other things. She curated recent exhibitions on the history of polio, acupuncture, medical devices for altering the human body, and on the disability rights movement. She is the author of *Fevered Lives; Tuberculosis in American Culture since 1870* (1996) and co-editor of *Artificial Parts and Practical Lives, The Modern History of Prosthetics* (2002) and of *Scrapbooks in American Life* (2006). Katherine also teaches graduate courses on material culture at George Washington University. Her current project is on the history and culture of skin.

Melanie Panitch is Director of the School of Disability Studies at Ryerson University, Toronto, a position she has held since the School was founded in 1999, and Co-director of the Ryerson-RBC Institute for Disability Studies Research and Education. She is the author of *Disability, Mothers and Organization: Accidental Activists*, a history of activist mothering in the Canadian Association for Community Living (Routledge, 2008). She curated 'Out From Under: Disability, History and Things to Remember' (with Catherine Frazee and Kathryn Church). The exhibit received the 2008 City of Toronto Access and Human Rights Award and Ryerson University's 2009 Teaching Award for Innovation.

Victoria Phiri is a social anthropologist at Livingstone Museum in Zambia specializing in Ethnic Studies. She has done extensive research on tradi-tional cultures in the urban context of Zambia. She holds a Masters degree in Indigenous Studies from the University of Tromso in Norway.

Richard Sandell is Director and Head of the School of Museum Studies at the University of Leicester. He has been awarded research fellowships at the Smithsonian Institution (2004/5) and the Humanities Research Center of the Australian National University (2008) to pursue his research interests which focus on museums and human rights and the social agency and responsibility of museums. He is the editor of *Museums, Society, Inequality* (2002), author of *Museums, Prejudice and the Reframing of*

Difference (2007) and co-editor (with Robert R. Janes) of *Museum Management and Marketing* (2007), all published by Routledge.

Shari Rosenstein Werb worked at the U.S. Holocaust Memorial Museum from 1991 to 2008 creating educational and public programs about the Holocaust and its implications for today's world. As Director, Institutional Outreach, she created the Harriet McBryde Johnson program – an event that helped shape her thinking about accessibility, universal design, relevancy, and collaborations with the disability community. She is currently Director of Education and Outreach at the Smithsonian Institution's National Museum of Natural History. Ms Werb earned her MS in Leadership in Museum Education from Bank Street College in New York.

ACKNOWLEDGMENTS

We would like to express our thanks to the many people and organizations who, in different ways and over many years, have shaped our approach to this book including Sarah Ballard, Molly Barrett, Zelda Baveystock, Liz Braby, Paul Bewley, Ciara Canning, Debra Cox, Tracey Crawley, Megan de la Hunt, Anna Dolecka, Sean Dryden, Mark Edwards, Siobhan Edwards, Thomas Elwick, Jonathan Evans, John Ferry, Maureen Finn, Brendan Flynn, Mat Fraser, Steve Gardam, Jackie Gay, Sam Groves, Martyn Hale, Caireen Hart, Tony Heaton, Cassie Herschel-Shorland, David Hevey, Samantha Heywood, Tom Hodgson, Rachel Hurst, Claire Jacques, Robert Janes, Reyahn King, Christiane Kroebel, Kath Landthaller, Kylea Little, Rebecca McGinnis, Crawford McGugan, Vicky Mair, Janet Marstine, Philippa Massey, Kylie Message, Jane Montgomery, Sarah Ogilvie, Victoria Osborne, Mark O'Neill, Dan Phillips, Katie Potter, Emma Pybus, Kate Richardson, Sari Salovaara, Sarah Saville Evans, Rebecca Shawcross, Arlene Stein, Darren Stevens, Melissa Strauss, Mark Taylor, Caroline Turner, Diana Walters, Sophie Weaver, Marcus Weisen, Nancy Willis and Alisdair Wilson. Additional thanks to Peter Carney, Julian Anderson, Barbara Lloyd, Tom Partridge, Amy Jane Barnes, CLMG, SHAPE and the staff of Birmingham Museum and Art Gallery; Colchester and Ipswich Museums Service; Glasgow Museums; the Imperial War Museum, London; Royal London Hospital Archives and Museum; Stamford Museum; Tyne and Wear Museums; Northampton Museum and Art Gallery; and Whitby Museum.

Jocelyn Dodd and Richard Sandell are grateful to students and colleagues in the School of Museum Studies, University of Leicester for sharing thoughts and insights over many years and to the Heritage Lottery Fund, National Endowment for Science, Technology and the Arts and Humanities Research Council for their financial support of research projects on which chapters 1 and 7 in this volume draw.

Richard Sandell would like to thank the University of Leicester for study leave during 2009 and the Research School of Humanities, Australian National University, for the award of a research fellowship in 2008 that supported his ongoing research into museums and human rights.

Rosemarie Garland-Thomson would like to thank Carla Melissa Anderson, Doug Auld, Riva Leher and Chris Rush for contributing their work, and Dean Lisa Tedesco and Dean Robert Paul at Emory University.

Finally the editors are enormously grateful to Matt Gibbons, Lalle Pursglove, Andrew Watts, Olly Cooper and Robbie Cooke for their support, advice and encouragement throughout the process of bringing this volume to fruition.

PREFACE

Recent decades have witnessed an expansion of the ways in which disability and disabled people's lives and experiences are publicly portrayed. Profound changes brought about by new social movements during the second part of the twentieth century and the growing global influence of broader human rights discourses, have enabled cultural representations that permit more progressive ways of seeing and understanding disability to appear in many different contexts. These alternative depictions of disability have set out to supplant or subvert narrow, delimiting and oppressive modes of portrayal widely found across a range of cultural and media settings.

Museums have entered this arena rather belatedly and with some considerable caution. Although the last two decades have seen growing concern amongst practitioners for the development of more inclusive approaches to representation – addressing, in particular, the exclusion and marginalization of women, minority ethnic and indigenous communities – attempts to counter the under- and mis-representation of disabled people within museum narratives have, until recently, been rare. The last few years, however, have seen increasing interest in the potential that museums and galleries might hold as sites for the staging of interpretive interventions intended to offer visitors, and society more broadly, progressive ways of understanding disability, shaped by a concern for equality and social justice.

The 28 contributors to this volume – academics and researchers, cultural practitioners and activists – approach this under-researched topic from productively diverse and international perspectives, drawing on disciplines including disability studies, museum studies, art history, sociology and social anthropology, cultural and media studies and the history of science and medicine. This plurality of perspectives inevitably produces variety in the ways in which disability is discussed, chapters very often reflecting the climate of disability politics within the contexts they examine. While being mindful of the political implications of language use, we have nevertheless resisted a temptation to impose uniformity in style, opting instead to respect the ways in which different contributions draw on different linguistic conventions. Although contributors write from wide ranging perspectives they are nevertheless linked by a shared concern for the ways in which representational practices can be deployed to offer more respectful, egalitarian narratives of disability.

The chapters are organized into three main sections. *New Ways of Seeing* explores the potential for museums – as organizations with the capacity to offer credible, permissible, authentic cultural narratives – to reframe the ways in which audiences, and society more broadly, perceive, understand and engage with disability. Drawing on different disciplinary, institutional and cultural contexts, the chapters in this section examine the potential for the construction of new narratives through modes of representation which subvert, resist and reconfigure the ways in which disabled people have most often been portrayed.

Museums' attempts to represent disabled people in ways that embody (and seek to elicit support for) a particular moral and political standpoint underpinned by a concern for human rights generate a set of complex interpretive challenges for which there are rarely straightforward answers. The chapters in the second section – *Interpretive Journeys and Experiments* – explore ways in which museums have sought to respond to these representational challenges, many of which are uniquely relevant to disability but others of which resonate more broadly with attempts to construct more inclusive narratives.

The final section – *Unsettling Practices* – explores the ways in which increasing interactions between museums and disability constituencies (activists, community groups, disability studies scholars and so on) are generating new opportunities for institutions that are open to experimentation. At the same time these interactions are demanding (and sometimes creating) new ways of working. These new approaches can be energizing and creative but can also operate to unsettle, or at least call into question, existing museum practices in ways which those working in the institution can find challenging.

Interwoven throughout each of the three sections are the related themes of activism and agency. Contributors explore the opportunities and challenges presented by the museum's engagement with activist perspectives and practices – with attempts to elicit support for particular ways of understanding disability. Similarly, each chapter sheds light upon the agency of different constituencies in shaping new cultural narratives and the unique role that museums might play in framing and informing individual and collective social understandings of difference.

The interdisciplinary and international conversation that emerges will, we hope, not only generate new insights into a developing field of study but, as importantly, stimulate and inform experimental, ethically-informed practice in museums and galleries.

Richard Sandell
Jocelyn Dodd
Rosemarie Garland-Thomson

Part I

NEW WAYS OF SEEING

1

ACTIVIST PRACTICE

Richard Sandell and Jocelyn Dodd

There has long been a sense within the disability rights movement and amongst disability scholars that representation matters; that public portrayals of disabled people have effects and consequences which – though slippery, diffuse and difficult to trace – are nevertheless ubiquitous and capable of powerfully shaping disabled people's lives in innumerable and very tangible ways.[1] Alongside struggles for employment and education rights, access to public services, political participation and so on, activists have, for more than two decades, argued that cultural representations are *constitutive* as well as *reflective* of ways of seeing, thinking and talking about disability (Gartner and Joe 1987; Hevey 1992; Oliver 1996). These predominantly negative and damaging conceptions have, in turn, shaped public policy, approaches to education, employment and welfare; they have framed interactions between disabled and non-disabled people and provided the justification for continuing forms of prejudice, discrimination and oppression.

Meanwhile in museums, a similar concern for the social and political effects of representation has emerged over recent decades and underpinned widespread shifts in practice towards the development of more inclusive processes of exhibition-making and the portrayal of diverse communities in more respectful and equitable ways (Bennett 2006; Sandell 2007). Practitioners have become increasingly concerned to include – in collections, exhibitions and displays – the histories, experiences and voices of communities that have tended to be marginalised from mainstream museum narratives although portrayals of disabled people have, until quite recently, remained markedly absent (Sandell *et al.* 2005).

This chapter examines the emergence of what might be termed an *activist museum practice*, intended to construct and elicit support amongst audiences (and other constituencies) for alternative, progressive ways of thinking about disability. We begin by highlighting the intersecting forces and concerns emanating from the arenas of disability studies, disability politics and rights activism that have helped to shape the production and circulation, in recent years, of a more protean range of images of disabled people in the public sphere. We then consider three particularly high-profile cultural

3

representations of disabled figures in the US and UK, embodied in highly visible public sculptures and statues – the aims and intentions behind their creation and the controversies that characterized their reception – to shed light upon the constitutive potential of public portrayals of disability. These portrayals, as we shall see, hold the capacity to provoke (and inform) strong opinions and to generate sometimes fierce media debates. Drawing on our experiences as action researchers – working in collaboration with disabled activists and artists to explore new approaches to representing disability – the last part of the chapter considers the challenges and opportunities posed by the staging of socially purposeful, interpretive interventions within museums and galleries. Here we highlight the challenges – moral, political and pragmatic – that museums have encountered in exploring this new territory and discuss the ways in which these might be addressed through ethically and politically informed approaches to representation, interpretation and audience engagement.

Representations and rights

Matters of representation are intricately bound up with the broader struggle for disability rights, perhaps even more so than for other civil and human rights movements. Central to the achievement of disability rights has been a desire to bring about a widespread and radical shift in the way disability is conceived – away from 'the cultural assumption that disability is equated with dependency, invalidity and tragedy', to 'the political demand that disability be defined [...] in terms of social oppression, social relations and social barriers' (Shakespeare 2006: 31). The conceptual drive behind this shift emerged in the late 1960s and gained momentum through the 1970s and 1980s in the form of politically progressive, social-contextual accounts of disability – developed by disabled people – that offered a radical critique of individualist and medicalised ways of seeing. As disability scholars Barnes, Mercer and Shakespeare explained:

> By the beginning of the twentieth century, the individual approach to disability – which sees its diagnosis and solution in medical knowledge – was securely entrenched. The focus is on bodily 'abnormality', disorder or deficiency, and the way in which this in turn 'causes' some degree of 'disability' or functional limitation ... This forms the basis for a 'personal tragedy' approach, where the individual is regarded as a victim, and as someone who is in need of 'care and attention', and dependent on others....
>
> In developing what became known as a social approach to disability, disabled people in Britain argued that it is society which disables people with impairments, and therefore any meaningful

4

solution must be directed at social change rather than individual
adjustment and rehabilitation.

(1999: 21, 27)

As the rights movement gathered momentum, the dominance of portrayals
in popular and news media that reflected individualized and medicalized
conceptions of disability became an issue of growing concern for disability
scholars. Activists became increasingly interested in challenging representations which operated to constrain the rights movement and in seeking to
supplant them with alternative portrayals that subverted negative stereotypes
and resisted the conception of disability as personal tragedy (Barnes and
Mercer 2003; Oliver 1996).[2]

This concern for how disability has been portrayed – and the ways in
which such portrayals can operate to reinforce and shape prejudice or conversely to foster more respectful and equitable understandings of difference –
has underpinned a series of investigations and analyses of modes of representation across a range of media including film (Norden 1994), broadcast
and news media (Barnes 1992), literature (Garland Thomson 1997) and
charity advertising (Hevey 1992). These analyses have built a picture of what
Stuart Hall (in his analysis of racialised representations in western popular
culture) terms the 'dominant regime of representation'. For Hall a regime of
representation refers to 'the whole repertoire of imagery and visual effects
through which "difference" is represented at any one historical moment'
(1997: 232). A given regime may comprise protean, fluid and contradictory
depictions of difference but, at particular historical moments, can also be
understood to take on a prevailing character. As Jackie Gay argues:

> Disabled people throughout the world are engaged with a long and
> complicated struggle with the way we are portrayed and the mean-
> ings attached to these portrayals that include disability as stigma, as
> a sign of a damaged soul, as being less than human, as dependent,
> weak, sexless, valueless.
>
> (Gay with Fraser 2008: 21)

Victims, villains, freaks and heroes

A number of common strands and themes emerge from these wide ranging
analyses of representational systems and meanings. More than twenty years ago
Alan Gartner and Tom Joe, for example, highlighted the historical ubiquity
of 'disabling images' which function to dehumanize disabled people:

> Images of the disabled as either less or more than merely human can
> be found throughout recorded history. There is the blind soothsayer
> of ancient Greece, the early Christian belief in demonic possession of

the insane, the persistent theme in Judeo-Christian tradition that disability signifies a special relationship with God. The disabled are blessed or damned but never quite human.

(1987: 2)

A number of studies have also highlighted the prevalence of images which emphasize specific physical differences at the expense of all other traits and which function to construct some disabled individuals as the extreme Others, generally perceived to be beyond the range of ordinary human appearance. This process, which David Hevey has referred to as 'enfreakment', is not solely confined to the freakshows that flourished in the late nineteenth century, in which individuals perceived to possess unusual or inexplicable bodies performed for and were stared at by the paying public, but has been found in literature, popular culture and, in Hevey's own study, in charity advertising. Alongside and frequently interwoven with the images that dehumanise and enfreak are a series of recurring negative stereotypes – the disabled person as pitiable, pathetic, dependent and vulnerable; as evil, criminal or otherwise villainous; as sexless or sexually deviant. These pervasive modes of depiction have been found in studies of wide ranging media in the UK, US and beyond (Barnes 1992; Gartner and Joe 1987).

Alternative frames and narratives

As human rights discourses have gained increasing global influence, as the politics of difference has brought about greater sensitivity over depictions of a range of minorities, and as the disability rights movement has gathered momentum, so these pernicious stereotypes have become less publicly acceptable and widespread (though, in some settings, remarkably persistent). At the same time, however, some have argued that the sensibilities that led to the demise of images that overtly associate disability with tragedy, pity, villainy and deviance have paved the way for alternatives that – while they may be welcomed by contemporary mainstream audiences – have done little to lend support to the reconceptualization of disability fought for by the disability rights movement. Charles Riley II, in his analysis of popular media in the USA, for example, argues that contemporary news stories very often continue to construct disabled people through a narrow set of clichéd roles, but ones which foreground heroism and bravery as individuals strive towards 'a quality of life that is less disabled, more normal' (2005: x). These damaging depictions, he suggests, function to reassure, to inspire pity and condescending admiration, while reinforcing a sense of superiority amongst non-disabled audiences.

Recent years, then, have seen an unravelling of the regime of representation that has been understood to dominate and govern cultural portrayals of disabled people and to construct and foster discriminatory ways of understanding disability (Barnes and Mercer 2003: 98). While it would be inaccurate to suggest that disability narratives have been wholly transformed – that negatively stereotypical images have been replaced with images that disabled people have uniformly welcomed – the repertoire of images and the representations that circulate in the first part of the twenty-first century are undeniably more protean and nuanced in their portrayals than those which have tended to predominate in the past (Garland-Thomson, this volume). These diverse depictions present a more complex narrative of difference and, though welcomed by many, have very often generated fierce controversies which throw into relief the different values, priorities and perspectives underpinning alternative ways of understanding disability.

In this next part of the chapter we consider the controversies that accompanied the unveiling of three very different cultural representations of disabled figures in the UK and USA, each revealing of the ways in which portrayals in the public sphere operate to provoke, frame and inform conversations about difference (Sandell 2007). Moreover, the controversies evoke the climate surrounding disability politics at the start of the twenty-first century and the character of the debates with which the museums, to which we turn shortly, sought to engage.

The President, the artist and the prime minister

In 2001 a new 'room' was added to the Franklin Delano Roosevelt memorial in Washington DC which featured a bronze statue of the President using his wheelchair. Four years later, Marc Quinn's sculpture of the artist and disabled woman – entitled *Alison Lapper Pregnant* – was unveiled in London's Trafalgar Square. The following year, in March 2006, a statue of Winston Churchill, depicting the British prime minister in a straitjacket, was put on display in Norwich, England. These very different public representations of real disabled individuals were, of course, conceived, commissioned, produced, viewed and debated in very different contexts and circumstances. Nevertheless, there are marked similarities in the ways in which those responsible for bringing these statues and sculptures to fruition articulated their underlying motivations and intentions. Perhaps more significantly, there are similarities evident in the ways in which different constituencies have responded to these cultural interventions and the character of the media controversies that each generated.

'A nod to political correctness'

Controversy surrounding the FDR memorial began even before the dedication ceremony held on 2 May 1997. Rosemarie Garland Thomson describes the views of disability rights activists and disability studies scholars at that time:

[We] had wanted to avoid repeating the persistent stereotypes of disability – the ones that tell us that disability is a shameful personal problem relegated to the private realm of charity and medicine, but inappropriate in the public sphere. We had wanted the memorial to tell the story of a man who was both disabled by polio and president of the United States for 12 years. ... But the only statue that even remotely referred to FDR's disability showed him seated, covered by a cape, on a chair with small wheels barely peeking out.

(2001: B11)

Those who were critical of the original memorial argued that decisions regarding the manner in which the President would be represented should be informed, not by the social mores and perceptions of disability in FDR's time, but rather by the post-civil rights values of twenty-first-century America. Those who opposed a new addition to the memorial accused disability activists of political correctness, but the views of disability studies scholars and the threat of protests from activists at the dedication spurred President Clinton to put in place plans for a new statue – clearly showing FDR in his wheelchair – which was subsequently unveiled in 2001. This addition was viewed by many as an important achievement, a contribution to the development of a more progressive public understanding of disability; one which drew on the realities of FDR's lived experience but which was framed in ways that challenged rather than reinforced prevalent contemporary negative stereotypes.[3] As the Chairman and President of the National Organization on Disability which had lobbied for the inclusion of a statue clearly showing FDR in his wheelchair later responded to critics: 'The statue is by no means a nod to political correctness. Instead, it is the accurate portrayal of a man who used a wheelchair every day of his presidency' (Deland 2005: 9).

'A repellent artefact'

The sculpture depicting artist and disabled woman – 'Alison Lapper Pregnant' – by the (non-disabled) artist Marc Quinn generated a similarly fierce debate when it was unveiled in London's Trafalgar Square in 2005. One tabloid newspaper led with the headline 'Travulgar Square', claiming that 'the art world was in uproar' about this statue of 'an armless pregnant woman' (Kennedy 2004). The debate which unfolded in newspapers over the following days and months saw supporters of Quinn's statue praising the quality of the artwork and highlighting its potential to challenge viewers' preconceptions about disabled people as well as limited notions of beauty and sexuality, while critics attacked the piece as a politically correct 'drab monument to the backward pieties of our age' (O'Neill 2007). Interestingly several critics, and also members of the public debating the statue on the online pages of national newspapers, described the statue as 'disgusting' and 'repellent' but most were at pains to point out that their objections were levelled not at the subject – Alison Lapper – but at the artist and at the commissioning panel. For example, Robin Simon, editor of the *British Art Journal*, commented: 'I think it is horrible. Not because of the subject matter, I hasten to add. I have a lot of time for Alison Lapper. She is very brave. It is just a repellent artefact.'

In a similar vein, Brendan O'Neill (2007) wrote in the *Guardian* newspaper online:

> I've grown to loathe the Alison Lapper Pregnant statue (not Alison Lapper herself, please note, who I'm sure has overcome great challenges to become both an artist and a mother). ... It shows we value people for what they are rather than what they achieve. In our era of the politics of identity we seem more interested in celebrating individuals' fixed and quite accidental attributes – their ethnicity, cultural heritage or in Lapper's case, her disability – rather than what they have discovered or done in the world outside of their bodies. We prefer victims to heroes.

The critics, in their eagerness to distinguish between their views of the sculpture and their views of Alison Lapper, arguably reveal more about their personal (as well as prevailing social) attitudes to physical difference than they might acknowledge. Nevertheless, the comments are illustrative of the capacity for images that confront entrenched ways of seeing, to provoke strong opinions.

'Insulting', 'pathetic', 'appallingly bad taste'

The year after 'Alison Lapper Pregnant' was unveiled in London, a 9ft-high statue of Sir Winston Churchill in a straitjacket went on display in the centre of Norwich, a city in the east of England, again prompting outrage and debate in the news media. The charity responsible for commissioning the work – mental health charity Rethink – made strong claims regarding the agency of the statue which, a spokesperson stated, was designed 'in order to portray a more positive image of people with mental illness'. They added:

'The message we want to portray is that it is possible to recover from mental illness and overcome it and be successful – because Churchill is an example of someone who was able to do that.'

This time, opposition to the statue focused largely on the perceived inappropriateness of depicting 'a great leader' in this way (echoing some of the debate surrounding the FDR memorial) and critical comments in the media suggested that many felt explicit public acknowledgment of Churchill's experiences of mental ill health sat uneasily alongside the honouring of his heroism and leadership. Conservative MP Ann Widdecombe, for example, was quoted as saying, 'I only hope this will be treated with the contempt it deserves ... This is very distasteful. It is an insult to his memory. He should be respected. He is a hero' (Quinn 2006: 33).

The artists, activists, scholars, commissioning bodies, and politicians behind the sculptures and memorials that eventually appeared in Washington DC, Trafalgar Square and Norwich, expressed (albeit in different ways) their desire to counter, contest or subvert entrenched negative ways of seeing disability. Despite the socially purposeful ambitions with which each of the works was imbued (and in some instances, perhaps *because* of the explicitly social messages they were perceived to embody), the responses they inspired were far from consensual. Whilst many responses reflected support for new ways of seeing, many expressed fiercely opposing views. This variety in response is unsurprising. As Rosemarie Garland-Thomson argues:

> New sights ask new questions that can lead to new under-
> standings ... The cultural work of these images is to make us look
> at them long enough to change our minds. We may be dis-
> comforted, moved, outraged, enlightened, or offended. But we
> cannot look away any more.
>
> (2009: 157–58)

It is this climate of controversy – surrounding not only differing representations of disability but also the role that cultural organizations and agents
might play in (re)shaping public understandings of difference – that provides
the backdrop for the growing interest in museums as sites in which portrayals of disabled people, underpinned by notions of social justice and
equity, might be constructed, staged and debated.

Audiences and narratives

Over the past two decades or so, disability (or, more precisely, disabled
people) has become an increasingly important topic within museums; the
subject of numerous articles in professional publications, many seminars and
conference sessions, training events and manuals. As part of a broader drive
towards the development of new (traditionally excluded) audiences, and
spurred on by government policy and new equality legislation, museums
have (with varying levels of commitment and success) explored ways of
making their buildings and programmes more accessible to disabled people.

Disability, then, has been narrowly associated with visitation and attention
has been focused on enhancing physical (and, to a lesser extent, sensory)
access for disabled visitors. Interestingly, initiatives designed to engage other
groups traditionally under-represented in museums' visitor profiles – notably
minority ethnic communities – have often centred around the programming

of events and exhibitions that reflect the histories, interests and contemporary lives of the target audience. Indeed the trend towards more inclusive practice has resulted in a proliferation of initiatives – oral and hidden history projects, contemporary collecting and so on – designed to better reflect community diversity within museums' narrative repertoires and, in turn, to increase levels of visitation amongst under-represented groups. For disabled audiences, however, a preoccupation with access has, it seems, paradoxically obscured the possibility of disability-themed content within exhibitions and displays.

Although the paucity of disability-related narratives and the skewed and partial character of representations of disabled people have been noted in both the US (Majewski and Bunch 1998) and the UK (Delin 2002), museums have nevertheless been slow to respond. Annie Delin, for example, suggests that

> Any casual visitor to museums in Britain would assume that disabled people occupied a specific range of roles in the nation's history. The absence of disabled people as creators of arts, in images and in artefacts, and their presence in works reinforcing cultural stereotypes, conspire to present a narrow perspective of the existence of disability in history.
>
> (ibid.: 84)

In 2003, Delin joined the Research Centre for Museums and Galleries (RCMG) at the University of Leicester which had recently secured funding to undertake a UK-wide investigation of both the material that existed within collections and the factors that could account for the under- and misrepresentation of disabled people within contemporary displays. The research set out to discover whether the absence of disabled people in museum narratives was explained by a corresponding paucity of disability-related material culture within existing collections or whether other factors were at play. The findings were surprising and, as we shall see, proved highly significant for establishing a future agenda for both research and experimental practice.

The project – entitled *Buried in the Footnotes* – surveyed collections of fine and decorative art, social history, costume, ethnography, military history and so on and found a range of material that had some relationship to disability or disabled people's lives – and on a much larger scale than anticipated.[4] The breadth, scale and quality of material identified suggested considerable potential for museums to develop rich and respectful representations of disabled people:

> As well as the expected asylum residents, freakshow performers, beggars, dependant invalids and recipients of charity funding, we also found evidence of disabled people fulfilling roles including those of

11

teacher, naval commander, parent, lover, collector, benefactor, painter, cooper, miner, musician, linguist, quilter, embroiderer, sculptor, fundraiser, radiographer, nursing educator, politician, merchant and so on.

(Sandell *et al.* 2005: 15)

The richness of material within collections was, however, rarely reflected in museums' public programmes. While a few notable exceptions had developed displays which included wide ranging experiences of disability and presented varied roles (historical and contemporary) enacted by disabled people, most museum narratives omitted disability-related material; failed to make an object's link to disability history explicit in interpretation; or presented material in ways which conformed to stereotypical and reductive representations of disabled people commonplace in other media (ibid.).

A fear of offence

Interviews with museum staff revealed a series of concerns and anxieties that operated to inhibit practice and constrain experimentation in this area. Many cited a fear of causing offence to disabled people, for example, by inappropriately drawing attention to or stigmatizing difference or by using language which might be judged disrespectful or outdated. Some were anxious to avoid creating settings which might be seen to encourage or permit unwelcome visitor behaviours (staring, ridiculing) or which might provoke shock, distress or discomfort (ibid.: 16; Sandell 2007: 160–63).

The concerns felt by staff were very often articulated in the form of interpretive dilemmas or challenges which, it seemed, prevented them from tackling an issue they were otherwise open to exploring. How could the invisibility of disabled people be addressed without recreating inappropriate forms looking reminiscent of the freakshow? Should an exhibition identify as disabled an historical figure who, in their own time, went to great lengths to conceal their impairment? Should the 'difficult stories' of disability – those pertaining to war injury and mutilation, freakshows, eugenics, histories of institutionalization and segregation – be explored in addition to celebratory and inclusive narratives? Although many interviewees were interested in exploring ways of incorporating accounts of disability within their displays, there was a perceived need for guidance that could enable them to move forward in this area.

Activist practice

Building on these research findings and fuelled by a range of factors including growing support within the sector for engagement with hidden histories; the emergence of empirical evidence of the social agency of museums in shaping understandings of difference; and an environment in which rights-related issues were subject to increasing public and political debate, RCMG subsequently developed a large-scale, multi-partner action research project designed to explore and evaluate new approaches to portraying disabled people in museums and galleries. *Rethinking Disability Representation,* which ran between 2006 and 2009, created nine experimental interventions in museums across England and Scotland which, though tremendously diverse in content, theming and interpretive approach, were nevertheless linked by a shared aim. Each of the nine participating museums worked with the research team and, crucially, a 'think tank' of disabled activists, artists and cultural practitioners, to construct a series of socially purposeful narratives – framed by the social model of disability – that could offer audiences new, progressive ways of seeing and frame the ways in which visitors engaged with and participated in disability rights-related debates.

The resulting projects – temporary and touring exhibitions, permanent displays, films and educational resources and sessions for schools – drew on diverse collections to address a broad range of topics. *Life Beyond the Label* (Figure 1.1), for example, used museum objects (from existing collections and newly acquired items), personal testimonies, films and artworks to develop an exhibition, at Colchester Castle Museum, that revealed the lives of local disabled people, past and present, and prompted visitors to consider current and historical perceptions of disability. The Imperial War Museum drew on the institution's rich and extensive collections and archives to create a series of

Figure 1.1 'Life Beyond the Label', Colchester Castle Museum. (Photo: Julian Anderson)

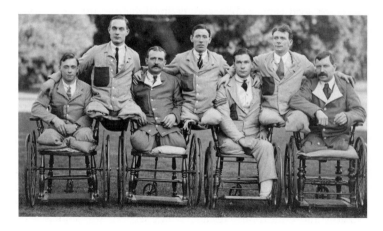

Figure 1.2 Limbless First World War veterans at Roehampton Military Hospital. (Photograph courtesy of the Imperial War Museum, London: Q108161)

educational sessions for secondary schools that addressed the relationship between disability and conflict and encouraged participants to reflect on their own (and broader social) attitudes towards disabled people (Figure 1.2). *Lives in Motion* at the Museum of Transport in Glasgow combined objects, humorous personal stories and comprehensive audio-visual resources to look at the ways in which transport can enable and disable people's lives, highlighting a series of con-temporary rights-related issues and debates.[5]

Together the nine projects sought to counter stereotypes by presenting richly textured and nuanced accounts of disability experience; to highlight and interrogate historical and contemporary modes of discrimination and oppres-sion; and to unsettle visitors' preconceptions in ways which were designed to facilitate new understandings. The process of creating these purposefully framed interpretive interventions revealed a series of challenges; some specific to the theme of disability representation but others which concerned, more broadly, the dilemmas presented by attempts in museums to engage with a range of contemporary (often contested) moral and social issues. This final part of the chapter examines the key interpretive, ethical and pragmatic challenges encountered during the process of shaping this activist practice.

Taking sides

Although the term activism has many connotations it can be understood, in the broadest sense, to refer to a set of actions designed to bring about social change, often in relation to an issue which is characterized by moral, social or political contestation. Activist practice, then, may take many forms but must inevitably entail the adoption of a particular moral standpoint in relation to issues that frequently hold the capacity to generate fiercely opposing views.

The adoption and use of the social model of disability as a device with which to frame the narratives that emerged in the nine museums (and underpin the moral position they embodied and sought to engender support for) prompted considerable discussion amongst the research team and museum participants. Often referred to as the 'big idea' of the British disability rights movement (Hasler 1993 cited in Shakespeare 2006: 29), the social model has strong activist credentials and a close association with broader frameworks of human rights – attributes which brought advantages but which also posed potential challenges for its use within the museum setting.

The social model of disability equipped each of the museums with a powerful conceptual tool with which to mould their interpretive experiments. In this sense it functioned as both a *moral compass* which – by virtue of its associations with human rights frameworks and discourses that enjoy widespread political and social acceptance at an abstract level – offered a trusted source of guidance and as a *lens* with which to establish an overarching narrative and to continually refine interpretive content and tone. However, while the social model brought clarity, focus and ethical instruction, its use also posed challenges. In particular, the notion of explicit allegiance with a specific set of ideas – with 'one side of the argument' – sits uneasily with more established approaches to museum work. The practice of exhibition-making, for many curators, involves actively avoiding the adoption of moral positions which lay the institution open to accusations of bias or of inappropriately taking up the role of advocate for a specific cause. Although there is increasing professional acceptance of the inherently political character of all museum displays, the desire for impartiality and balance remains powerful (Sandell 2007: 177). Other concerns, as we shall see, centred around the danger of presenting disability experience in reductive, overly simplistic and potentially misleading or inaccurate ways – of flattening disability experience in an attempt to follow 'social model thinking' and to guide visitors towards understanding of, and support for, this particular viewpoint.

Complexity and nuance

Trends in museum communication and learning in recent decades have seen a move away from a behaviourist, transmission model – which views knowledge as transferred from museum to visitor in a straightforward, linear and unidirectional manner – towards constructivist approaches which acknowledge the visitor's active role in the construction of meaning. As John Falk, Lynn Dierking and Marianna Adams explain:

> From a constructivist perspective, learning in and from museums is not just about what the museum wishes to teach the visitor. It is as much about what meaning the visitor chooses to make of the museum experience.
>
> (2006: 325)

15

How then could unequivocal support for social-contextual, progressive ways of thinking about disability – embodied in the social model – be combined with approaches to interpretation and visitor engagement that could resist 'moralising didacticism' (Sandell 2007: 196) and instead open up rather than close off multiple possibilities for visitors to engage? This question was discussed at length during the first year of the project and especially at a residential meeting where the research team and museum partners explored creative approaches to interpretation and audience engagement. International examples of innovative practice, from the United States Holocaust Memorial Museum (Rosenstein Werb and Hartmann Squire, this volume) the Anne Frank House and the International Coalition of Sites of Conscience provided examples of museum settings in which the institution's ethical and moral position was made clear but, at the same time, could be combined with a range of interpretive devices and styles in an attempt to avoid overly tendentious and prescriptive messages.

Members of the 'think tank' were strong advocates for social model thinking as a basis for underpinning and shaping the museum narratives that would emerge. Indeed, adherence to this political and philosophical position – coupled with a rejection of individualist and medicalized ways of portraying disabled people – was seen as critical to the success of the project. At the same time, however, the projects that emerged, while implicitly (and sometimes explicitly) articulating their adoption of a social-contextual understanding of disability, also sought (with varying degrees of success) to exploit the unique qualities of the museum as an informal learning environment and to deploy diverse interpretive approaches in order to resist overly dichotomous, neat and reductive narratives.

Plurality and authenticity

The interpretive approach that proved most helpful in capturing complexity and conveying the diversity of perspectives that characterize contemporary disability communities (Snyder and Mitchell 2006: 176) was the presentation of disabled people's own voices, opinions and experiences, sometimes alongside (and, very often, in place of) the mediating curatorial voice of the museum. The significance of these authentic modes of storytelling for enabling visitors to construct new meanings around disability was also revealed during the in-depth evaluation across each of the nine projects.[6]

Though projects were conceived through the application of social model thinking, the individuals whose experiences were featured in the exhibitions, films and educational resources that emerged not surprisingly talked about their experiences of disability in a range of ways and using a variety of terms. So, while we hoped to privilege a social-contextual understanding of disability, we simultaneously sought to acknowledge the presence of alternative viewpoints rather than falsely imposing or implying a consensus. Moreover, in a number of the projects, the inclusion of multiple perspectives operated to highlight the contestation inherent in different approaches to understanding disability.

This layering of perspectives was perhaps most visibly structured in the project developed using the fine art collections at Birmingham Museum and Art Gallery. *Talking about ... Disability and Art* created a trail through the museum's permanent galleries by taking eight paintings – each of which featured depictions of disabled people or reflected in some way the artist's own experience of disability – and offering visitors a series of audio commentaries to accompany them (Figure 1.3). These diverse interpretations of each painting were created through a collaborative process between museum staff and a specially recruited group of six disabled artists. Visitors could choose to listen to all or some of the following: background information on the painting provided by a curator; an interpretation – developed by the six disabled artists – exploring how the painting could be understood in relation to contemporary disabled people's lives; a personal story or artistic response by one of the disabled artists inspired by the painting; and an audio description of the painting developed for visually impaired visitors.

These interventions, threaded throughout the gallery, constituted a markedly different approach to the interpretation that accompanied the majority of paintings on display. Perhaps most significantly, the interpretations developed collaboratively by the artists were intentionally designed to offer explicitly politicized responses to the paintings through connections with contemporary lived experiences of disability. The collaborative response to *The Blind Men of Jericho* (Plate 1.1), a copy of a painting by Nicholas Poussin, (1650–1700), for example, includes the following commentary:

> *The Blind Men of Jericho* shows Jesus performing a miracle, surrounded by his followers. He is restoring sight to a blind man.
>
> This painting demonstrates the Christian belief, and the belief of other religions too, that miracles can and do happen. The message of the Bible story illustrated seems to be that disabled people will only get better – will only experience a miracle – if they believe in Jesus. It appears to illustrate an accepted truth that believers have been healed in the past so it must be true. This makes it difficult to challenge.
>
> Disabled people today still have to deal with this attitude. The history of how disabled people are viewed seems to have its roots in these Bible stories. Some of us have had recent experiences of people calling on God and Jesus to heal us. This behaviour and the painting also imply that all disabled people want to be 'cured'. This wrongly suggests that there is something 'ill' or 'not right' with us. [...]

While these collaborative responses frequently privileged a *politicised* reading of the painting, the individually authored solo responses inspired by each

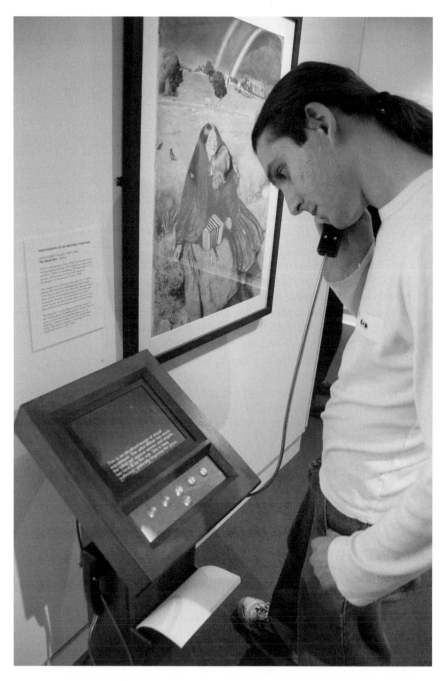

Figure 1.3 'Talking about ... Disability and Art', Birmingham Museum and Art Gallery. (Photo: Peter Carney)

work very often featured highly *personalized* stories. Zoë Partington-Sollinger, for example, offers visitors an emotive and, at the same time, humorous response to the same painting drawing on personal experience:

> ... My first impression of this painting was of a group of men in luxurious robes set against a less detailed backdrop. It felt very theatrical. Then I noticed the person with his hand on the kneeling man's head – and it becomes obvious that it was the hand of Jesus – and that he was healing a blind man.
>
> I started to feel uneasy about the image and became deeply concerned about the painting's message – in particular the 'healing' part and making 'the blind' better. It started to resonate with my own experience of losing my sight and the obsession of the people around me to 'fix' me and find a medical miracle to get my sight back. [...]
>
> When I stood back, I saw the painting's set-up in a different light. It made me laugh – these men lined up ready to see 'the great one'! This is my annual experience when I visit the eye clinic in Manchester – a place with very unattractive carpets and seating that don't reflect modern day décor; Blind and partially sighted people looking desperate and very grey in a depressing overcrowded setting.
>
> We are lined up in rows waiting to see the guru who will repair us and save our sight and give us independence. The nurses stand like the disciples and chat amongst themselves. [...]
>
> I won't ever be able to attend my clinic again without recalling the image of *The Blind Men of Jericho*. I feel a personal connection to these men and a frustration that modern day imagery still depicts blind and partially sighted people as tragic, heroic, bad or unattractive.
>
> Many adverts put out by leading disabled charities continue to use these stereotypes. They do not recognise the significance of the iconography and messages in their own advertising campaigns, and the negative stereotyping this reinforces.

These unconventional, alternative readings, that foreground the political and the personal, sit alongside the more measured curatorial accounts with which most gallery visitors are familiar. The presentation of multiple viewpoints helps to reveal the contestation surrounding alternative conceptions of disability although the inclusion of the unfamiliar (and frequently strident) voices of disabled people within the museum setting also posed a number of challenges for staff. Liz Braby and Melissa Strauss, museum staff who worked on the project, commented:

> We had to be careful about references to other communities. The group associated Christianity and three religious-themed artworks

with negative stereotypes and views, including the idea that disability was seen by some as a judgement from God, and as warranting charity and pity. We felt it was important not to offend Christian visitors, but also to engage with the issues raised and not censor the participants' views. We addressed this by making it clear that the interpretations are not 'definitive', but rather the personal, and joint, views of the participants.

(2008: 93)

A place for debate

Activist practice can be seen to demand careful navigation through a relatively new terrain; one that is potentially fraught with ethical pitfalls. The ways in which audiences respond to initiatives designed to garner support for particular moral standpoints (underpinned by concern for social justice) remain relatively under-researched but our experience suggests that exploring contemporary (often contentious) topics opens up exciting possibilities for museums to engage audiences.

Of course, visitors will respond in tremendously varied ways to the representations they encounter, however carefully the museum might craft them. Learning in museums, as we have seen, is no longer conceived as a means of transmitting knowledge to the (passive) visitor bur rather 'a process of active engagement with experience. It is what you do when you want to make sense of the world' (Museums, Libraries and Archives Council 2008). At the same time, research suggests that while audiences are undoubtedly highly active in the process of constructing meaning out of their visit, their responses and modes of engagement are nevertheless framed and informed by the museum and the moral standpoints it is perceived to embody.

Ultimately the projects that comprised *Rethinking Disability Representation* evolved in ways that sought not to offer prescriptive, fixed and didactic ways of seeing but rather to engage visitors in a dialogue and debate about disability and social justice. At the same time, the use of the social model of disability – as both moral compass and interpretive guide – was an attempt to set parameters around the meanings that visitors might make out of their encounter; to establish the *moral coordinates* within which the debates between and amongst visitors could occur.

Museums, we conclude, might most appropriately be understood not as sites of moral coercion but rather as learning environments in which infinitely diverse meanings can be constructed; but meanings which are generated out of engagement with a set of credible, authentic and ethically informed interpretive resources. This conception of the museum may do little to reassure practitioners anxious about the implications of lending support to a particular moral standpoint but, in response, we would point out that there is no neutral position. Just as visitors will create meanings

20

out of the purposeful interpretations they encounter, they will also draw conclusions from the marked absences, awkward silences and skewed representations surrounding disability that they currently find in most museums.

Notes

1 Disability studies literature contains discussion of the influences of media portrayals on both disabled people's own sense of identity and on the broader understandings of disability amongst non-disabled audiences. Michael Oliver, for example, draws attention to research which suggests that negative media portrayals have played a part in socializing young disabled people into dependency (1996: 70). Barnes and Mercer, though mindful of the debates surrounding media 'effects' within the broader fields of media and audience studies highlight, 'a widespread assumption that the media's negative stereotypes of disabled people reinforce existing patterns of discrimination' (2003: 100).

2 Well known examples include the demonstrations by disabled people in both the US and UK against the charity show Telethons which led to their demise in the early 1990s (Oliver 1996).

3 This new intervention itself provoked further controversy amongst scholars and activists unhappy with the selection of a quotation that would be inscribed in the wall behind it. Rosemarie Garland-Thomson subsequently wrote, 'Many of us in disability studies wish to register our dissent from the choice of the inscription for the new room of the FDR memorial. Pleased as we are with the statue itself, we worry that this memorial to our first markedly disabled president ultimately replicates the segregation and privatization of disability' (2001: B12).

4 For a full account of the research design and findings see Sandell *et al.* 2005.

5 For details of all nine projects see Dodd *et al.* 2008.

6 See Dodd *et al.* 2008 for a detailed account of the findings from the evaluation and Dodd, Jones, Jolly and Sandell, this volume, for discussion of the ways in which visitors engaged with (drew upon, resisted, appropriated) the museum projects they encountered.

References

Barnes, C. (1992) *Disabling imagery and the media: an exploration of principles for media representation of disabled people*, Halifax: (BCODP) British Council of Organisations of Disabled People, Ryburn Publishing.

Barnes, C. and Mercer, G. (2003) *Disability*, Cambridge: Polity Press.

Barnes, C., Mercer, G. and Shakespeare, T. (1999) *Exploring Disability: A sociological introduction*, Cambridge and Maldon, MA: Polity Press.

Bennett, T. (2006) 'Civic seeing: museums and the organisation of vision' in S. Macdonald (ed.), *A Companion to Museum Studies*, Malden, MA and Oxford: Blackwell Publishing.

Braby, L. and Strauss, M. (2008) 'Talking about … disability and art' in J. Dodd, R. Sandell, D. Jolly and C. Jones (eds) *Rethinking Disability: Representation in Museums and Galleries*, Leicester: University of Leicester.

Deland, M. R. (2005) 'Correspondence', *Wilson Quarterly*, Autumn: 9.

Delin, A. (2002) 'Buried in the footnotes: the absence of disabled people in the collective imagery of our past' in R. Sandell (ed.), *Museums, Society, Inequality*, London and New York: Routledge.

Dodd, J., Sandell, R., Jolly, D. and Jones, C. (eds) (2008) *Rethinking Disability Representation in Museums and Galleries*, Leicester: University of Leicester.

Falk, J. H., Dierking, L. D. and Adams, M. (2006) 'Living in a learning society: museums and free-choice learning' in S. Macdonald (ed.), *A Companion to Museum Studies*, Oxford: Blackwell, pp. 323–39.

Garland-Thomson, R. (1997) *Extraordinary Bodies: Figuring physical disability in American culture and literature*, New York: Columbia University Press.

—— (2001) 'The FDR Memorial: who speaks from the wheelchair', *Chronicle of Higher Education*, 26 January 2001.

—— (2009) *Staring: how we look*, Oxford and New York: Oxford University Press.

Gartner, A. and Joe, T. (eds) (1987) *Images of the Disabled, Disabling Images*, New York: Praeger.

Gay, J. with Fraser, M. (2008) 'Why does representation matter?' in J. Dodd, R. Sandell, D. Jolly, and C. Jones (eds) *Rethinking Disability Representation in Museums and Galleries*, Leicester: University of Leicester.

Hall, S. (ed) (1997) *Representation: Cultural Representations and Signifying Practices*, London, Thousand Oaks, New Delhi: Sage Publications Limited.

Hasler, F. (1993) 'Developments in the disabled people's movement' in J. Swain, S. French, C. Barnes and C. Thomas (eds) *Disabling Barriers – Enabling Environments,* London: Sage.

Hevey, D. (1992) *The Creatures That Time Forgot: Photography and Disability Imagery*, London: Routledge.

Kennedy, S. (2004) 'Travulgar Square', *The Sun,* 16 March, p. 27.

Majewski, J. and Bunch, L. (1998) 'The expanding definition of diversity: accessibility and disability culture issues in museum exhibitions', *Curator*, 41(3): 153–61.

Museums, Libraries and Archives Council (2008) *Inspiring Learning: an improvement framework for museums, libraries and archives*, Online. Available http://www.inspiringlearningforall.gov.uk (accessed 27 June 2009).

Norden, M. (1994) *The Cinema of Isolation: A History of Disability in the Movies*, New Brunswick, NJ: Rutgers University Press.

Oliver, M. (1996) *Understanding Disability: from theory to practice*, Basingstoke: Palgrave.

O'Neill, B. (2007) 'Statue of Limitations', *Guardian,* Online. Available http://www.guardian.co.uk/commentisfree/2007/may/17/statueoflimitations (accessed 27 June 2009).

Quinn, B. (2006) 'Outcry over this "insult" to Churchill', *The Daily Mail*, March 11, p. 33.

Riley II, C. R. (2005) *Disability and the media: prescriptions for change*, Hanover and London: University Press of New England.

Sandell, R. (2007) *Museums, Prejudice and the Reframing of Difference*, London and New York: Routledge.

Sandell, R., Delin, A., Dodd, J. and Gay, J. (2005) 'Beggars, freaks and heroes? Museum collections and the hidden history of disability', *Museum Management and Curatorship*. 20(1): 5–19.

Shakespeare, T. (2006) *Disability Rights and Wrongs*, London and New York: Routledge.

Snyder, S. L. and Mitchell, D. T. (2006) *Cultural locations of disability*, Chicago and London: The University of Chicago Press.

2

PICTURING PEOPLE WITH DISABILITIES

Classical portraiture as reconstructive narrative

Rosemarie Garland-Thomson

Pictures are visual narratives.[1] They tell stories to viewers about what they depict. Pictures tell their stories not with words but through visual elements and conventions. The stories that public pictures tell shape the way we understand one another. The images that surround us both reflect received perceptions and mould new ways of thinking about one another. Until recently in the USA, a limited range of public visual narratives constricted the way we view people with disabilities. The most prevalent pictures of people with disabilities have come to us through the genres of freak show photography, charity campaigns or medical photography. These images portray disability narrowly as sensational, sentimental or pathological.

Ways of seeing disability have expanded, however, as people with disabilities have entered into the newly accessible public realm. The public visual landscape has enlarged in the wake of the legal, material and social changes that the larger civil and human rights initiatives of the last 40 years have brought about in the USA and Europe. Laws, policies and the built environment assure full integration and participation by mandating the removal of material and institutional barriers that excluded people with disabilities from the civic arenas of employment, politics, education and community life. As people with disabilities have literally come out of nursing homes, segregated schools, and other restrictive environments, they have simultaneously come out politically to advocate for social justice and disability rights. As more people with disabilities have become visible in the public eye, so too have varied images emerged that tell a broader range of stories about people with disabilities. An ethic of multiculturalism and a politics of diversity influence the public images available to viewers and tell potentially fresh stories about disabled people and the lives they lead. Varied images of people with disabilities that do not replicate the corrosive old stories of suffering, inferiority, pity or repugnance appear routinely now in ephemeral print advertisements, on television and in films, and in the visual arts.[2] Public pictures of people with disabilities that tell positive stories, that show disabled people as valued citizens with meaningful and satisfying lives, work against damaging received master visual narratives about disability.

This chapter focuses on a number of formal portraits of people with disabilities that have appeared in public places in the decades around the turn of the twenty-first century. These portraits can be seen as examples of what Jackie Leach Scully calls 'reconstructive narratives' (Scully 2008: 128). That is, they accomplish the cultural work of providing 'alternative and morally less harmful accounts' that serve to 'displace more damaging portrayals' of people with disabilities (ibid.: 129). By closely reading the stories these portraits present about their subjects, this chapter shows how a conservative representational genre can act in the service of a progressive politics of inclusion. The argument here is that bringing representations of people with disabilities into the public realm via traditional portraiture is an act of sociopolitical integration. To be recognized as a member of a traditionally socially discredited group such as 'the disabled' reduces one's social capital. In contrast, being the subject of a public portrait symbolizes membership in a high status group, literally framing the subject as an appropriate member of the public sphere who is worthy of contemplation and commemoration.[3]

To illustrate the ways in which these portraits confer symbolic capital on disabled subjects, the analysis here details how the portraits accord dignity and authority to unconventional subjects by using the conventions of classical portraiture to reconstruct what it means to be a person with a disability. To do this, the chapter uses the critical method of close reading to reveal how these portraits use several fundamental elements of traditional portraiture – frame, pose, costume, and likeness – to portray disabled subjects in a way that re-narrates disability, making it legible in new ways. The central claim here is that by achieving a recognizable likeness of their subjects as people with disabilities, these portraits make it possible for viewers to understand disabled people as citizens worthy of public recognition and hence of inclusion in the public arena.

Classical portraiture is an elite, highly convention-bound genre of public art that is both influential and conservative. A portrait is an object that bestows cultural capital not only on its owner but also on its subject. The portraits we see in public places such as museums, libraries, board rooms, governmental and educational spaces, and even elite private spaces generally do the work of supporting the status quo by representing, through familiar aesthetic forms, individuals who have power and value in the ascendant political and social order. Typically a progressive political agenda appears, in contrast, expressed through forms such as the avant-garde, outsider art, or art that is in some way formally transgressive. One thinks, for example, of George Grosz's grotesque antifascist paintings, Picasso's Cubist *Guernica*, Cindy Sherman's parodic feminist porn photography, or even the activist performances of The Guerrilla Girls. A good deal of what makes the portraits under discussion here of interest is that they mobilize a very conservative artistic genre in the service of a radical purpose. These representations 'breach portrait conventions' by presenting people whom Shearer West terms 'the unknown and the underclass' rather than society's 'prominent members' (West 2004: 97). At the same time, however, the portraits confirm the commemorative function of the genre that the formal conventions convey. In other words, form and content are at odds in these visually arresting, yet conventionally rendered, portraits. Another way of saying this is that these pictures offer unexpected, even disturbing content in an expected, undisturbing form. This discrepancy intensifies the potential effect of the pictures by juxtaposing the unfamiliar and the familiar, eliciting in viewers a kind of visual vertigo that offers new meanings to the representation of disability.

What portraits want

In his book, *What Do Pictures Want?* W. J. T. Mitchell suggests that pictures have ontological authority, meaning that the picture itself establishes a relationship with the viewer that exceeds the intention of the author or any rhetorical message the picture carries. Portraits, I suggest, have this iconic quality because of their capacity to stage face-to-face relationships with the viewer that capture elements of living interpersonal relations. Through what art critic Lorne Campbell terms 'individualization', a portrait 'stresses those particular aspects of [the] sitter that distinguish him from the rest of humanity' (Campbell 1990: 9). As portraits, the paintings thus announce that their subjects are worthy of public commemoration, important enough to look at and to recognize as particular individuals. In other words, portraits don't just communicate a message but rather act as intentional embodiments that seek to establish a relationship of communication with the viewer about the subject. To use Mitchell's concept, portraits want to be seen. These pictures demand recognition. Portraits themselves – apart from the intentions of the artist or subject – say, 'Look at me and see who I am.'

Portraits command recognition via a set of traditional visual conventions that depend for their effect upon viewers recognizing not just the subject of the portrait but the fact that they are viewing a portrait. So a portrait tells viewers a story in two ways: first, it shows the distinctive characteristics of its subject in order to make that subject as legible as possible to the viewer; second, it tells viewers that the subject of the portrait is worthy of commemoration and honour because a portrait has been made of that person. This is what classical portraits do, then: they confer dignity, value and recognition on their subjects. Portraits accomplish this cultural work through what can be termed visual intertextuality. That is, they depend for their effect on the viewer having seen other portraits and understood the cultural work of portraiture as an elite form of representation. The content, in other words, is legible to the viewer by way of the form. Visual intertextuality, then, is key to the cultural work of classical portraiture in that these pictures refer to another image for their meaning as much as, or perhaps even more than, any material referent. Another way of saying this is that seeing portraits has taught us how to see portraits; knowing what and how a portrait means is part of our collective acculturation. Portraits do their storytelling through a set of familiar conventions that make a portrait mean. We examine here the interrelated elements of frame, pose, costume and likeness through which portraits do their cultural work.

Frame

We begin with frame. Classical portraits are enclosed in a literal frame which serves to clip out, as it were, the subject from its surrounding environment and to recontextualize it in another space. The act of framing establishes meaning in several ways. First, it selects aspects of the person portrayed and their surrounding environment by eliminating some elements and including others. This sorting process gives emphasis and symbolic status to the selected props, pose, costume, background and so on and attenuates the significance of other aspects of the subject that do not appear in the picture. In other words, framing structures the elements of the visual narrative the portrait presents to the viewer.

Part of the frame of meaning in a classical portrait is the convention of oil painting. Oil is an elite medium that bespeaks an elite process requiring deliberation, resources, sitting time, studio space and the support of others to produce a classical oil-painted portrait. Much unacknowledged labour went into supporting the material situation that enabled these portraits. Someone, in other words, built the studio, prepared food, produced the materials, and secured the privilege of time and space necessary for both the artist and subject to come together to make this painting.

Classical portraiture entails, then, the aesthetic act of decontextualizing or 'cropping out' a figure along with selected surroundings from everyday life and recontextualizing or literally framing that figure in a public space of honour, often complete with elaborate gilt frame, artistic signature and reverential viewers. Take, for example, the framing function of Gilbert Stuart's famous 1810 portrait of George Washington, which institutes our shared iconic image of who we recognize as an important American (Plate 2.1). Indeed, this version of what we have learned is the prototypical picture of a founding father has been enforced through the dissemination of this image on the American one dollar bill. More than simply a picture of Washington, this portrait bespeaks through the medium of oil paint and heavy gilded frame that it is a deliberate and enduring substantial material object properly presented in an honoured public setting.

The 2005 portrait by Doug Auld, which is from his series *State of Grace*, achieves part of its cultural work from visual intertextuality with the familiar portrait of George Washington. The subject of Auld's portrait is Shayla, a black woman with significant facial burn scars (Plate 2.2).[4] Auld uses the familiar conventions of traditional portraiture – such as realism, texture, colour, pose and likeness – to portray very unconventional subjects. Shayla's image is cropped and posed in a familiar portrait configuration, quite similar to that of Washington in both Gilbert's famous portrait and the one dollar bill. Both are partial profile, bust poses. Both subjects appear against a staid, rich brown, dignified background which accentuates their distinctive faces. Both portraits accentuate hair and facial features to achieve the particularity that creates resemblance. Both employ the distinctive texture and colour produced by oils and brushstrokes. All this visual intertextuality establishes pictorial authority for Shayla's portrait at the same time that it highlights subtle differences between the two pictures. Washington's head is crowned with a wig that marks eighteenth-century European-American masculine high status. Shayla's hair similarly marks her distinct status as a woman of African heritage and a burn survivor. The textured swirls of colour that represent scars scatter among the coils of tight, intricate braids that sprout from her scalp. Another subtle but significant difference in the twin portraits is that Washington's partial profile bust pose invites a distanced eye contact between viewer and subject, suggestive of monarchical, disengaged superiority, and his upper chest displays a dress collar that marks him not as a king but as an elite citizen. Shayla, in contrast, faces in the opposite direction, suggesting the disconcerting resemblance of a mirror image. More important perhaps is that Auld frames Shayla more closely in a much more engaged, indeed insistent, eye comportment. This intense eye-to-eye engagement with the viewer can make a subject seem to reach out of the picture with pre-emptive ocular ardour.

Shayla is, in fact, staring back at her viewer, demanding the visual connection through which the mutual recognition and reciprocal accord of shared humanness occurs. Refusing to wilt under another's stare is a way to insist on one's dignity and worth. Shayla's eyes are steady on us, emerging from beneath furrowed brows out of a stern face variegated with intricate brushstrokes and colours which announce the residues of burning. Her look refuses the poor victim role or the distanced medical subject. As the realism of portraiture does its work of making a likeness, we come to recognize the effects of burning on flesh. The iconic aspects of Shayla's portrayal literally frame the viewer's reception of a visual subject rarely seen outside medical textbooks or charity pleas – but never through the conventions of elite art.

Pose

As we saw with Doug Auld's portrait of Shayla, expected poses announce to viewers that subjects are dignified and worthy of commemoration. In a series of formal drawings called *The Lost Portraits* artist Chris Rush pictures 'unusual children and adults' in studies from life done at a facility for disabled people where he volunteers.[5] Rush's drawings use the conventions of classical portraiture, especially pose, to confer dignity on subjects who have traditionally been seen through the conventions of medical or scientific representation. Like Auld's burn survivors, Rush's subjects bear the visual characteristics of pathologized conditions, here those stigmatized as mental retardation. Whereas Auld uses bold texture and colour to render scarred flesh less shocking but still compelling, Rush softens the presentation of his subjects' particularities through the medium of conte crayon and poses them with great dignity.

One of Rush's most arresting drawings presents a young woman in the regal profile pose characteristic of the familiar commemorative portraits of the Italian Renaissance (Figure 2.1).[6] Rush's *Swim II* draws meaning from the visual reference to many canonical works of art such as the *Portrait of a Young Woman* by Antonio del Pollaiuolo, painted in the late fifteenth century (Figure 2.2). Like her Renaissance predecessor, this young woman's individual likeness, as well as her social status, emerges from the sharp line her stately features form against the background. Her nose and chin lift imperiously; her eyes gaze impassively out on the world beneath her. Her head is turbaned with a richly coloured and ornately patterned aristocratic headdress, and her shoulders reveal an elegant brocade gown. Yet, along with the familiar comportment of the Renaissance lady, we glean something different about this portrait. The turban in Rush's picture is, in fact, a bright beach towel wrapped around her hair, the gown a simple bathing suit, her adornment a simple heart tattooed on her shoulder, her eyes in a faraway reverie, and in her profiled face we see the distinct features of a person with Down's syndrome. The same conventions of portraiture that frame, pose and costume the recognizable aristocratic Florentine beauty, work together to grant a similar contemplative dignity and social capital to a subject for whom it is usually denied. Indeed, Rush's towel-turbaned woman belongs to a group of people whose lives are thought to be unlivable and unworthy enough to merit the development and use of routine technological tests to detect them in advance and eliminate them from our human community. The common narratives of inferiority, misfortune and devaluation that accrue to people with developmental disabilities cannot sit comfortably upon a woman presented by this portrait. As such, *Swim II* mediates between our collective cultural images of elite beauties and the ostensibly retarded and misshapen.

Pose, then, is crucial to a portrait's meaning but also to its legibility, to the process of recognition of the subject by the viewer that is fundamental to the cultural work of portraiture. As we have seen, frame and costume augment the

Figure 2.1 Chris Rush, *Swim II*, Conte crayon on paper. Portraits are life size in scale.

work of pose so that the entirety of the subject's presentation functions as a single legible image. The portrait of artist and disability activist Susan Nussbaum, painted by Riva Lehrer in 1998 as a part of the series *Circle Stories*, brings together pose and costume – what might be called comportment – and offers an intertextual reference that increases the portrait's legibility (Plate 2.3a). Lehrer costumes Nussbaum casually, marking her with an artsy, ethnic-looking

Figure 2.2 Antonio del Pollaiuolo, *Portrait of a Young Woman*, c. 1465. Oil on poplar, 52.5 x 36.5 cm. (Photo by Joerg P.Anders, Gemaeldegalerie, Staatliche Museen zu Berlin, Berlin, Germany. Bildarchiv Preussischer Kulturbesitz/Art Resource, NY.)

shawl and surrounding her with the floating objects of her trade, history and status, as is conventional in portraits. Most distinctive of Nussbaum's costuming is her wheelchair, in which she is deeply settled with her arthritis-shaped hands comfortably and casually foregrounded. The particularity of her hands and wheelchair, along with the surrounding objects, assure an idiosyncratic rather than generic reading of her figure.

To counter the persistent cultural narrative of wheelchair users as 'bound' or 'confined' by disability, Lehrer's portrait invokes visual intertextuality to impose on Nussbaum the comportment of renowned authorship established by Pablo Picasso's famous 1906 portrait of Gertrude Stein, one of twentieth-century modernism's most recognized authors (Plate 2.3b). Nussbaum's pose replicates Stein's Buddha-like solidity, the engaged forward-leaning body and the eager, capable yet distinctive hands. These are no delicate, ultra-feminine Barbie-esque girls so valued in contemporary masculinist society, but rather they are generative, womanly, fertility goddess figures. Picasso's icon of modern authorship overwrites the pitiable image of the cripple that a wheelchair calls up in almost any viewer acculturated by telethons, charity campaigns and images of street beggars.

Costume

Another portrait in Riva Lehrer's *Circle Stories* series of disability rights movement leaders uses wheelchairs as the canonical symbol of disability in costuming Chicago activists, Mike Ervin and Anna Stonum, in the 1998 double portrait of the couple (Plate 2.4a). Whereas Nussbaum's sense of solid presence comes from her bodily comportment, Ervin and Stonum gain material authority through their seating in throne-like power wheelchairs. The portraiture convention of emphasizing status through symbolic back-ground continues here in the extravagant lightning display in the sky behind the couple's power wheelchairs, creating a visual play on the concept of power. Even though Ervin and Stonum are costumed in the jeans and casual shirts of contemporary counterculture activist artists, an intertextual refer-ence to aristocratic or even monarchical costuming and pose characteristic of the traditional double portrait ensures that viewers do not read this couple as street beggars or hospital residents. Indeed, Lehrer's portrait imposes on Irvin and Stonum the distinction and status conveyed in double portraits such as an anonymous, seventeenth-century portrait from the French School, which typically picture a high status couple posed at equal height, dressed similarly in the attire of their rank, and touching hands to signify the unity and sharing of their power and position (Plate 2.4b).

Likeness

In portraits of people with disabilities, the canonical disability costume of a wheelchair can be used to produce the likeness essential to the cultural work of portraits. Likeness enables identification of the subject by representing the particularities of the subject's face and body, including costuming, props and bodily decoration, through realistic conventions so as to have the 'general effect' of authenticity (Gage 1997: 119). The portrait of Christopher Reeve by Sacha Newley painted in 2004 shortly before Reeve's death uses likeness to achieve recognition, perhaps most apparently of the examples here, by rendering its subject's distinctive particularities. In doing so, Reeve's portrait exemplifies the potential for traditional portraiture to confer dignity and authority on subjects from which they have been traditionally withheld (Plate 2.5b).[7] Reeve was a recognizable celebrity in the popular media before he became a disabled wheelchair user. Newley's conventionally rendered and framed portrait, displayed in the contemporary area of the National Portrait Gallery, Washington DC, presents a recognizably disabled Reeve in a full body pose typical of the formal official portraits that fill these classic spaces of national honour. With Reeve's portrait, however, conventional forms present unconventional content. As in traditional portraits, the pose displays the symbols of the subject's status. Instead of the business suit, the usual uniform of modern power, Reeve wears a power wheelchair, the canonical costume of contemporary disability. As an emblem of his status, his wheelchair functions symbolically as a substantial high-tech throne crafted to the particularities of his body to sustain his regal bearing. Another insignia of his status as a person with a disability is Reeve's respirator, resting with dignity at his throat like a contemporary man's tie or George Washington's collar. Reeve's shaved head simultaneously suggests the fashionable look of contemporary male athletes and the baldness resulting from medical treatment. The monarchical pose brings forward as the centre of attention Reeve's legs and feet, supported amply by his chair. His hands rest in nests that conform comfortably to their shape. His face – the usual site of recognition – retires to the background, the noble head crowned by a modest headrest curving from behind his ear. Like the subjects of traditional elite portraits, the setting emblematizes Reeve's status, placing him in a private but formal space graced with an Oriental rug with which he shares a sculpture of a sailboat, all brightly lit by large windows in the background. This contrasts sharply with the stereotypical image of the so-called 'wheelchair-bound' street beggar or medical patient. The medium of oil painting textures and colours Reeve's image, alluding to Impressionist alfresco painting and pastoral settings, countering the common assumption that disability confines or secludes.

The wheelchair is, on the most obvious level, of course, a symbol of his status as a person with a disability. Reeve is the only explicitly, that is to say visibly, marked person with disabilities in the National Portrait Gallery, which is how the portrait invites viewers to read him. I would invite us to read Reeve's presentation here – and this is the important distinction – not as a symbol of vulnerability as disability, but rather as a materialization of the relationship between body and environment we all share equally. The cradling of all Reeve's appendages, from head to feet, in material mediations between flesh and world literally renders a picture of our shared human experience of embodiment, of flesh accommodated by world, of a sustaining fit between self and situation. Moreover, because the work of portraiture is to present a figure at once recognizable yet representative, the picture invites viewers to identify with Reeve as a figure both above them and of them, as less the exception and more the rule. The boldness of this portrait is that it enlists a conventional visual genre to make explicit what is usually hidden by dominant representations. This traditional portrait presents the truth of our enfleshment, of our universal need for sustenance, and accords that truth dignity and status.

Reeve's portrait at the National Portrait Gallery calls to a relationship of visual intertextuality with his former iconic role as Superman, which circulated widely in a variety of media and popular culture, imprinting in the collective cultural imagination the image of the fantastical flying super-abled superhero (Plate 2.5a). Clad in a futuristic red and blue leotard and cape with a signature yellow 'S' power crest on the chest, the figure of Superman emerged as a mythic comic book hero in 1938 and continued as a 'man of steel' endowed with superhuman strength, flight capability, and an extraterrestrial genealogy in various media and commercial incarnations continuously up to the present. Superman's capacity to transform from the mild-mannered, near-sighted, unremarkable reporter, Clark Kent, into the extraordinarily-abled, gravity-defying hero, took an ironic turn when the actor, who had occupied the role of Superman from 1978 to 1987, instantaneously transformed in 1995 into a person with quadriplegia as a result of the sporting accident in which the all too human Reeve was bested by the forces of gravity that his fictional persona of Superman would have easily transcended.

The residual iconic image of an airborne, rocket-like Superman in a hyper-masculine, fist-forward pose of indomitable thrust informs our collective reception of Sacha Newley's serene and dignified 2004 portrait of Christopher Reeve who becomes, through this juxtaposition, a 'man of steel' in a very different way. Newley's representation of Reeve retracts and re-choreographs Superman's phallic pose, offering up in the picture's foreground soft fleshly hands and legs that are supported by – rather than forged from – rigid, unforgiving iron. The literally penetrating head of Superman recedes to the background of Newley's quieted and contemplative Reeve, rendering him as Everyman rather than Superman. The cultural work, then, of this portrait depends on the reference to, and contrast with, the widely disseminated image of Reeve as Superman that haunts the viewer's reception of the aesthetic act of commemoration and honouring that such a formal portrait confers.

Likeness, then, renders legible not only the individual person a portrait displays, but also the group memberships to which the subject of the portrait belongs through either self-identification or social ascription. The conventions employed render the particularities of the subject and its surrounding context to accomplish this recognition. In other words, Newley's portrait wants viewers to simultaneously recognize Reeve the celebrity and Reeve the person with quadriplegia.

A final example of disability portraiture brings forward issues of gendered identity in conversation with disabled identity. From September 2005 to April 2006, a statue called *Alison Lapper Pregnant* occupied the Fourth Plinth in London's Trafalgar Square, a public place of honour that had been vacant for 150 years and is dominated by the towering memorial to Lord Nelson (Figure 2.3). A controversial, juried work of public art by British artist Marc Quinn, *Alison Lapper Pregnant* puts forward a very unconventional subject through the very conventional classical realist form of a marble statue of a nude woman on a pedestal. Quinn's statue strikingly departs from customary nudes by portraying an actual woman rather than a generic ideal figure. Indeed, the figure of Alison Lapper posed and rendered so traditionally by Quinn's statue jars in its contrast with the classical ideal by presenting a heavily pregnant and disabled Lapper, who displays uncommonly short arms and unusually shaped legs and feet.[8] The marble statue becomes a portrait, then, by rendering a specific individual (who is recognizable as such) rather than a generalized subject.

To publicly commemorate a female figure bearing the seldom exposed pregnant belly flanked with its heavy breasts and atypical limbs presents a version of womanhood that is exceptional not so much in truth but rather in its exposure to public view. Both pregnancy and the human variations of disability are, in fact, common aspects of actual women's bodies, that are almost never displayed publicly and certainly never through the medium of the classical nude.[9] *Alison Lapper Pregnant* thus invites consideration of the disjunction between Woman in the cultural imagination and women as immanent, distinctly individual beings.

By portraying Lapper via the conventions of the traditional nude, the statue also insists on the question of which female bodies are esteemed and which are discredited. What Lapper's marble portrait asks is how what classical art has presented as beauty might be crosshatched by what we think of as ugly – a pregnant, disabled female body. Lapper's is the kind of body that is often assumed to disqualify someone from the privileges and responsibilities of proper womanhood. *Alison Lapper Pregnant* engages in a visual conversation with such common social attitudes by asserting that a woman with significant disabilities who is evidently sexual, about to become a mother, and possibly reproducing herself is worthy of being seen in Trafalgar Square.

These inquiries about female beauty and proper womanhood that *Alison Lapper Pregnant* poses become clearer through the statue's visual intertextual reference to the iconic image of female beauty in the Western world: the classical Greek era's *Venus de Milo*, who graces another public place of honour

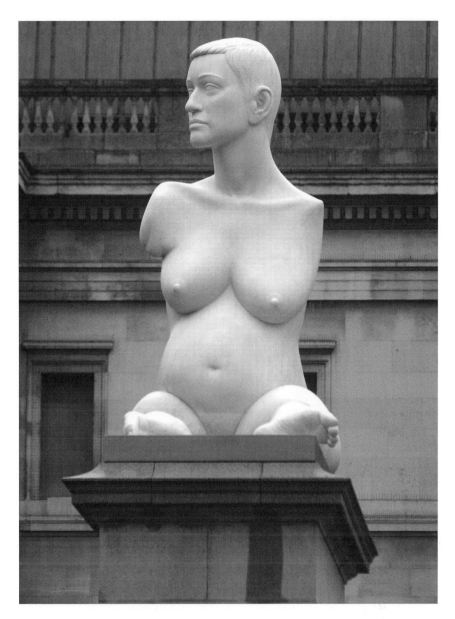

Figure 2.3 Marc Quinn, *Alison Lapper Pregnant*. British artist Marc Quinn's white, 13-ton statue inspired by artist Alison Lapper who was born armless and with shortened legs,
was installed in central London's Trafalgar Square, 15 September 2005. Lapper
posed naked for Quinn when she was eight months pregnant, in what the artist says
was a tribute to motherhood and people with disabilities. The sculpture remained
in place for 18 months. (AP Photo/Lefteris Pitarakis)

Figure 2.4 *Venus de Milo*, frontal view. Marble, c. 100 BCE. Hellenistic. (Photo by
Hervé Lewandowski. Louvre, Paris, France. Réunion des Musées Nationaux/Art
Resource, NY)

in Paris's great art museum, the Louvre (Figure 2.4). The visual conversation between the two marble nudes invites us to consider Lapper in relation to female beauty and the Venus de Milo in relation to disability. *Alison Lapper Pregnant* suggests that we read the *Venus de Milo* as an amputee whose arms are foreshortened by the vagaries of her individual history, by some chance encounter with a force of the environment. The *Venus de Milo* suggests that we read Alison Lapper as a beautiful woman. This connotative connection between the two works of art allows us, then, to view each statue in new ways. This intertextuality functions as a visual exclamation point commanding more firmly and clearly consideration of the questions suggested by the Lapper statue alone.

The likenesses achieved in the portraits of both Reeve's stilled body and Lapper's unusual shape are emblematic of the ordinary transformations of body, mind and senses that we call disabilities and that occur in some way to nearly everyone over a lifetime. This shared human experience of disability is a forbidden yet compelling sight. Both portraits are hybrids of the to-be-looked-at and not-to-be-looked-at, just as Lapper herself, as at once a woman and a person with significant disabilities, is a hybrid of the to-be-pregnant and the not-to-be-pregnant.

Recognition

What Bryan S. Turner terms 'critical recognition theory' focuses our attention on how aesthetic products such as portraits can accomplish ethical and progressive political work (Turner 2006: 54). Turner argues that '[c]are and respect for other people and their cultures cannot take place without a prior recognition of them as human beings' (Turner 2006: 54). By making possible recognition of subjects as worthy and – at the same time – disabled, these portraits enable us to recognize disability in new and progressive ways. The political philosopher Nancy Fraser argues that recognition is essential not simply for individual self-realization but, more importantly, as the cornerstone of an ethical political society. Recognition is, according to Fraser, 'an ideal reciprocal relation between subjects in which each sees the other as its equal and also as separate from it. This relation is deemed constituent for subjectivity; one becomes an individual subject only in virtue of recognizing, and being recognized by, another subject' (Fraser and Honneth 2003: 10).[10] The cultural critic bell hooks similarly affirms the potential of 'the direct unmediated gaze of recognition' as a conduit to a relation of mutual equality. What hooks terms 'the look of recognition that affirms subjectivity' is precisely the cultural work these portraits invite (hooks 1992: 129–30).

The key in the recognition process that enacts Fraser's 'ideal reciprocal relation between subjects' is for the majority to perceive the minority's 'distinctive characteristics' (Fraser and Honneth 2003: 10, 29). In other words, to be recognized is to be seen as one is. The 'distinctive characteristics' of disability are highly discredited embodied traits and ways of interacting with the world which are represented largely negatively in public culture. Thus disability is a state of being and a social assignment to which no one goes willingly and which few embrace or even accommodate. As such, being labelled as 'disabled' can distort one's subjectivity. The contradiction between Fraser's call to affirm the 'distinctive characteristics' of minority groups and this collective aversion to disability makes it difficult to imagine disability as a positive form of human variation that can yield a valued, or even tenable, identity.

Social injustice gets legitimated, in part, through patterns of representation that impart subordinate status, that perpetuate disrespect learned via stereotypical images. In Fraser's understanding, the way this works is that 'it is unjust that some individuals and groups are denied the status of full partners in social interaction simply as a consequence of institutionalized patterns of cultural value in whose construction they have not equally participated and which disparage their distinctive characteristics or the distinctive characteristics assigned to them' (Fraser and Honneth 2003: 29). If representations are a part of the 'institutionalized patterns of cultural value' that legitimate social injustice, they can also counter it. According to Fraser,

> [T]he remedy for injustice is cultural or symbolic change. And this could involve upwardly revaluing disrespected identities and the cultural products of maligned groups; recognizing and positively valorizing cultural diversity; transforming wholesale societal patterns of representation, interpretation and communication in ways that would change everyone's social identity.
>
> (Fraser and Honneth 2003: 13)

By realistically rendering through the convention of likeness and positively valuing through the cultural narrative of portraiture the particularities of the body that we understand as disabilities, these portraits of people with disabilities invite viewers to recognize what we have collectively learned through our common acculturation to understand as devalued human variations.

By invoking the authority of a highly convention-bound traditional visual genre in the service of representing individuals and a cultural group that has been historically discredited and undervalued, these portraits do progressive cultural work. That work is 'recognition of the distinctive perspectives' of people with disabilities and the 'affirmation of group specificity' (Fraser and Honneth 2003: 7, 12). In terms of Pierre Bourdieu's theory of the material expression of economic capital, these portraits institutionalize new cultural capital as they bestow it on the subjects by publicly pronouncing, through 'conferring institutional recognition', that the person portrayed is now an official member of the valued class (Bourdieu 1986: 248). Moreover, this work takes place as an encounter between viewer and a subject that is seldom posed through aesthetic mediations such as traditional portraiture, which is

38

understood as a conservative genre. The portraits considered here thus make newly intelligible devalued forms of human embodiment and promote new forms of cultural literacy by rendering subjects into esteemed public figures and teaching us how to value them.

Offered here, then, is a strong claim that these portraits accomplish ethical work as well. By enacting 'the look of recognition that affirms subjectivity' these portraits ask viewers to recognize the distinctiveness of disability not as diminishment, but as testimony to our shared humanness. These portraits counter damaging dominant visual master narratives of disability, what Jackie Leach Scully calls 'toxic identity stories' (Scully 2008: 129). By presenting an alternative to these corrosive stories, the portraits give aesthetic form to the collective 'ethical responsibility' Scully calls for 'to keep the fullest possible range of nontoxic narratives of identity in circulation, and in accessible forms, and to ensure that toxic ones are identified, and countered or replaced, where ever they arise' (Scully 2008: 130).

Notes

1 I am grateful to Emory College of Arts and Sciences and The Graduate School of Emory University, which generously provided resources for the illustrations in this chapter.

2 For examples of analysis about media representations of disability see, for example, Snyder, Brueggemann, and Garland-Thomson (2002), Haller and Ralf (2003), and Norden (1994).

3 For an explanation of social and symbolic capital, see Bourdieu (1986).

4 The motivation for the series of portraits came from a scene of staring Auld experienced 30 years before he began to paint burn survivors. Ambling through an outdoor market, the young Auld encountered a vision he was not 'prepared for', he told a *New York Times* reporter in 2006. He caught sight of a young girl who was significantly burned. Her face shocked him into staring, imprinting a vivid image that stayed with him over the years. He struggled to make sense of her face. So challenging was this task and so unprepared was Auld, however, that he withdrew his stare, short-circuiting his inquiry into her humanity. When the girl looked back at the man whose eyes were locked on her face, he lost his voice and did 'what everybody else did. I turned my head away' (Newman 2006: 1.25). Haunted for years by this broken connection, Auld decided to address his regret with his art. He approached the Burn Center at St. Barnabas Medical Center in Livingston, New Jersey, in order to contact former patients to seek permission and cooperation in painting their portraits. Auld means his subjects to be looked at, to give viewers 'the chance to gaze without voyeuristic guilt at the disfigured, [so] they may be more likely to accept them as fellow human beings, rather than as grotesques to be gawked at or turned away from' (Newman 2006: 1.25).

5 According to the description of *The Lost Portraits* series, Rush's pictures attend carefully to viewers' perceptions of their subjects by gratifying viewers' 'deep curiosity' while at the same time inviting 'empathy' and 'sensitivity'. The exhibition narrative explains that the portraits invite viewers 'to draw close to their strangeness and see something of ourselves waiting there'. They show what to many is the 'strangeness' of disability in the familiar frame of a portrait ('Permission to Stare' 2006). See also the artist's website at http://chrisrushartist.com/.

6 For an art historical account of the development of pose in the Renaissance and also the development of the double portrait considered later in this chapter, see Campbell (1990).

7 Newley painted a triptych of Reeve shortly before his death, which includes two head portraits. Newley describes the work on his website at http://www.sachanewley.com.

8 Alison Lapper is herself an artist and a single mother. Abandoned to a foundling home for disabled children at birth, she eventually earned a First in Fine Art at Brighton University and became a successful artist. In her youth, she discovered increased freedom and flexibility by discarding the prosthetic limbs she was encouraged to wear. She works for The Mouth and Foot Painting Artists Association designing greeting cards that are sold in 73 countries. She also has made a series of photographic self-portraits and in 2006 published an autobiography with Guy Feldman called *My Life in My Hands*.

9 Recently, however, pregnant celebrities have appeared in high fashion magazines. See, for example, Annie Liebovitz's controversial *Vanity Fair* magazine cover photo of pregnant Demi Moore published in August, 1991.

10 For more on the political and ethical aspects of recognition, see Taylor (1994).

References

Bourdieu, P. (1986) 'The forms of capital' in J. G. Richardson (ed.), *Handbook of Theory: Research for the Sociology of Education*, New York: Greenwood Press, pp. 241–58.

Campbell, L. (1990) *Renaissance Portraits: European Portrait Painting in the 14th, 15th and 16th Centuries*, New Haven, CT: Yale University Press.

Fraser, N. and Honneth, A. (2003) *Redistribution or Recognition? A Political Philosophical Exchange*, London: Verso.

Gage, J. (1997) 'Photographic likeness' in J. Woodall (ed.), *Portraiture: Facing the Subject*, Manchester and New York: Manchester University Press, pp. 119–30.

Haller, B. A. and Ralf, S. (2003) 'Current perspectives on advertising images of disability' in G. Dines and J. Humez (eds), *Gender, Race and Class in Media*, Thousand Oaks, CA: Sage, pp. 293–301.

hooks, b. (1992) *Black Looks: Race and Representation*, Boston: South End Press.

Lapper, A. and Feldman, G. (2006) *My Life in My Hands*, London: Simon & Schuster.

Mitchell, W. J. T. (2006) *What do Pictures Want? The Lives and Loves of Images*, Chicago: Chicago University Press.

Newman, A. (2006) 'Facing their scars, and finding beauty', *New York Times*, 18 June: 1.25.

Norden, M. F. (1994) *The Cinema of Isolation: A History of Physical Disability in the Movies*, New Brunswick, NJ: Rutgers University Press.

Rush, C. (2006) 'Permission to stare', online. Available http://www.jackthepelicanpresents.com/rushpr.html (accessed 18 August 2006).

Scully, J. L. (2008) *Disability Bioethics: Moral Bodies, Moral Difference*, Lanham, MD: Rowman and Littlefield.

Snyder, S., Brueggemann, B. and Garland-Thomson, R. (2002) *Disability Studies: Enabling the Humanities*, New York: Modern Languages Association Press.

Taylor, C. (1994) 'The politics of recognition' in A. Gutman (ed.), *Multiculturalism: Examining the Politics of Recognition*, Princeton, NJ: Princeton University Press.

Turner, B. S. (2006) *Vulnerability and Human Rights*, University Park, PA: Penn State University Press.

West, S. (2004) *Portraiture*, Oxford and New York: Oxford University Press.

3

AGENTS AT ANGKOR

Lain Hart

From the civil war of the 1960s and 1970s to the killing fields and the Vietnamese invasion, political oppression and brutal conflict racked Cambodia while violence came to characterize the image of the country abroad. The imminent threat of death or dismemberment remained a reality in Cambodia long after the military defeat of the Khmer Rouge as a result of their efforts, and those of their enemies, to deploy the weapon for which Cambodia has become infamous: the anti-personnel land mine.

Beginning in the 1990s, the country opened up to international tourism as well as global institutions of charitable funding and investment. The development of Angkor Archaeological Park, Cambodia's own 'World Heritage Site', transformed the sleepy town of Siem Reap into a mecca for both international tourists and local economic migrants. Today the impact of international involvement in Cambodia is the subject of analyses belonging to the growing body of academic literature that deals with post-Khmer Rouge Cambodia. Tim Winter is one scholar who has chosen to focus on cultural tourism, national heritage, and the commodification of Cambodia's past (see Winter 2004, 2006).

People with physical disabilities feature prominently in the publicity materials issued by charitable organizations involved in Cambodia and, in fact, there may be no other nationality associated so specifically with people with disabilities in the way that Cambodia is associated with amputees. However, in academic treatments of contemporary Cambodian society, one aspect that has been consistently overlooked is the way in which Cambodian people with disabilities have asserted their ownership of national heritage and used international cooperation in the field of Angkorean cultural preservation in order to access an improved quality of life.

While the other studies in this volume have for the most part discussed the representation of disability in the urban museums of industrialized societies, this chapter shifts attention to the notion of disability within a rural, developing nation. It deals with a community of people with disabilities living in the town of Siem Reap. Like most of the other residents of this town, members of the community depend for their livelihoods upon the tourists who arrive in buses from neighbouring Thailand, or who land at Siem Reap's new airport, streaming in their millions to the nearby ruins of Angkor Wat. This chapter focuses on a number of people with disabilities, as well as two able-bodied Cambodians involved in Angkor Archaeological Park's Land Mine Museum and the Angkor Association for the Disabled.

My intention here is not to recapitulate individual experiences, nor to generalize about the experience of being physically disabled in Cambodia, but rather to illustrate how Cambodians with disabilities negotiate the challenges that arise in the course of their involvement with the tourist industry and the cultural sector. I also consider the ways in which disabled individuals influence the narrative of heritage told at Angkor Archaeological Park, and how they shape the tourist experience at Angkor while, at the same time, challenging prejudices about disability. For this I have relied in part on the efforts of Lindsay French, an anthropologist who worked with Cambodian refugees on the Thai border between 1989 and 1991. Attributions appear where I reference her work, whereas the information and quotes that appear here without attribution refer to the research that I conducted in Siem Reap over the course of 2008.

Coming of age under the Khmer Rouge

In a turn of events that took many Cambodians by surprise, guerrilla forces under the leadership of Pol Pot seized the capital city of Phnom Penh in 1975. Intent upon transforming all aspects of life in Cambodia, Pol Pot and the Khmer Rouge implemented a comprehensive plan modelled on the Cultural Revolution in China.

For the generation that came of age under this regime, formal education was non-existent. Merely being suspected of practising traditional religion or playing folk music could mean a death sentence, and reading and writing were very nearly lost arts in Cambodia. Even after the Vietnamese invasion of 1979, and as the looming possibility of execution or imprisonment receded with the crumbling power of the Khmer Rouge, brutal combat across the country splintered Cambodia into murderous factions and battered an already enfeebled economy.

With so few opportunities available for social or economic security, many young Cambodians sought stability by joining the army. There, the officers commanded their loyalty, but this arrangement was more of a patron–client relationship: in exchange for enlisting, soldiers received from their commander uniforms and weapons, as well as the possibility of promotion. Enlistment might lead to a position within a powerful local system of authority, though the rank-and-file troops were rarely paid, and they were often forced to supplement their rations by foraging. Most importantly, however, a commander might be able to find a place for a soldier's family in one of the many refugee camps located on the country's borders, which were explicitly aligned with one or the other faction. Whether pro-Vietnamese, anti-Vietnamese, pro-Khmer Rouge, anti-Khmer Rouge, monarchist, socialist, liberal democrat or communist, the political allegiances of the troops and their families were generally imposed upon them by their commanders.

Being the most expendable of resources available to military leaders, the youngest recruits were often tasked with mine-laying or mine-detecting. Since much of the combat during this period involved small units of poorly trained troops and villagers fighting along jungle paths, mines and booby-traps could be deployed to maximum effect. However, anti-personnel land mines are often only powerful enough to inflict injury, not death. Like the manufacturers of land mines in Europe, the Middle East, the former Soviet Union, as well as China, Vietnam, and the United States, Cambodian commanders were aware of the fact that wounded men, women, and children occupy more of the enemy's resources than dead ones, and by transforming them into amputees, the land mine also serves as a terrifying weapon of psychological warfare.

In this way, for more than a decade, Vietnamese-backed forces struggled against the Khmer Rouge and their allies. Sem Sovantha was one young man who joined the Vietnam-backed faction as a teenager, serving as a captain from 1982 to 1990, when he went into battle against Khmer Rouge guerrillas to the south of Phnom Penh. There, he lost both his legs to a land mine. In this condition he was no longer useful to his commander. Captain Sovantha became a refugee, and he survived by begging in camps along the Thai border.

In the pro-Khmer Rouge refugee camps in which she worked with amputee veterans during the 1990s, French found that many of the soldiers there had perceived their relationship with the commanders to be one of moral obligation and reciprocity. And yet, when soldiers like Sovantha were injured, military leaders failed to provide for them. As one disabled veteran told French: 'Our commanders just need people who can do their work for them. When we cannot work anymore, they just throw us away' (French 1995: 79).

When I met Sovantha in 2008, he highlighted for me the social and psychological dimensions of his disability. Feelings of worthlessness and powerlessness are acute among disabled Cambodian men, who have been taught that they have a moral obligation to provide for their parents, wife, children, and even their extended family. In Cambodia, 'Considerable shame accrues to a man who cannot provide his family with the resources to live at the level to which they are accustomed' (ibid.: 80).

The Angkor Association for the Disabled

In the mid-1990s, the international community backed the Vietnamese-led government, United Nations organizations launched vast nation-building projects in Cambodia, and many refugees came home. Sovantha returned to Phnom Penh. By sitting underneath the window outside a classroom where lessons were being held, he learned to speak English, then made his way to Siem Reap. In 2003 Sovantha established the Angkor Association for the Disabled (AAD). An AAD outreach effort in 2007 found about 40 people with disabilities living on the streets of Siem Reap, all of them migrants born in outlying rural areas. Perhaps pressured to leave their home communities by poverty or social stigma, many Cambodians seek out a new future in Siem Reap, often with their families in tow. One of AAD's priorities has been to provide school materials like books and uniforms to the children of disabled members of the community. AAD also undertakes outreach efforts in communities around Angkor Wat in order to promote alternatives to begging.

The organization's longest-running employment programme is also the one that visitors to Angkor Archaeological Park see in action at the temple of Banteay Kdei. It was established the year before the foundation of AAD, when Sovantha struck up a friendship with a musician who lived next door named Leng Yom. He and Sovantha put together a programme to provide musical instruments and training to people with disabilities. Since then Sovantha's old neighbour has helped provide disabled Cambodians access to a better livelihood as their music teacher.

AAD musicians start work at Banteay Kdei almost every day at 8 o'clock. Yom and his students set up on a wooden platform just inside the main temple gate. Seated nearest the gate is Voo Un. Like Sovantha, he is a husband, father and an ex-soldier. As a young man he was blinded by a rocket. He cradles a string instrument called a *tro*, a two-stringed violin made of wood and snakeskin. Beside Voo Un is another veteran holding a drum, and another man ready with the cymbals. Yom sits behind a piano-like instrument called a *khim*, and together they wait for the first tourist of the day to emerge from the entrance to the temple grounds. Elsewhere within the park, two other traditional music ensembles composed of disabled Cambodians set up at other temples. They are affiliated with different non-governmental organizations.

The first visitors of the day are often Cambodian. Especially in the cool hours of the morning, families from around the country make their own tours of Angkor's temples. Crowds of local people dominate the space during religious festivals. For them, admission is free, and when they arrive at Banteay Kdei, Voo Un and the rest of the AAD's musicians perform a celebratory folk song.

There is a tremendous variety to Cambodian music. Sounds range from the struck keys and gongs of court music to the dance rhythms of popular tunes. *Pinn peat* is the music of the elite, an accompaniment to classical dance and religious ceremonies. Monasteries often possess a *pinn peat* ensemble. Other formats feature different instruments and arrangements, like *pleng kar*, the music of marriage. Village entertainment might also take the form of *ayai* repartee singing, or a *chrieng chapey* ballad. Classical arts tend to reference

44

Buddhist stories and the Khmer version of the *Ramayana*, while the images conjured up by the lyrics of folk songs more often relate to the animist beliefs that existed in Cambodia long before a pre-Angkorean period of Indianization. In their encounter with today's tastes and economic necessities, the diverse sub-genres have fared variously. Whereas the classical formats of Cambodian music have, for the most part, benefited from government patronage and international support throughout the 1980s and 1990s, folk music has begun to fade from village life.

The proliferation of foreign technologies brings problems as well as benefits. Pricey traditional instruments like the *khim* rarely feature in village performances today. More and more often, even at monasteries during Buddhist festivals, Thai pop music blares from Chinese-made speakers. The kinds of songs that AAD musicians play have been associated with village festivals for generations, and most local Cambodians know them by heart, but if not for the AAD's CD-burning efforts, many of these songs might never have been recorded.

AAD sells CDs at Banteay Kdei and at the local market, where Cambodians and foreigners both buy copies. Interestingly, tourists almost always opt for CDs of folk dance songs, whereas Cambodian buyers tend to favour recordings of wedding music. One employee of AAD speculated that perhaps this was due to the fact that the wedding songs call to mind fond memories of past matrimonial events, which are traditionally very lavish celebrations involving entire villages.

Intent upon preserving a folk art form he practised from the age of fourteen, Voo Un has over thirty traditional wedding songs memorized. He and the other AAD musicians do occasionally make adjustments to their repertoire to accommodate the tastes of their audiences. For instance, when a group of five Chinese tourists appeared at the gate at Banteay Kdei, they were greeted with a fanfare. They ignored the quartet, and disappeared into the temple ruins. When the Chinese tourists re-emerged, Yom led his group in playing a famous Chinese folk song. The tourists recognized it, and one approached with a shy smile to drop a dollar in the AAD donation box.

Working next to under-age vendors who sell statues, scarves and photocopied guidebooks indistinguishable from the souvenirs boys and girls sell at the gates of almost every other temple, and elsewhere, the AAD musicians are participants in a thriving and mostly unregulated heritage industry. Voo Un and the other disabled musicians are performing primarily in order to make a living, and their ensemble is not strictly traditional. Especially when playing for foreign tourists, troupes of Cambodian musicians with disabilities will often reinterpret familiar melodies and play with phrases and motifs in much the same way that Western jazz musicians do. Furthermore, an indispensable aspect of the performance is visual. For instance, on Siem Reap's 'Bar Street', where a number of foreign-owned restaurants, pubs, and hostels are located, one group of musicians with disabilities plays behind a sign proclaiming them to be land mine survivors. Sitting next to the sign is a quadruple amputee, whose job it is to handle CD sales with his teeth.

The musicians' bodies are part of the performance. They are artifacts of war. History has inscribed on their bodies a narrative thick with social and personal tragedy and each disabled musician has expanded the group's agency by taking on the role of curator and conservator of an indigenous artistic tradition. It is as a combined expression of Cambodian heritages – ancient, modern, Angkorean, pre-Angkorean, Khmer Rouge – that the musicians singularize their performance and re-enchant traditional music. In the sacred space of Angkor, they challenge contemporary ideas about disability and the way in which they use Cambodian heritage speaks to Winter's recommendation that, 'rather than viewing Angkor as a monumental landscape of the "ancient" past', the authorities responsible for the site should consider it 'a form of "living heritage" pivotal in the articulation of contemporary cultural and national identities' (2004: 331).

Disability and karma

In many cultures, when either able-bodied people or people with disabilities struggle with depression, they may find solace in spiritual dedication or religious community. However, the religious life of Cambodia depends upon a hierarchy of merit, in which people with disabilities figure as decidedly lesser beings.

Since the fall of the Khmer Rouge, Cambodia has experienced something of a Buddhist renaissance. To be more specific, it is a Theravada Buddhist renaissance, a resurgence of feeling for the particular Buddhist sect long considered a key element of Khmer identity. Perhaps to a more stringent extent than the devotees of other Buddhist traditions, Cambodian Theravada Buddhists conceive of karmic 'purity' and 'contamination' as opposite forces involved in the struggle 'between the Buddha and demons, dhamma and adhamma, order and disorder, coherence and fragmentation' (Hinton 2008: 78). Theravada Buddhism can also be distinguished from other Buddhist sects partly on the basis of the emphasis practitioners place on accruing merit by participating in the ritual life of the monastery.

The reasons able-bodied Cambodian men give when seeking ordination tend to be as pragmatic as they are religious. In one survey, for instance, a novice monk admitted that what appealed to him about life in a religious community was the regular availability of food, and many more monks cited increased opportunities for education – foreign visitors to a Cambodian monastery might even find themselves discussing the progress of a monk's Master's Degree in Business Administration (Ledgerwood 2008: 151). According to the scholar who published the survey, 'the lives of educated monks are now associated with learning English, having access to computers, cell phones and other technology, and perhaps the possibility of foreign travel' (ibid.: 152).

Thanks to contributions made by Buddhists around the world, thousands of new and renovated Theravada Buddhist monasteries have sprung up across the country in the wake of the retreat of the Khmer Rouge. In fact, joining a monastery now constitutes one of the few opportunities for individual social and economic advancement in Cambodia, but it is one from which men may be excluded purely on the basis of their physical impairments. The regulatory framework of monastic life, or *vinaya*, expressly bans men and boys with physical impairments from seeking ordination, and in some cases an able-bodied monk who becomes impaired may be compelled to leave the monastery (French 1995: 84). The only other official impediments to ordination are debt, mental deficiency and disease. All of these are signs of bad karma.

According to Winter, Angkor could be improved by re-situating it in 'Pan-Asian historical, religious, and cultural contexts' and re-inventing it 'as a leisure space, as an active religious site, as a place for local community formation, and as a space of national heritage' (2006: 150–51). However, nowhere in the portion of his work under consideration here does Winter mention Cambodians with disabilities. Instead, he urges Angkor Archaeological Park authorities to conserve certain Angkorean sites as Theravada Buddhist monasteries (Winter 2004: 342). He encourages Cambodians, foreign tourists, and especially the park management to associate Angkorean monuments with the religious heritage of the majority – exactly the form of heritage from which people with disabilities have been excluded.

International agencies

Theravada Buddhist monasteries are a part of Cambodian heritage, but they are more than that. The religious system provides monks with a livelihood, and positions of recognized authority. In these particular ways, it is no different from the army. More opportunities for reliable work and positions of influence that have emerged in post-Khmer Rouge Cambodia lie in political parties and the police.

The government has no official policy on busking at the temple of Banteay Kdei. Instead, AAD's musicians ensure their protection by paying the police 10 per cent of what they make. Established in 1997 and trained by international law enforcement agencies, Angkor's Heritage Police are meant to be the country's most elite and least corrupt. According to Sovantha, on some days they demand all of the money the musicians have collected from CD sales and donations.

To survive in a society in which corruption is routine and employment opportunities are in short supply even among the able-bodied population, people with disabilities adopt various strategies. Sometimes they do not just survive, they thrive by becoming involved in the cultural sector, and just as it is with monks, the military, the bureaucracy and the police, one of the most effective strategies adopted by people with disabilities in this field has been to make useful arrangements with foreigners.

Inside their office in Siem Reap, Sovantha and the AAD's able-bodied accountant work together at a computer donated by the Australian agency Aus AID. Outside, some equipment for a woodworking shop was furnished by ABILIS, a Finnish agency for people with disabilities, though the tools themselves were made locally from old car parts. Deum, the woodcarving teacher, was impaired by polio, and he trained under Catholic missionaries, who encouraged him to perfect a 5-inch Madonna-and-Child piece, though Angkorean bas-reliefs were clearly the inspiration for the style of his other sculptures.

Woodcarving and music are two commercial activities Sovantha has pursued with AAD which clearly involve people with disabilities in the artistic interpretation of Cambodian heritage, although they are no longer as lucrative as they were when the country first opened up to international tourism in the 1990s. At the time of the onset of the global recession in late 2008, Sovantha was energetically pursuing international funding for several more or less feasible alternative schemes for the employment of the other members of AAD, including farming and weaving.

In January of 2009, an American volunteer organized a meeting between Sovantha and a representative from the international volunteer organization Openmind Projects. The programme they put together will bring international volunteers to classrooms in Cambodia to give people with disabilities training in information technology. The object is to help them launch careers as web developers, programmers or graphic designers. As a tech-savvy workforce emerges in Southeast Asia to meet the demands of western corporations eager to outsource contracts, many AAD members are optimistic about the opportunities that may arise in the course of their participation in an internet-based economy. Sovantha is also exploring the possibility of training people with disabilities as official guides at Angkor Archaeological Park.

The Land Mine Museum

Angkor Archaeological Park contains the Land Mine Museum. Not far from Banteay Kdei, fat fern fronds and banana tree leaves shade a corner of the museum grounds where a strand of barbed wire and red skull-and-crossbones signs mark a phony minefield. Beyond, different kinds of rusted metal discs, some as small as a child's yo-yo, lie bereft of their high explosive content and scattered like trash in the overgrown grass.

Aki Ra served as a child-soldier in the Khmer Rouge. As a boy, he was forced to lay thousands of mines. Once he had escaped the Khmer Rouge, he dedicated the rest of his life to finding and removing as many of the buried weapons as he could. In the forests of Northwest Cambodia, in the fields nearby, on the grounds of Angkor Archaeological Park, and in no small part thanks to his efforts, thousands of land mines turned up. Many of them became objects on display at the museum he founded in 1999.

Exhibits inside Aki Ra's museum connect different kinds of land mines to the various phases of Cambodia's wartime history. Plaques of text provide some details on their destructive capacities. Almost all of the information is technical. It focuses the visitor's attention on timelines and facts about the international weapons trade. Land mine survivors do not feature prominently except on a wall next to the gift shop entrance, where there are a number of typed pages tacked up next to photographs. With the help of the Canadian government, the Land Mine Museum Relief Fund supports several boys and girls from poor, rural communities. Each of these sheets gives a few words about one of the children living on the museum's residential compound, and Hak was one of them.

Hak does not belong to the same generation as Sovantha, Voo Un and Leng Yom. Too young to remember the reign of the Khmer Rouge, he grew up about an hour away from Siem Reap near a large seasonal lake. He was 8 years old when he set off one day with his younger brother to graze the family livestock. Since the season was dry, and the water was low, Hak was able to lead the way to an island nearby. They ventured into the shade of a copse of sugar palm trees, and Hak stepped on an anti-personnel land mine. He has no recollection of the immediate aftermath; to this day, neither Hak nor his own parents know who brought him to the hospital. Once he was there, however, it was clear that his foot would have to be amputated. Back in the shade of the trees, Hak's brother was dead.

In 1998, when Hak was twelve, he met Aki Ra. At the time, Hak was malnourished and his thumbs were dislocated from repeatedly falling on his crutches. Aki Ra proposed to Hak's parents that they allow him to come to Siem Reap and live with other land mine survivors at the new museum, where he could work and study for a job in the tourist industry. An international agency provided Hak with a prosthetic lower leg. Hak set himself to studying English and Japanese, and stayed at the Land Mine Museum for seven years. Then, at the age of 19, he tried to find a job in Siem Reap.

Disability and community

Opinions offered online by travel bloggers who have visited Cambodia as tourists frequently contrast the 'glory' of ancient Angkor to the 'tragedy' of modern times, and perhaps Cambodia's popularity as a tourist destination, especially among youthful backpackers, lies in the fact that some of the complexity of human experience finds here a tidy expression in courtly elegance and rugged adventure, ancient ruins and anarchic nightlife, meditative monks and land mine signs, and the breadth of a dichotomy that reaches, on the one hand, to the splendour of a mysterious Angkorean past, and on the other, to the mass graves and machinery of destruction unique to modern times.

The promotional literature of the travel industry has tended to emphasize the 'glories' of a Cambodia denuded of its more difficult wartime heritage. For example, before Aki Ra found powerful allies in the Canadian government, Cambodian authorities tried to shut down his museum. Concerned that it would not put forward the most pleasant, tourist-friendly image of Cambodia, they 'demanded money, threatened closure, and pulled down the museum's signs along the road to Angkor Wat' while accusing Aki Ra 'of selling arms and stockpiling weapons for use against the government' (Mack 2002).

When Hak left the Land Mine Museum to make room for new arrivals and move into his own apartment in Siem Reap, he struggled to find work in the local community. Even though Hak had studied English and Japanese, the owners of hotels, restaurants and souvenir shops in Siem Reap refused to employ him once they discovered he was an amputee. Hak was forced to leave his apartment and return to his village. There, he said he felt like a burden on his father. He was glad to be able to return to Siem Reap when Sovantha gave him a job at AAD in 2008.

Five days a week, Hak arrived at the AAD office in the morning and made an inventory. He also made translations and helped arrange the sale of woodcarvings and CDs at the market. A teacher paid for Hak to travel to Japan to tell a group of students about life as a land mine survivor in Cambodia. By the time I met him in 2008, he had a motorbike, pocket translator and the groomed, professional appearance of a young businessman. Hak carried a briefcase everywhere he went, and his cell phone rang constantly — either a girlfriend calling, or one of his many teachers checking up on the progress of his language lessons.

In 2008 ten people with disabilities were living and working at AAD, some of them with their wives and children. Sovantha organized micro-credit programmes, lessons in reading and writing Khmer, and English instruction as well as training in music and woodcarving. At its height, AAD's carving programme included six girls and four boys, ranging up to 23 years of age. Of all ten, only three were impaired by land mines, the rest by polio.

When I visited the Land Mine Museum in 2008, several of the biographies displayed on the gift shop wall mentioned polio. One young girl was blinded in a childhood accident. In fact, only one boy living at the museum in 2008 was injured by a land mine. After more than ten years, mine clearance efforts like Aki Ra's are at last succeeding, and the demographics of disability are changing.

Since young men and boys like Hak were traditionally responsible for jobs on the edge of the farm or village like clearing away the forest, it was typically they who encountered left-behind land mines. In de-mined Cambodia, women and girls are much more widely represented among the disabled community. Often it is as a result of having been impaired by polio or traffic accidents. In fact, Cambodia's renovated roadways become more crowded every year, while the number of accidents soars (The Bangkok Post 2008).

People with disabilities belong to a community of people and things, a world of Cambodians and foreigners, disabled and able-bodied people, computers and prosthetic limbs. Within this community Cambodians with disabilities are reaching out to other Cambodians with disabilities to offer technological, financial, and emotional support. And yet, as one NGO reported, most deaf Cambodians have never met another deaf person (Thomas 2005: 32). NGOs like AAD and the Land Mine Museum are forging connections among people and things to improve the material and emotional wellbeing of Cambodians with all kinds of disabilities.

Agents at Angkor

In the images of Cambodia circulated abroad to inspire pity and encourage charitable donations, crippled bodies betoken a crippled society. This is disability as tragedy, and disability as dependence. Images like these have achieved the same iconic status as the serene, half-smiling faces carved into the turrets of temple ruins like Banteay Kdei, which are featured in the websites and brochures of the travel industry. Not just as survivors, but also as workers and artists, the musicians of AAD defy the prejudices of Cambodians and tourists alike.

As I have described in this chapter, people with disabilities have been excluded from many of the opportunities for social and economic advancement that able-bodied Cambodians enjoy, and the specific ways in which people with disabilities have dealt with that exclusion have depended on associations with foreign organizations, involvement in the conservation of Cambodian heritage, and the construction of strong, inclusive communities. Organizations like AAD and the Land Mine Museum are serving people with disabilities in Cambodia, though land mines and the country's wartime heritage no longer define the lives of people with disabilities.

In the academic literature dealing with Cambodia today, not enough emphasis has been given to marginalized groups. A better understanding of the impact of international investment and the tourist industry in Cambodia, as well as more effective uses of foreign influence and resources, would result from a more thorough consideration of the capacities of marginalized groups, like people with disabilities, to interpret the past and author the future of Cambodia.

References

The Bangkok Post (2008) 'Cambodia traffic the most deadly in Asean'. Online. Available http://www.bangkokpost.com/breaking_news/breakingnews.php?id=130046 (accessed 10 November 2008).

French, L. (1995) 'The political economy of injury and compassion: amputees on the Thai–Cambodia border' in Thomas Csordas (ed.), *Embodiment and Experience: The Existential Ground of Culture and Self*, **Oxford**: Oxford University Press, pp. 69–99.

Hinton, A. (2008) 'Truth, representation, and the politics of memory after genocide' in Alexandra Kent and David Chandler (eds), *People of Virtue: Reconfiguring Religion, Power and Moral Order in Cambodia Today*, Copenhagen: Nordic Institute of Asian Studies, pp. 62–84.

Ledgerwood, J. (2008) 'Buddhist practice in rural Kandal Province, 1960 and 2003. An essay in honor of May M. Ebihara', in Alexandra Kent and David Chandler (eds), *People of Virtue: Reconfiguring Religion, Power and Moral Order in Cambodia Today*, Copenhagen: Nordic Institute of Asian Studies, pp. 147–79.

Mack, E. (2002) 'Grisly Gallery: Cambodia's Land Mine Museum Shows War Is Hell'. Online. Available http://www.utne.com/2002-09-01/GrislyGallery.aspx?page=1 (accessed 10 November 2008).

Thomas, P. (2005) *Poverty Reduction and Development in Cambodia: Enabling Disabled People to Play a Role*, Disability Knowledge and Research Programme. Available http://disabilitykar.net/research/pol.cam.html.

Winter, T. (2004) 'Landscape, memory and heritage: New Year celebrations at Angkor, Cambodia', *Current Issues in Tourism*, 7(4–5): 330–45.

—— (2006) 'Bakheng tourism: setting new standards for Angkor', Phnom Bakheng Workshop on Public Interpretation. Siem Reap: APSARA & World Monuments Fund.

4

'SEE NO EVIL'

Victoria Phiri

Disabled people are largely absent from the narratives of Zambian life and culture presented in the country's national museums. This chapter explores perceptions of and attitudes towards physical and mental difference within both historical traditions and cultural beliefs and contemporary values and perspectives in Zambia and considers how, in turn, these social under-standings of disability might have influenced representational practices within Zambia's National Museums. It further considers how increasing concern for disability rights within Zambia might offer possibilities for informing alternative representational forms and practices.

I consider shifting understandings of disability from Zambia's colonial past,[1] through the early period of independence and from the late 1970s onwards, a period in which both conventional medicine and Christianity have had widespread influence.[2] To do this I draw on a number of Zambian studies as well as literature from Western countries. To supplement the literature-based research and to gain an insight into contemporary attitudes I also conducted in-depth interviews with 40 individuals between August and November 2008 from the towns of Livingstone and Lusaka[3] including persons with disabilities and non-disabled individuals, professionals and parents of disabled children as well as interviews with curatorial staff at the National Museums of Zambia.

Disability and Zambian cultural beliefs

Zambia is situated in south central Africa with a population of approximately 9.7 million (as at 2000 census) and comprising 72 Bantu-speaking ethnic groups. Recent estimates suggest that disabled people in Zambia constitute 2 per cent of this population (Phiri 2008: 14) although, as Kisanji has argued, attempts to gather such statistics in different parts of the world are always problematic because 'perception of impairments is culture-bound and culture-sensitive assessment instruments are yet to be developed' (1998: 3). Indeed, as Devlieger (2000) states, disability is a cultural reality that is bound by both time and place such that definitions may be different from one social grouping to another and different from one historical period to another.

Disability and the supernatural

Early writers on the traditional beliefs held by various societies within Zambia highlighted the prevalence of the attribution of disability to supernatural or spiritual causes. Gouldsbury and Sheane (1911: 119), for example, found that among the plateau people of Northern Zambia, disability was attributed to external and usually supernatural influences such as angry ancestors, evil spirits or witchcraft. For instance, albinos were said to be born of wandering spirits. A birth of twins was also looked upon as an abnormality and a bad omen that required the entire community in which such a birth occurred to be purified by special rites together with the parents of the children. Gouldsburg and Sheane (1911) also documented the practice of human sacrifice amongst the Bemba people and their accounts suggest that people with physical impairments were the preferred targets for these practices which were only stopped by the spread of Christianity. Furthermore, Smith *et al.* (1968: 239) wrote that the Ila people attributed 'unexplained illnesses' (such as mental illnesses) to punishment by ancestral or 'bad' spirits. Epilepsy was believed to be caused by an animal whose name was not even allowed to be mentioned; it was merely called 'Shibandilwabana', meaning 'it is not to be mentioned in the presence of children'.

While understandings of disability in Zambia have changed considerably, a number of studies in recent decades have found that traditional beliefs about the causes of physical differences persist and have argued that these play a part in maintaining the stigma, isolation and discrimination linked to contemporary experiences of disability. For instance Phiri, in his 1979 study of attitudes towards disabled people in Zambia, found that pregnant women were not allowed to look at or associate with disabled people for fear that they would give birth to a disabled child. Similar attitudes were found in a subsequent study by Phiri (2008: 22), who found that, in many rural areas of Zambia, a disabled child is still viewed as a curse upon the family to the extent that, if the impairment is severe, the child may be hidden away from society.

Disability as punishment

The association of disability with the idea of punishment is also demonstrated in the folklore of Zambia. One of the most common folktales still found in many Zambian societies is a story about a group of jealous young mothers who trick their friend into killing her child. After discovering that she has been tricked, the young mother goes away from her home into the wilderness where she meets with a goddess who rewards her misfortune with a very beautiful baby to replace the one that was killed. Upon returning to her community, her friends – who are consumed with envy over her new baby – deliberately kill their own children and venture out into the wilderness hoping to receive equally beautiful babies. However, the goddess punishes them for their trickery and deceit by giving them babies with one eye, one arm and one leg. The young mothers are so horrified at the sight of these babies that they try to get rid of them by abandoning them in the forest before setting off for home. To their disappointment and horror the babies follow them into their village where their families, appalled by their misfortune, banish the young mothers and their babies from the village.

Joseph Kisanji argues that such folkloric representations of physical difference can help us to understand contemporary attitudes and behaviours. 'Folklore', he suggests, 'provides the raw material for explaining a community's behavior towards one another or one section of a community towards another. Since it is metaphoric and embedded within the day-to-day life, folklore can also be considered to provide the community's account for its actions in a way that is intelligible and justifiable to its members' (1998: 5). Following Kisanji, this tale might therefore be understood as reflecting and reinforcing a negative view of disability as a form of punishment, as something abhorrent, something to be ashamed of or to get rid of.

Shifting attitudes

Predominantly negative perceptions of disability which appear to be under-pinned by traditional Zambian beliefs appeared in a number of the interviews I conducted during 2008. Several interviewees referred to the belief that when a dying person breathes on an expectant mother, the child she is carrying will be disabled. Others suggested that disability was caused by the breaking of a taboo by a pregnant woman (for example, promiscuous behaviour or the eating of something forbidden) or that disability was a form of punishment by bad spirits or angry ancestors for an individual having done something wrong or committing an act of evil. Still others suggested that disability can be caused by magic or witchcraft performed by an individual with supernatural powers motivated by vengeance or envy.

However, other interviewees suggested that these beliefs which associate disability with the supernatural or spiritual are no longer widely supported. For example, Malia, a 19-year-old 'born again Christian' from Lusaka, believed that contemporary Zambian society, which is largely Christian, views disability as simply 'differently able' and Ngosa, a 42-year-old nurse from Livingstone, commented that 'all people are created by a good, loving God'.

Disability and Christianity

Although it has been argued that the widespread influence of Christianity in Zambia has played a part in countering negative attitudes towards physical difference it would be misleading to suggest that conceptions of disability, underpinned by Christianity stand in stark (positive) contrast to those shaped by so-called traditional Zambian cultural beliefs. Indeed, van Kampen, van Zijverden and Emmett's account of the influence of Christian thinking on perceptions of difference highlights the problematic nature of what has been termed a 'religious model' of understanding disability:

> In a Western, Judeo-Christian society, the roots of understanding bodily difference have been grounded in Biblical references, the consequent responses and impact of the Christian church, and the effect of the Enlightenment project underpinning the modern era. These embodied states were seen as the result of evil sprits, the devil, witchcraft or God's displeasure. Alternatively, such people were also signified as reflecting 'the suffering Christ', and were often perceived to be angelic or beyond human status, to be a blessing for others.
>
> Therefore, themes which embrace notions of sin or sanctity, impurity and wholeness, undesirability and weakness, care and compassion, healing and burden have formed the dominant bases of Western conceptualizations of, and responses to, groups of people who in a contemporary context, are described as disabled.[4]
>
> (2008: 26)

Van Kampen, van Zijverden and Emmett go on to explicitly draw similarities between conceptions of disability underpinned by Christian beliefs and those found in so-called 'traditional' African religions and beliefs. Understandings of disability within Zambia therefore might be most appropriately conceptualised as arising out of a complex blend of influences which shape individual and community behaviours and actions. While it is possible to see an ongoing legacy of influence stemming from belief systems which can be traced back many generations, through time these have been overlaid with other influences. For example, Audrey, a 26-year-old woman I interviewed in Livingstone, whose child has cerebral palsy, has pursued both conventional medical care (at Livingstone Hospital) and spiritual healing. She explained that the various spiritual leaders she has consulted from different churches have all confirmed that her child's condition is 'the work of the devil' and 'needs prayers'. Indeed, three out of the five mothers I spoke with whose children are receiving physiotherapy treatments at Livingstone Hospital confirmed having prayers with church spiritual healers to cast away the evil spirits believed to be affecting their children.

The extent to which cultural beliefs which view disability as arising from supernatural or spiritual causes continue to hold sway remains contested and unclear. For example, a recent Editorial in the *Times of Zambia* (2008: 1), one of Zambia's main newspapers, suggested that the lack of attention to the needs and rights of disabled children was a product of the traditional beliefs and cultural attitudes that still continue to provide answers for the causes of disability in many parts of Zambian society. The report regretted that many parents still regard disability as a form of misfortune, a curse or punishment, and argued that these regressive attitudes helped to explain the continuing discrimination, isolation and stigma experienced by disabled children today. This, the newspaper argued, has resulted in disabled children missing out on educational opportunities and becoming beggars on the streets. The report was highly critical of the government; in particular policies which have seen schools and other institutions established which segregate disabled people, further contributing to isolation and stigma.[5] This view of the continuing prevalence and influence of attitudes which view disability in wholly negative ways is also supported by Phiri (2008).

I return shortly to the growing concern for disability rights in Zambia – and the possibilities this might hold for changing societal attitudes – but first I turn attention to the Zambian National Museums (and the Livingstone Museum in particular) to consider the ways in which representations of disability have been shaped by the complex and shifting blend of influences described in the first part of the chapter.

Museums and disability in Zambia

The National Museums Board of Zambia was instituted in 1966 through an Act of Parliament and mandated to control, manage and develop museums in the country. The Act replaced the Northern Rhodesia Government Notice 17, first introduced in 1946 to serve Livingstone Museum, the only national museum established during the colonial period in 1934. Through the 1966 Act,[6] the National Museums Board of Zambia, on behalf of the Government, established museums for the education, enjoyment and development of the nation through research, collection and preservation of Zambia's heritage.[7] The Livingstone Museum is Zambia's largest museum in terms of collections, exhibitions and personnel. The Museum is multi-disciplinary and the permanent exhibitions (in prehistory, history, natural history, and ethnography and art) mainly depict the development of Zambian society from prehistoric times to the present day.

In recent years there have been efforts to make the building and its programmes more accessible to disabled visitors. In 1993 an exhibition especially designed for blind visitors was created and, in 2006, a ramp and accessible public conveniences were constructed. However, the inclusion of disabled people does not extend to the museum's displays or exhibitions. Indeed, representations of disabled people are almost entirely absent from the various scenarios depicting Zambian society through the different disciplines of the museum.

The Ethnography and Art galleries depict the cultural evolution of Zambia through time and space. Here, large dioramas inhabited by life-size models of people performing various tasks and activities have been used to recreate village scenarios in rural settings as well as dwellings in the urban centres of Zambia. The rural scenarios show the main activities of village life such as food processing, which is mainly done by women, and craftsmanship such as basketry and blacksmithing, that is mainly done by men. The urban centre scenarios depict life and culture in the towns – tarred roads, industrial activity, banks, huge housing complexes, traffic, the police, telephones and electricity. They also depict the challenges associated with major urban centres in the country such as water pollution by industries, overcrowding and poverty in the form of shanty compounds or slums, street vending and makeshift street shops. In the depictions of both rural and urban life, there are no representations (models or images) of disabled people. In many ways this might seem unsurprising.[8] Yet the absence of disabled figures from Livingstone Museum's urban dioramas is perhaps especially striking since the major town centres in Zambia are characterized by streets lined with people with disabilities (especially blind people) begging – a feature that is effectively erased despite the Museum's concern within these galleries to highlight a variety of social and environmental issues.

At the far end of the gallery is a space called 'the museum' in which 'traditional' artifacts associated with Zambian culture and the circle of life from birth to death are presented. Displayed here are objects linked to traditional birth rites, rites of passage, traditional food production, crafts, medicines, witchcraft and burial rites. Facing the section of the display concerned with witchcraft, sorcery and burial rites is the figure of a man with a heavily distorted body carved out of wood. The figure has one arm which is holding a medicine gourd on his head while the other arm extends from his shoulder and ends as a foot. His face is also severely disfigured. The carving, done by a prominent artist who has provided art works for the Livingstone Museum since 1958, is called 'the diviner'. The medicine gourd on the figure's head, the rattle he holds and the charm around his neck confirm his trade as a diviner. While 'the diviner' is an artist's response to the theme of the display (rather than a representation of a real individual) it is perhaps significant that the museum's only depiction of bodily difference is displayed in a way which operates to confirm an association with witchcraft and the supernatural.

The absence of representations of disabled individuals within the Livingstone Museum's history galleries is similarly striking, although for different reasons. Here the displays show the historical development of Zambian society from the period of Bantu migration to the present day through a wide range of images and objects. The history displays depict personalities, situations and major events that relate to landmarks in the history of the nation such as Kingdom formation, the slave trade, colonialism, the struggle for Independence, and the first, second and third republics. One part of the gallery features a display entitled 'The People of Zambia' – a map of the country that has been populated with pictures of prominent members of society; individuals who have made significant contributions to the country's social, political and cultural development over time. This 'wall of achievement' – intended to show a wide range of people who have contributed to the development of the country in various fields such as politics, sport, music, arts, education and so on – features no disabled individuals.

Interviews with curatorial and management staff at the Livingstone Museum, conducted during November 2008, revealed a variety of views on, and explanations for, the absence of disabled people within the museum's narratives. One senior manager felt that drawing particular attention to disabled people by making them part of the exhibitions would be inappropriate since, in his opinion, Zambian society is very inclusive of disabled people. These concerns around the appropriateness of drawing attention to difference were echoed by another curator who felt that including disabled figures within, for example, a display of traditional dress would operate to distract visitors from the main narrative focus on costume and textiles. More pragmatic issues were raised by another curator who felt that prevalent attitudes towards disabled people, which meant that many were hidden away from public view, made it difficult to include them in stories of Zambian life. In this way, the museum's displays were felt to reflect the invisibility and segregation of disabled people in some aspects of Zambian life.

These pragmatic concerns were echoed by another curator who attributed the absence of disabled people from the 'People of Zambia' exhibit to a lack of space, highlighting the difficulty of including all the prominent individuals who had been nominated for inclusion during the process of exhibit development. However, he believed that there were a number of disabled persons who deserved a place. He noted, in particular, the significant achievements of Lazarus Tembo, once Zambia's most popular folk singer and a blind man who was not only a successful musician but the country's only disabled person to become a Minister in the Zambian government during the late 1980s, and another prominent blind musician, P. K. Chishala. The curator explained that he had suggested the names of these two individuals for a position on the 'wall of achievement' but that they were eventually not selected for inclusion by the exhibition team.

An artist who worked on the permanent history exhibition lamented that it was very difficult to change the view of the team of experts that decided what would be included within the displays and what would not. Interviewed in November 2008, he argued that there are a number of disabled people who should have been featured amongst those individuals who have made important contributions to Zambian life and culture: 'They should have at least included Tembo, if not for society in general but for us, the disabled. He was our role model and we are so proud of what he was able to achieve in a society where disability is quite often misunderstood.'

His views concerning the value of including disabled individuals within the museum's celebration of extraordinary individuals who have shaped

Zambian culture and life were supported by others working in the field of disability, also interviewed in this study. According to members of the Association of Disabled People in Zambia, Tembo offered them a glimpse of hope in a society where disabled persons are marginalized. Tembo also gave them dignity as he demonstrated that disability need not necessarily mean exclusion from public life. Interviewees also claimed that Tembo's prominent public office position helped to challenge some of the prevalent negative perceptions surrounding disability.[9]

Disability rights in Zambia

What part then might Zambia's museums play in nurturing more progressive social attitudes towards disability and what challenges are likely to be encountered in any attempts to redress the invisibility and marginalization of disabled people in the stories the museum tells about Zambian life and culture? Although the development of more inclusive narratives within the museum is not without its difficulties, the increasing concern for and discussion surrounding the rights of disabled people in Zambia might usefully be drawn upon to inform the process.

The earliest organization focused on the needs of disabled people in the country – The Northern Rhodesia Society for the Blind – was formed by volunteers in 1952. Since then a number of disability organizations have been formed, many of which have operated to secure rights for disabled people and have functioned alongside organizations that have campaigned for civil and human rights for a range of groups. In common with other rights campaigns in Europe and America, as described by British disability studies scholars Colin Barnes and Geoff Mercer (2002), disability rights campaigns in Zambia have directed government attention to the effects of social and environmental barriers on people with disabilities, highlighting issues such as access to education, employment and buildings as well as the pernicious and pervasive effects of discriminatory attitudes and beliefs. Indeed, these campaigns have yielded some significant results in government policy and legislation. The Zambian government has developed a human rights policy which gives support to a range of rights for disabled people including the right to education, to economic and social security and to participate in all social, creative and recreational facilities (Phiri 2008: 27). Moreover, to ensure that disabled people have access to their rights, the government of Zambia established a legal framework in the form of the Disability Act of 1996 through which all discrimination on the basis of disability is banned and a series of strategies designed to support the achievement of full rights were put forward.

Although the principle of rights for disabled people is now established in the political arena, the extent to which these rights might be successfully realized remains open to considerable debate. Phiri (2008: 30) argues that there are a number of hindrances that make the implementation and observation of these human rights impossible. For instance, he observes that the right to education is hindered by a lack of accessible schools, colleges and universities and a shortage of appropriately trained teachers; problems that are, in turn, compounded by related issues of inaccessible transport systems and rural isolation. Phiri further observes that a lack of access to education may, in turn, lead to a failure to attain other human rights such as the right to economic and social security and the right to information. Similarly, the right to participate fully in all social, creative or recreational facilities is hindered by the prevalence of discriminatory social attitudes which restrict disabled people's opportunities for social interaction in the public sphere.

Supporting rights in the museum

Despite – or perhaps because of – these barriers to the attainment of rights, museums alongside other public institutions have a potentially important part to play in contributing towards the greater inclusion of disabled people. The Livingstone Museum, for example, might redress the paucity of images and objects that reflect disabled peoples' lives throughout the displays and include material portraying disabled individuals in ways which challenge dominant negative attitudes. Attempts to represent social and cultural diversity in the People of Zambia exhibit, for example, might usefully be extended to include prominent disabled figures.

In addition, there exists an opportunity to draw attention to the discrimination, stigma and disadvantage experienced by many disabled people. Indeed, the Livingstone Museum's displays that focus on urban centres and attempt to highlight the social issues and challenges they face – especially those linked to poverty – have a particular role to play. In most urban centres of Zambia, poverty is largely made visible by the many disabled persons who line the streets as beggars. As Devlieger (1998: 436) explains, people with disabilities in Africa tend to be involved in the lower-status occupations and activities such as small-scale crafts businesses, street vending and begging. Phiri also notes that 'poverty and disability are linked in a vicious cycle of cause/effect paradox' (2008: 26). He explains, for example, that disabled people in Zambia are much more likely to live in poverty and deprivation as compared to non-disabled people. This is largely attributed to the fact that disabled people have limited employment opportunities arising from inadequate access to education and training and a mainly inaccessible environment with discriminatory cultural and attitudinal barriers. The Museum's engagement with these very real social challenges would help to raise public and political awareness of the experiences of Zambia's disabled population.

Even though it seems that the inclusion of disabled people in museum narratives in Zambia might play a part in supporting the realization of

61

human rights for people with disabilities, there are nevertheless a number of challenges, both pragmatic and ethical, that potentially constrain museum engagement with these issues. The invisibility, exclusion and segregation of disabled people in many parts of Zambian culture pose challenges to curators in terms of collecting objects and supporting images that could be used to interpret disability-related stories. These practical challenges are compounded by concerns about community and visitor responses that might be generated by attempts to increase the visibility of disabled people – people who, for the reasons explored in this chapter, are often purposefully hidden from public view.

This situation poses a series of especially difficult questions for museum staff. Should the museum, for example, prominently display that which some visitors, especially those for whom disability is firmly linked to the supernatural, steadfastly want to avoid looking at? Just as importantly, how would disabled visitors respond to exhibitions that highlight disability-related themes in a society where many have learnt that their place is in the private, not public, realm? These are just some of the challenges that museum practitioners reflected upon during the interviews I conducted for this chapter and which continue to operate to constrain the museum moving forward on these issues. Further research is needed to explore ways in which the museum might negotiate these ethical challenges but until the exclusion of disabled people from the stories of Zambian life and culture is redressed, the institution risks perpetuating wider negative social attitudes towards difference.

Notes

1 The colonial period in Zambia lasted from 1890 to 1964 (1890–1924 under the British South African Company and 1924–64 under the British Colonial Office). This period is important to this study in shedding light on Zambian society before the arrival of Christianity and conventional medicine, factors which have had an enormous impact on social and cultural change.

2 This period shows the widespread influence of Christianity with about 98 per cent of Zambians being Christians and, by 1991, Zambia being declared a Christian nation (Gifford 1998). In this period, there was also growth in the practice of conventional medicine and the establishment of health institutions throughout the country. Phiri (2008: 13) indicates that, by 2008, there were about 1,285 health institutions which included central hospitals, specialized hospitals, general hospitals, district hospitals, rural health centres, urban health centres and military hospitals. In this period the government also showed commitment to the provision of health care to its citizens through health care reforms that have improved general health indicators.

3 Although it did not prove possible, due to resource constraints, to carry out additional interviews in rural areas I have purposely drawn on existing studies of attitudes concerning disability outside of the urban centres of the country to ensure a variety of perspectives are considered.

4 This view of the role that Christianity has played in underpinning negative attitudes towards disability has also been discussed by scholars within the field of disability studies. See, for example Barnes, Mercer and Shakespeare (1999).

5 Institutional solutions to the 'problem' of disability are not, of course, unique to Zambia. Barnes, Mercer and Shakespeare (1999), for example, describe the ways in which processes of industrialization and medicalization in Britain in the nineteenth and twentieth centuries led to increasing segregation of disabled people within a range of institutions.

6 Government of the Republic of Zambia (GRZ) Act No. 10 of 1966, Section 4 (2).

7 See also *The Livingstone Museum Annual Report for the period 1st January to 31st December 1965,* held by the Livingstone Museum Archives.

8 Indeed, recent research in the UK has found similar omissions throughout museums and galleries of all kinds. See, for example, Sandell *et al.* (2005).

9 These comments were made during interviews with staff from the Disabled People's Association of Zambia and Women for Change in Zambia, carried out between August and September 2008.

References

Barnes, C., Mercer, G. and Shakespeare, T. (1999) *Exploring Disability, a Sociological Introduction,* Cambridge: Polity Press.

Barnes, C. and Mercer, G. (2002) *Disability,* Cambridge: Polity Press.

Devlieger, P. J. (1998) 'Representations of physical disability in colonial Zimbabwe: the Cyrene Mission and *Pitaniko, the Film of Cyrene*', *Disability and Society,* 13 (5): 709–24.

Devlieger, P. J. (2000) 'Rejoinder: The culture and disability perspective on disability', *Disability and Rehabilitation,* 20(11): 526–27.

Gifford, P. (1998) *African Christianity: Its Public Role,* London: C. Hurst and Company.

Gouldsbury, C. and Sheane, H. (1911) *The Great Plateau of Northern Rhodesia,* London: Edward Arnold.

Government of the Republic of Zambia (1966) *The Livingstone Museum Annual Report for the period 1st January to 31st December, 1965,* Lusaka: Government Printer.

Kisanji, J. (1998) 'Culture and disability: an analysis of inclusive education based on African folklore', Paper presented to *The International Expert Meeting and Symposium on Local Concepts and Beliefs on Disability in Different Cultures,* Bonn, Germany, 21–24 May 1998. Online. Available http://www.eenet.org.uk/key_issues/cultural/culture_disability.doc (Accessed 20th May 2009).

Phiri, D. C. (2008) 'Adopted Physical Activity', Unpublished thesis, Halmstad University, Sweden.

Phiri, N. L. (1979) *Problems of the Handicapped: An Assessment of Attitudes Towards the Disabled and Implications for Rehabilitation in Zambia,* Lusaka: Lusaka Institute for African Studies.

Sandell, R., Delin, A., Dodd, J. and Gay, J. (2005) 'Beggars, freaks and heroes? Museum collections and the hidden history of disability', *Museum Management and Curatorship,* 20(1): 5–19.

Times of Zambia (2008) 'Editorial', *Times of Zambia,* 22 September 2008: 1.

van Kampen, M., van Zijverden, I. M. and Emmett, T. (2008) 'Reflections on poverty and disability: a review of literature', *Asia Pacific Disability Rehabilitation Journal,* 19(1): 19–36. Online. Available http://www.aifo.it/english/resources/online/apdrj/apdrj108/poverty_disability.pdf (Accessed 15 May 2009).

5

GHOSTS IN THE WAR MUSEUM

Ana Carden-Coyne

Museums of war, conflict and genocide have to manage complex histories of war – pertaining to its conduct, meaning, and national and personal legacies. Highly politicized institutions, with intricate funding relationships to governments and donors, war museums are mindful of their diverse constituencies, embracing relationships with veterans, families and the wider public. While they display a great capacity to discuss violence and death, especially within the context of heroic remembering, the subjects of maiming and disability are more problematic. Despite the fact that wounding and physical and psychological disablement remain major legacies of war, museums often avoid discussing this impact on soldiers and ignore the disablement, rape and torture of civilians.

Recent work on 'atrocity museums' offers a global map based on observations of shared discourses, noting their exponential growth in the 'global rush' to commemorate through memorial museums (Williams 2007). States are willing to fund such museums for a range of reasons, both local and global, for instance promoting human rights and reconciliation discourses alongside tourism. When war museums are examined through the concept of 'dark tourism' (Stone 2006), visitors are transformed into macabre tourists invoking less the call to commemorate, and more a global, cultural and media preoccupation with death and suffering. However, scholars have argued for a more nuanced understanding of the consumption aspects of dark tourism, beyond that of supply (the museum) and demand (the visitor), suggesting that audience appeal is also about finding ways to confront death in modern societies (Stone and Sharpley 2008: 574). This is especially when the meaning of war is complicated by conflicting ideals of national duty and heroism versus the reality of wounding and the longer-term consequences of economic and social dislocation for traumatized and disabled people.

The representation of wounded and disabled people mirrors these contradictions. Although historically poignant, the interpretation and symbolism associated with wounding is open to political exploitation and emotional manipulation, while the disabled figure is often entirely absent from the war narrative. This chapter compares and contrasts a range of museums, examining the political uses and abuses, absences and presences of disabled people in contexts of conflict and genocide. Drawing upon evidence from Britain, the United States, Vietnam, Cambodia and Rwanda, this chapter explores the politics of representation in culturally diverse museological practices that are framed by both local contexts and global narratives about the meaning of conflict and genocidal violence.

Globalized museological trends

Museums of war, conflict and genocide operate within an international context of geopolitical relations, trade and tourism, alongside local audiences and employed museum staff. In some former war zones, humanitarian aid and non-governmental agencies constitute a major visitor-base and help to generate global tourism of young people curious about war and genocide, especially when particular conflicts have been imagined through media and filmic representations, such as with the Holocaust and events in Vietnam, Rwanda and Cambodia. War museums thus mediate local needs within wider, globalized narratives that interpret the meaning and legacy of war and genocide. The intertwining of the local and global within museum displays, and at the point of the audience–exhibition encounter, requires a more complex understanding of the way that the 'dream spaces' (Kavanagh 2000) of war museums are entrusted with confronting and healing the violent past. This dual project is formulated in a web of local and transnational interrelations that shape how disabled people are either represented or silenced in war museums in both Western and non-Western societies.

Scholarship on Cambodia, for instance, highlights global discourses of 'human suffering' (Duffy 2001) and the mobilization of genocidal narratives for political purposes (Hughes 2003a; Williams 2004). In the capital Phnom Penh, the Tuol Sleng Museum of Genocide Crimes, housed in the former prison S21, has been viewed as offering a 'master narrative of the successor state' (Ledgerwood 1997); an emblem of Vietnamese intervention that was politically important in exposing to the international community the genocide of Pol Pot's Khmer Rouge revolution. Holocaust museological practices were critical in re-narrating Cambodia as the victim and Vietnam as the rescuer, both at Tuol Sleng and at the Vietnam War Remnants Museum. The original curator of the latter, the retired Vietnamese Colonel Mai Lam, had toured the sites of Auschwitz and consulted with its curators. Representation in Cambodia, then, borrowed from both the Vietnamese perspective of the 'American War' and the Euro-American case, while also embedded in the politics of Cambodia's national reconstruction in relation to Vietnam's role as an 'occupying liberator'. In both museums, graphic images of prisoner torture and its material culture (chains, gallows, water tanks, identity photographs) operated as politicized global 'envoys' of the deeply traumatic past (Hughes 2003b).

Scholars of the Vietnam War – researching entirely from an American perspective – have discussed the 'entangling of memory': a web of contests between personal recollection and 'organised forgetting' (Sturken 1997). Examining Vietnamese war museology, however, anthropologists emphasize the diverse and plural field of 'transnational memory' (Schwenkel 2006). In much global memory work, the dead and the dying are valorized while the disabled are largely ignored. While scholars of the memorials of the two world wars have demonstrated the way the 'absent dead' haunted the minds of the living, and how this was borne out in material culture and sacred spaces (Moriarty 1995; Inglis 2005), museums – like memorials – often avoid the consequences of war for those who live on. In the global war commemoration culture, there are few memorials dedicated to men and women disabled in conflicts, whether combatants or civilians. To be effective educational and community spaces, war museums have an opportunity to confront not just death and injury, but the living legacies of conflict – disabled soldiers and civilians – in order to resist the 'social amnesia' (Nora 1996; Forty and Kuchler 1999) of war's real and ongoing consequences and, at the same time, address the issue of the social exclusion of disabled people. Facing the plight of the war disabled could also be an effective way of creating greater awareness of society's vulnerable citizens.

Instead of the living disabled, however, war museums and memorials focus on commemorating the dead, side-stepping the way that war maims and traumatizes people, and avoid the significant impact of conflict on disabled people's lives, such as the interruption and endangering of care for disabled adults and children in homes and institutions. The war in Bosnia, for instance, has warranted a culture of commemoration, especially following the international community's willingness to recognize the genocide in Srebrenica. Despite humanitarian efforts to shift discriminating attitudes, the experience of disabled adults and children in the former Yugoslavia, especially those resident in state institutions during the war, remains hidden (Hastie 1997: 93–121). Museum representation often mirrors this; disabled people's stories are largely lost in comprehending conflicts that deeply impact them.

By contrast, scholars of the Holocaust have revealed the targeting of disabled children for forced euthanasia and extermination. In Berlin, an 18-month operation provided the first gas chambers to euthanize more than 70,000 disabled people labelled as 'lives not worth living' and 'useless eaters' (Lifton 1986; Friedlander 1995; Bryant 2005). Recent scholarship highlights how disability was fundamental to Nazi culture, mobilizing images about veterans, hereditable disease, and disabled civilians. Carol Poore contributes new information on how German disabled people's organizations negotiated between collaboration, self-advocacy and resistance (Poore 2007: 67–138). At the United States Holocaust Memorial Museum (Washington DC), the permanent exhibitions miss the chance to educate visitors on the way that cultural representations of disability were continually circulated to reinforce the Third Reich's racial goals. Moreover, the significance of euthanasia targeted at disabled people – beginning with German 'Aryan' children – in framing the Final Solution remains a significantly undeveloped area for education. While genocidal violence, for instance in Rwanda or Darfur, is explored to some extent, the impact on disabled people rarely features within the analysis, or the comprehension of war's impact on vulnerable groups. What, then, are some of the challenges museums face in addressing the absence of disability in museums of war and conflict?

Spectacularization and the 'failure to see'

The numbing circulation of Holocaust imagery, as Barbie Zelizer argues, has operated to both aestheticize genocide and anaesthetize viewers' responses to images, inducing social amnesia; a remembering that only serves to forget (Zelizer 1998). Violent imagery is 'publicly framed' through 'media pandemonium' that 'aestheticizes' rather than communicates the complex realities of war, famine, or repression. Yet in both the media and the museum, violated bodies can become exhibition objects that reinforce the spectacle of 'distant suffering' (Boltanski, 1999: 3–13). The effect of pity eclipses any discussion of the complexities of justice. How, then, can museums engage with the physical and psychological disabilities caused by war without perpetuating the 'failure to see' (Sliwinski 2004)? Curators may fear using images of disabled people, aware that photography presents a false promise of 'awakening social conscience', and might cause distress from the 'spectator's inability to respond', or cause offence to disabled audiences (Sliwinski 2004: 150). How can this 'failure to see' be addressed in relation to the presence and absence in museums of those disabled in war, especially given the complex histories that shape the way disabled people have been represented, excluded and politicized?

For many museums, the wounded body is a necessary object through which the story of war is told. Whether in paintings or photographs that transform intimate violations through framing or enlargement on exhibition boards, the wounded body symbolizes a multitude of themes: suffering and victimhood; triumph and heroism; military values; the rightness of a cause; victory and the conquering of an enemy. Wounded symbolism is not just a result of the photograph's attempt to 'represent' the materiality of the body, objectifying painful flesh as a museum exhibit with a supplied narrative. The transformation of a person's physical wounds into a visual object is also part of a wider desire to 'see' the pain of war. Such photographs, as Susan Sontag writes, provide a mythic documentary proof that atrocities are verifiable; audiences increasingly require technology to authenticate the truth, especially when violence is denied or obfuscated by politics (Sontag 2003). While visual culture is fundamental to curatorial practice, the pain of 'others', at times, can operate to distance rather than inform audiences. Moreover, I would argue that the spectacle of photographs of wounded bodies (which become objects) often supplants the museum's ability to critically interrogate the social, economic and political responsibility for violence.

Wounding is the principal aim of arms manufacture and the conduct of war. Both the practice of wounding (hitting targets) and, conversely, heroically sustaining wounds are glorified in military culture. In a different sense, consumer culture has also encouraged war's 'pleasure culture' in boys' literature, toys and digital games, for instance, generating mythic representations of 'soldier heroes' (Paris 2000; Dawson 1994). At the same time, war museums, as educational facilities, rely on school-age audiences and play to the desire for 'horrible histories'. Museum shops sell military paraphernalia from toy jet fighters to khaki teddy bears, normalizing war through harmless consumerism. Other constituencies include ex-servicemen, widows and families. How then does the war museum negotiate the range of potentially conflicted constituencies? Some will be more amenable to heroization and 'just cause' militarism, while others might be peace or anti-war audiences. The expectations of these groups mean that the impact of war is often explored without challenging the principle of conducting war, for risk of offending. Why is it that wounding is a story told, but that disabled soldiers are so often missing from the main narrative? If war museums are conduits of memory, why do many museums (Western and non-Western) forget the reality that one of war's major outcomes is not just death, but maiming – and that in modern warfare, most people survive. Is the war museum uncomfortable with the political and social consequences of war because audiences, too, evade these painful issues?

Audience responses

Enabled and disabled audiences will have complex personal responses to representations of war and maiming. According to Anne Delin, in most museums 'disabled people might find not a single image of a person like themselves – no affirmation that in the past people like themselves lived, worked, created great art, wore clothes, were loved or esteemed' (Delin 2002: 85). When the museum purports to commemorate war, how can the absence of injury and disability be understood? Delin suggests that this 'hidden history' is the result of a suite of intersecting prejudices, those of both the past (which shaped the formation of collections) and the present day (ibid.: 86). Museums may also be wary of offending; silence and ignorance might seem preferable to incurring community wrath. Curators are sometimes uncertain of how to deal with historical terms like 'cripple' that are frowned upon in contemporary usage. Contemporary concerns about disability can also be projected onto disabled people living in the past (ibid.: 86) and, as a result of such sensitivities, complexity in understanding disabled peoples' lives can be lost through the prism of contemporary politics.

Indeed, people living with war disabilities are often stereotyped to embody archetypal victims or heroes (whose difference is erased and normalized), and curators may worry about how this is interpreted. Moreover, women and children disabled in conflict are largely absented from such discourses, incongruous with the masculine enterprise of war. In relation to the Holocaust, Dominick LaCapra warns of 'fetishizing' traumatic histories or totalizing them into cohesive narratives. He suggests 'empathetic unsettlement' in order to prevent the creation of falsely uplifting stories that enforce closure and endorse the political motives of reconciliation (LaCapra 1999). Delin also asks an important question, 'whether in forgetting the disability of some of our heroes, [we are] slowing the process of inclusion for today's disabled people?' (Delin 2002: 90). Practices of concealing and revealing frequently operate in museums – but, as Delin's analysis highlights, these are not always in the service of disabled people.

The politics of absence and presence

War museums have a great ethical responsibility to represent and engage with disability for two main reasons. First, the legacies of colonial violence fundamental to war and empire-building continue to function today in the forms of social exclusion and racial discrimination. Second, one of the most significant consequences of war is the disablement of soldiers and civilians, yet this aspect is rarely a focus in exhibitions. Why are war museums – often charged with a memorial mission to commemorate the dead – silent about the effects of war on those who continue to live afterwards and whose struggles do not end with the cessation of hostilities? Why is it that death and violent weaponry can be confronted – even spectacularized in photographs and objects – and yet disability maintains a powerful absence?

The absence of disability is especially significant given that recent years have seen museums increasingly concerned to take seriously their responsibility in educating audiences and framing social debates, empowering visitors to construct their own meanings whilst seeking to maintain impartiality and balance. Museums mediate the divergent needs of communities, while communities trust the reliability of museum sources (testimonies and documents) and expect that a balanced view of conflict will be presented more than in the mass media or the political arena.

Reframing disability

Some evidence suggests that the museum is a potentially powerful site in which audience perceptions of an issue, a prejudicial view, or a socially accepted memory – even one that is deeply ingrained – might be challenged and altered (Sandell 2002, 2007). What part, then, might museums play in challenging the powerful and prevalent frames through which disability is viewed, especially given the reliance on medicalized ways of seeing the impaired mind or body? Disabled people are often shown in relation to medical phenomena, the history of surgery, cure, prosthetic aids and rehabilitation. The medical model of disability looms large amongst curators in museums, assuming a natural link between medical collections and material culture and the disabled person (Delin 2002: 87). In relation to this potential for museums to function as agents of change, Delin poses an important challenge for museums of war and conflict: to humanize rather than medicalize and to include the war disabled beyond the stereotypes of the social outcast, heroic victim or noble symbol of national sacrifice.

Between 2006 and 2008, I consulted on an exhibition, jointly curated by the Wellcome Trust (London) and the Deutsches Hygiene Museum (Dresden), on *War and Medicine* (22 November 2008–15 February 2009). The curators made a concerted effort to engage in complex debates about the conduct of war and the myths of medical progress, the role of doctors, patients' perspectives, and the long-term consequences for wounded and disabled soldiers and their families, engaging with recent scholarship on war disability and military medical ethics, and seeking dialogue with men and women recently wounded in war. The catalogue essays also illuminated patient experiences and life after hospitalization. Colleen Schmidt, Curator of the Deutsches Hygiene Museum, discussed 'Life Without Arms' and the role of Carl Hermann Unthan – a congenitally disabled travelling violinist – in motivating the rehabilitation of disabled soldiers in Germany after the First World War. Joanna Bourke wrote about 'Suffering and the Healing Profession' during both world wars. Wolfgang Eckart explored Stalingrad as a case of 'Wounded Bodies and Souls', while I discussed patient experiences of military medical bureaucracy and their self-perceptions as mere 'Soldiers' Bodies in the War Machine' (Larner, Peto and Monem 2008). The exhibition attempted to write wounded and disabled people into the narrative of war, and to weave a more complex dialogue between social and medical/institutional models of disability, an important context for military medicine. Nevertheless, the exhibition did not entirely eschew narratives of medical progress and the practitioner's heroism.

On the one hand, the absence of disabled bodies in war museums reveals its own form of politics – the social amnesia of war disablement that the museum inadvertently replicates. On the other hand, the politicization of disabled bodies appears to be thrown into high relief in cases where the presence of disabled people (including civilians) captures the meaning of the conflict or its genocidal origins, such as in the Kigali Centre, Rwanda, or the Cambodian Land Mines Museum (Siem Reap). In the Vietnam War Remnants Museum (Ho Chi Minh City), photographs of extreme cases of children who acquired impairments from toxins contained in the herbicide Agent Orange reflect the wider political aim to educate international visitors on 'crimes' committed during the 'American War'. The museum, however, has undergone several transformations as diplomatic relations between the former enemies altered. In 1975, the museum was known as 'The House for Displaying War Crimes of American Imperialism and the Puppet Government of South Vietnam' and was then changed to the Museum of American War Crimes. By 1993 it was renamed the War Crimes Museum, and is now known as the War Remnants Museum, reflecting closer geopolitical relations between Vietnam and the United States. Nevertheless, the use of child victims of Agent Orange in the museum turns them into symbols of government 'anti-imperial' discourse. Mounted and framed photographs of children disabled in the 1970s tell us nothing about those people – now adults – today. Instead they become objects or 'remnants' of war like the other objects in the museum of the same title. Disabled people's humanity is diminished for the sake of geopolitical rhetoric.

The political use of disability in the Vietnamese museum context raises important issues; however, there is a danger in drawing the contrast of presence and absence of disabled bodies along national and cultural, or Western and non-Western, lines. Indeed, such false dichotomies potentially conceal useful lessons that Anglo-European museums can learn about their own tacit forms of propaganda or their avoidance of injury and disablement as a major legacy of war.

Combating social and representational exclusion

Some museums have actively explored their capacity to address social and cultural inequality. The Imperial War Museum North, for example, has a successful outreach programme with local disadvantaged and 'at risk' children. As a means of bridging generational gaps, it uses storytelling and other programmes to connect children to grandparents or family members who experienced war. However, when the Museum first opened, it displayed only one object relating to disability – a shiny, metallic prosthetic leg in a glass wall-cabinet. The prosthetic had no label, existing merely as a signifier of technological masculinity and medical mastery. The display inadvertently repeated historical attitudes to disabled soldiers that forced them to 'overcome' their disabilities (Anderson and Carden-Coyne 2007). In isolation, the object implied that disabled soldiers simply accessed such technology, substituting for an explanation about how disabled people actually lived.

Lessons can be drawn from the Cambodian Land Mines Museum (CLMM), Siem Reap, established in 1997 by Aki Ra, a former Khmer Rouge soldier who worked as a UN mine-clearer from 1994. (See Hart, this volume.) The museum focuses on the impact of land mines on children and adults and on informing visitors about mine safety and the process of the Ottawa Treaty ban (1997), highlighting survivors' stories and encouraging activism. Initially CLMM housed military hardware and detritus: decommissioned mines, bombs and explosive weapons. By 2001, the Museum was managed by a Canadian war photographer who set up the Cambodian Landmine Museum Fund. In 2007, the Museum re-opened in new, architect-designed facilities further out of Siem Reap. Separated from the exhibitions on mine safety, the site includes residential accommodation for disabled children and an educational facility where local staff and some volunteers teach Khmer, English, music, art, and computers. The Museum is also the home of Aki Ra's family who continue field de-mining or work in the administration office.

There are no cyborg fantasies here; thirty disabled children who reside in the museum grounds have little access to prosthetic legs or advanced physical therapies to improve their mobility. In the past, the children often begged for money when visitors came, although the facility managers no longer allow this practice. As well, the sign asking visitors not to photograph the children was put in place to prevent the children from becoming a spectacle in the 'dark tourism' industry, which also encouraged begging rather than education. The children's separation from the museum is supplemented with many photographs and life stories that realize the impact of land mines and weapons displayed nearby. While their stories lend significance and interpret the meaning of the material culture on display in this unique Museum and outreach centre, the physical absence of the disabled children nevertheless generates a powerful curiosity that is part of the Museum's attraction to visitors.

The Museum's founder, Aki Ra, has claimed the site as a social agent, describing his mission as a deeply personal one: 'I want to make my country safe for my people.' Indeed, Aki Ra hoped the Museum could combat local inequality and assist disadvantaged groups, while educating the wider visitor public at a global level. The ad hoc style of the displays and labels – a deliberate anti-aesthetic – incorporates personal photographs, including Aki Ra's activism. Volunteers can also live in the community for a minimum of one month; a rule established by the NGO management. While CLMM enjoys considerable internet and media profile – due to the mediatization of the story of Aki Ra's transformation from Khmer child soldier and mine layer to UN de-miner – the Museum itself might not appear to bear the 'cultural weight' of other (more established) museums as agents of cultural change reaching to build 'an inclusive, equitable society' (Macdonald, 1998: xi).

While 'social inclusion' is embedded in UK museum practices, through government policy, it is curious that war museums have largely avoided the representation and participation of disabled people and their families. Pioneering work by educators at the Imperial War Museum is a notable exception (see Sandell and Dodd, this volume). Although critics of museum engagement with the inclusion agenda argue that such an approach could render the museum an instrument of governmental social control, eroding museum autonomy, the glaring absence of the war disabled in conflict museums could also be understood to reinforce government concerns to avoid the political consequences of soldiers and civilians maimed in war.

While the goal of inclusion is situated within the problem of facing up to war, in museums disabled veterans rarely have a distinct voice. Part of that problem is also that disabled groups and individuals do not necessarily constitute a community or an identity that can be readily accessed. Disabled veterans in Britain have a long tradition of having to negotiate their economic and social participation framed by 'embodied citizenship' (Cohen 2001; Carden-Coyne 2009). Disabled veterans were often impoverished as a result of their war service; the combination of physical and economic incapacity often prevented full participation in society. While disabled soldiers might appear the logical constituency of war museums, this is not always apparent. Indeed, the museum can imitate wider social practices of exclusion. While scholars imagine the museum's potential to enable individuals to 'negotiate a sense of identity that is located within a collective identity of citizens', in the case of disabled veterans and civilians, this is elusive (Newman and McLean 2002: 61). Certainly exclusion is a key component in group-identity formation, yet disabled veterans may also react to the lack of consultation when representing war without reference to their experiences. As institutions develop comprehensive 'disability equality policies' for staffing and visitors, it is hopeful that exhibition practices will become more inclusive, consultation with disabled groups will be actively pursued, collections will become more diverse, and the consequences of war will be addressed in the representation of violent conflict.

Back at the Cambodian Land Mines Museum in Siem Reap, international visitors have reported finding the images of disabled children 'hard to look at' and the unrefined curatorial style somewhat confronting. One visitor, for example, who described himself as 'a late 20s geek from the UK residing in Kuala Lumpur' and working in computer security, wrote in his blog entry for 2 March 2006:

> There are stories, photos and paintings around the place illustrating this, they aren't for the weak-stomached. Some of the stories you read about these very children are heartbreaking, one young boy for example was playing near his home when he found some unexploded ordnance, of course he didn't know what it was, so he picked it up … It blew both of his hands off. What's worse … his 2 brothers heard the explosion and ran to help him, they ran into a tripwire triggering another explosion and were both killed.[1]

Museum visitors are mostly world travellers and backpackers, who might upload their experiences and impressions on the web in the form of visual blogs, with photos and video as well as links to NGOs, volunteer sites and fundraising events. Within this globalized field, CLMM aims to educate foreign visitors in anti-mine action, and 'horror stories' are aimed at inciting a humanitarian ethos of volunteer action. Although the 1974–79 Cambodian genocide and civil war was the period in which mines were laid, the historical and current local political context is distinctly absent from the museum; instead the international 1990s campaign to ban land mines is a main concern. Arguably, the memory of the civil war is too raw, especially when justice is only just beginning in the form of war crimes trials (2009).

Traumatic representations

By contrast in Rwanda, the Kigali Memorial Centre has three permanent exhibitions specifically documenting the genocide, plus a children's memorial and an exhibition on global genocide and violence. The Centre was established in the year of the tenth anniversary of the genocide (2004) by the Kigali City Council and the Aegis Trust, UK, and is built over a burial site of 250,000 victims. The Education Centre and Memorial Garden educates and remembers the attempted genocide of the Tutsi community in 1994. James Thompson argues that this memorial museum delivered a 'strategic memory' shaped for foreign visitors, aid workers and tourists (Thompson 2009: 97–100): the narrative of murdered children was critical both to the accusation of international complicity in colonialism, and the 'political project' – 'the master narrative' – of national reconciliation.

Research into the psychosocial consequences of the genocide states that 70 per cent of survivors were women: some were widowed without property rights, many were raped and left pregnant, and 100,000 children were orphaned. International psychosocial rehabilitation efforts were often insensitive to local customs or lacked coherence between military, humanitarian, and political agendas. Most people still live where the atrocities took place, and maimed and disabled people are constant reminders of the genocide. In 2002, 80 per cent of people with disabilities lived in rural areas with little access to treatment and experienced great difficulty reintegrating. Land mines continue to injure; access to rehabilitation and prosthetics is limited; and residual social problems include inability to work and marry, social stigmas, ostracism and withdrawal (Palmer 2002: 18–20). The impact on Rwandan society is marked; the complexities of local systems (*gaçaca* trial) and international justice (war crimes tribunal held in Tanzania) have hampered the healing process. These critical issues are not addressed in the Museum.

While the international community has been concerned with justice, activists have questioned the lack of discussion about disabled people. Questions have been raised about how deaf, blind and impaired Rwandans were targeted during the genocide, and what specialized care remains for them now. At the Gatagara Centre for disabled people outside Kigali, most of the patients and staff were killed regardless of their ethnicity (Masakhwe 2004). While services for disabled people have improved since 1994, with the increase in land mine cases, assistance and rehabilitation is still a problem and there is a perceived lack of government involvement, while disability organizations lack funding to meet the shortfall.

Given the problems with rehabilitation facilities in Rwanda, it is important to reflect on how images of disabled people are mobilized in the Museum. While it is politically problematic, – especially while justice remains a critical issue – to expect the Museum to function as a site of reconciliation, how are survivors and disabled civilians incorporated into its mission? If the Museum is a political site, does it reiterate government rhetoric and insist on an official memory of war? If the memory of the genocide is shaped for foreign visitors, how are disabled survivors included in or excluded from the official representation?

In recent years there has been a growth of experimental practices in museums, exploring their potential to function as therapeutic agents (Silverman 2002), even though disadvantaged groups are rarely seen as 'potential visitors'. Some museums lack the institutional experience of working with marginalized people, although a growing number are working in institutional partnerships to design exhibits and increase consultative processes (ibid.). Some Western museums have resolved this issue by working with mental health professionals, social workers and therapists. Yet in recent years, constructions of 'trauma' and 'recovery' have come under radical critique, especially when linked to social healing, reconciliation and when applied to non-Western communities (Bracken and Petty 1998; Summerfield 2001, 2002). Contradictions about mental illness abound. In Britain, First World War shellshock is eulogized in the media and mobilized in museums as an acceptable narrative of war as pitiful. Yet, people diagnosed with Post-Traumatic Stress Disorder or combat trauma are largely absent from museum representations. While experimental practice has explored the potential for museums to function as a form of therapy that builds community trust and social inclusion, and evaluations suggest that working with mental health professionals provides useful social outcomes (Silverman 2002: 75), this approach presents a further set of complex challenges for museum practitioners to navigate.

In the case of disabling traumatic memories, the museum negotiates a difficult path through the potential for individual visitors to find comfort through the 'currency of communication' while, at the same time, some may find talking about the past 'painful and unnecessary' (Kavanagh 2002: 115). As Gaynor Kavanagh suggests, museums must accept that, when confronting difficult histories, pain and sorrow will be triggered in exhibitions:

> We live in a society damaged by wars and their after effects, one in which hate continues to fuel discrimination and fear limits the ability to change or accommodate other ways of thinking. However prosperous and forward moving it may be, the abilities to put the past into perspective, or leave it behind, and live tolerant lives are not universally shared.

> (ibid.: 116)

Although Kavanagh argues that museums cannot play a major role in this area she suggests that museums and collections might be of some value to people who are dealing with difficult memories:

> Through working with both the memories *and* the people to whom they truly belong, museums can bear witness to the best and worst, the extraordinary and mundane, the innovative and the traditional. They can enable others in their own explorations of life's experiences.
>
> (ibid.: 120)

Yet for some museums the trauma is so recent and present that it would be impossible for them 'to encourage debate and to elicit audience responses in relation to challenging issues of prejudice and discrimination' or to 'engender support for the concept of equal human rights for all' – roles which are increasingly pursued and explored by museums (Sandell 2007: 1). Indeed, the imposition of Anglo-European ways of addressing trauma onto museums operating in very different contexts is deeply problematic. In the case of the Rwanda museum, for example, practices are steeped in still-unresolved issues of justice and reparation – and global forgetting.

In conclusion, museum representations of people wounded and disabled in war and genocide might, in different settings, be developed with a number of aims in mind including consciousness-raising, the sacralization of victims, an ameliorating effect on contemporary communities and an attempt to engender in visitors empathy and values of peace and tolerance (Williams 2007: 153). Yet the activism of remembering may also be inverted, inducing selective forgetting and repeating existing problems of social exclusion. While it might be a misleading dichotomy to pitch the sanctity of dead soldiers in commemorative cultures against the forgetting of the living disabled, important questions remain for museums as much as society. Soldiers have killed and been wounded; civilians have been maimed and raped by soldiers, and many people are traumatized and economically disadvantaged as a result of conflict. Problematically, war museums attempt to heal while also avoiding these 'difficult histories'.

Museums and curators will need to be creative and daring in the future if they wish to tackle the significantly omitted subject of the relationship between war and disability. Museums will need a greater commitment to comprehending disability as a politics of war and its aftermath, thoughtfully engaging with the legacies of violence without turning disabled people into exemplary victims or heroic bodies redeemed in narratives of false uplift. Until these absences are thoughtfully addressed, wounded and disabled people will remain ghosts in the war museum.

Plate 1.1 The Blind Men of Jericho, a copy of a painting by Nicholas Poussin, 1650/1700. (Courtesy of Birmingham Museums and Art Gallery)

Plate 2.1 Gilbert Stuart, *Portrait of George Washington*, c. 1810. (Private Collection. Art Resource, NY)

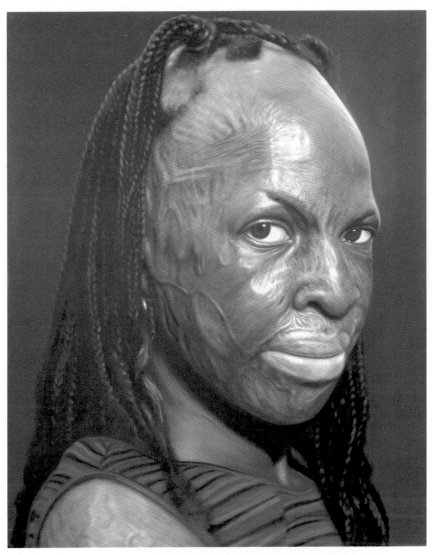

Plate 2.2 Doug Auld, *Shayla*. Oil on canvas, 40 × 50 inches (© Doug Auld (2005) from his series 'State of Grace' – Portraits of burn survivors. www.dougauld.com)

Plate 2.3a Riva Lehrer, *Circle Story #3: Susan Nussbaum*, 1998, acrylic on panel, 16 × 26 inches.

Plate 2.3b Pablo Picasso, *Gertrude Stein*, 1906. Oil on canvas, 39 × 32 inches (100 × 81.3 cm). Bequest of Gertrude Stein, 1946. (Image copyright © The Metropolitan Museum of Art/Art Resource, NY)

Plate 2.4a Riva Lehrer, *Circle Story #5: Mike Ervin and Anna Stonum*, 1998, mixed media on paper, 22 × 21 inches.

Plate 2.4b Anonymous, seventeenth-century double portrait, French School, c. 1575–1600. Oil on wood, 73 × 96 cm. (Photo by C. Jean/ J. Schormans. Louvre, Paris, France. Réunion des Musées Nationaux/Art Resource, NY)

Plate 2.5a Image of Christopher Reeve as Superman, Warner Bros. 'SUPERMAN: The Movie' (© Warner Bros. Entertainment Inc. All Rights Reserved)

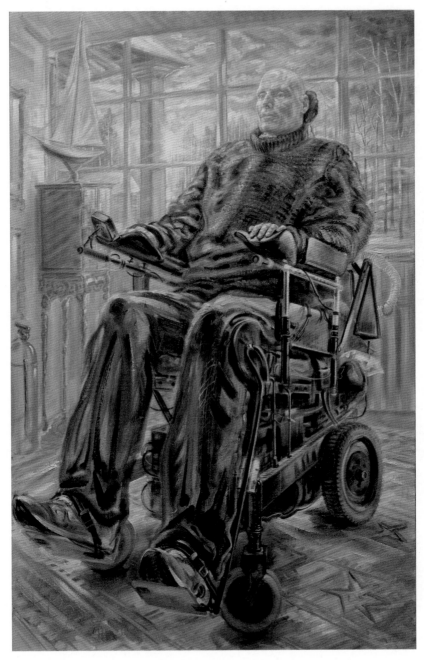

Plate 2.5b Sacha Newley, *Christopher Reeve*, 2004, oil on linen, 172.7 × 111.8 × 3.8 cm. (68 × 44 × 1 1/2 inches). (National Portrait Gallery, Smithsonian Institution; gift of Mr. and Mrs. Sacha Newley; © 2004 Sacha Newley)

Plate 6.1 Behind the Shadow of Merrick. (© Royal London Hospital Archives and Museum, University of Leicester and film maker David Hevey)

Plate 7.1 Visitors to the exhibition, 'One in Four', Tyne and Wear Museums. (Photo: Peter Carney)

Plate 7.2 'Life Beyond the Label', Colchester Castle Museum

Plate 7.3 'One in Four', Discovery Museum, Tyne and Wear. (Photo: Peter Carney)

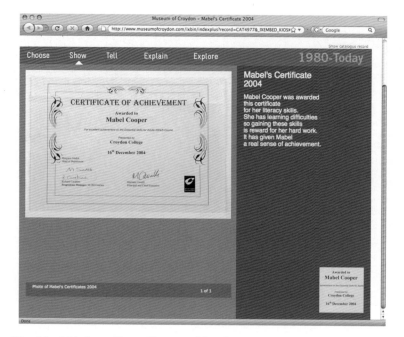

Plate 8.1a Mabel's certificate, Museum of Croydon

Plate 8.1b Madeleine's celebrities, Museum of Croydon

Plate 11.1 Denise Beckwith, *The Little Mermaid*. (Courtesy of Belinda Mason)

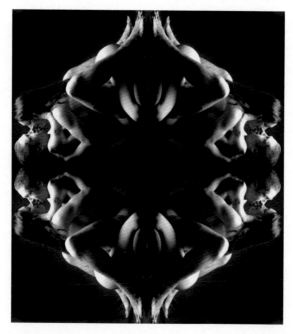

Plate 11.2 Mat Fraser with partner Patou Soult, *Entwined*. (Courtesy of Belinda Mason)

Plate 13.1 Mark Gilbert *Mazeeda B. (Post op.)*, 1999. Oil on Canvas, 1524 ×1524 mm. (© Mark Gilbert. Printed by kind permission of The Facial Surgery Research Foundation)

Plate 13.2 Mark Gilbert, *Henry De L. IV*, 1999. Oil on Canvas, 1981 × 1486 mm. (© Mark Gilbert. Printed by kind permission of The Facial Surgery Research Foundation)

Plate 19.1 Grave marker of Bertha Flatten from Faribault State School and Hospital, Faribault, Minnesota. (Collections of the Smithsonian Institution's National Museum of American History)

Note

1 The full entry is available online at http://www.shaolintiger.com/2006/03/03/cambodia-day-4-an-afternoon-at-the-cambodian-land-mine-museum/.

References

Anderson, J. and Carden-Coyne, A. (2007) 'Enabling the past: new perspectives in the history of disability', *European Review of History*, 14(4): 447–57.

Boltanski, L. (1999) *Distant Suffering: Morality, Media and Politics*, Cambridge: Cambridge University Press.

Bracken, P. and Petty, C. (eds), (1998) *Rethinking the Trauma of War*, London and New York: Free Association Books.

Bryant, M. (2005) *Confronting the 'Good Death': Nazi Euthanasia on Trial, 1945–1953*. Boulder: University Press of Colorado.

Carden-Coyne, A. (2009) *Reconstructing the Body: Classicism, Modernism and the First World War*, Oxford: Oxford University Press.

Cohen, D. (2001) *The War Come Home: Disabled Veterans in Britain and Germany, 1914–1939*, Berkeley: University of California Press.

Dawson, G. (1994) *Soldier Heroes: British Adventure, Empire and the Imagining of Masculinities*, London: Routledge.

Delin, A. (2002), 'Buried in the footnotes: the absence of disabled people in the collective imagery of the past' in R. Sandell (ed.), *Museums, Society, Inequality*, London: Routledge: 84–97.

Duffy, T. (2001) 'Museums of "human suffering" and the struggle for human rights', *Museum International*, 53(1): Jan–March, 10–16.

Forty, A. and Kuchler, S. (eds) (1999) *The Art of Forgetting*, Oxford: Berg.

Friedlander, H. (1995) *The Origins of Nazi Genocide: From Euthanasia to the Final Solution*, Chapel Hill: University of North Carolina Press.

Hastie, R. (1997) *Disabled Children in a Society at War: A Casebook from Bosnia*, London: Oxfam.

Hughes, R. (2003a) 'Nationalism and memory at the Tuol Sleng Museum of Genocide Crimes, Cambodia' in C. Hodgkin and S. Radstone (eds), *Contested Pasts: the Politics of Memory*, London: Routledge, pp. 175–92.

——(2003b), 'The abject artefacts of memory: photographs from Cambodia's genocide', *Media, Culture and Society*, 25(1): 23–44.

Inglis, K. S. (2005) *Sacred Places: War Memorials in the Australian Landscape*, Carlton, Victoria: Melbourne University Press.

Kavanagh, G. (2000) *Dream Spaces: Memory and the Museum*, London: Leicester University Press.

——, (2002) ' Remembering ourselves in the work of museums: trauma and the place of the personal in the public', in R. Sandell (ed), *Museums, Society, Inequality*, London: Routledge, pp. 110–22.

——(ed.) (1996) *Making Histories in Museums*, London: Leicester University Press.

LaCapra, D. (1999) 'Trauma, absence, loss', *Critical Inquiry*, 25, Summer: 696–727.

Larner, M., Peto, J. and Monem, N. (eds) (2008) *War and Medicine*, London: Black Dog Publishing.

Ledgerwood, J. (1997) 'The Cambodian Tuol Sleng Museum of Genocide Crimes: national narrative', *Museum Anthropology*, 21(1): 82–98.

Lifton, R. J. (1986) *The Nazi Doctors: Medical Killing and the Psychology of Genocide*, New York: Basic Books.

Macdonald, S. (ed.) (1998) *The Politics of Display: Museums, Science, Culture*, London and New York: Routledge.

Masakhwe, P. W. (2004) 'The disabled and the Rwanda genocide: The untold story', *Disability World*, 23 April–May. Online. Available http://www.disabilityworld.org/04–05_04/news/ rwanda.shtml (accessed 20 December 2008).

Moriarty, C. (1995) 'The absent dead and figurative First World War memorials', *Transactions of the Ancient Monuments Society*, 39: 7–40.

Newman, A. and McLean, F. (2002) 'Architectures of Inclusion: museums, galleries and inclusive communities' in R. Sandell (ed.), *Museums, Society, Inequality*, London and New York: Routledge, pp. 56–68.

Nora, P. (1996) *Realms of Memory: The Construction of the French Past, Volume One Conflicts and Divisions*, translated by Arthur Goldhammer, New York: Columbia University Press.

Palmer, I. (2002) 'Psychosocial costs of war in Rwanda', *Advances in Psychiatric Treatment,* 8: 17–25.

Paris, M. (2000) *Warrior Nation: Images of War in British Popular Culture, 1850–2000*, London: Reaktion.

Poore, C. (2007) *Disability in Twentieth-century German Culture*, Ann Arbor: University of Michigan Press.

Sandell, R. (2002) 'Museums and the combating of social inequality' in R. Sandell (ed.), *Museums, Society, Inequality*, London: Routledge, pp. 3–23.

—— (2007) *Museums, Prejudice and the Reframing of Difference*, London: Routledge.

Schwenkel, C. (2006) 'Recombinant history: transnational practices of memory and knowledge production in contemporary Vietnam', *Cultural Anthropology*, 21(1): 3–30.

Silverman, L. H. (2002) 'The therapeutic potential of museums as pathways to inclusion' in R. Sandell (ed.), *Museums, Society, Inequality*, London: Routledge, pp. 69–83.

Sliwinski, S. (2004) 'A painful labour. Responsibility and photography', *Visual Studies*, 19 (2): 150–61.

Sontag, S. (2003) *Regarding the Pain of Others*, London: Penguin.

Stone, P. (2006) 'A dark tourism spectrum: Towards a typology of death and macabre related tourist sites, attractions and exhibitions', *Tourism: An Interdisciplinary International Journal*, 52 (2): 145-60.

Stone, P. and Sharpley, R. (2008) 'Consuming dark tourism: a thanatological perspective', *Annals of Tourism Research*, 35(2), April: 574–95.

Sturken, M. (1997) *Tangled Memories: the Vietnam War, the AIDS epidemic, and the politics of remembering*, Berkeley: University of California Press.

Summerfield, D. (2001) 'The invention of post-traumatic stress disorder and the social usefulness of a psychiatric category', *British Medical Journal*, 322: 95–98.

——, (2002) 'Effects of war: moral knowledge, revenge, reconciliation, and medicalised concepts of "recovery"', *British Medical Journal*, 325: 1105–7.

Thompson, J. (2009), *Applied Theatre and the End of Effect*, Basingstoke: Palgrave Macmillan.

Williams, P. (2004), 'Witnessing genocide: vigilance and remembrance at Tuol Sleng and Choeung Ek', *Holocaust and Genocide Studies*, 18 (2): 234–54.

——(2007) *Memorial Museums: the Global Rush to Commemorate Atrocities*, Oxford and New York: Berg.

Zelizer, B. (1998) *Remembering to Forget: Holocaust Memory through the Camera's Eye*, Chicago: Chicago University Press.

6

BEHIND THE SHADOW
OF MERRICK

David Hevey

In 2006 I was invited to work with the Royal London Hospital Archives and Museum to create a new film that would draw on the institution's rich history and collections to offer visitors and viewers new ways of seeing disabled people and thinking about disability.[1] As I immersed myself in the archives and talked with museum staff, ideas for the film gradually took shape. I wanted to make a film that would be viewed and would resonate far beyond the walls of the Royal London Hospital Museum, a film that entered into the huge discourse surrounding the hospital's most famous resident, Joseph Merrick (more widely known as 'The Elephant Man'), a film that entered into even bigger discourses of diversity and difference and was therefore able to be viewed – and to be meaningful – across time, platform and country. In other words, I wanted to make a film specific to one place and one person and yet to tell universal stories about difference, image, history and how people need to be seen as they see themselves – which is what Merrick wanted, which is what we all want. The film, *Behind the Shadow of Merrick* (Plate 6.1), was completed in 2008.[2] This chapter explores the aims and intentions that shaped the film and reflects on the interpretive and filmic devices deployed to prompt viewers to see disability in new ways.

Often, Merrick lived at the harsher end of human experience but he responded with humility and humanity, in part because he had a first-class brain but also, in part, because he met people who understood him beyond the 'elephant man' label. The Royalty of the time, and others who took an interest in Merrick, did not have an interest in him as a freak – that is to say, a spectacle to be put down or diminished – but as someone who lived on the borders, in the way that explorers, soldiers and scientists lived on the borders in the late-Victorian era. Even the English freak show owner for whom Joseph worked – remembering that it was Merrick himself who applied for the job – seems to have, like most people, come to respect Merrick the man, beyond Merrick the phenomenon. Since his death, many have re-freaked Merrick; I tried to get him back to his essential humanity, truth and lived-experience, but alive now, through the empathy and identification of others. And Joseph's actual story is more interesting than the many fictional stories that have been made about him, especially when re-examined from the point of view of those who share Merrick's life the most – disabled people.

Early on in the project, Jonathan Evans, the curator and archivist at the Royal London Hospital Museum, made the point to me that the various Joseph Merrick interpretations, from the well-known film by David Lynch, to the opera, to other creative works, often reveal much about the creators in their quest for 'the Elephant Man' but say less about the real Joseph Merrick. The filmmaking process, for me, begins with finding the true story, immersing myself in the material, in the museum, in the search for a new way of showing old stories, a plausible, realistic and true way of telling something anew. We set out to find a truth. Very early on it was apparent to me that, in the cacophony of voices who told versions of Merrick's story, the one voice not heard was that of those most like him – disabled people.

Inside the museum

The Royal London Hospital Archives and Museum has a small collection of artefacts left by Joseph Merrick after he had lived in rooms at the hospital, including his veil and *carte de visite*. It also has medical engravings, the memoirs of Sir Frederick Treves, who wrote about 'the Elephant Man' having been Merrick's physician, and many books and papers concerned with aspects of Merrick's life. Having ploughed through much of this material, sourced for me by Jonathan Evans and Kate Richardson, I came across a paper by Jonathan which turned out to be the key to the development of the film because it showed how the stages of Merrick's life echoed the stages of millions of disabled people's lives: impairment, awareness of impairment, negative response, familial ambivalence, social isolation, lack of education, medical intervention, workhouse/charity, hounding, finding peace in a place of one's own (known today as independent living), self-representation as a way of showing the world how you see yourself, and, finally, being seen by the world as one sees oneself. As Merrick lived, so do millions of disabled people.

The one who went first

The key stages of Merrick's life – the facts of what we really know actually happened to Joseph Merrick – were all condensed in Jonathan's paper for the sake of clarity and truth and they formed a link to the experiences of disabled people today. Every project that sets out to be original, innovative, worth doing and to make an impact has that eureka moment when you find the new story to tell. Jonathan Evans' insightful paper provided that because it showed that Joseph Merrick, far from being the ultimate outsider, the freak of history, was in reality the disabled archetype, the one-who-went-first. Once I'd realized that Merrick was not as many had portrayed him – a strange outsider 'Super-crip' with no relevance to disabled people's lives – but the archetypal disabled person, it was possible to distil from Jonathan's factual account a series of questions with which to interview disabled people about their lives and for them to filter their particular feelings about Merrick, which were of course distinct and unique.

Through the interviewing, I began to see how Merrick casts a real shadow on many disabled people's lives. Many had a strange affinity with him, yet kept clear of him through fear of negative association. The interview progressed along the following line of enquiry: this happened in Merrick's life (increasing awareness of impairment, isolation, spectacle, medical intervention, unemployment, gaining a level of acceptance, beginning to be seen as he saw himself and so on); have you had similar experiences in your own life? Then I sought another level of response to the questions: if this happened in *his* life and it happened in *yours*, how do you think he felt during each episode? The interviews unfolded, bouncing to and fro through history, creating a reflection on Merrick and a reflection on disabled people linking to his life through empathy. Thus, I developed a film around what Joseph Merrick went through, not based on sentiment or projection or myth, but on people who live similar parts of similar lives now, which is how it became their film, too: as he did then, they do now.

Merrick had been imprinted on many disabled people's consciousness in subjective ways. Disabled people I interviewed for the film talked about their experiences and how, as children, they learned about Merrick. In one interview, Rowen recalled her dread and fear of ending up in a museum as an exhibit herself; it's unlikely that a non-disabled person would take on and internalize the Merrick fable in this way. Others were fascinated and keen to explore the museum and Merrick's presence within it, like touching the relics or mementoes of a distant relative, again exhibiting a connection perhaps deeper than non-disabled people might feel with the story.

What I had, therefore, was a line of enquiry; a few museum-artifacts (in Merrick's veil, calling card and poem); a museum which is a little like Doctor Who's Tardis (small on the outside but, inside, a resource which is hugely influential and important for understanding the real Joseph Merrick); my skills as a filmmaker; and brilliant and profound contributors who empathized with Merrick.

Rowen, Tim and Tina

The stories in the film are dramatic. Rowen told of how, as a child, she'd known distantly of the Elephant Man and feared that she, too, would end up in a museum: only she'd be there as a live specimen, not a dead specimen. Tim, a blind man who went to blind school, talked of how 'being a Merrick' was a school insult; it meant the lowest-of-the-low in disability terms and it was an insult he and his fellow students hurled at one other. Tina (Figure 6.1)

Figure 6.1 Tina, Behind the Shadow of Merrick. (©Royal London Hospital Archives and Museum, University of Leicester and filmmaker David Hevey)

talked of how she, like Joseph Merrick, received visitors in the dark. The story of Merrick mattered intensely to Tina and this changed the nature of the film; not by capitulating to one voice but by enabling a deeper exploration of Merrick's status as an archetype. Tina knew Merrick in a way that was beyond factual and archival knowledge (though she knew a lot about him); her identification was through empathy, identity and understanding what he had been through – because she had been there too.

As Merrick had often lived in the dark, so had Tina. In the film, Tina tells a story of how, when she met her first husband, he often used to come round to her house at night as a friend and sit and talk in the dark with her, before she had the courage to reveal her appearance. As Merrick had been hounded, so had Tina. As Merrick had worn a veil, so Tina wore a hooded sweatshirt. As a filmmaker, one seeks to add levels of truth to a film if one can get to them; Tina enabled this because it was obvious she could almost transcend time in her identity with Merrick.

Merrick was seen as different, as Tina, Rowen and Tim in the film are seen as different. Tina is a burns-survivor and an extraordinary woman, not necessarily because of her impairment but because of her articulacy about human nature, about living in the modern world and about the shortcomings of humanity, as she has experienced them at the sharp end. The 'shock' of the film (which I don't see but which I understand) is that Tina, Rowen and Tim are the willing, visual descendants of Merrick; his accomplices in turning his challenging life in the past into a means of challenging their world today.

Tina, Tim and Rowen make explicit that which is visually communicated in the film by articulating their commonality with Merrick, the deep emotional detail of being Other and the shared experience of living apart, isolation, fear and segregation. Tina, perhaps more than anyone, shows that Merrick was the forefather, not the freak.

Performing the props

The museum and its collections are central to the film, particularly Joseph Merrick's veil, calling card and poem. These items, all currently displayed in the museum, formed part of his possessions when he came to the hospital and stayed with him until the end of his life. In the process of filmmaking, these artifacts functioned as powerful triggers to fresh inquiry.

I felt that conventional talking-head documentary would not work; we had to show the active, conscious participation the film's participants brought to their rediscovery of Merrick. Working in a space between drama and documentary, I directed performances-from-truth, rather than observations. Tim, Rowen and Tina played with the veil, they examined the card and they read the poem out loud; performing, but at the same time keeping their exploration of Merrick's life deep, emotional, moving and true. It is powerful to see someone who is different explore another who is different, but even more powerful to hear their articulate, emotional and yet in-control voices talking through what they see, feel and desire.

I decided that we had to see the contributors physically explore and inhabit the artifacts that were the material traces of Merrick's life – to put on his veil, closely study his photograph, reinterpret his poem – to convey a notion of 'living-again' in and for Merrick, rather than Merrick tawdrily dying again in yet another interpretation of Merrick-the-victim.

The card

The first artifact we used was Merrick's *carte de visite* (Figure 6.2). As Jonathan Evans (Figure 6.3) explains:

> A *carte de visite* portrait photograph of Joseph Merrick, wearing a suit, c. 1889 is also featured in the film. The contributors handle a replica of the photo, the original of which is in The Royal London's collection and which has become the most familiar image of Merrick since it was first published in 1970. This is a personal item which Joseph had printed and which he gave to Reverend Tristram Valentine, the Hospital Chaplain, who is someone he would have seen regularly when he was resident at the London Hospital. The disabled contributors look closely at the *carte de visite* and it inspires them to make revealing comments – Tina, for example, ponders whether Joseph would have been accepting of her appearance. The small photograph is one of the last visual representations of Merrick, taken about a year before his death when he was aging and his health was failing. It is a touching image.

Figure 6.2 Carte de visite photograph of Joseph Merrick, c. 1889. (Courtesy of Royal London Hospital Archives)

In the image on the card Merrick wears a suit, he does not hide away. It is interesting because it is shameless; no veil to hide behind, and no games with the focus. This image of Merrick is especially intriguing because in it he demonstrates, dare I say it, pride. It reminds me of the freak-show archives which, far from being freaky, show pictures of performers, such as Tom Thumb, who controlled their own images, were clearly proud of themselves and who sold these cards by the tens of thousands. And remember, the 'freak show' label was put on by the showman – to this day, horror is one of the biggest selling genres of storytelling – but it was not particularly ever present in the photographs that the performers themselves had made, and the image of Merrick is no exception.

Figure 6.3 Jonathan Evans, Behind the Shadow of Merrick. (© Royal London Hospital Archives and Museum, University of Leicester and filmmaker David Hevey)

As Robert Bogdan (1988) points out in his classic text, *Freak Show,* there is a huge tradition of 'freak show' performers in which disabled people controlled their self-image and, as a result, portrayals very often showed a powerful combination of self-control, self-styling and a strong sense of self. Bogdan makes it clear that while circus owners often added 'freaky-text' to project their own meanings onto the casts they exhibited, disabled, diverse or different performers often produced and sold their own circus calling-cards. These images – portrayals of how people saw themselves, minus the 'freak' label – convey very different meanings to audiences than those crafted by the freak show promoters.

Merrick's *carte de visite* was his self-image, not hiding his difference, not grotesquing, just normal-to-himself. In the film, as Rowen and Tina study the card, we see beyond their differences into their sense of self; the shots show how they identify with Merrick, but humanize all of them at once.

The veil

An enormously important artifact in the film was Merrick's veil. It is huge, the eye-slit narrow, like the window of a pillbox bunker. I used an exact replica of the original which is in the museum's collection and which he wore in the freak-show and, presumably, on those days when he couldn't face the staring. Maybe the veil also functioned as an access tool? Maybe Joseph could walk around with the veil hiding his difference? Certainly, Tina very much identified with this and her use of long hair and a hooded sweatshirt to do much the same.

The replica of Merrick's veil is handled and donned by each of the disabled contributors to the film. Each removes it in revelatory fashion to show the person concealed underneath. In contrast, Jonathan Evans presents the original veil and hat on its mount. He wears white gloves, a feature which emphasizes his professional (rather than personal) relationship to the object and the fact that the item on the mount is the original artifact: it is not otherwise made clear to the viewer that the hat and veil the disabled actors try on is a replica. The object is a visual reminder of how Merrick hid his appearance from the public gaze when travelling. He combined the hat with a floor-length opera cloak and oversized carpet slippers. The size of the hat reminds the visitor that Joseph's head, with its overgrowth of bone and flesh, was the circumference of a man's waist, and that he had difficulty in supporting it.

As Tim put on Merrick's veil, as Rowen hung Merrick's veil on her wheelchair arm, as Tina wore the veil, poking her tongue and arm through the eye slit, they each explored what hiding away meant to them. In visual terms, the act of these people playing with the veil is itself shocking to the viewer who sees that they hold no special reverence for it as an historical object, although they clearly hold enormous reverence for the man who wore it. It was important in our film for the disabled contributors to play with the veil, the card and poem, to physically re-inhabit Merrick, to live the world as he lived it. His life was not remote to Tina, Tim and Rowen and the film clearly shows that sense of shared experience. The one thing that people rarely see is those who are different actively changing their image. Seeing Tim, Tina and Rowen explore Merrick's veil certainly broke notions of victimhood for them and for Merrick.

The poem

Joseph Merrick also left behind his version of a poem, which concludes, 'the mind's the standard of the man' (Figure 6.4). I directed two of my three

Figure 6.4 Poem, Behind the Shadow of Merrick. (© Royal London Hospital Archives and Museum, University of Leicester and filmmaker David Hevey)

contributors to inhabit this poem, which they did in very different and distinct ways. Tim's performance was about the mental clarity and control which the Victorian Merrick might have felt, knowing he had such a good mind. Tina's was, in contrast, more emotional; a soap-box oration for change. Tim's performance was a command, Tina's was a plea. I could have simply had an actor read the poem but the audience would have learned very little because nothing would have moved them. The way we did it, with the disabled contributors entering the poem in the way that actors enter a role, brought it to life. It gave the audience yet another layer of possibility about Merrick and possibility about all difference (and the toleration of difference).

Unsettling viewers

How then are viewers intended to respond? What filmic devices and interpretive strategies are deployed to move the viewer towards greater understanding? *Behind the Shadow of Merrick* is *visual* first, creating *mise en scène* face-scapes. It is *drama* second, as the viewer fights to keep at an intellectual distance but is drawn in emotionally through people's testimony that operates more deeply than the film's thematic structure. Finally, the film is *art with purpose*, because it seeks to change the way we view difference.

It is narrated by the 9-year-old child of one of the contributors. This, in itself, is something of a departure from the conventional museum film, which more often than not will be narrated by an actor – an adult with an authoritative voice. The child's voice functions by inviting the visitor to think about the universality of disability.

The museum objects play a critical role. People are obsessed with tracing their ancestors, but our ancestors live in our genes. It was as if we were using the card, the veil and the poem to trigger a sort of genetic memory in the film's disabled contributors; to live again inside Merrick – his cares, his thoughts, his passions and his strength – and, in turn, for him to live inside Tina, Rowen and Tim; his heirs to difference.

Behind the Shadow of Merrick works on several levels and should be viewed several times but, at the same time, it is clear and 'up-front' in its approach. It is not a dry documentary, it uses real people, their real lives, fears and emotions. It is not a drama, but the people nevertheless perform. In the end, the uses of imagery, story and editing are all at the service of telling a new truth. If people want to learn more of the facts of Joseph Merrick's life they might learn them here, but not dates and times. Rather they might learn how he might have felt. Many viewers have responded by saying that the film reverberates in their thinking; they find it difficult, once viewed, to 'police' it in their heads.

It may seem an obvious thing to state, but *Behind the Shadow of Merrick* is a film. By that I mean it is primarily *visual and moving*. The story moves along visually and aurally and it is not radio-with-pictures, an accusation so often thrown at bad television and film. It captures visually the response that Tina,

Rowen and Tim have to the unfolding story of Merrick in their midst and in their consciousness and, while the film's visuals are underpinned by dramatic stories, the primary level is about changing one's *visual* view of Merrick and – by their obvious and willing association – changing our visual view of all people who are different in the way he was different.

Behind the Shadow of Merrick is a film that shocks some viewers, but what interests me is truth and how to show and tell it; not tricks, spectacle or shock. I did not set out to shock; I set out to uncover the long shadow of Merrick, work out why it is still cast into our times and what he still tells us. Indeed, I was 'shocked' how large Merrick is in the lives of disabled people and how keen to tell their tale of him so many were. So, when some people are shocked by the film, I wonder if it is the film's visualization of Merrick-and-Tina-and-Rowen-and-Tim – their commonality and shared experience – that actually shocks. Some people might wish to have seen a more mythologizing or intellectualizing film but, perhaps, not one that works in a primarily *visual* way?

In film, truth is delivered in many ways: what you show, how you show it and what the characters say and do within that. Once I knew what interviewees were going to say, and I knew how a few artifacts and a simple location would be to our advantage, the issue was then how to make something people felt *compelled* to view, rather than *moralized into viewing*.

Authenticity and agency

The film's power lies in its use of authentic personal experience. At one point, the young girl's voice-over says: 'Sometimes Joseph Merrick lived in the dark. You have to feel strong to take on the staring' and Tina responds:

> Oh, I completely understand that, that Merrick didn't want to come out, except for at night. I went through a few years where I would only let people come to my house if it was past ten o'clock, when the light had gone down, the light had faded and it was dusk, and I could join the vampires. And come out and play.

Similarly, towards the end of the film, the young girl poses a question: 'What would disabled people say to him now, if they could talk to him across time?' And, as she plays with Merrick's veil, Tina responds:

> If I met Merrick today ... but Merrick might not like me when I think about it, because he'd probably be looking for the perfect woman, the so-called, y'know, someone who's beautiful and certainly without scars. I fear that that would be the case, but if he wasn't like that, even if he was like that, it wouldn't matter, but I would tell him to hold his head up high. Merrick made his mark on

this planet and it was a pretty good one and I think he's a role model for a lot of us crips.

At this point, Rowen takes up the commentary:

> Knowing that Merrick was around as a disabled person, not always hiding who he was but being out and proud, as an individual, feels as though I've got ancestry. He is my ancestor and I am part of his family. Knowing that I am still dealing with the issues that he was dealing with over a hundred years ago makes me feel sad in some ways but also proud. It's as though he's a forefather, he went before me, and hopefully there'll be generations like us who'll go after us.

If audiences allow themselves to feel their way through the film, and not be scared by the obvious raw authenticity of some of the contributions, then these raw and authentic testimonies can operate in a powerful way to challenge one's pre-existing notions of those who are different.

I personally do not see *Behind The Shadow of Merrick* as shocking, but the film is unsettling. Many people hate their patterns to be broken and the film sets out to break patterns; the cinematography is 'in your face'; extreme close-ups, portrait after portrait, a few establishing wide shots, then back to portraits and eyes. The editing underscores the pattern-breaking feel by being 'off the beat'; the images cut suddenly; images which are beautifully shot on film and graded to hover in our consciousness, to be beautiful images of people who do not normally have beauty bestowed on them, as Merrick did not. Just when you get comfortable and feel safe, a cut comes in to move you to a new and unknown image.

Why reclaim Merrick?

It was the merger of two things in Merrick that gave him his historical presence: the huge 'outsiderist' body, with a huge 'insiderist' brain. It is clear he could operate in all levels of society, from the freak-show booth to the Royal booth at the opera. While there is something of the Old Testament about him – all is vanity – there is also something of the Modern about him – the striving to find a role for one's difference. There is something of the fighter in him; he kept going. There is celebrity; he featured in *The Times* and met Royalty. He pushes many buttons. But the film represents the first time Joseph Merrick has been claimed by those who are the most like him – disabled people – and not just claimed fancifully but based on the key stages of his life being the archetypal key stages of many disabled lives. By showing this process of claiming, the film challenges those who, in the past, have enfreaked disabled people and who continue to do so today.

Ultimately, in this new version of Merrick's story, he represents that shifting shoreline between mainstream and outsiderism, between beauty and the beast, between being meaningful and being meaningless in life *as judged on one's body*. We all want to leave our mark: Merrick did and I think he knew he would. Merrick will still be discussed and revisited in a hundred years, because he casts a shadow on the nature of life: difference, fear, outsiderism, and the fight we all have to be seen as we see ourselves. These things are classic, universal and contemporary and he represents them more than most – as do Tina, Rowen and Tim in the film.

Merrick's quest was about his ascension, not a flattening of society and class. He understood himself as an outsider, but he tried to enter and scale the hierarchies of his day, which he did with some success. In my opinion, Merrick understood that we live on a hierarchical planet but he also understood that nobody's label is fixed. He tried to find out how and where he could shine, as we all should. I personally believe what intrigued non-voyeurs was Merrick's combination of his mind and his body: a mind that was sharpened by knowing how base humankind can be. Others sought out both his body *and* his mind. Princess Alexandra was a regular visitor to him and was not, I believe, visiting him as a specimen, but as *difference*, creating width in her life as well as his. When Princess Alexandra met him, I do not think she thought, 'My God, what a freak', but rather 'What a man!'

Difference and diversity break patterns, something which can make many people uncomfortable. Merrick is a hint of that shamanistic quality that *difference* and *diversity* (the words I much prefer over 'disability') bring to mainstream normality: that of knowing how to survive shape-shifting life, how to value both difference-in-normality and normality-in-difference: how to search for one's own label, how to keep going.

It should be obvious to most people that human beings have more in common than they have differences. Exploring diversity and difference should actually be about finding the common bonds; about taking difference away, which is what I believe Merrick wanted. Part of the reason Merrick lives on is because somehow – with his suits, his *carte de visite*, his mentions in *The Times*, his friendships with Royalty, his sense of self as valid in the world – he shows how difference and normality are complementary and serve one another. So, the film is not really about diversity, difference and disability: it is about finding human archetypes. *Behind the Shadow of Merrick* is a contemporary beauty-and-the-beast story, but Beauty and the Beast change places. Or, in fact, become one, as those opposites become one in all of us.

Merrick's story and its intertwining with the stories of Tim, Rowen and Tina is important because he is significant to understanding diversity in contemporary society: he straddles the outsider and the insider, the stranger and the archetype, the beauty and the beast. He speaks to issues of difference and belonging which are alive today and more pressing than ever in debates over identity, race, ethnicity and diversity.

Notes

1 The project was one of nine interpretive interventions that comprised Rethinking Disability Representation in Museums and Galleries, a large action research collaborative project led by the Research Centre for Museums and Galleries at the University of Leicester (see Sandell and Dodd, this volume). It was decided that the intervention developed for the Royal London Hospital Museum would be a film since the museum has limited display space for additional exhibitions and because there is a pre-existing cinematic set-up in the main gallery – a screen, a series of short films and documentaries related to medical history and the history of the institution, and seating for visitors to view them.

2 The 17-minute film can be viewed within the museum itself and was circulated for independent viewing online (from the Rethinking Disability Representation pages of the Research Centre for Museums and Galleries website at http://www.le.ac.uk/ms/research/rcmg.html and on DVD within Dodd, Sandell, Jolly and Jones (2008)).

References

Bogdan, R. (1988) *Freak Show: Presenting Human Oddities for Amusement and Profit*, Chicago: University Press of Chicago.

Dodd, J., Sandell, R., Jolly, D. and Jones, C. (2008) *Rethinking Disability Representation in Museums and Galleries*. Research Centre for Museums and Galleries (RCMG), Leicester: University of Leicester.

7

DISABILITY REFRAMED

Challenging visitor perceptions in the museum

Jocelyn Dodd, Ceri Jones, Debbie Jolly and Richard Sandell

What happens when visitors to museums and galleries encounter displays, educational programmes and other interpretive projects that are designed to offer and elicit support for new ways of understanding disability? How do visitors respond to these socially purposeful interventions? How, if at all, do these encounters unsettle, reconfigure or call into question existing understandings of disability and perceptions of disabled people? This chapter considers these under-explored questions by examining and reflecting upon findings from an in-depth qualitative evaluation of visitor responses to a range of museum and gallery projects in the UK, each developed in partnership with disabled people to open up new ways of understanding, thinking and talking about disability.

Rethinking disability representation

Rethinking Disability Representation in Museums and Galleries was the title of a large-scale, multi-partner action research project[1] which set out to explore – through collaboration, experimentation and evaluation – alternative approaches to representing disability in museums and galleries (Sandell and Dodd, this volume). A key aim of the project was to develop a series of narratives – embodied in exhibitions, displays, films and educational sessions (Figure 7.1) – that could support audiences in developing new understandings of disability and frame the ways in which they participated in and contributed to (sometimes controversial) present-day debates linked to disability. A critical feature of the project was the establishment of a 'Think Tank' comprising disabled activists, artists, and cultural practitioners, which played a leading role in shaping the content and tone of the different interpretive interventions that eventually appeared in nine different museums in the UK during 2008.

The project can be seen as part of a broader trend within international museum practice towards greater social engagement and an increased concern amongst practitioners for developing displays and exhibitions that offer more respectful and equitable ways of representing different communities, many of

Figure 7.1 'Life Beyond the Label', Colchester Castle Museum. (Photo: Julian Anderson)

which have, until more recently, been omitted from (or marginalized within) museum narratives (Sandell 2007). Despite this trend, relatively little is known about the social effects and consequences of these purposeful interpretive interventions. Indeed, the research findings presented here constitute some of the first empirical evidence of the ways in which audiences in museums engage with newly emerging representations of disability.

Framing

The nine projects, diverse in terms of narrative, media and the objects featured, were nevertheless connected by their use of the social model of disability as a means of viewing collections and framing the content and tone of the interpretations. Although there has been a lively debate within disability studies in recent years concerning the social model there is, nevertheless, consensus amongst activists and scholars surrounding certain principles and conceptual approaches. In particular, the social model of disability has been widely recognized as a key conceptual tool for the advancement of the rights of disabled people.

For the greater part of the twentieth century, disability has been viewed within western societies as a 'personal tragedy' (Oliver 1983), an approach that dominated public policy and practice within a range of educational and charitable settings. As Barnes and Mercer (2003) explain, this approach

... encompasses an individual and largely medicalized approach: first, disability is regarded as a problem at the individual (body–mind) level; second, it is equated with individual functional limitations or other 'defects'; and third, medical knowledge and practice determines treatment options. From a societal perspective, disability is dysfunctional...

(2003: 2)

From the late 1960s, however, disabled people began to challenge this deeply entrenched and oppressive view of disability, developing what has become known as the social model. As Michael Oliver states, the social model

does not deny the problem of disability but locates it squarely within society. It is not individual limitations, of whatever kind, which are the cause of the problem but society's failure to provide appropriate services and adequately ensure the needs of disabled people are fully taken into account in its social organisation.

Hence disability, according to the social model, is all the things that impose restrictions on disabled people; ranging from individual prejudice to institutional discrimination, from inaccessible public buildings to unusable transport systems, from segregated education to excluding work arrangements, and so on.

(1996: 32–33)

Although the social model and other sociopolitical, progressive accounts of disability are today widely supported by rights activists and disability studies researchers (and have had considerable influence on policy development and legislation in many parts of the world), 'individual model' thinking nevertheless retains a powerful hold on the public imagination and continues to shape negative attitudes towards disabled people and to underpin ongoing prejudice and discrimination. As a starting point for framing the interpretive approaches developed by each of the museums, the social model therefore presented the opportunity to revolutionize the display and interpretation of objects connected to disability and to challenge culturally dominant norms of disability representation which tend to rely on (and reinforce) reductive stereotypes of disabled people.

Rethinking Disability Representation was shaped by the notion that museums can counter prejudice by 'reframing, informing and enabling society's conversations about difference' (Sandell 2007: 173). In this way the museum is conceived as an agent of social change which, by taking up a particular moral stance on disability – one underpinned by support for human rights – and by representing disabled people in more equitable and respectful ways, holds the capacity to inform the ways in which visitors construct meaning related to disability out of their museum visit.[2] Capturing and analysing the ways in which audiences engaged with and responded to the experimental interpretations created by the Think Tank and the nine museums was, therefore, a critical aspect of the project.

Cultural narratives and representations of disability

Limited research has been conducted into examining the presence (and modes of portrayal) of disabled people in museums and galleries. However, a recent study in the UK found that while museum and gallery collections contained a wealth of material linked to disabled people's lives, representations of disabled individuals were rarely included in displays and exhibitions. Where disabled people did appear, their depictions very often conformed to a limited set of stereotypes commonly found in other media (Sandell *et al.* 2005).

Although museums have received relatively little attention, a number of studies and reports have explored the ways in which disabled people are represented in news media, in film and television (Barnes 1992), literature (Garland-Thomson 1997) and charity advertising (Hevey 1992). The findings of these studies inevitably vary from setting to setting, but most have found a prevalence of overtly negative and reductive stereotypes which portray disabled people as objects of pity and sympathy, as passive, sexless, dependent or, conversely as brave and heroic 'supercrips' (Barnes, Mercer and Shakespeare 1999). Reflecting this limited and limiting spectrum of ways of seeing disability, public perception has been found to range from 'imaginative concern, [to] mawkish sentimentality, indifference, rejection and hostility' (Thomas 1982: 4). Indeed, while prejudice directed at disabled people can manifest itself in the form of hate crimes and other violent acts, it can also be expressed in less explicitly aggressive and malevolent ways. 'Unlike racial, ethnic and sexual minorities', Catherine Kudlick argues, 'disabled people experience attacks cloaked in pity accompanied by a widely held perception that no one wishes them ill' (2003: 768). Such discriminatory attitudes, supported by negative stereotypes, are rarely addressed in the public arena and are often deep-seated and challenging to overcome. How then would diverse audiences respond to more complex and nuanced portrayals of disabled people in museum settings? And how would visitors react to the adoption by museums of a moral and political position underpinned by a concern for disability rights?

Capturing visitor engagement and response

Visitor responses were collected from across the nine museums that participated in *Rethinking Disability Representation*. Qualitative research methods were felt to be the most appropriate for capturing the complexity and detail of audience responses. In developing a suitable research tool, there were some challenges to enabling the generation of comparable data across nine very

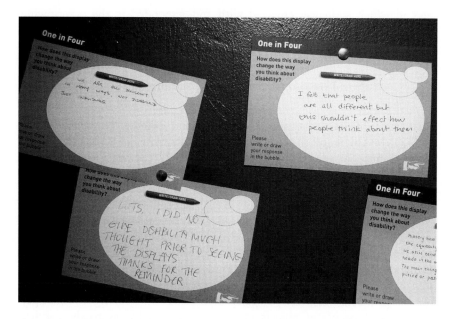

Figure 7.2 Response cards, 'One in Four', Tyne and Wear Museums.

different museum projects. The tool needed to be suitable for use with a diversity of audiences and interpretive methods including exhibitions, displays, schools education programmes and a specially commissioned film. To facilitate this process, a generic response card was designed that would elicit responses from visitors to a single, open-ended question (Figure 7.2). After much discussion and a pilot investigation at one of the sites, the following question was chosen as it proved to be the most effective at prompting visitors to think directly about issues around disability and representation:

How does this display change the way you think about disability?[3]

On the reverse of the card, visitors were asked to provide demographic details. The response cards were designed to combine accessibility and appeal and were distributed and administered by the museums involved (Plate 7.1). During the period of evaluation, a total of 1,784 response cards were completed. Additionally, a total of 43 semi-structured interviews were carried out to explore visitor responses in greater depth,[4] along with two case studies of schools visiting the Imperial War Museum in London and two focus groups with postgraduate students to gauge their reactions to the film created for the Royal London Hospital Archives and Museum, *Behind the Shadow of Merrick* (see Hevey, this volume). Responses obtained through these methods were analysed using data analysis software through a rigorous process whereby recurring themes and patterns were identified and grouped together into new categories; a process that was repeated, developed and refined until a series of themes for visitor responses emerged.

Visitor responses: an overview

From the analysis emerged a very rich and complex picture of disabled and non-disabled visitor responses to the nine museum projects, which included drawings, affective statements, personal experiences and lengthier commentaries. Furthermore, while the question on the card certainly focused visitors upon thinking about their own attitudes towards disability, the range of responses outside of this stimulus – gathered through interviews, case studies and focus groups – suggested that visitors engaged with the projects in a variety of ways and felt able to discuss and respond to the issues that they themselves found important.

Visitor interest and support

Overall, there was significant support from the majority of visitors for the nine projects and most seemed willing to engage with what they had seen and experienced in the museum. A typical comment is the following from Steven (26–35 years, non-disabled),[5] a visitor to Colchester Castle Museum's touring exhibition, *Life Beyond the Label*, who was both supportive of the exhibition and showed evidence of engaging with principles underpinning the social model of disability (a theme which we shall return to in greater detail):

> A very worthwhile exhibition. Everybody should be aware of the challenges disabled people have to face within Society.

Many others, for example Jane (36–45 years, non-disabled) who visited Northampton Museum, commented that it was the first time that they had thought about the issues raised in the project:

> Fantastic and engaging and truly absorbing. Thank you for making me think about this for the first time – a revelation.

Some expressed their support through statements which highlighted the importance of the museum as a site for learning (for example, about social issues) or a forum for the discussion of (potentially challenging) topics. For example Pam (46–55 years, non-disabled), interviewed at Birmingham Museum and Art Gallery, commented:

> Well, museums and galleries are where you can talk about anything really; any aspect of life should be explored through art I think.

Michael (46–55 years, disabled), also interviewed at Birmingham, considered that the inclusion of disability as a theme within the museum setting ensured it had 'some kind of authority stamped upon it'. As a result, he continued, museum visitors would 'give it more credence than if they saw it in a bar or a café or something … it just gives it more authority and more power'. The perception that museums were places of authority, with the capacity to offer credible ways of thinking about a topic, was often coupled with a sense that the interpretive stance within the projects was well balanced. For example William, a disabled visitor to Birmingham Museum and Art Gallery, commented:

> the opinions were good, I enjoyed the opinions, it was nice to hear an opinion, especially a well-balanced one, cos sometimes you get … people have some strange opinions of people with disabilities. I've disabilities myself. I've worked with a lot of people with a lot of different disabilities, but like some people have a very narrow view and don't really understand what disabilities are about … They sort of have a label and they forget that people are behind these disabilities. So it's nice to hear quite a balanced view wasn't it?

For many visitors the cultural authority of the museum[6] was significantly enhanced by the inclusion of the real voices and 'real life' experiences of disabled people. We return to these important issues pertaining to authenticity and authority in greater detail later in the chapter.

Personal connections

Within the evaluation, visitors who identified as disabled (and many who chose to highlight their connection with disability through disabled family members or friends) were generally very positive about encountering, within the setting of a museum, a topic that was important to them on a personal level. Rowena, a disabled woman aged 46–55 who visited the exhibition *One in Four* at Tyne and Wear Museums, commented:

> We really need more of these exhibitions, make people aware of the barriers. Anything to help people be included. Brilliant exhibitions!

While a minority expressed concerns and reservations,[7] the majority of disabled visitors' comments were supportive, reflecting (and sometimes explicitly highlighting) recognition that the interpretations in each of the projects, and the messages they were perceived to convey, had been shaped by disabled people themselves. Many comments suggested that – by addressing the topic of disability within a public space perceived to be authoritative – the projects conferred value upon disabled people's views and experiences. For example Elaine,

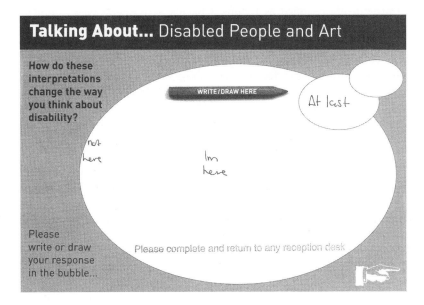

Figure 7.3 Response card, Birmingham Museum and Art Gallery.

a disabled woman at Birmingham Museum and Art Gallery, wrote: 'At last …
I'm here [in the centre] … not here [at the margins]', revealing her views on
the political significance of the museum's belated attention to disability issues
(see Figure 7.3).

'My attitudes haven't changed'

Although the overall picture emerging from the evaluation was encouraging, it
was also evident that the challenge of countering deeply ingrained and dominant ways of viewing disability remained, not surprisingly, a substantial one. As
previous studies have found, perceptions of difference are unlikely to be wholly
transformed by a single exhibition visit but, at the same time, museums have
been found to occupy a unique position in the mediascape that affords them a
particular role in countering prejudice (Sandell 2007). Moreover, as we discuss
more fully below, some responses contained complex and contradictory elements
which could not be neatly categorized as wholly 'positive' or 'negative'.

While a significant number of visitors demonstrated – through their responses – evidence of a change in the way they understood disability issues, some
were reluctant (and a very small number seemed offended) to consider that the
museum might have changed or influenced their thinking. In some cases, visitors
highlighted their (pre-existing) progressive views, for instance Holly (36–45
years, non-disabled), who commented after her visit to Colchester Castle Museum:

Hasn't really changed as I think I have a very liberal view – don't judge people on their abilities or how they look anyway.

Other visitors felt that the approach taken by the nine projects would be beneficial for raising awareness amongst those whom they perceived to be less informed than themselves about disability issues. Brendan (26–35 years, non-disabled), a visitor to Colchester Castle Museum, linked his understanding of disability issues to the experience of having a disabled family member:

Have great respect for all people with disabilities; in fact have someone in my family. May be good for people who have not had or known people. But only if they give it the time to look!

These modes of response, in which visitors demonstrate an eagerness to declare their own (progressive, tolerant, unprejudiced) position, have been found in earlier studies. Sandell, for example, in his analysis of visitors' engagement with displays purposefully designed to counter prejudice, found that:

Many visitors explicitly declared their support for concepts they identified in the museum's displays, such as equality, 'tolerance' and 'the importance of learning from the past' … many seemed eager to condemn discrimination, to 'perform' their own tolerance.

(2007: 35)

However, the explicit denial of a change in attitudes might also be explained, at least in part, by the character of prejudice which is generally directed towards disabled people. A recent study of prejudice in the UK found that subjects would not openly acknowledge that they held prejudiced attitudes based on disability, even though the language that they used reflected perceptions of disabled people as individuals who lacked competence, were vulnerable and deserving of pity. The authors of the study describe this type of prejudice – whereby individuals strongly believe that they do not hold negative views about disabled people even if the ways in which they discuss disability reveal a different picture – as 'benevolent prejudice' (Valentine and MacDonald 2004).

Similarly, the analysis of visitor responses to the projects in our evaluation revealed that expressions of overt hostility against disabled people were rare. However, as we shall see, the ways in which people discussed disability sometimes revealed perceptions which were at odds with the sociopolitical standpoint taken to frame each project.

Confrontation and unease

Some visitors were also uncomfortable about the ideas pertaining to disability that they encountered in the projects and the ways in which these were interpreted and presented to visitors. Aiden – a non-disabled visitor to Colchester Castle Museum – found a series of photographic self-portraits of disabled people, in which they asserted and articulated different aspects of their identity by writing words onto their faces, somewhat discomforting (Plate 7.2). It seemed from his responses that he found some elements of the display challenging because they did not appear to fit into his conception of how disabled people should be, or how they should behave. Throughout the interview he repeatedly expressed his discomfort with elements of the exhibition which showed people claiming and asserting their disabled identity. Some of the images, it seemed, unsettled him because they emphasized people's differences in a way which he felt was too confrontational:

> It's as though they're throwing you a challenge. Throwing it back to you – 'now get over it'. Well there's nothing to get over really. You're just a person the same as I am. So I just think those … those pictures are a little bit … I suppose they're thought provoking, that's the whole idea of it. I just find that they're almost 'in your face'.

Another example came from Fiona, a non-disabled visitor to Birmingham Museum and Art Gallery, who found the museum's interpretive approach – through which disability was explicitly highlighted – to be inappropriate and somewhat unhelpful to advancing an equality agenda.

> I'm never too keen on making a big … why have an exhibition about disability? It's a bit odd really, as if it's making a big thing about it. I don't think it helps inclusion at all.

Language

Sometimes the language visitors used was evocative of discriminatory and stigmatizing ways of referring to disability which, to contemporary activists and politically informed constituencies, appeared outdated and offensive. Therefore, although responses in this chapter are presented in their original, unedited form, we acknowledge that the language used by visitors may not always conform to contemporary expectations of what is deemed appropriate.

At the same time, guided by discussions within the 'Think Tank', we have attempted to avoid condemning visitors for their views or for not using the 'right' language. Rather, we argue that visitors are 'most appropriately conceived of not as "prejudiced" or "unprejudiced" but rather as struggling to manage anxieties about difference' (Sandell 2007: 174). Response cards also tended to be completed immediately after a visit and therefore represent visitors' raw, immediate thoughts, which might have been expressed very differently had they been given more time for reflection. Indeed, some responses seemed to suggest that visitors were grappling with 'new' ways of

101

conceptualizing disability that they had encountered in the museum. As a result, some responses contained what might be seen as discriminatory or negative attitudes intertwined with more egalitarian and respectful ways of thinking about disability.

Disability reframed?

We now turn to examine some of the significant themes which emerged from the analysis of visitor responses; evidence is drawn from both the response cards and visitor interviews throughout. In the following section, we discuss the key ways in which visitors were prompted to think and talk about disability as a result of their visit.

A social-political understanding of disability

One of the chief aims of *Rethinking Disability Representation* was to begin to move visitors' thinking away from individualized and medicalized under-standings of disability – which view the 'problem' of disability as arising from an individual's impairments or bodily difference (Oliver 1990) – towards understanding the oppressive and discriminatory effects of multiple barriers (physical, sensory, attitudinal) on disabled people's lives. The most commonly recurring mode of response (explicitly or implicitly) indicated that there had been fostered in visitors' minds a greater recognition of these social barriers, suggesting that many were receptive to the social model thinking that framed and underpinned each of the museum interventions.

Across the nine projects, visitors showed an increased appreciation of the barriers to participation that disabled people face in all spheres of life. For example, Ruth (56–65 years, non-disabled), a visitor to Glasgow Transport Museum's exhibition, *Lives in Motion,* commented that the exhibition

> ... highlights how long it took for progress to be made for people with a disability to be included in the plans for public transport and public life in general. Although great improvements have been made it is obvious that there is still a lot to be done to allow dis-abled people to be fully integrated into the general transport scheme in our country.

The exhibition *One in Four* (Tyne and Wear Museums) (Plate 7.3) enabled Mollie (26–35 years, non-disabled), to grasp one of the key concepts underpinning the social model – that society effectively 'constructs' disability:

> The exhibition was excellent. It reminds you how far society has come – but also still to go – and that it is society that causes disability i.e. not adapting to individuals.

102

The nine projects, however, went beyond an examination of the visible, physical barriers that exclude disabled people and visitor comments showed some evidence of understanding the potentially disabling effects that 'invisible' barriers, such as negative attitudes, can have on the lives of disabled people. Examples of this include Laura (46–55 years, non-disabled), a visitor to Colchester Castle Museum, who could see the potential of the exhibition to impact more widely upon public perceptions of disabled people:

> Glad that display is prominent. Helps to highlight the problems and attitudes that disabled people may face. Hopefully the public will see people with disabilities in a more positive light.

The following visitor to Northampton Museum, Katherine (36–45 years, non-disabled), showed evidence in her response of coming to a new realization about the different opportunities that society affords disabled and non-disabled people:

> This display challenges assumptions we all make about disabled people. It also highlights how limited resources restrict people's choices & therefore impacts so much on people's everyday lives & quality of life …

Behind the Shadow of Merrick, a short film developed for the Royal London Hospital Museum (see Hevey, this volume), used objects, documents and stories related to Joseph Merrick to examine issues and attitudes surrounding disability in the past and present day and evoked many emotional responses from viewers. The following comment from Sarah (36–45 years, non-disabled) captures her surprise at how little attitudes seem to have changed since the nineteenth century:

> A person is much more than a physical representation. It is quite humbling. I couldn't help but think that if I was disabled how angry I would be that people would make judgements based purely on personal appearance – I am much much more than my physical appearance. Times have changed since Merrick but frighteningly attitudes haven't.

Engagement with the projects provided many visitors with both concepts and a language with which to articulate their increased understanding of the barriers faced by disabled people in society. The predominance of responses that reflected understanding of (and support for) the social model was viewed by the research team as compelling evidence of the potential for museums to offer visitors credible and permissible ways of understanding disability.

Equality and social justice

In the second largest category of response that emerged from our analysis, visitors referenced and drew upon a discourse of rights and social justice to discuss disability. The rights and equality discourse consists of a number of factors including the right to equality of opportunity, equal access to services, the right to voice dissent and the right to respect and dignity. Several of the museum projects documented and discussed specific histories and 'real-life' examples of rights struggles which, on the basis of the evidence from the response cards, enabled visitors to connect both with tangible issues – such as the impact of poor access to public transport systems – and with more abstract rights-related concepts.

Many comments expressed, in basic terms, their support for an equality agenda such as the following response from Patricia (36–45 years, non-disabled), a visitor to Colchester Castle Museum:

> Proves people should be treated as equal & not differently.

Some visitors used their response card as a 'call for action' – on the part of individuals, society in general and governments in particular – to address the inequalities generated by the physical and attitudinal barriers highlighted by a social-contextual approach to disability. For example, Emily (26–35 years, non-disabled), who visited Tyne and Wear Museums, commented:

> It just strengthens my thoughts that the government [spends] more money on telling us how to treat people but does not provide the funding needed for disabled people to live full, rewarding lives without having to overcome obstacles. EVERYONE has the right to realize their full potential. We live in a wealthy country so funding should never be an issue.

Other visitors articulated their opinions by drawing explicitly and directly on concepts that they had been exposed to during their museum visit. The following comment, by Katy – a 13-year-old, non-disabled pupil – shows how the Imperial War Museum's education programme helped to frame and inform the way in which she perceives disabled people:

> I think disabled people should be recognised as equals and should be given equal opportunity – before I thought if someone was disabled they should stay at home but my views are very different now!

Support for equality was often expressed through an emphasis on 'sameness', tied to the notion that disabled people are 'just like everyone else'. While some visitors stated this as a matter of fact – as something they had always

104

thought – for some younger visitors, like Chloe, a 12-year-old, non-disabled visitor to Tyne and Wear Museums, it was presented as a new perspective:

> I think it [has] made me realise that everyone is the same and dis-ability people are the same as us and should be treat[ed] the same.

Discussions with members of the Think Tank revealed different opinions on the relative desirability of these comments that emphasized 'sameness'. While such comments were interpreted by some as empathetic expressions of support for disability rights, others raised concerns about the impact of conflating the experiences of disabled and non-disabled people in ways which potentially denied the particularity of lived experience, the history and the distinct political identity of disabled individuals. Certainly, some responses seemed to suggest a difficulty for some visitors in reconciling ideas of sameness and difference between disabled and non-disabled people. Alice, a 15-year-old, non-disabled visitor to Colchester Castle Museum, wrote:

> I always thought people with a disability are still the same as us but it's a really nice thing to see that their opening up to other people. It makes me feel upset that their saying everyone is different. They shouldn't have to feel that way because their still the same as everyone else without disability.

Impairment as tragedy: a hegemonic and persistent discourse?

Just as some visitors struggled to reconcile concepts of sameness and differ-ence, others – especially in this next category – responded in ways which suggested a dissonance between the images of disability they were accus-tomed to seeing (which generally reflected an individualized, medicalized perspective) and the representations of disability put forward in the museum project which were shaped by a social model.

Using the social model to frame the interpretation of collections related to disability and the lives and experiences of disabled people was seen, by the Think Tank and research team, as a means by which to resist – and indeed to directly challenge – representations that had the potential to provoke fear or patronizing sympathy in visitors. Stereotypical representations presenting disabled people as passive victims, dependent on others, or as objects of pity, were to be avoided and, indeed, actively countered. Considerable efforts, therefore, were made across the nine projects to avoid narratives that equated impairment with tragedy and to offer alternative readings of the experience of disability.

Despite these efforts, it is perhaps unsurprising that a significant number of responses reflected the conception of disability as 'personal tragedy' (Oliver 1990), since this way of seeing – this framing of impairment – continues to dominate and is 'infused throughout media representations, language, cultural beliefs, research, policy and professional practice' (French and Swain 2004: 34). This understanding of impairment as tragedy was manifest in a number of ways. For instance Harriet (46–55 years, non-disabled), a visitor to Colchester Castle Museum, considered herself to be fortunate because she was not disabled:

> It makes me realise how lucky I am. I admire the way disabled people cope.

While Zara (16–25 years) had a similar response to the film *Behind the Shadow of Merrick*, though interestingly she sensed that this was not the aim of the creators:

> I feel sorry for the people in the film and I am glad I am not disabled, although I am not sure this is what the film makers intended.

The disposition towards 'feeling lucky' not to be disabled was sometimes linked with the concern that one could become impaired (and so disabled) at any time which, as some researchers have suggested, might be viewed as an entirely rational, cognitive response to the possibility of impairment within a society that continues to discriminate and oppress disabled people (French and Swain 2004). Such concerns tended to be expressed by older visitors, such as Brenda (56–65 years), who visited Glasgow Museum of Transport:

> I just feel fortunate I am not in the same situation but who knows what is round the corner of life ...

It is important to recognize, however, that there was not always a clear distinction between those elements in visitor responses that could be attached to the individual model and those which reflected understanding of social model thinking. Contradictions could arise as visitors struggled to accommodate new ways of thinking about disability with those that continue to dominate across cultural and media settings. In the following comment, Samantha (16–25 years, non-disabled), a visitor to Colchester Castle Museum, both references the negative stereotype of the disabled person as dependent and in need of care and, at the same time, appears to move towards a cognitive reconstruction of disabled people via the recognition of 'sameness':

> It made me realise a lot more about disabled people and how much more care and help they really need. I would love to get involved or to help to make a difference to a disabled person – they are the same as non-disabled people so why treat them any differently?

Comments such as this generated an especially lively debate during the process of analysis and interpretation as to how they should be interpreted. In this 'grey area' where visitors may be seen as negotiating between what are regarded as culturally dominant, negative, representations of disability and alternative perspectives as framed by the social model, they may often continue to rely on and use language associated with prejudice and disablism. Should such comments be regarded as offensive and patronizing, at odds with the aims of the project or, conversely, can it be argued that some of these comments might be better understood as empathetic and illustrative of the first steps towards a more respectful understanding of disability, even if the language and tone might be considered problematic?

Heroic survivors and other stereotypes

This fourth category of response highlights not the tragedy of impairment but rather the individual's heroism in overcoming the challenges impairment brings. This conception of the heroic survivor, or 'super-crip' (Barnes, Mercer and Shakespeare 1999) can be seen to reflect individual or medical model thinking by emphasizing the individual's role in 'overcoming' the limitations posed by their own impairment through acts of heroism and bravery. Such conceptions of disability sit well in the cultural imagination, and particularly in the popular media, where disabled people are often referred to as 'brave', 'cheerful', 'wonderful' or 'inspiring'. While this is often meant as a compliment on the ways that people cope, it usually focuses on the individual impairment rather than the myriad social barriers that disabled people experience and, in doing so, reflects an individualized way of understanding disability issues and, crucially, one which operates to undermine claims of equal rights.

While efforts were made by the nine museum projects to resist overly celebratory and naïve views of disability (and, indeed, to actively counter them), narratives of 'heroism' and 'bravery' continued to persist in visitor responses in a similar way to the 'tragic' narratives discussed above. For example, Zoë (26–35 years, non-disabled), commented after her visit to Colchester Castle Museum:

> I've always been aware and interested in learning about disability. It's a good idea to have this display to help people understand what these inspiring people go through and how they deal with life.

Discussing these responses, some members of the Think Tank argued that it was possible, in some instances, to highlight narratives which revealed individual disabled people's bravery without succumbing to damaging stereotypes. Despite the dangers inherent in reproducing familiar stereotypes, narratives highlighting bravery, they suggested, should not automatically be avoided by museums since heroic acts are as much a part of disability history as they are of mainstream history. What was regarded as important, however, was to understand the context within which visitors' comments are made when analysing their significance. For example, comments from students who took part in educational sessions at the Imperial War Museum around the theme of 'Disability and Conflict' not surprisingly referenced bravery and heroism; responses which Think Tank members viewed as positive and linked to a progressive understanding of disability issues. For example, Libby, a 15-year-old, non-disabled student who participated in a session which explored the attitudes of people towards Second World War pilots who sustained severe facial injuries, later commented:

> The session strongly reinforces the bravery and strength of the men that were part of the Guinea Pig club. After all the horrific events they have been involved in, they still enjoy life and smile. I think that is something to be greatly admired.

In contrast, comments which suggested that visitors endowed some disabled people with heroic qualities simply for their ability to manage the disabling barriers they encountered in life were viewed as rather more problematic.

This overview of the evaluation carried out across the nine projects demonstrates the richness, diversity and complexity of visitors' responses to the representations of disabled people and the interpretations of disability-themed narratives that they encountered. While visitors responded to the exhibitions, displays, films and educational sessions in myriad ways, the evaluation powerfully revealed the museum's capacity to offer ways of seeing which have considerable influence on visitors' thinking. Many left the museum talking about disability differently, in ways that reflected the project's overarching aim.

Part of the evaluation attempted to explore not only the ideas, concepts and messages that visitors identified within the projects and took away from their visit but also the interpretive strategies and devices that were most effective in engendering support for the project's broader aims. The strongest of these to emerge from the analysis of visitors' responses was the significance and agency of disabled people's own voices and experiences.

Authenticity, agency, authority

Threaded throughout the data from comments cards, interviews and focus groups were numerous references – tacit and explicit, implied and direct – to the museums' use of real voices and the real-life experiences of disabled people across the nine interpretive experiments. The inclusion and privileging of these authentic narratives was enormously significant to visitors and, we would argue, played a key role in enabling them to construct altered understandings of disability. For instance, Emma, a non-disabled visitor

108

interviewed at Colchester Castle Museum, considered that reading about the real-life experiences of disabled people

> brings it down to a personal level, whereas, you know, a lot of the time disability's talked about on a general level and it doesn't, you know … a personal experience of it is much more hard hitting than something that's generalised.

Visitors talked about how they valued the personal experiences of disabled people and how the inclusion of these perspectives conferred authenticity upon the content. Keira, a classroom assistant who accompanied a group of students to the Imperial War Museum, also considered that the message was more powerful when conveyed by a real person experiencing the phenomenon in question, 'Because it brings the message home, you know, somebody talking from personal experience'.

The power of personal stories, many of which spoke of a struggle against discrimination, to elicit emotional responses from visitors was also evident in the evaluation. Responses suggest that people often engaged deeply with the ideas and stories they encountered in ways that inspired empathy, surprise, awe, horror, anger, pleasure, gratitude, understanding and reflection. Highly emotional reactions were perhaps most frequently expressed in response to the film *Behind the Shadow of Merrick*. Catherine, a disabled woman and student, contacted RCMG after viewing the film and commented:

> I think 'Behind the Shadow of Merrick' is a very powerful and moving film. It has an emotional rawness that both engages the viewer and, more importantly, holds them beyond the screening … For most non-disabled people, Merrick is 'the other' and 'the outsider' but for your participants in the film he is the epitome of the insider: he knows the cold, harsh reality of not visibly belonging and of being the eternal stranger.

Personalizing the topic of disability – by giving faces and names to people who shared their experiences with visitors – meant that the issues raised by each of the projects were seen from the point of view of disabled people themselves. It appeared that, for some visitors especially, this was a powerful approach, enabling them to empathize with (and understand) the topic from a new, more authentic perspective. The impact of the highly personalized and socially relevant narratives that appeared throughout the projects reflects the close involvement and collaboration of each of the museums with disabled people in their development, both centrally through the 'Think Tank' – which played a key role in framing their overarching approaches – and, in many cases, extensive consultation with disabled people at a local level. Joe, a non-disabled visitor interviewed at Colchester Castle Museum, seemed to identify and value the way in which he perceived disabled people to be in control of their representation in the *Life Beyond the Label* exhibition:

> I imagine it's themselves, because the feeling I get is that ... the people involved have been active, not passive. It's not been done to them, but they've collaborated.

Conclusion

The analysis of data from comments cards, interviews and focus groups subsequently revealed a complex tapestry of visitor responses to the nine museum projects. As we have seen, some visitors reported fundamental shifts in their perceptions of disabled people and a greater understanding of more progressive (social-contextual) ways of understanding disability. However, the prevalence of negative and stereotypical views of disabled people throughout many aspects of social life and the media meant that some responses continued to reflect viewpoints grounded in the individual and medical models of disability. Some visitors showed evidence of negotiating between both perspectives, others struggling to reconcile the notion of 'difference', and an assertive political identity for disabled people, with the notion that disabled people are the 'same' as non-disabled people and equally deserving of rights.

Rethinking Disability Representation set out with an undeniably ambitious set of aims. Ubiquitous and deeply ingrained representations of disabled people may have proved stubbornly resistant to the efforts of the nine museums but, at the same time, the evaluation revealed considerable evidence of the capacity for museums – as culturally authoritative institutions – to offer new, progressive and egalitarian ways of understanding disability. It is only through more self-conscious approaches to representation, grounded in genuinely collaborative practice with disabled people, that museums can begin to tap their potential to contribute towards broader social changes. The empirical evidence gathered from across these nine interpretive experiments presents a tantalizing glimpse of the changes that are indeed real and possible.

Notes

1 The project was initiated by the Research Centre for Museums and Galleries (RCMG) and funded by the Heritage Lottery Fund, National Endowment for Science, Technology and the Arts and the University of Leicester, with support from the nine participating museums: Birmingham Museum and Art Gallery, Colchester and Ipswich Museums Service, Glasgow Museums, the Imperial War Museum, London, Royal London Hospital Archives and Museum, Stamford Museum, Tyne and Wear Museums, Northampton Museum and Art Gallery and Whitby Museum.
2 For a detailed discussion of the agency of museums in (re)framing visitors' conceptions of difference, see Sandell 2007.

3 The term 'display' was changed at some sites to make it suitable for specific projects. For instance the response cards used at the Imperial War Museum, where the project took the form of educational sessions for secondary schools, asked: 'How does this session change the way you think about disability?'

4 The interviews took place at four museums: Birmingham Museum and Art Gallery, Colchester Castle Museum, South Shields Museum and Discovery Museum, Newcastle-upon-Tyne.

5 All names have been changed to protect respondents' confidentiality.

6 For a fuller discussion of the cultural authority of the museum see Karp and Kratz (2000), Kratz (2002) and Sandell (2007).

7 See Dodd *et al.* (2008) for a detailed discussion of visitors' responses.

References

Barnes, C. (1992) *Disabling Imagery and the Media: An Exploration of the Principles for Media Representation of Disabled People*, British Council of Organisations of Disabled People (BCODP), Halifax: Ryburn Publishing.

Barnes, C., Mercer, G. and Shakespeare, T. (1999) *Exploring Disability: A Sociological Introduction*, Cambridge and Maldon, MA: Polity Press.

Barnes, C. and Mercer, G. (2003) *Disability*, Cambridge: Polity Press.

French, S. and Swain, J. (2004) 'Whose tragedy? Towards a personal non-tragedy view of disability' in J. Swain, C. Barnes, S. French and C. Thomas (eds), *Disabling Barriers, Enabling Environments,* 2nd edition, London, Thousand Oaks, CA and New Delhi: Sage, pp. 34–41.

Garland-Thomson, R. (1997) *Extraordinary Bodies: Figuring Physical Disability in American Culture and Literature*, New York: Columbia University Press.

Hevey, D. (1992) *The Creatures That Time Forgot: Photography and Disability Imagery*, London: Routledge.

Kudlick, C.J. (2003) 'Disability history: Why we need another "Other"', *American Historical Review*, 108(3): 763–93.

Oliver, M. (1983) *Social Work with Disabled People*, Basingstoke: Macmillan.

—— (1990) *The Politics of Disablement*, Basingstoke: Macmillan.

—— (1996) *Understanding Disability: From Theory to Practice*, Basingstoke and New York: Palgrave.

Sandell, R. (2007) *Museums, Prejudice and the Reframing of Difference*, London and New York: Routledge.

Sandell, R., Delin, A., Dodd, J., and Gay, J. (2005) 'Beggars, freaks and heroes? Museum collections and the hidden history of disability', *Journal of Museum Management and Curatorship*, 20(1): 5–19.

Shakespeare, T. (2004) *Disability Rights and Wrongs*, London and New York: Routledge.

Thomas, D. (1982) *The Experience of Handicap,* London: Methuen.

Valentine, G. and MacDonald, I. (2004) *Understanding Prejudice: Attitudes towards Minorities*, London: Stonewall.

Part 2

INTERPRETIVE JOURNEYS AND EXPERIMENTS

8

TO LABEL THE LABEL?

'Learning disability' and exhibiting 'critical proximity'

Helen Graham

The Museum of Croydon's recently developed permanent displays explore the history of Croydon, south London, through specific people's objects and stories. Two among the many stories presented are *Mabel's Certificate* (2004) and *Madeleine's Celebrities* (1960–79). Mabel Cooper's choice of object, her own account of its importance and the descriptive text offered by the museum, all refer in some way to 'learning difficulties'. In contrast – though in common with many of the other stories on display – Madeleine Gardiner's oral testimony and the museum-authored supporting interpretation draw on no specific identity or classification to 'explain' Madeleine's memories of celebrities coming to Croydon's Fairfield Hall.[1]

Whether or not to 'label the label' – to attach a widely recognized descriptor that denotes membership of a particular identity category to an individual's story or object – is an ongoing problematic. Recent initiatives in museums designed to enhance the visibility of disabled people within exhibition narratives have generally relied on the mobilization of recognizable classifications. 'Labels' – for example 'disabled people' in the UK and 'persons with disabilities' in the USA – are often deployed to promote disabled people's rights and to draw attention to inequalities. The use of such labels as markers of identity can engender powerful feelings of belonging and worth, they can operate to communicate a positive sense of shared group membership and be mobilized to effect political and social change. But, at the same time, labels can work to differentiate groups and, in doing so, they can stigmatize. These concerns are also linked with questions regarding the capacity of such classifications to reflect the subtleties and complexities of daily life experiences; a growing emphasis on identity categories as mutable and contingent on circumstance, and a sense that classifications are not simply *descriptive* but also *productive,* have meant labels are being approached with increasing caution.

One of the reasons for this caution lies in the epistemological consequences of labelling – specifically how we make sense of the relationship between individual people's actions, memories and objects and 'larger contexts' or 'wider social and historical explanation'. In recent years the emphasis has shifted away from museum exhibitions which mobilize 'meta-narratives' that aim to assimilate and explain multiple objects and lives within a unifying framework. In the place of such meta-explanation, there has been a call for a 'de-centering' of the museum voice, an increased use of dialogic and multi-vocal approaches to interpretation and for museums to be places for the representation of 'cultures-in-difference' (Bennett 2006) or to function as cross-cultural 'contact zones' (Clifford 1997).

Such shifts are reflected in the Museum of Croydon. No grand narrative of Croydon's development is attempted; instead multiple people's objects and stories are divided into decades. 'Croydon' is not expressed as one coherent, whole place but rather perceived as something fluid and changing and *made up* of many different people whose radical multiplicity is represented through the stories in the gallery. However, the exhibition does not fully abandon the explanatory register; instead, explanations are located at the bottom of the interpretive hierarchy. Audiovisual 'touchscreens' offer visitors access to information about an object through the choice of different options – 'Show', 'Tell', 'Explain' and 'Explore'. The person whose object appears in the display case 'Tells' the visitor about the object through oral testimony, while the museum voice first 'Shows' the object and then 'Explains' it. Unlike 'explanation' when located at the top of an interpretive hierarchy, the Museum of Croydon's use of explanation does not aim at synthesis and cohesion. Rather, multiple explanations are mobilized for specific objects and people, which do not coalesce but rather work as unreconciled pathways of explanation – of one amongst several contexts, for one part of one person's life, as one aspect of 'Croydon'.

The de-centred, multi-vocal approach to understanding our pasts has, however, been criticized – the perception being that if you lose analysis and explanation then politics too is in danger of being lost. A strand of this basic argument has been developed by Gayatri Chakravorty Spivak who argues for a 'strategic essentialism' which recognizes both the dangers of naturalizing difference and, at times, the necessity for mobilizing around collective identities in order to make political contest possible (1987: 205). At the same time, the dangers of fetishizing the authenticity of experience have also been noted (Scott 1992). Through the prioritizing of people's stories in their own words, and complemented by optional explanatory interpretation, the Museum of Croydon's approach represents a subtle and effective response to these dilemmas. Yet there remains scope for exploring further the implications of the decision whether to label or not, and to identify alternative approaches.

Taking a close reading of Mabel's and Madeleine's stories as its focus, this chapter locates the decision whether or not to invoke identity labels as a particular expression of concern over how the relationship between specificity (of an object, a memory, an event) and social and historical explanation can be understood *as politics*.[2] In this chapter I suggest that social history in museums might be renewed by supplementing fidelity to individuals' own vocabulary for describing their lives by 'redistributing', in Bruno Latour's terms, 'the local' – and thereby neither treating individual people's words as the locus of pure authenticity nor jumping to meta-explanation which erases specificity. Instead, following Latour, I suggest politics be relocated through tracing the networks and associations (via movements of people, objects and ideas) that maintain differentiation, hierarchy and inequality. I conclude by suggesting that museums no longer need to locate themselves 'above' the people and events they represent (through standing back and setting out the big picture) nor aim only to create 'dialogue' between locales. Rather through an epistemological shift, museums can replace critical distance with visitor experiences of 'critical proximity' (Latour 2005: 253).[3]

Labelling objects and labelling people

Object labels have traditionally been classificatory; they have tended to contain information about the object's 'name, date, material, scientific name [and] accession number' (Serrell 1996: 28). Equally, the labels of 'mental deficiency', 'mental handicap', 'learning disabilities' and' learning difficulties' have emerged and developed over time through similar logics of definition and differentiation. Indeed, the connections between museum display and intellectual disability are not solely confined to contemporary concerns with the representativeness of audiences, collections and displays. As Nélia Dias has argued in relationship to the development of French anthropology collections in the late nineteenth century, in the 'search for differentiating characteristics of the skull and of the face in human groups, anthropological studies focused on the Other – inferior races, idiots, criminals' and through this 'confirmed the latter as objects of difference and otherness' (1998: 38).

The mutual development of museums and understandings of human evolution was motivated not only by the generation of new knowledge but – significantly – also by the desire to effectively communicate 'a means of making difference visible to the public and inscribing it in the memory of visitors' (Dias 1998: 38). In fact, Dias argues, the prioritization of communicating with the public actually shaped the production of knowledge as museum display was 'a major reason why the comparative anatomy of human races and the study of physical remains (skeletons, skulls, crania) was privileged over physiology and the study of functions and processes in the living' (ibid.: 38). It was for these reasons that while the 'meticulous study of objects' was seen as key to a new rational method of knowledge production (Hooper-Greenhill 2000: 105–6), the *display* of objects required some deliberate shaping for the sake of effective teaching (Bennett 1998). The 'clear and detailed labelling of exhibits' was developed precisely so that exhibitions would be 'auto-intelligible' and so that 'the working man was not ... wearied by his visit and sent away dissatisfied' (ibid.: 26, 27).

The 'labelling' of objects or people cannot therefore be understood outside of the desire to communicate something. In essence any naming device aims to 'stabilize' meaning for the purposes of its transmission to others. Bruno Latour with Michael Callon has discussed this process as one of creating 'black boxes'. This is a term widely used in Science and Technology Studies to refer to things – or ideas – that are treated as if their content 'no longer needs to be reconsidered' (1981: 285). An example often given is of a computer, whose complex chains of production, or the workings which make typing or internet connection possible, are largely forgotten as we go on with our jobs until, that is, the computer stops working and suddenly some of those networks which made the computer work are revealed. Even though, Latour and Callon argue, 'black boxes never remain fully closed or properly fastened', stabilizing meaning does offer people the opportunity to cease to 'negotiate' every experience 'with equal intensity' (ibid.: 285). Certainly, stabilized meanings – in the form of categories of identity – have been tactically mobilized (women, Black, Scottish, mothers and so on), gathering people together as a means of expressing commonalities and using this stability to move on to communicate a political challenge. While this has been effective for a number of social movements, the labels associated with intellectual disability have been problematic because reclaiming and owning their meaning has proved very difficult. In fact, unlike the contexts of feminist or Black politics where the term 'labelling' is not generally used to refer to 'identity', 'labelling' is regularly used in learning disability politics, professional practice and academic research precisely to express anxiety about the implications of the use of 'learning disability/difficulties' (McClimens 2007).

The chief cause of this anxiety is that 'learning disability' has been very difficult to 'black box'. In recent years, the pathological basis of learning disability as an underlying explanatory factor has been challenged:

> Clinical conventional wisdom suggests that in only 25–30 per cent of cases so diagnosed is intellectual disability associated with an identifiable organic pathology ... In other words, the bulk of the category consists of people who have been categorised as significantly less bright than the general population average, without there being any clear diagnosis or understanding of the reasons for their incompetence.
>
> (Jenkins 1998: 9, 10)

Moreover, social explanations of disability that have emerged through critiques of the 'medical model'[4] have stressed the contingent and unfixed nature of 'intellectual ability' (Goodley and Roets 2008). This has been coupled with an increasing focus on the *work* done by the act of labelling; as

Ian Hacking puts it in more general terms, 'human beings and human acts come into being hand in hand with our invention of categories labelling them' (Hacking 1986: 236).

One of the key concerns has been about the impact of categorization and differentiation. As Robert B. Edgerton – whose pioneering work on deinstitutionalization in the 1960s has greatly influenced thinking around 'labelling' – characterized the problem, the 'label of mental retardation not only serves as a humiliating, frustrating and discrediting stigma ... it also serves to lower your self-esteem' (Edgerton 1967: 145). This analysis has also underpinned 'normalization' theory, which remains influential in social care practice and aims to counter stigmatization through associating learning-disabled people with 'valued' (non-learning disabled) people and places. Normalization has been criticized by those working in the tradition of the social model of disability for not critiquing the ways in which the organization of our society itself creates certain kinds of learning disability and for not enabling a positive political identity to emerge. Research has also shown that many individuals described as learning disabled do not themselves recognize the term (Goodley 2001: 216–17). Self-advocates have challenged labelling through the slogan, 'label jars, not people' (Walmsley 1997) with some choosing 'learning difficulties' as a preferred identity. Yet, at the same time there is no doubt that being classified as 'having learning disabilities' by social care professionals very often remains essential to being considered eligible for welfare services and, in the process of classification, clinically produced knowledges such as IQ are considered alongside social factors.

In the context of the changing configurations of 'the natural/biological' and 'the social' outlined above, museums are no doubt left in a difficult situation in approaching issues of classification and explanation. Some of the problems and ethical concerns associated with mobilizing specific classifications or labels were identified in recent research looking at representations of disabled people in UK museum and gallery collections and displays, where anxiety was expressed by curators over when to 'out' a specific person as disabled (Dodd *et al.* 2004: 16). The term 'outing' refers to the public disclosure of a person's impairment (when they may have gone to great lengths to conceal it) or the attachment of the label 'disabled' to a person who may not have self-identified as such in their own lifetime (Sandell 2007: 165–66). The researchers Jocelyn Dodd, Richard Sandell, Annie Delin and Jackie Gay – while recognizing the need to consider a range of contextual factors when deciding on the appropriateness of 'outing' – tended to oppose 'sidestepping' the issue. They saw making explicit reference to disability as an opportunity either to develop positive representations of disabled people that might 'complicate reductionist and totalizing understandings of disability' (Sandell 2007: 169) or to tell difficult stories about prejudice and exclusion (Dodd *et al.* 2004: 17–18).

The issue of 'outing' (this time in the context of lesbian and gay history) was an issue facing Croydon in their development of the *Lifetimes* gallery (the predecessor to the Museum of Croydon) in 1995. Staff involved in the gallery expressed the hope that – with more than 300 voices presented in the gallery, each drawing on 'the authority of personal experience' to present their accounts of the past – 'lesbian and gay experience can be presented not as an anomaly, but as one aspect of complex lives' (Rachel Hasted quoted in Vanegas 2002: 103). Indeed, Hasted further argued that, 'since sexuality is only one aspect of a person's life, the stories only mention it when it is appropriate' (ibid.: 103). However, while this inclusive approach was striven for, there was also a concern that 'lesbians and gay men will become invisible within the exhibition' (ibid.: 103). It was also suggested that where donated objects did not immediately express themselves as being related to lesbian and gay history, a searchable database (and freely available pamphlets in the gallery) should allow the objects' connections to such history to be highlighted (ibid.: 103). Through this, the aim was to conceptualize lives as articulated at different times by different identities and to discover how, without over-determining the specific story individuals offered, to allow the diversity of social groups represented in the gallery to be 'find-able' or recognized by visitors.

However, while Vanegas describes a useful technical fix to this conundrum there remains a conceptual problem. Dodd *et al.* do assume that including the label of 'disabled' in exhibition interpretation is directly linked to introducing a political reading into the display (2004: 12, 18) and suggest that building a positive 'new cultural identity' is at stake in this decision (ibid.: 16). This position is a clear response to the ongoing erasure of disabled people in public contexts. But is the explicit use of such a label necessary to generate a political reading of the impact of 'disability'?

Here it is helpful to draw on a debate shaping contemporary sociology, concerning the utility of sociological classifications – such as 'class', 'gender', 'sexuality' – for describing, analysing or, indeed, changing the world. Latour – who sees himself as conducting a 'sociology of association' (sometimes called 'pragmatic sociology') – counsels against the 'instant sociology' and 'ready explanations' he associates with what he calls 'critical sociology'. He argues that the danger of the analytical use of 'black boxed' categories/ structures is that they become mobilized in such a way that any given specific interaction becomes *because of* and *explained by* (for example) class, capitalism, or patriarchy. Instead he argues that sociologists should 'not stabilize' and allow the concepts of those people being studied to be 'stronger' than those 'of the analysts' (Latour 2005: 30). Where 'critical sociology', he argues, tends to look for what is 'behind' action and psychoanalytical approaches search for unconscious motivations, the job of the sociologist of association is to trace these connections as they are created through both actions and articulations. Key to Latour's approach is to see that people 'are constantly at work', justifying their groups' existence 'invoking rules and precedents and ... measuring up one definition against all the others' (ibid.: 31). In terms of approaching museum display, the challenge is to be guided by the specific terms people themselves use to describe their own lives, yet not erase or 'side-step' the complex formations of differentiation, hierarchy and inequality which flow through their daily life experiences.

Mabel's certificate: communicating differentiation and inequality

So it is this complex work – and the implications of mobilizing labels – to which we return via Mabel Cooper's literacy certificate, displayed and interpreted in the Museum of Croydon (Plate 8.1a). Here, Mabel's story has a very coherent, clear and generally explanatory narrative. Unlike some of the gay men and lesbian women who chose objects which were not about their sexuality for the *Lifetimes* gallery, Mabel has chosen an object which specifically allows the museum to represent 'learning difficulties'. In her oral history, Mabel expresses the importance of the certificate by placing it in the context of her experience of school where 'she went for a little while' until they told her 'you can't come back again' because 'you can't learn, you're not able to learn'. In the second part of her oral testimony Mabel speaks about going to Croydon College and learning to read 'a little bit', especially with the help of her friend, Gloria. Mabel's account achieves its effect by using a comparison between the past and the present. First, the over-determination of her lack of ability to learn is questioned, therefore destabilizing 'learning disability' (or as it would have been 'mental deficiency') as a 'black box'. Second, however, a less fixed notion of learning difficulties remains implicitly important to make sense of the support from Croydon College provided to help her get her certificate.

However, the museum-voice interpretation offered at the 'Show' and 'Explain' levels of the audio-visual gives different explanations for the certificate. The 'Show' element – the first of the categories on the touchscreen – describes Mabel as having 'learning difficulties so gaining these skills is a reward for her hard work', going on to say that learning to read 'has given Mabel a real sense of achievement'. The evocation of learning difficulties at the 'Show' level is mobilized in the sentence quoted above as if it is an *explanation* of why Mabel needed to 'work hard' to learn to read and write. Drawing on Mabel's own autobiographical writings,[5] the 'Explain' level of the touchscreen – located after 'Show' and 'Tell' – accounts for the importance of 'studying at Croydon College' by the introduction of Mabel's history, specifically her experience of being held at St Lawrence's Hospital in Caterham. Here, the significance of Mabel's achievement is further reinforced by attaching to it a history of segregation and oppression. Learning difficulties are not simply the meta-explanation of 'finding it hard to read', but rather segregation and discrimination are also evoked as 'explanations'.

In many ways the difference in what is 'collected' and 'stabilized' – to use Latour's terms – at each of the interpretive levels is best understood through following the different use of the idea of 'reading'. Reading at the 'Show' and 'Explain' levels is treated positively. So at the 'Show' level, learning to read is a 'big achievement' that took 'hard work' and at the 'Explain' level it is because of classes at Croydon College and Gloria's help that Mabel has learned to 'read *properly*' (emphasis added). Mabel, in her oral history extract, however, offers a much more equivocal and non-binary understanding of reading. The opening sentences of her oral testimony extract suggest that it was precisely at 'reading' as a site (located at school) that she was first classified as 'unteachable'. Although clearly the critical framework of comparison of past and present shows the failure of that set of pedagogical and clinical systems as they operated through the vehicle of 'reading', this does not mean that 'reading' is embraced by Mabel herself as a sign of either redemption or success. In the audio of her oral history, Mabel actually sounds a bit ambivalent about reading. She says 'I *should* learn to read' and through this introduces some sense of compulsion and external expectation. Unlike the first section of the oral history where Mabel is strident, in the second section her voice sounds quieter and less forceful. Where being able to read is represented as a binary state at the 'Show' level of the audio-visual interpretation, before Mabel started at Croydon College she tells us that she could already do 'two letter words' and now can do a 'few more' words. In fact, for Mabel the certificate does not mark the end of the journey but is rather just one point along the way as, with Gloria's help, it 'is coming on'. Where at the 'Show' and 'Explain' levels 'reading' demarcates achievement and acts as a validation of Mabel's ability, 'reading' does not operate at all as a 'black box' for Mabel. It is both hard and a competency which is *in progress* but, crucially, it also remains a site through which she is judged. If understood through the lens of the social model of disability it would be precisely the organization of our world around literacy that gives specific form to Mabel's 'difficulties'. When thought about in this way, the binary state of reading (learn to read, learn to read *properly*), at the interpretation levels, actually works to set up a binary reading of Mabel herself (*now* she can read), even though her words complicate and break down the connections, associations and practices which make up 'reading' and her classification as someone who has 'learning difficulties'.

Mabel's story makes 'learning difficulties' visible and legible and through this enables a critical reading of the effects of the over-determination of someone's capacity. The museum interpretation certainly works to give a kind of political punctuation to Mabel's critical framework of comparison of past and present by evoking the history of institutionalization. That said, and taking Latour's advice of allowing Mabel's terms to be stronger than the terms of the museum voice, it is possible to see that there are some erasures at work. While Mabel's main argument was reinforced through the 'Explain' label, the interpretation did not follow the detail of how Mabel compared then and now – and the implications of that for the politics of reading itself. Because of this, the label worked to re-stabilize both 'learning difficulties' and 'reading', the latter seeming to be the very site of differentiation, hierarchy and inequality to which Mabel's oral testimony draws our attention.

Madeleine's celebrities: communicating the complexity of experience

Unlike Mabel, Madeleine did not choose a literacy certificate for her object case. Instead she chose programmes representing the celebrities she saw at the Fairfield Halls where she used to work. At no point does she classify herself in any way, and neither does the museum voice interpretation. Where Mabel's story set up an interpretive context via the use of 'learning difficulties', Madeleine's account leaves us with what Latour calls 'vast oceans of uncertainty' not even speckled with 'a few islands of calibrated and stabilized forms' (2005: 245). The 'Show' touchscreen label introduces the programmes as showing 'some of the celebrities Madeleine Gardiner met at the Fairfield Halls' while she worked there (Plate 8.1b). The 'Explain' level places Madeleine's story in the context of the history of the Fairfield Halls by explaining that 'entertainers visited the site over a hundred years before the Halls were built. The Fair Field hosted dancing bears, jugglers and acrobats at Croydon's Great Fair.'

The museum voice – with its focus on explaining 'Madeleine's celebrities' with a general history of the Fairfield Halls – drives the visitor away from any reading of Madeleine's story which might speak to 'learning disability' specifically or 'differentiation' and 'inequality' in a more general way. Yet the precise edit of Madeleine's oral history, I think, suggests a Museum commitment not to erase some of the complexity of her account. Madeleine's account is structured around two encounters, the first with the celebrities like 'Peggy Mount, Gordon Jackson, Richard O' Sullivan, Gilbert O'Sullivan, who else, Richard Todd, and that one whose name I can't remember. Barbara Windsor, Ronnie Corbett, Matt Monroe, Gene Pitney, oh, quite a few of them.' She comments: 'I wasn't supposed to, they would come down for their meals, and I used to go round the table and ask them for their autographs. They were very good.' The second encounter is with her mother who, Madeleine tells us, 'threw [the autographs] away, didn't she? Because she said it was rubbish.' Taking the same approach as the *Lifetimes* galleries, the Museum of Croydon did not mobilize any label to describe Madeleine. This is highly appropriate as the objects in the story were not 'about' learning disabilities/difficulties and because in the whole of the longer interview recorded between Madeleine and interviewer Ian Buchanan, neither the phrase 'learning disabilities' nor 'learning difficulties' was mentioned once.

But while there appears to be an understandable representational discomfort in locating the complexity of Madeleine's account through a 'structural' or classificatory explanation (e.g. her autographs were thrown away because she has learning difficulties), there remains something in the display strongly driving the visitor *towards* this kind of 'context' – specifically the sound of Madeleine's voice. Madeleine's voice, her intonation and some of her phrasing indicates *difference* just as surely as do other elements of the display, such as photographs of Mabel's certificate, Sislin Fay Allen in her police uniform (the first Black woman officer in the Metropolitan Police) and Roger Fisher dressed as a cowboy with his arm on his partner Ron. The vocal difference acts as a kind of analytical pointer for making sense of the two encounters. Neither not being supposed to approach celebrities nor her mother throwing the autographs away *equal* or *add up to* the classification of 'learning disability'. Yet both sites do act as moments of tension, concrete social moments through which differentiation, hierarchy and inequality can be traced.

As is also visible in Dodd *et al.*'s (2004) desire to make sure disability isn't 'side-stepped' in displays, there has been a general sense that it is through this notion of analysis, explanation and the mobilization of specific identities that politics itself is seen as emerging. Certainly, specific social accounts – especially those as richly complex as Madeleine's – immediately resist the sense that they are simply specific. As Latour puts it: 'any given interaction seems to *overflow* with elements which are already in the situation coming from some other *time*, some other *place*, and generated by some other *agency*' (2005: 166, emphasis original). As a result there is a tendency – especially if you want specific people's memories to have a political impact of some kind – to jump to context (the 'so what?' prized in exhibition interpretation strategies). Challenging the sense that a sweatshop can be *explained* by capitalism, Latour concludes that the problem with structure is that it is nowhere tangible and because of this is 'very powerful and yet much too weak and remote to have any efficacy' (ibid.: 168). Although there is a constant pull between specificity and unmanageable and ineffective 'context', Latour argues that there is some specific empirical work that can be done which might actually start to account for the many things which made a specific event happen. Latour describes this as replacing critical distance with 'critical proximity' – that is, working with the intimate specificity of experience but moving outwards to consider the political contexts which make a specific experience possible. A key methodology in Latour's strategy for 'critical proximity', and for addressing the erasures created by classificatory explanations, is to 'localize the global' and 'redistribute the local'. What Latour means by this is that, while 'no place is self-contained enough to be local' (ibid.: 204) and every place or interaction is made possible through multiple networks, at the same time, those places cannot be accounted for by reference to a dominating global 'underlying structure' which itself cannot be located. Defending the political purpose of his approach, Latour argues that 'it does not require enormous skill or political acumen to realize that if you have to fight against a force that is invisible, untraceable, ubiquitous, and total, you will be powerless and roundly defeated' and that 'localizing the global', by breaking down and identifying the 'skein of weak ties' and 'surprising connections' that make up our social worlds, is 'the only way to begin contemplating any kind of fight' (ibid.: 250, 252).

I'm not suggesting here that all this work of tracing – if done – could be used in exhibition interpretation. But approaching the explanation of specific encounters by tracing material practices and specific ideas outwards (rather than starting with top line key messages and working down) might enable an approach which neither ignores differentiation, hierarchy and inequality opened up by the complexity of oral/first-person accounts nor flattens complexity through over-determined labelling and classification. To return to Mabel's oral history, a skeletal tracing of associations would allow 'reading' to be pulled out as a way of generating more responsive interpretation. 'Reading' could then be used to introduce the history of the emergence of mental deficiency as a 'problem' after universal schooling was introduced in 1870 (Thomson 1998: 13). This historical locator might then be used to introduce a social model of disability reading of literacy and to ask the visitor to consider whether a world where reading wasn't necessary would change understanding of 'learning difficulties'. From there, Mabel's critique of the fixed nature of both 'learning difficulties' and of 'reading' as a set of specific practices which are in process could be reinforced.

In Madeleine's case, there are multiple ways this local moment could be redistributed. There is a strong materiality to this story. There are autographs, some on serviettes, all once kept in autograph books. The autographs were slowly built up encounter by encounter with specific celebrities in the Fairfield Halls dining room. We know she 'wasn't supposed to', but how was this prevented? Was this prevented for everyone, or were extra attempts made to stop Madeleine approaching the celebrities? Of the staff at the Fairfield Halls, Madeleine says it 'was more or less me' who collected autographs. Using this as a starting point it might be possible to trace the development of celebrity culture in this period. Which celebrities came to Croydon? How many autographs were collected and by which people? How were the autographs circulated and when did a market in autographs develop? This would offer material ways for understanding better the lack of value placed on them by Madeleine's mother.

Key to Madeleine's oral history is how her mother came to be in a position to make decisions over Madeleine's belongings. One way of approaching this would be to consider the link between control over belongings and adulthood. This specific history could be traced via some of the labels associated with intellectual disability discussed above, as one of the main features of the long stay hospitals was not having your own clothes[6] and ensuring people defined as 'having learning disabilities' now have control over their own belongings is, in theory, core to current policy and professional practices (Department of Health 2001, 2007). Listening to the specificity of Madeleine's accounts and asking questions like these could then facilitate the opening up of her oral testimony as a location for understanding political inequalities while still following her own use of language and sense of priorities. Although actually tracing all the networks and associations which make up a specific memory would be incredibly difficult and time consuming, Latour's approach does suggest a set of helpful reconceptualizations which might re-animate the political nature of the personal in museum displays.

Not only a label: interpretation and critical proximity

Labels can work to generate differentiation, create ranked hierarchies and perpetuate inequalities. Labels as identities can also generate shared understanding and collective articulations. They also, crucially, work to stabilize meaning for the purposes of communication. For all these reasons, labels both remain a crucial part of the way we all make sense of our social worlds and – because of their power to classify and stabilize – also need to be approached with care. As I have shown, the label of 'learning disability' poses specific problems not least because 'learning disability' has been described as 'labelling' precisely because of concerns over stigmatization, yet becoming labelled still remains necessary to ensure access to state resources.

However, the specific debate over invoking the 'learning disability' label is just one example of a more widely applicable question over the relationship between specific people's objects or memories and 'context' or 'explanation'. It has been thought that the best way of generating critical and political readings is through using meta-explanatory terms such as 'capitalism' or 'patriarchy' or explicitly mobilizing identity categories. However, while these labels allow you to see some elements of daily life, they also potentially erase the rich complexity of social experience. Instead, and following Latour, I have made two specific suggestions which might allow a 'critical proximity' to develop. First, great care should be taken to follow the terms people use to describe their own lives. Second, by following the specific concerns of specific people the 'local' can be redistributed and the networks which make up a specific experience can be partially traced and represented. In the case of Mabel's account of learning to read, it is 'reading' itself which could be drawn out as a problematic site which itself contributed towards her specific experience of 'learning difficulties'. In Madeleine's oral history there were opportunities to explore the difference and inequality pointed to by her voice and words by tracing the devalued place of celebrity culture in the late twentieth century or by investigating the importance of belongings and the link between having your own things and notions of adult personhood.

The increasing trend towards beginning interpretation from the object, a specific historical moment or a specific person's experience, offers us the beginnings of a more satisfyingly complex and intimate interpretive approach. Critical distance only ever took politics so far; it is through following people outwards through the specificity of their lives that 'critical proximity' (Latour 2005: 253) will emerge.

Notes

1 The issue of how to use people's names is of immense importance when writing about those who have been defined as having a 'learning disability'. In this chapter, I introduce Mabel Cooper and Madeleine Gardiner using their full names. After this I only use their first names. There is a very real danger that in using only first names – rather than the more formal second name that is conventionally used to refer to writers and public figures – the infantilization which has characterized the worst institutionalized 'care' is perpetuated. However, in this chapter I have taken this route to reflect the intimate and personal approach which is used across the Museum of Croydon and for all the people they represent. It is, in part, this intimacy that makes the exhibition so successful and makes the Museum of Croydon such an important case study for exploring the mediation between specific people's experiences and accounts, and the idea and implications of 'explanation'.

2 I would like to thank the editors for their comments and suggestions and Katie Graham and Michael Terwey for reading earlier drafts of this chapter. I would also like to thank Rob Shakespeare at the Museum of Croydon for the permission to use the images included and The Open University's Social History of Learning Disability group for their pioneering work on 'inclusive history'.

3 Bruno Latour and others associated with Actor-Network-Theory (ANT) have developed a much more extensive analytical and methodological infrastructure than I have drawn upon here (see also Law and Hassard 1999). In this chapter, I have simply taken key conceptual insights offered by ANT to illuminate this chapter's specific empirical focus on 'the label'. With its focus on materiality – and as has been shown by Kevin Hetherington (e.g. 2003) and Andy Morris (2003) – ANT offers rich potential for further analysing museums and their audiences.

4 The social model of disability has come to be widely recognized within the field of disability studies and amongst disability campaigners and activists as a key conceptual tool for the advancement of the rights of disabled people. Whereas the medical model presents a highly individualized, medicalized, pathologized understanding of disability – where disability is located 'on the body' – the social model rejects this understanding of disability and instead locates the issue not with the individual and their impairment but with the many barriers within society that operate to restrict and oppress disabled people (Dodd *et al.* 2008).

5 See Cooper 2001 written with Dorothy Atkinson.

6 See, for example, Ferris 2001.

References

Bennett, T. (1998) 'Speaking to the eyes: Museums, legibility and the social order' in S. MacDonald (ed.), *The Politics of Display: Museums, Science, Culture*, London: Routledge.

—— (2006) 'Exhibition, difference and the logic of culture' in I. Karp, C. A. Kratz, L. Szwaja and T. Ybarra-Frausto (eds), *Museum Frictions: Public Culture/Global Transformations*, Durham, NC and London: Duke University Press.

Callon, M. and Latour, B. (1981) 'Unscrewing the Big Leviathan: how actors macrostructure rea-
lity and how sociologists help them to do so' in K. D. Knorr-Cetina and A. V. Cicourel (eds),
Advances in Social Theory and Methodology: Toward an Integration of Micro- and Macro-Sociologies,
Boston, MA: Routledge and Kegan Paul.

Clifford, J. (1997) *Routes: Travel and Translations in the Late Twentieth Century*, Cambridge,
MA: Harvard University Press.

Cooper, M. (2001) 'Mabel's story', *Learning Disability History*, Faculty of Health and Social
Care, The Open University. Online. Available http://www.open.ac.uk/hsc/ldsite/mabel/
index.html (accessed 21 November 2008).

Department of Health (2001) *Valuing People: A New Strategy for Learning Disability for the 21st
Century*. Online. Available http://www.archive.official-ocuments.co.uk/document/cm50/
5086/5086.pdf (accessed 21 November 2008).

—— (2007) *Valuing People Now: From Progress to Transformation*. Online. Available http://
www.dh.gov.uk/en/Consultations/LiveConsultations/DH_081014 (accessed 21 November
2008).

Dias, N. (1998) 'The visibility of difference: nineteenth-century French anthropological collections' in Sharon MacDonald (ed.), *The Politics of Display: Museums, Science, Culture*,
London: Routledge.

Dodd, J., Sandell, R., Delin A. and Gay, J. (2004) *Buried in the footnotes: the representation of
disabled people in museum and gallery collections*, University of Leicester. Online. Available
https://lra.le.ac.uk/handle/2381/33 (accessed 21 November 2008).

Dodd, J., Sandell, R., Jolly, D. and Jones, C. (2008) *Rethinking Disability Representation in
Museums and Galleries*, University of Leicester.

Edgerton, R. B. (1967) *The Cloak of Competence: Stigma in the Lives of the Mentally Retarded*,
Berkeley: University of California Press.

Ferris, G. (2001) 'Gloria's story', *Learning Disability History*, Faculty of Health and Social Care,
The Open University. Online. Available http://www.open.ac.uk/hsc/ldsite/gloria/index.
html (accessed 21 November 2008).

Goodley, D. (2001) 'Learning Difficulties, the social model of disability and impairment:
challenging epistemologies', *Disability and Society*, 16(2): 207–31.

—— and Roets, G. (2008) 'The (be)comings and goings of "developmental disabilities": the
cultural politics of "impairment"', *Discourses: Studies in the Cultural Politics of Education*, 29
(2): 239–355.

Hacking, I. (1986) 'Making up people' in T. C. Heller, M. Sosna and D. E. Wellbery (eds),
Reconstructing Individualism: Autonomy, Individuality and the Self in Western Thought, Stanford,
CA: Stanford University Press.

Hetherington, K. (2003) 'Accountability and disposal: visual impairment and the museum',
Museum and Society, 1(2): 104–15.

Hopper-Greenhill, E. (2000) *Museums and the Interpretation of Visual Culture*, London:
Routledge.

Jenkins, R. (ed.) (1998) *Questions of Competence: Culture, Classification and Intellectual Disability*,
Cambridge: Cambridge University Press.

Latour, B. (2005) *Reassembling the Social: An Introduction to Actor-Network-Theory*, Oxford:
Oxford University Press.

Law, J. and Hassard, J. (eds) (1999) *Actor Network Theory and After*, Oxford: Blackwell.

McClimens, A. (2007) 'Languages, labels and diagnosis: An idiot's guide to learning disability',
Journal of Intellectual Disability, 11: 257.

Mohanty, S. P. (1989) 'Us and them: on the philosophical bases of political criticism', *The Yale Journal of Criticism*, 21: 1–31.

Morris, A. (2003) 'Redrawing the boundaries: questioning the geographies of Britishness at Tate-Britain', *Museum and Society*, 1(3): 170–81.

Sandell, R. (2007) *Museums, Prejudice and the Reframing of Difference*, London and New York: Routledge.

Scott, J. W. (1992) 'Experience' in J. Butler and J. W. Scott (eds), *Feminists Theorize the Political*, London and New York: Routledge.

Serrell, B. (1996) *Exhibit Labels: An Interpretive Approach*, Walnut Creek, CA and Oxford: Altamira.

Spivak, G. C. (1987) *In Other Worlds: Essays in Cultural Politics*, London and New York: Routledge.

Thomson, A. (2008) 'Oral history and community history in Britain: personal and critical reflections on twenty-five years of change', *Oral History*, 36(1): 95–105.

Thomson, M. (1998) *The Problem of Mental Deficiency: Eugenics, Democracy and Social Policy in Britain 1870–1959*, Oxford: Oxford University Press.

Vanegas, A. (2002) 'Representing lesbian and gay men in British social history museums' in R. Sandell (ed.), *Museums, Society, Inequality*, London: Routledge.

Walmsley, J. (1997) 'Including people with learning difficulties: theory and practice' in Len Barton and Mike Oliver (eds), *Disability Studies: Past, Present and Future*, Leeds: The Disability Press.

Woodward, K. (1997) 'Concepts of identity and difference' in K. Woodward (ed.), *Identity and Difference*, London: Sage.

9

HURTING AND HEALING

Reflections on representing experiences
of mental illness in museums

Joanna Besley and Carol Low

The idea of the museum as a therapeutic agent with the potential to contribute to the health and wellbeing of communities has attracted increasing interest amongst both practitioners and researchers in recent years (Silverman 2002; Dodd 2002). At the same time, however, experimental avenues of practice exploring the museum's therapeutic potential are generating new ethical challenges and demanding from practitioners sets of skills and ways of working that are different from those traditionally valued in museum work (Kavanagh 2002; Silverman 2002).

This chapter contributes to this developing discourse by exploring the potential healing role which a museum can play through engaging, as participants in the process of exhibition-making, people who have experienced considerable trauma in their lives. By focusing on the experiences of people living with mental health difficulties who took part in the exhibition *Remembering Goodna: stories from a Queensland mental hospital*, we aim to highlight both the value of this mode of practice and the curatorial challenges posed by the presentation of often traumatic, sad and intensely painful personal stories.[1]

Demanding histories

The exhibition held at the Museum of Brisbane, Australia from November 2007 to March 2008, explored the complex and difficult 150-year history of Goodna mental hospital, Queensland's largest and longest-operating mental health facility.[2] Its history, one that embodies recurring themes of separation and integration, care and neglect, aspiration and apathy, is one which resonates across many parts of the Western world where similar institutions have existed. Founded in 1865 as the Woogaroo Lunatic Asylum, the institution was constantly re-named, reflecting both changing ideas about psychiatric care and repeated attempts to escape the stigma associated with an institution for 'the insane'. Name changes track the stages of the institution's history, from a colonial asylum, one of the very first public institutions maintained by the newly self-governing colony of Queensland, through moral therapy, mental hygiene and then a long period of de-institutionalization from the post-war period to today.

Woogaroo Lunatic Asylum became Goodna Hospital for the Insane, followed by Mental Hospital Goodna, then Brisbane Special Hospital, then Wolston Park Hospital. It is now called The Park Centre for Mental Health. To simplify matters in the exhibition, we simply referred to the place as 'Goodna', which is how it was known colloquially in Queensland for many years – often spoken in hushed tones or used pejoratively as a schoolyard taunt.

Patients came to the hospital from all over Queensland and, over the life of the institution, more than 50,000 people were admitted. By the mid-1950s, Goodna was the largest single mental hospital in Australia, with over 2,500 residents (on a daily average) and a staff of nearly 800. Like many such institutions, Goodna was a self-contained world, with a close symbiotic relationship to the adjacent village (later, suburb) of Goodna where most of the staff lived. In many instances, the hospital was the place of employment for generations of the same family. The hospital farm produced food, the powerhouse generated electricity and an extensive staff of tradespeople built and maintained everything on-site. Strikingly, the hospital site was also the product of the labour of its inmates, as patients worked in all areas of the hospital's operations until the 1980s.

At the beginning of the 1990s, the institution remained one of the largest psychiatric facilities in Australia. Over ten years, reforms determined by the National Mental Health Policy were implemented and Wolston Park Hospital formally closed in 2001, to be succeeded on site by The Park Centre for Mental Health. The Park now provides a diverse range of mental health services, including mental health research and education as well as extended in-patient care, albeit for a much smaller number of people.

As one former patient described it in the exhibition, the place 'is a ghost of its former self'. Buildings other than those deemed to be of heritage significance have been demolished, community organizations have moved into some of those left, but most remain empty, becoming increasingly derelict and forlorn. New buildings reflect current thinking, and patients live in small group homes or individual units, many doing their own cooking, cleaning and washing. However, the institution retains its power and prominent position in the public imagination. Many Queenslanders who live with mental health difficulties today were among the hundreds of patients confined there in the past. Others have recovered, but their time at Goodna continues to resonate, as it does for their friends and family members. It was a history that needed to be told or, as one visitor to the exhibition subsequently remarked, 'this was an exhibition demanding to be made'. Yet *Remembering Goodna* was the first project to bring the history of the hospital to light.

Interdisciplinary strengths

The exhibition had its genesis in a research project, led by historian Mark Finnane of Griffith University and funded by the Australian Research Council, which subsequently evolved as a partnership between the university, Museum of Brisbane and The Park Centre for Mental Health. Museum of Brisbane, a young organization which opened in 2003, is a city museum (operated by the local authority, Brisbane City Council) which has a strong commitment to collaborating with the community, presenting multiple viewpoints, and drawing on community collections.[3] It presents an eclectic changing programme of social history and visual arts exhibitions exploring the city's history and contemporary cultures and, in many ways, the proposed exhibition appeared to be a 'natural fit'. Yet, in dealing with a social issue as complex as mental health, *Remembering Goodna* took the museum into new territory both in terms of our professional practice and our experiences of community engagement.

The formal partnership between the hospital, university and museum provided museum staff with institutional backing, support and expertise. More crucially, an inter-disciplinary curatorium of medical staff, advocates, a historian, a community development worker, an arts worker and curator was formed to shape and guide the exhibition. This collection of individuals with diverse skills, professional experiences and wide ranging but complementary forms of expert knowledge, proved to be critical to the success of the project.[4] Of greater significance, however, was the participation in the development of the exhibition of people who had lived and worked at the hospital. These people's experiences were central to the project but the sad and often intensely painful stories they shared also presented the most powerful challenges to traditional curatorial methods.

Private into public: museums and the process of healing from trauma

Museums – as civic institutions in the public sphere in which difficult issues and ideas can be presented and debated – can play a unique and important role in the process of healing. When the act of telling has been constrained, even forbidden, by the sheer horror of re-living personal experience, and when testimonies have been suppressed by those with power (whether in the family or by the state), the bringing into the light of day that which has hitherto been private or hidden can be of powerful therapeutic value. Indeed, there is a growing body of literature examining the role of museums in relation to processes of memorialization, healing and reconciliation, for example, in relation to Holocaust museums (Young 1994) and museums in post-apartheid South Africa (Coombes 2003). Furthermore, the museum as memorial has been identified as a distinct form for contemporary remembering (Williams 2007).

In Australia, the potential for museums to engage in (and contribute to) broader processes of reconciliation is still at a nascent stage. When the National Museum of Australia opened in 2001, conservative critics and the Federal government alike savaged its treatment of Australian history, which was purposely provocative and open-ended. Key exhibits about disputed topics such as massacres on the frontier have since been removed under the direction of a government-appointed committee. Likewise, the refusal of successive governments, until 2008, to apologize to Aboriginal people for the policies that sanctioned the removal of children from their families and communities is indicative of the slow progress of reconciliation in this country. Yet the contested nature of national history in relation to race is still much more widely and openly discussed than the histories of the many people who were institutionalized because of mental ill health.

Where the effects of oppressive and discriminatory policies and practices towards indigenous Australians have often been debated (although frequently openly disputed) in the political and public sphere, the traumatic effects of institutionalization have, for the most part, been ignored. There has been one national and a number of state-based inquiries into the experiences of Australians who were institutionalized in psychiatric facilities as children and these have begun to raise public awareness of the brutality of these places and the systems which supported them. These inquiries, however, have not led to broader, community-based reconciliation processes. The traumatizing practices of psychiatric institutions have received relatively little public attention and individuals have often been left to struggle alone with their memories and experiences. In bringing these struggles to public view, the *Remembering Goodna* exhibition was a first in Australia. In many ways, the significance of the endeavor was not recognized until after the exhibition was over.

That the exhibition was aimed not solely at professionals with a specialist interest in the subject matter – lawyers, doctors or government officials – but at the wider community, was significant. For one of the participants who is living with mental health issues, the exhibition meant that '[ordinary] people can see how we suffer with mental illness and how the environment was'. Another contrasted her experience participating in the exhibition with those of interacting with the government:

> I have been distressed writing my submissions in respect to apply-
> ing for consideration under the Redress Services of the Communities
> Department[5] – for those abused in children's homes. It triggers a lot
> of pain writing about the effects abuse in the children's homes had

on my health and my life. *Remembering Goodna* was a healing time and it helps. It will live in our hearts and minds. Thank you for it and I am grateful to everyone who helped to set up the exhibition. Didn't it get fabulous responses?

Judith Herman, a psychiatrist and researcher who has written on trauma and healing, states that 'remembering and telling the truth about terrible events are prerequisites both for the restoration of social order, and for the healing of individual victims' (Herman 1992: 1). It is here that the civic nature of museums really matters. Museum of Brisbane is located in City Hall. To have their stories told in this foremost civic space was important to the participants. 'I am grateful and honoured to have my picture on the TV and my name on the wall', wrote one former patient. Many former staff of the hospital also expressed their views that taking part in the exhibition provided an opportunity to explain to others the nature of their work, that is often not well understood by the rest of the community.

In presenting the exhibition in City Hall, the Museum (and, by extension, Brisbane City Council and the state government, through Queensland Health and The Park as project partners) was acknowledging that the history of the treatment of mental illness was significant to the history of the city and the state. The exhibition was very consciously presented as being about 'us' – all of us, the Queensland community – not 'them', the people with mental illness. The history of Goodna was presented as a shared story and mental illness as a widely shared experience, and visitors to the exhibition acknowledged this:

> I feel Queensland people can move on now and start to accept all people who have a mental illness or condition. This is just the start to integrate all people with every health issue they have so that we can start to understand each other and live all together in this lovely community.
>
> (Male visitor aged 56, East Brisbane)

For those who were patients in the facility, the exhibition came some way to meet a need to commemorate, by bringing back the past, allowing an opportunity for mourning in a context of public acknowledgement, and also for reclaiming their lives. Clendinnen (1999: 51), writing on Holocaust commemoration, describes this process as 'exorcism: to turn memories into meaning'. Indeed, several participants reported that the experience of participating in the project's development and also of subsequently visiting the exhibition elicited some sense of shedding, of moving on, of exorcising some of the demons of the past. 'I feel like I have crossed another bridge', said one former patient. 'I'm almost ready to close the book', said another.

One participant who had been sent to Goodna as a teenager, and who had multiple experiences there of solitary confinement, of being put in a strait-jacket and of witnessing physical abuse and neglect, described how she felt her life had been 'on hold' but since participating in the exhibition she found she was able to begin to move on. Of particular significance for this participant was the display of straitjackets. There were two on display, one canvas and leather straitjacket made by the hospital saddle-maker and a 'soft' jacket, made of denim.

When she first saw them at the opening, she was very concerned that the museum staff had put one straitjacket on the mannequin in the wrong way. She was able to have this corrected. It was on her second visit to the exhibition that she found that she kept coming back and back to this part of the display.

> It was the straitjackets funnily enough, that gave me closure [...] seeing them there and knowing I would never go back in one of them again, and that I would not ever go back to Goodna again, or *any* mental institution.

'Artifacts', as Lois Silverman argues, 'have an undeniable power to elicit responses from people. Objects serve as symbols of ourselves, our relation-ships, and our lives' (Silverman 2002: 77). In this case, the straitjacket was very real to the participant in bringing back the trauma of her past in Goodna. It also progressively became the symbol for her release from this past, which had gripped her for so many years.

Other powerful artifacts, specific to a mental hospital, were also on display in the exhibition. Electroconvulsive therapy (ECT) machines, the massive syringes used to administer early anti-psychotic medications, bundles of keys, cigarette lighters with chains to attach them to the wall, plastic cut-lery, the hospital mortuary trolley and one of hundreds of nameless concrete gravestones from the former hospital cemetery, were some of the more potent objects. In all cases, these artifacts were presented together with personal stories to emphasize their connection with lived human experience. As an example, an ECT machine was accompanied by Edward's story:

> In the earlier years, I received shock treatment. I would be laid out on a bed; things similar to earphones would be placed over my ears and a spoon sort of thing between my teeth. Five or six male nurses would hold you down. You would wake up about two hours later to eat something. Nowadays, you are given a needle before, so you are unconscious when you get the shock. Sometimes male warders would tease the patients by saying they were going to the electric chair. This was in the earlier days. The shock treatment has made me lose my memory in some areas. For instance, I can't even

visualize my wife and children's faces in my mind anymore. All I can say is that there must be a lot more in a similar state to mine.

These very compelling artifacts were displayed alongside innocuous, everyday items such as mosquito nets, work boots, cigarettes, bureaucratic memos and toys made in the craft rooms. This juxtaposition – of the extreme with the quotidian – is what captured and conveyed the real nature of the place; this place where people experienced the extremes of human existence but also the place where, as one patient put it, 'nothing ever happened, I didn't hear a dog bark the whole eight years I was there'. Juxtaposition and adjacency, as opposed to continuity and sequence, were the organizing principles of the final form of the exhibition enabling conflicting and contradictory stories to be placed side by side. Rather than recreating the rigidities or claustrophobia of the institution, the exhibition was designed to create a sense of spaciousness to allow visitors room to reflect and feel.

Healing from trauma – participants have their say

In her significant text *Trauma and Recovery: from Domestic Abuse to Political Terror* (1992), Herman gives us three stages of healing. The first concerns the provision of a safe environment where the individual who has experienced trauma can gain control; a place from which the past can be named and the silences surrounding it can be broken. The second stage is one of remembrance. Here the story is told in depth and in detail, enabling a reconstruction of narrative and an opportunity for mourning what has been lost. Also important at this stage is acknowledgement from others of the individual's experiences. The third stage is one of reconnection. Here, the individual reconciles with themselves and reconnects with others; they can learn to stand up for themselves ('fight', not 'flight') and, potentially, find a 'survivor mission' to carry forward the healing to other contexts, or with other people for a more hopeful future. Museums, we would argue, can potentially play a role in providing opportunities for people to move through these stages of healing described by Herman. In reflecting upon their participation after the exhibition, a number of people reported feelings and experiences which might be understood in relation to this transition.

A number of former staff, for example, spoke about the high levels of stress that they experienced while working at the hospital and how they were unable to talk about these experiences with anyone. As one woman explained:

I was 18 or 19 when that happened, those kinds of things. I just never ever will get those kinds of images out of my head. You didn't talk about those things to anybody, not the group of nurses that you were with, not your supervisors. It was such a closed environment ... I wasn't game to talk about those kinds of things to anybody.

For many, the exhibition was their first opportunity to break the silences surrounding their difficult experiences. Working at the hospital produced a strong collective identity among the staff that continued into retirement with regular reunion lunches and morning teas. This group identity was built around a sense of camaraderie and support, making the expression of weakness or fear difficult. Following the exhibition, participants reported that their former colleagues expressed gratitude that, from their perspective, a fuller story had been told.

Although participants told how hard it was to revisit the past, this seemed to be outweighed by the healing they reported from their experience of participation. One woman who was a patient in Goodna for six years (time she said she spent 'knitting and crocheting 24/7') found visiting the exhibition, 'personally quite draining'. She is now a consumer advocate in the mental health sector and took part in a series of public programmes held at the museum during the exhibition where those living with mental health issues told something of their lives, their hospital experiences, and of recovery. Although sharing her own life experiences in this public way is commonplace in her advocacy and education roles, the act of sharing within the context of the exhibition was much more difficult:

> Talking that day really upset me; I felt re-traumatized as there were families in the audience that I hadn't seen for many years whose loved ones had sadly passed away. Also I think having the exhibition next door made me feel very vulnerable, the grief and loss, remembering all the people who had died, seeing the belongings and memorabilia of some of the people I knew and lived with.

Another former patient who had appeared before the national Senate Inquiry[6] and who now works in peer support for people experiencing mental health problems (Herman's 'reconnections stage') purposefully used the exhibition to advocate for justice for people who had been institutionalized as children. In her filmed interview she did not just tell her own story but also recounted stories of people she had known at Goodna who did not have the capacity to speak for themselves, either because of their ill health or because they had since died. One of the stories involved an instance of abuse by a member of staff on a fellow patient that she had witnessed. Speaking about this event for the exhibition motivated her to make a formal report to the relevant authorities.

Indeed, through the process of research for the exhibition, many former patients shared memories with curatorial staff which were painful, disturbing and sometimes enormously challenging to us on both personal and professional levels. In this final part of the chapter, we consider the impact of these disclosures on our museum practice.

Reconciling our own practices

In her thoughtful and provocative analysis of the challenges surrounding reminiscence work in museums, Gaynor Kavanagh (2002: 111) argues that what is needed in museum practitioners 'is a kind of emotional literacy, an ability to work sensitively and astutely with the thoughts and feelings of others'. This way of working and the acquisition of new skills is not always straightforward. Indeed, *Remembering Goodna* demonstrated that it can be challenging to reconcile the slow, developmental, trust-building processes needed for collaboration with those who have experienced trauma with the museum environment which is generally preoccupied with the challenges of interpreting difficult concepts and communicating them to visitors, all within a framework of limited resources and tight deadlines.

The strategies for creating spaces for 'permitted and supported remembering' (ibid.: 118) that the Goodna project used included the employment of a community development worker, as well as a community arts worker with direct experience in the mental health sector. They were able to link into networks of consumer groups and consumer advocates to contact people who were given the choice to participate freely or not. Some individuals and groups rejected the invitation to take part, because they did not want to be re-traumatized. We therefore anticipated that those who agreed to get involved were already equipped with some coping strategies (ibid.: 115) and indeed many were (or had been) involved in activism around psychiatric disability, treatments and community and systemic change.

At the developmental phase of the exhibition, it was crucial to address the expectations of the community participants directly. Without knowing how their stories would eventually be represented in the exhibition, it was important that participants did not have unrealistic expectations of either how their own story might appear in relation to the exhibition as a whole, or of the personal and public outcomes that might emerge from the unveiling of these inhumane and appalling pasts. Most participants were ready to tell their stories straight away to the community worker, well before the curatorial decisions were made about the content, structure and theming of the exhibition. Listening and spending time were the two most important strategies for building trust.

Initially, concerns about individuals' privacy were thought to be significant by museum staff. However the participants dismissed these as secondary to the necessity for their stories to 'get out there'. It became clear that the exhibition needed to convey directly the personal impact of the stigma of mental illness, and the grief and loss that people experience when they are institutionalized. One of the slogans of the disability movement – 'nothing about us, without us' – became a guiding principle for the exhibition. More than simply offering the opportunity for people to participate, this was taken to mean that the exhibition could not use or perpetuate paternalistic, disabling methods of representation or language. It meant that the exhibition strove to present the unmediated voices of people who themselves live with mental health difficulties or had worked at the institution. People had to speak for themselves, not have their stories heavily interpreted and re-presented by a curator. The curatorial role shifted from creator to enabler.

Filmed interviews were one of the main ways chosen to achieve this. Four 20-minute documentaries, loosely grouped in themes, were produced. Staff and patient stories were presented together to avoid a 'them and us' approach.

Supporting the participants while they prepared the parts of their stories they were going to share on camera and thinking through how they wanted to be supported on the day of filming was essential. This meant regular contact by the community worker and, increasingly, with the curator and project manager, as the initial trust built and the relationships formed were broadened out to include museum staff. This contact was maintained before, during and after the entire process on a one-on-one basis.

The second way that participants communicated directly was the 'First Aid Box' art project. Standard metal first aid boxes were emptied of their medical contents and filled instead with significant and meaningful items – 'the things that get you through'. These were created by people who experience mental health difficulties today. Several of them had spent time at Goodna. Visitors responded strongly to these very direct and yet symbolic representations of peoples' lives:

> Our favourite was the first aid boxes, they are very real and touching, even when you haven't been through what they have, you feel like you somehow know them, beautiful.
> (Female visitors aged 16, 19 and 14, Brisbane)

Visiting the display brought tears for many – former patients, those who had had loved ones in Goodna or similar institutions, those who had worked in such settings, as well as visitors from the general public who were often very moved. Over 60,000 people visited the exhibition and about 650 of these left substantial written comments. Visitors spent a great deal of time contemplating the depth of material uncovered in the exhibition and the emotions often reflected in the comments they left, suggesting that the exhibition addressed a history that people wanted to know and understand. Many responses suggested that visitors had not only gained new insights but also deeper, empathetic understandings of the experiences of people with mental health difficulties past and present, that had resulted in changes in their thinking:

> Having been to The Park and seen the old buildings there I was haunted by what must have gone on. This is a very important

exhibition because it acknowledges the pain and suffering those people went through. It must not be kept behind closed doors. Finally it has come out into the open. It is important not to forget what went on there.

(Female visitor aged 25, Brisbane)

I've never felt so ashamed! I'll never look at anyone in the same way again.

(Male visitor aged 21, Brisbane)

Anticipating that many visitors would find the experience of visiting an upsetting one, museum staff had initially hoped to have someone on hand in the exhibition at all times. This subsequently proved unsustainable and, instead, the idea of a 'chill out room' – common in the mental health field – was adapted for the exhibition. The 'living room' as it became known, was furnished with sofas, coffee table and rug and a conscious attempt was made to create a domestic (as opposed to institutional) feel. Here, visitors could take time to reflect and feel but it was also a space that attempted to connect museum visitors with practical information about mental health. During the process of exhibition development, one woman whose husband experienced mental distress when he returned from the Second World War had told us how bewildering the experience had been: in part, because it had been so difficult to access information – 'there were no brochures in the doctor's surgery in those days'. Mindful of the ongoing stigma surrounding mental health difficulties, numerous brochures, promotional and educational material related to mental health services were provided in the 'living room'.

Training and support for all museum staff connected with the project also had to be considered. Several sessions took place with a member of the curatorium who has worked at the hospital for many years and is also a psychologist. These took the form of open-ended discussions that took place throughout the project so that museum staff, particularly front of house staff, could discuss their own feelings and ways to approach visitors who needed support. These were also regular opportunities for curatorial staff to discuss with their colleagues their intentions, the challenges they were encountering and their proposed strategies for dealing with these. The curatorium, which brought together people with different areas of expertise and knowledge, was also an important resource for supporting colleagues in dealing with the traumatic stories they encountered during the exhibition development.

There is no doubt that *Remembering Goodna* was a powerful experience for participants, visitors and museum staff alike. It demonstrated the huge potential for museums to take an active part in changing community perceptions and understanding of mental health and mental illness. Essential to the exhibition's success was the involvement of those who lived and worked at the hospital. How, for example, could the three large aluminium teapots that were among the eclectic collection of objects in the exhibition be made meaningful to visitors without knowing that the tea came in the pots with milk and sugar already mixed-in – that patients didn't even have a choice in how they liked to drink their tea?

Visitors' responses, feedback from participants and public recognition of the exhibition[7] all emphasized the important commemorative and healing role the exhibition performed for the whole community, as well as for participants in the exhibition. A number of visitors expressed hope for the future after visiting the exhibition:

> Thought-provoking and inspiring to see how people have survived and lived despite the conditions. On the other hand, it's a sad history for some people and their families that ought not to be forgotten. So well done to this exhibition for remembering it all – good, shocking, devastating but strangely hopeful for the future.
>
> (Male visitor aged 30, Brisbane)

For those of us who work in museums, *Remembering Goodna* highlighted the importance of supportive teamwork and the value of inter-disciplinarity and collaboration. By means of processes and approaches borrowed from areas of practice such as community development and social work, we learned the necessity for listening and taking time for relationships to develop. From working together with the mental health sector, we learned the importance of accepting one's own incompleteness and fallibility when seeking to understand and represent the experiences of others. This learning resulted in the privileging, within the exhibition, of participants' own voices.

As Silverman (2002: 69) describes it, there is a need in museums for 'opportunities to learn, to reflect, restore, and perhaps most importantly of all, to affirm sense of self and continued connections to others in the face of difficulty'. With *Remembering Goodna*, the learning began with the museum's own staff and broadened out to encompass the wider community as the stories of those who experience mental health difficulties were shared and acknowledged.

Notes

1 The authors would like to thank the participants in *Remembering Goodna* for their ongoing support of the project and for sharing their reflections and critique for this chapter.

2 Brisbane is the capital city of the state of Queensland in Australia.

3 Museum of Brisbane does not actively collect, although it is the custodian of the city's visual arts collection. The museum borrows from members of the community and other institutions for its social history exhibitions.

4 The members of the curatorium were Nadia Beer, advocate at the hospital for over 35 years; Joanna Besley, Carmen Burton, Louise Denoon and Leanne Kelly (Museum of Brisbane); Mark Finnane, historian, Griffith University; Deborah Gilroy, former psychiatric nurse at the hospital; Carol Low, community worker; and Neal Price, community arts worker and former psychiatric nurse.

5 The Redress Scheme was established by the Queensland Government in response to the Forde Inquiry into the Abuse of Children in Queensland Institutions. The scheme was established to provide ex gratia payments to people who experienced abuse and neglect as children in these institutions.

6 In March 2003, the Australian Senate established an Inquiry into Children in Institutional Care. Many individuals and organizations submitted written reports or appeared before the Inquiry. Two reports were published, *Forgotten Australians* in 2004 and *Protecting Vulnerable Children* in 2005.

7 *Remembering Goodna* has won a number of awards, including the Queensland Gallery and Museum Achievement Award 2008, the National Trust of Queensland's John Herbert Award for Most Outstanding Heritage Project and a Queensland Mental Health Week 2008 Achievement Award.

References

Clendinnen, I. (1999) *Reading the Holocaust*, Cambridge: Cambridge University Press.

Coombes, A. E. (2003) *History after Apartheid: visual culture and public memory in a democratic South Africa*, Johannesburg: Wits University Press.

Dodd, J. (2002) 'Museums and the health of the community' in R. Sandell (ed.), *Museums, Society, Inequality*, London and New York: Routledge, pp. 182–89.

Herman, J. L. (1992) *Trauma and Recovery: from domestic abuse to political terror*, New York: Basic Books.

Kavanagh, G. (2002) 'Remembering ourselves in the work of museums: trauma and the place of the personal in the public' in R. Sandell (ed.), *Museums, Society, Inequality*, London and New York: Routledge, pp. 110–22.

Silverman, L. (2002) 'The therapeutic potential of museums as pathways to inclusion' in R. Sandell (ed.), *Museums, Society, Inequality*, London and New York: Routledge, pp. 69–83.

Williams, P. (2007) *Memorial Museums: the global rush to commemorate atrocities*, Oxford and New York: Berg.

Young, J. E. (ed.) (1994) *The Art of Memory: Holocaust memorials in history*, Munich and New York: Prestel-Verlag and the New York Jewish Museum.

10

HISTORIES OF DISABILITY AND MEDICINE

Reconciling historical narratives and contemporary values

Julie Anderson and Lisa O'Sullivan

Museums of science often perform a dual role. They attempt to make sense of the past, offering audiences a unique way to view and understand objects relating to the history of science. At the same time, many are also places in which visitors can discover more about new directions in scientific research and explore complex social and political issues surrounding contemporary science. This dual role can sometimes generate tensions and interpretive and ethical challenges to which this chapter speaks.

In March 2009, the Science Museum in London launched a major online educational resource, *Brought to Life: Exploring the History of Medicine.*[1] The website, primarily designed for teachers and students working on the history of medicine and related subjects in secondary schools and universities, provides access to a huge array of images of objects from the Museum's extraordinary medical collections, accompanied by detailed descriptions and introductions to major themes in the history of medicine.[2] Although designed with users from formal educational settings in mind, the website also aims to appeal to broader interested audiences through a variety of engaging media.

Early in the project's development, it was decided that disability would be a significant theme.[3] Questions of illness and impairment are central to the social and cultural approach to the history of medicine taken by the curators and, moreover, the Museum's collections include a diverse array of objects and technologies associated with disablement. Early examples of prosthetics are joined by the vast collection of artificial limbs from the Roehampton collection.[4] This includes numerous prosthetics issued to soldiers and many specially designed for the changing needs of children born to women who were prescribed thalidomide in the 1950s and 1960s. These objects are powerful educational resources for informing visitors to the website about developments in the history of medicine as well as changes in attitudes towards disability in different times and places. They are also objects which can be challenging to contemporary sensitivities surrounding disability representation.

The web offers new possibilities for access with technologies to ensure that a site is available to as many users as possible. From a content perspective, the Museum's collections offered a chance to include objects which could be interpreted (or, indeed, reinterpreted) with questions pertaining to the relationships between medicine and illness, impairment, disability and health. However, in the context of contemporary disability politics both in the UK and beyond, the use of medical history as a means to shed light on disability brings with it inherent tensions.[5] This chapter will explore these particular tensions and examine how they were played out in the development of the Science Museum's online educational resource. It will address a series of questions that are pertinent not only to museums of science but also to wide ranging institutions that have collections linked to medical practices. What understandings of disability are created by the medical gaze? To what extent are museums concerned with histories of medicine able to create spaces for alternative and personalized understandings of disability? How can respect for contemporary ideas about disability, identity and agency be balanced with museological and historiographical concerns for representing the past in accurate and truthful ways?

Science museums, historical truths and contemporary controversies

Museums are increasingly recognized as institutions capable of crystallizing and communicating important shared narratives – especially those of national and social belonging – through their interpretation of material objects (Hooper-Greenhill 2000; Macdonald 1998). This understanding of museums as 'guardians' of national stories, with the capacity to reify 'official' narratives, has led to increasing contestation over their depictions of the past (Dubin 1999). Museum practice over recent decades has moved away from the presentation of didactic 'facts' – an approach which has tended to position visitors as passive consumers rather than active participants – towards the inclusion of multiple viewpoints and interpretive devices designed to encourage individual interpretations and responses (Macdonald 2002, Sandell 2007).

The idea that museums offer trustworthy depictions of 'how things used to be' takes on particular significance when the subject matter and the collections involved are scientific in nature. While science exhibitions have often been viewed and understood (by both those who have created them as well as those who visit) as somehow objective or neutral (Macdonald 1998), contemporary museum practice in interpreting the history of science is increasingly concerned to address the internal and external drivers and politics which have always characterized the practice of science and, in particular, the

144

nature of scientific controversy. These trends have influenced museums' attempts to portray the history of medicine by making explicit the issues and contestation surrounding the ethics and nature of medical practice. Museums of science have been increasingly compelled to examine these controversies through a range of exhibitions and other media.

These shifts in museological practice, which have seen hegemonic, monolithic stories challenged and replaced by multiple narratives, have generated a set of challenges for curators and other museum professionals. One tension which has emerged through these new approaches to practice is the desire, on the one hand, to invite audiences to make up their own minds while, on the other, attempting to control meanings through the information that is displayed (Sandell 2007). This tension is heightened by the fact that many audience members rely on and expect museums to tell an authoritative story (Arnold 1998). Through their presentation of multiple interpretations, museums are effectively seeking to guide visitors who are attempting to understand complex concepts or histories, towards a more active interpretive role. This goal of allowing freedom or agency in interpretation is often mediated by the simultaneous attempt to convey a message, or set of messages, with specific sociopolitical goals.

A further issue which has complicated approaches to interpreting the history of science in museums concerns the increasing emphasis in contemporary museum practice on the museum's relationship to diverse communities and to broader issues of social justice. There is a growing professional assumption that museums will be self-aware in their construction of narratives and a belief that, as institutions, they can and should have a role in challenging social injustice. One of the outcomes of this movement has been the increasing attention paid to the ways in which museums represent minority or excluded groups, including disabled people. How then have more democratic approaches to both audience engagement and community representation shaped the ways in which museums have interpreted histories of science and medicine?

Medical history and models of disability

The history of medicine emerged as an academic discipline largely written by and about medical professionals. As such, narratives pertaining to disability tended to highlight the role and agency of the medical practitioner rather than the disabled person and focused on individuals being cured or overcoming their impairment, often while under the care of a benevolent doctor. However, during the 1980s, social historians began to focus more on the doctor–patient relationship. These new approaches were heavily influenced by the new social history which had emerged in the 1960s and which attempted to reconstruct the lives of those who had, up until that time, fallen below the historian's radar (Thomas 1966). The most high-profile practitioner of this new type of social history of medicine was Roy Porter (1985) who called for more patient-centred histories.

Despite this shift and increasing interest in these 'histories from below', historians of medicine who research disability have nevertheless continued to attract criticism. Some scholars, particularly those working in the field of disability studies, extend their criticisms of the ways in which medicine has represented disablement to historians working in this field who are sometimes viewed as necessarily complicit in the promotion of what are considered within disability studies to be regressive conceptions of disability; those which focus attention on and emphasize the need to cure physical or mental 'deficits'. To understand the controversy that still surrounds the place of disability in the history of medicine it is helpful then to consider more broadly relations between disabled people and medical practice.

Critical to the position of doctors as authority figures has been their power and ability to define – if not necessarily to cure – pathology and difference (Canguilhem 1991). For the medical profession, disability has essentially been viewed as a failure of medical intervention – an inability to completely cure a person to a state of 'wellness'. Hence, the medical profession has come to be criticized, particularly within the field of disability studies, for pathologizing disabled people as physically or psychologically lacking and for identifying individuals within medicine and in society more broadly, primarily – if not exclusively – in terms of their impairment or condition.

In the 1980s sociologists and writers in the emerging field of disability studies such as Oliver (1990) and Finkelstein (1980) critiqued and theorized this individualized, medicalized, pathologized understanding of disability. An alternative view of disability, that has come to be widely known as the social model, subsequently emerged. The social model, which Hasler (1993) has described as 'the big idea' of the disability movement and which continues to underpin contemporary disability activism in the UK, 'shifts attention from individuals and their physical or mental deficits to the ways in which society includes or excludes them' (Shakespeare 2006: 29). This and other related social-contextual conceptions of disability subsequently emerged to challenge the historical dominance of the medical profession and the use of medical definitions, categorizations and diagnoses as the primary way in which disability was understood (ibid.).

Over the past two decades a dialectic has been constructed between the medical and social models as disability scholars have attempted to 'rescue' disabled people from the perceived overarching dominance of the former. Whilst the social model continues to have considerable support within contemporary disability activism and disability studies in the UK, more recently critiques have emerged which challenge aspects of social model thinking. Disability academic and activist Tom Shakespeare, while recognizing the continuing value of social approaches in advancing disability equality, has pointed out that the construction of a stark dichotomy between the medical

146

and social models is, in many ways, reductive and limited in terms of its explanatory power partly because it allows disability studies to sideline issues surrounding the relationships between disability and impairment, pain, illness and suffering (ibid.). Similarly, Catherine Kudlick, in her address to the Society of the Social History of Medicine in 2008, suggested that within social history, the history of medicine does have something to offer to understanding disability apart from what she calls 'the pathology/deficit model' (Kudlick 2008). If the medical model is seen as highly problematic by many disability activists and theorists, the strong political overtones of the social model have limited its use as a tool for understanding disability in an historical framework. In fact, both models are primarily contemporary in their focus. We would therefore argue that new approaches in social and cultural medicine, which are sensitive to power dynamics and inequalities, agency and patient–practitioner interactions, offer a useful and nuanced way to capture the embodied experience of disabled people and their interactions with the objectifying medical gaze.

Disability on display

The historiographical approach to the development of the Science Museum's online resource, *Brought to Life,* was to try to marry an understanding of new medical technologies and practices within their cultural context and their implications for the user or patient. For instance, the iron lung – used to help patients with limited lung function – is an iconic object of medical intervention, most closely associated with the treatment of polio. Being placed within an iron lung was, for users, an often alienating and distressing experience. Patients were enclosed in an airtight chamber, with only their heads free. Pumps controlled the air pressure within the chamber, decreasing and increasing pressure so as to cause movement in the chest and mimic the action of the lungs. Many people spent months, if not years, immobilized inside the lung. In order to capture the experience of the iron lung, it was chosen for one of the site's multimedia pieces. The voice of a patient describing his experience of using the iron lung is interspersed with an explanation of how the technology works, and its impact. Thus, while online visitors can turn off the sound of the machine, replicated in the interactive experience, they are reminded that someone inside the iron lung did not have this option. The point that is emphasized is that medical technologies may be alienating or dehumanizing, but they also take the form of (often life-saving) objects with which people create a mediated relationship.

As Annie Delin has argued, the assumption of a 'natural link' between medical artifacts and disability is very much present in contemporary curatorial practice (Delin 2000: 87). Like many in disability studies, Delin argues that this tendency to equate disability with its medical technologies – rather than any other aspect of a disabled person's life – is evidence of a

147

tendency towards a medicalized vision of disability. Yet, as for any group of individuals, the physical artifacts with which disabled people have interacted are an important trace of their life experience. For a medical collection and indeed medical history, they bear witness to the relationship of disabled people with the medical profession, its technologies and its beliefs. The focus on technologies of enablement, such as prostheses for example, is not necessarily one which attempts to disregard the individual experience of disability. Rather, it reflects the material focus of museum collecting. Moreover, as curators know, it is through the stories that can be told about objects that they become meaningful. The documentation of the 'life' of an artifact is also that of the life of its user(s). Individuals have relationships with their prostheses that are often intimate and enduring. The collection of memories and the turn towards oral histories therefore enriches the possibilities presented by artifacts in isolation.

For instance, one of the objects featured in *Brought to Life* is a prosthetic leg, dated 1914–18, that was originally issued to a First World War soldier who had his leg amputated. The object has clearly been mended many times by the application of cement and plaster. Considered in isolation, without accompanying interpretation, the many repairs might be (mis)understood as evidence of a lack of resources made available to replace the worn-out prosthetic. The accompanying interpretation, however, reveals that the fibre leg – known as a pylon – was often a temporary limb. In fact the owner, a roof thatcher and tiler, either refused a new limb or never claimed it, preferring instead to repeatedly mend it using home repairs for a period of over 40 years as he was used to the feel and weight of his mended version. When finally agreeing to be fitted with a far more technologically sophisticated limb, he needed extra weights placed in the limb in order to replace the feel of the hugely heavy original prosthesis. While the leg is the material trace left in the museum collection, this should not be read as implying that the object's material presence has been taken as defining its user. Rather its interest lies in the meanings imposed on it by its user, highlighting the need to continue to preserve the multiple stories that come with objects.

A focus on disabled people as passive recipients of medical intervention has rightly been interrogated and unquestionably should not be the only way that they are represented. There is no doubt that disabled people should, and could, be featured in collections and displays that address social change, creative exploits and scientific discoveries. However, many disabled people have experienced medical intervention in their lives, and the records of this intervention remain a useful method of understanding the historical nature of disability. Moreover, we would argue that it is possible for museums to display and interpret items of a medical nature and depict and interpret their association with disabled people while still being mindful of the institutions' social and ethical responsibilities.[6] For instance, how might historical photographs of disfigurements showing progressive reconstructions of the

face be displayed and interpreted in ways which remain sensitive to contemporary values? The photographs may have limited contextual information
attached to them – the individual may be identified only by a number and
all that is known about them is the nature of the surgical processes they
underwent. Arguably, this may say as much about the protocols of scientific
records and publication as the position taken by researchers towards
their subjects. As has been explored in the philosophy of science, especially
through feminist critiques, scientific publications are highly constructed
(Rossiter 1982). They present a deliberately reductive narrative which strips
subjectivity – whether of subject or author. Medical practice, aligning itself
ever more closely with science from the late nineteenth century, followed
these conventions (Bynum 1994). Museums, we would argue, provide a
unique space in which these medical and scientific conventions – and their
impacts on individuals – might be made explicit and explored.

New museology, contemporary values and the past

The rise of an explicit audience focus within museums in recent decades aims
to respond to the demands and wishes of visitors concerning the types of
stories that are represented, and the perspectives from which they are told.
This has led to some laudable outcomes, with a new emphasis on uncovering
previously 'untold' stories, whether of women, minority ethnic groups, or
disabled people. Such new stories have been part of a broader drive towards
museums becoming inclusive spaces with the capacity to drive social change
and counter prejudice. Within this context, the desire for celebratory narratives which foreground stories that can serve to counter negative stereotypes
can be at odds with the realities of the past. This tension is not unique to the
telling of stories about disabled people – the same unease is evident in
museums' attempt to deal with issues of slavery, warfare and to reveal other
'hidden histories' linked to minority identities.

There is now intense discussion, as Sandell (2007) has highlighted, surrounding the social role of the museum, with an increasing assumption that
this includes a commitment to fostering positive social change and the
empowerment of previously disenfranchised communities. With an awareness of the implicitly political nature of museum displays, as Sandell states,
'museums, alongside many other institutional and individual agents, must
consider their impact on society' (Sandell 2002: 23). And yet, at the same
time, research on how audiences respond to messages designed to counter
prejudice suggests that such readings can easily run counter to the intent of
curators (Sandell 2007). In other words, texts may effectively take on meanings and interpretations unintended by their authors and this process is in
the control of individual readers (Barthes 1978). Despite this acknowledgement of the agency of the visitor, museums may explicitly tailor their
texts to deliver predetermined 'messages' and, as Sandell points out,

replacing one authoritative voice with a variety of perspectives does not necessarily negate the possibility of 'misunderstandings'. Instead, there is a danger that the multiple perspectives presented (which have inevitably gone through a selection process themselves) can act as substitutes for the single curatorial voice, allowing museums to avoid being seen to adopt or lend support to any one position (Sandell 2007).

Language past and present

One of the fundamental concerns surrounding the representation of disability in the context of medical history is that of language. Many historical medical terms used to describe disability and disabled people have unarguably been dehumanizing. Museums therefore must be mindful of the terms that they use and attempt to avoid the use of language which perpetuates approaches to disability which today are viewed as demeaning and oppressive. Yet, it does not inevitably follow that the language of the past should be completely avoided. As Raymond Williams demonstrates, words take on multiple meaning and usages within a historical period, and over time. Terms have specific histories of usage and definitions and, within any given context, 'we find a history and complexity of meanings; conscious changes, or consciously different uses; innovation, obsolescence, specialisation, extension, overlap; transfer' (Williams 1976: 15). There is a real risk that contemporary meanings and associations attached to a term can be assumed to be historical constants unless these issues are explicitly explored. For instance, during the development of *Brought to Life*, medical curators at the Science Museum were surprised by negative (contemporary) reactions to the use of historically accurate names to describe institutions such as the Cripples Hospital, Lunatic Asylums, or the use of terms such as leper, insane or mad. These emerged as problematic since such terminology was viewed by some contemporary users as perpetuating outmoded language and hence legitimating the attitudes perceived to be associated with it, as opposed to a careful attempt to represent both historically accurate categories, and the meanings attached to them in context. Indeed, working within the dichotomy of the medical/social models, such terminology is often assumed to be imposed on disabled people by external actors. However, the use of specific language can also arise out of the agency of disabled people themselves and preferences they and their carers express. For instance, in 1924, at the Crippled Children's Week which was instituted at the Wingfield Hospital, those in charge were asked by the relatives and friends of patients to use the word 'cripple' as opposed to 'orthopaedic' as the latter was found to have 'frightened people away' (The Cripples Journal 1924: 17).

Museums, Sandell has argued, 'must consider their impact on society and seek to shape that impact through practice that is based on contemporary values' (2002: 21). The challenge then for the historian and curator is to mediate between these contemporary values and the depiction of accurate historical representation. There is a danger that attempts by curators to avoid confrontation or distress to visitors may act to distort the realities of the past and, in doing so, blunt our awareness of the experience of historical actors – effectively removing a sense of their agency. How then are historians and curators able to reconcile tensions between contemporary values and historical modes of description and representation of disabled people? As Jim Bennett, a curator of the history of science, has suggested:

> A museum that takes its collections seriously as historical resources must [...] allow what is recoverable from the past to refine our understanding of both the past and the present.
>
> (1998: 181)

Drawing on Bennett's arguments, we would argue that, despite – or perhaps because of – contemporary sensitivities, it is important for museums to give visitors an historical understanding of the ways in which both medical practitioners, and society more broadly, viewed and treated disabled people. To dissociate disabled people from the terminology used to describe them in the past is to rob them of their historical construction – in essence to de-historicize them. Part of the historical identity of many disabled individuals is the nature of language used to understand, describe and, in many cases, remove some of their agency from them. As Christine Ferguson has recently argued in relation to Joseph Merrick (widely known as the Elephant Man):

> We risk blurring the representational violence historically perpetuated against people like [Joseph] Merrick if we wish away the invidious terms used to define them and replace them with gentle anachronisms that were never used in the 19th century.
>
> (2008: 130)

It is not necessarily wrong for people in different historical times to understand events and people in ways which differ from contemporary constructs. However, there has been a tendency within some disability studies to present a Whiggish sense of history, in which respect and sensitivity towards difference in various past times is measured against the present – and invariably found wanting. For a historian to ask whether 'cripple' as a label was necessarily used in a negative or demeaning way is not to try and unpick the very real advances made by disability advocates in demanding that disabled people today be treated with respect. Rather, it is an attempt to generate a more nuanced understanding of the correlations and meanings associated with the category in a specific historical time and place, and how that informed the lives and treatment of individual people.

It is not clear how, or indeed if, social approaches to the understanding of disability that attempt to dismiss or sideline the role of medicine in the construction of the 'disabled person' can be used to describe situated historical stories without disrespect to the experience of historical actors. It is similarly uncertain whether such social approaches can deal with the fact that, for many, experience of disability was more acted upon than acted. For the historian, the priority is to describe the experience of those in the past, and it is precisely the historical disenfranchisement of disabled people that needs to be highlighted.

Conclusions

The web has opened up opportunities for museums to reach wider audiences and the potential for online learning resources such as *Brought to Life* afford the Science Museum a wide range of possibilities to display collections in new and innovative ways. Object interpretation, narratives and multimedia activities allow online users the scope to actively engage with the collection and, through this, to develop new understandings of complex and controversial subjects. At the same time, the sensitivity and care needed to create appropriate physical exhibitions must also be deployed with virtual resources to ensure that audiences understand the context of objects on display and the accompanying narrative.

The term 'disability' encompasses a wide range of experiences and circumstances. It cuts across a wide range of historical time frames and contingencies and the experience of disability can be permanent or temporary. Indeed, there is a rich vein of potential research to be undertaken which examines how the experience of disability has been shaped by other (non-medical) factors such as gender, class, or the social meanings attached to a particular impairment or condition in a particular historical time and place. With this in mind, the experience of museum staff working on *Brought to Life* made it clear that, for a website principally concerned with historical material, the dialectic embodied in the social versus medical models of disability was less helpful for informing approaches to interpretation of its collections than other frameworks of analysis. Far more fruitful was the process of engaging with questions of disability, illness and health as *culturally and historically contingent* – an approach which enabled an understanding of the agency (or disempowerment) of those individuals who were subject to medical attention as mediated by an array of different factors.

Historical investigation of medical practice remains an important way to access and understand the experiences of disabled people in the past. Although the stories such investigations uncover reveal treatment of disabled people by the medical profession, and by society more broadly, that are out of step with contemporary values, it nevertheless remains the responsibility of both museum curators and historians to accurately depict the lives of disabled people within structures, embodied experience and social life. Understanding the way that aids or prosthetics were used – or not – can help contemporary audiences better understand how disability was constructed in historical terms. However, the ability to capture and communicate the experience of the past will always be limited and influenced by the types of records or material traces left as sources for the historian. Many museum objects bear witness to medical interventions in the lives of disabled individuals. At the same time, those objects can be interpreted in new ways that take account of, but are not overly determined by, contemporary values. Such approaches to interpretation emphasize the impact of objects, positive or negative, on the lives of their users. The centrality of medicine to the historical experience of disability is a useful reminder that the past must be represented with awareness that it is never merely a kind of morality play for the present but remains, in part, unknowable.

Notes

1 The resource can be accessed at http://www.sciencemuseum.org.uk/broughttolife.
2 Key themes with content relating explicitly to disability include 'Surgery, diseases and epidemics', 'Treatments and cures', 'Understanding the body' and 'War and medicine'.
3 This decision was also informed by the Museum's broader policy of audience-led programming whereby the targeting of an under-represented audience forms part of each major project.
4 Queen Mary's Roehampton was opened in 1915 as a hospital and limb fitting centre for amputees from the First World War. See Alper (1997).
5 See, for example, Barnes, Mercer and Shakespeare (1999).
6 See, for example, the account of the interpretive strategies in the exhibition *Whatever happened to polio?* at the Smithsonian's National Museum of American History in Sandell (2007).

References

Alper, H. (1997) *A History of Queen Mary's University Hospital Roehampton*, Richmond, Twickenham and Roehampton: The Trust.

Arnold, K. (1998) '*Birth and Breeding*: politics on display at the Wellcome Institute for the History of Medicine' in S. Macdonald (ed.), *The Politics of Display: Museums, Science, Culture*, London and New York: Routledge.

Barnes, C., Mercer, G. and Shakespeare, T. (eds) (1999) *Exploring Disability: A Sociological Introduction*, Cambridge and Maldon, MA: Polity Press.

Barthes, R. (1978) *Image–Music–Text*, New York: Hill and Wang.

Bennett, J. (1998) 'Can science museums take history seriously?' in S. Macdonald (ed.), *The Politics of Display: Museums, Science, Culture*, London and New York: Routledge.

Bynum, W. (1994) *Science and the Practice of Medicine in the Nineteenth Century*, Cambridge: Cambridge University Press.

Canguilhem, G. (1991) *The Normal and the Pathological*, Boston: MIT Press.

The Cripples Journal (1924) 'The dreaded word', *The Cripples Journal*, 1(1), July.

Delin, A. (2002) 'Buried in the footnotes: the absence of disabled people in the collective imagery of the past' in R. Sandell (ed.), *Museums, Society, Inequality*, London and New York: Routledge.

Dubin, S. C. (1999) *Displays of Power: Controversy in the American Museum from the Enola Gay to Sensation!*, New York: New York University Press.

Ferguson, C. (2008) 'Elephant talk: language and enfranchisement in the Merrick case' in M. Tromp (ed.), *Victorian Freaks: The Social Context of Freakery in Britain*, Ohio: Ohio State University Press.

Finkelstein, V. (1980) *Attitudes and Disabled People*, New York: World Rehabilitation Fund.

Hasler, F. (1993) 'Developments in the disabled people's movement' in J. Swain, S. French, C. Barnes and C. Thomas (eds), *Disabling Barriers – Enabling Environments*, London: Sage.

Hooper-Greenhill, E. (2000) *Museums and the Interpretation of Visual Culture*, London and New York: Routledge.

Kudlick, C. J. (2008) 'Disability history and history of medicine: rival siblings or conjoined twins?', Unpublished plenary paper given to the Society for the Social History of Medicine, Glasgow, 3 September.

Macdonald, S. (1998) 'Exhibitions of power and powers of exhibition: an introduction to the politics of display' in S. Macdonald (ed.), *The Politics of Display: Museums, Science, Culture*, London and New York: Routledge.

—— (2002) *Behind the Scenes at the Science Museum*, Oxford and New York: Berg.

Oliver, M. (1990) *The Politics of Disablement*, London: Macmillan.

Porter, R. (1985) *Patients and Practitioners: Lay Perceptions of Medicine in Pre-Industrial Society*, Cambridge: Cambridge University Press.

Rossiter, M. W. (1982) *Women Scientists in America: Struggles and Strategies to 1940*, Baltimore, MD: Johns Hopkins University Press.

Sandell, R. (ed.) (2002) *Museums, Society, Inequality*, London and New York: Routledge.

—— (2007) *Museums, Prejudice and the Reframing of Difference*, London and New York: Routledge.

Shakespeare, T. (2006) *Disability Rights and Wrongs*, London and New York: Routledge.

Thomas, K. (1966) 'The tools and the job', *The Times Literary Supplement*, April 7, 275–76.

Williams, R. (1976) *Keywords: A Vocabulary of Culture and Society*, London: Fontana/ Croom Helm.

11

REVEALING MOMENTS

Representations of disability and sexuality

Elizabeth Mariko Murray and Sarah Helaine Jacobs

Discussions of sex take place, for the most part, in the private realm. Shining a light on these private moments and engaging visitors in the exploration of the cultural significance of human sexuality has been a speciality of the Museum of Sex since it opened in 2002 in New York City. Five years later, in July of 2007, the museum hosted a small installation by Australian-based photographer Belinda Mason, drawn from the series, *Intimate Encounters: Disability and Sexuality,* a project undertaken to debunk the myth 'that a person with a disability had no sexual identity or desires' (Mason 2002). The resulting images were as diverse as the participants; realistic depictions mingled with fantasy scenarios and graphic sensuality gave way to tender emotional scenes. While the images were compelling, we wondered how they would be received by audiences.

Recent research has highlighted curators' anxieties surrounding the representation of disabled people and the ways in which these operate to constrain practice in this area (Sandell *et al.* 2005).[1] These concerns are, not surprisingly, heightened when disability is coupled with the topic of sex and sexuality since the latter has often remained too controversial for state and federally funded institutions in the USA to tackle. And yet, the topic of disability and sexuality, though rarely publicly discussed, is one with significance to the broader disability rights movement. Although sex and sexuality are very much personal affairs, the expression of sexual identity is an intensely social activity and, as Anne Finger has argued, can be another locus of exclusion for persons with disabilities.[2]

> Sexuality is often the source of our deepest oppression; it is also often the source of our deepest pain. It's easier for us to talk about – and formulate strategies for changing – discrimination in employment, education, and housing than to talk about our exclusion from sexuality and reproduction.
>
> (1992: 9)

Entering uncharted territory can be a daunting task for the museum; complications, pitfalls and mistakes are practically guaranteed. This chapter then offers an honest account of the challenges, ethical and pragmatic, the Museum of Sex encountered in mounting the exhibition, *Intimate Encounters*, the mistakes that were made and the approaches we used to address these. By sharing our experiences, we hope to allay some of the concerns involved in confronting politically charged and taboo topics and encourage other institutions to develop more inclusive practices.

Histories of representation

Placing the human body on display has always involved a complex negotiation of power and authority, subject and meaning and, when those bodies are nude and the topic is sexual in nature, the line between exhibition and exploitation can become increasingly blurred. Contemporary work such as Belinda Mason's photographs needs therefore to be understood in relation to historical and dominant modes of representing disability.

Historically, the medical community has relied on terminology and ideologies that have construed the bodies of persons with disabilities as imperfect or damaged, resulting in imagery which is fraught with destructive undertones. Often associated with a medical condition, charity advertisements have similarly used images of disability which emphasize helplessness and suffering in search of support for their cause (Hevey 1992: 367). These medicalized, disempowering ways of representing persons with disabilities, it has been argued, have tended to encourage viewer responses which can be characterized as oppressive, condolatory or disparaging (Sandell 2007).

Similarly, images of the nineteenth-century 'freak show' in which physical differences are highlighted to produce spectacles for the non-disabled viewer, linger in present-day consciousness (Sandell *et al.* 2005). This particular gaze, as manifested in the art realm, is perhaps best exemplified in the work of the photographer Diane Arbus. Drawing her subjects from the margins of society, Arbus' work centred on the experience of difference, often using visible physical impairments as a metaphor for internal pathologies (Hevey 1992: 370).

Although more than two decades have passed since the emergence of the disability rights movement in the 1980s, still the non-disabled public expresses surprise at the very notion of disabled sexuality. Marc Quinn's sculpture of the artist and disabled woman, *Alison Lapper Pregnant*, for example, generated a great deal of controversy when it was erected in Trafalgar Square, London in 2005. Simultaneously celebrated as a powerful statement on femininity, disability and sexuality, and denounced as an eyesore, the intense emotions expressed by viewers and media commentators are reminders of the continued absence of representations of disabled people as sexual individuals in both the arts and popular media. Indeed, the absence of media portrayals of people with disabilities in healthy, positive relationships reinforces societal notions that recognize value within a very narrow set of physical and mental parameters.

Prior to the staging of *Intimate Encounters*, the stories and bodies of people with disabilities were largely absent in the Museum of Sex. Where present, the bodies on display were clearly deviant, and of interest specifically *because* of their difference. In fact, with exhibitions on such diverse topics as the sexual history of New York City, the erotic art of Japan, and modern commercial design, it was surprising to realize that the only mention of disability had been in an examination of exotic fetishes entitled *Kink: Geography of the Erotic Imagination*. With *Intimate Encounters* we had the opportunity to redress the absence of disabled people within the museum and to show images that directly challenged the exploitative and oppressive imagery of historic modes of representation.

Intimate encounters

Belinda Mason, a non-disabled artist, began the project *Intimate Encounters* after photographing the Australian disability activist Dominic Davies. 'United We Sit' was the result of three months of discussions between Mason and Davies – their attempt to represent his passionate political and emotional statements in a single image (Figure 11.1). The following is an extract from the interpretive text that accompanied the image within the exhibition:

United We Sit
Dominic Davies and Lee Adams

Participating in this project we are making the personal political. There is a dearth of empowering, positive, sexy images of disabled people and we want to be a part of the movement to change this. We chose 'United We Sit' as our slogan to emphasize our solidarity with other disabled people and to challenge the norms. Dominic often needs to use a wheelchair and so we wanted to incorporate his impairment into the image too.

Dominic is an activist, editor, author, and Visiting Fellow at Nottingham University and a Visiting Lecturer at Leicester University.

Lee is a curator and interdisciplinary artist who works extensively in sculpture, theatre design, film, video, live performance, and installation. He has exhibited widely, including shows and screenings at the Tate Gallery, Liverpool; Museum of Modern Art, Oxford; Museum of the Moving Image, Hoax, The Foundry and The Nunnery in London; and the Mura Clay and Tap Gallery in Sydney.

Dominic has scoliosis and chronic pain.

Figure 11.1 United We Sit, Dominic Davies and Lee Adams. (Courtesy of Belinda Mason)

Through Davies, Mason became acquainted with other prominent members of the disability activist community in the United Kingdom, Australia, New Zealand, Canada and the United States. Mason worked collaboratively with her subjects, each of whom actively participated in how they would be portrayed. Their personality, interests and stories provided the inspiration and concept for each image. The resulting body of work was diverse; no single aesthetic element or treatment dominated the set, emphasizing the unique experiences across the group of subjects. A personal statement accompanied each photograph, along with an extensive biography and a note identifying the individual's disability. The inclusion of the latter would prove to be especially controversial in the museum installation in New York, an issue we return to later in the chapter.

The series included people with a range of experiences of disability. Through the accompanying interpretation, personalities emerged; individuals telling their own stories and experiences, all the while resisting and sometimes explicitly challenging prevalent stereotypes. The interpretation intended to resist medicalized discourses and narratives associated with the telling of more familiar 'disabled tales' (such as those which focused on 'surmounting obstacles'). Much of the project's impact resided in the individuality of each story, with the personal statements adding tremendous weight to the images. When viewed out of context, the unifying thread of 'disability' would be near invisible. When the images were viewed with their accompanying text, it became clear that the subjects were directing the action and that Mason had assumed the role of artistic interpreter. Most of the participants were, and continue to be, active in the fields of advocacy and disability rights. Frequently incorporating the visual or performing arts into their work, they were well versed in the politics of representation.

Mason began working on *Intimate Encounters* in 1998 and, following completion of the set in 2001, the exhibition toured extensively through Australia, England and Spain, to overwhelmingly positive reviews. In 2006, the Center for the Study of Gender and Sexuality (CSGS) at New York University (NYU) organized a year-long series of events dedicated to disability and sexuality and several images from the *Intimate Encounters* series were used to illustrate the events calendar. Don Kulick, Professor of Anthropology and then Director of CSGS, originally brought Mason's work to our attention.

Despite having received strong support and positive reviews throughout Australia and Europe, there had been difficulties finding an appropriate and willing venue in the USA. The precise reasons for this remain unclear but the exhibition's frank treatment of sexuality (which can be problematic for any institution receiving State or Federal funding), and disabled sexuality in particular, undoubtedly played at least some part in the story. The USA has generally been more conservative than many other nations regarding issues of sexuality and, at times, less progressive in the field of disability rights.

The track record of the Museum of Sex in tackling contentious subjects and its status as a for-profit, private museum located in New York City made us optimistic that public and community responses to *Intimate Encounters* would be enthusiastic and perhaps even enable us to attract new visitors. We found ourselves uniquely placed to take on such a project.

159

The Museum of Sex

The Museum of Sex was founded with a mission to explore the history, evolution and cultural significance of human sexuality. It was not the first erotic museum – the oldest among those is still in operation: Amsterdam's Venus Temple, which opened in 1985 – but it differs from its predecessors and contemporaries in theoretical perspective. The Museum's primary goal is not to titillate, but to inform and provoke discussion. In doing so, traditionally private acts are drawn into the public sphere.

Shedding light on covert behaviours has frequently revealed hidden objects and histories. The museum's permanent collection has been compiled through both acquisitions and donations which often arrive in unconventional ways. On a regular basis, as often as once a week, the museum receives a phone call from an individual with a recently deceased friend or family member who, upon going through the deceased's belongings, stumbles across hidden collections of erotica. These discoveries generally result in surprise, which soon gives way to confusion over the best way to dispose of the material – these are not your typical heirlooms. It is to their credit that friends and family members pause to consider options, rather than simply throwing everything away and erasing this often ignored history. This peculiar donation strategy has resulted in a museum collection that is largely composed of historical ephemera, erotica and pornography. While the museum is actively seeking to balance its holdings, we also recognize that there is value to this erotic history and that we are in a unique position in being able to collect, preserve and exhibit it.

Soon after the museum opened, it had become clear that our visitors interpreted the material on display in intensely personal ways. Patrons exhibited a strong desire to see themselves represented, perhaps more so than in other social or ethnographic museums where there is an expectation of viewing the 'other'. In line with our desire to provide a space for everyone, it became clear that we had not yet addressed the needs of people with disabilities. In taking steps towards greater social responsibility, the Museum of Sex has aimed to become an active agent of social change rather than an institution which merely reflects social mores. *Intimate Encounters* presented us with an opportunity to share voices from the disabled community which, up to this point, had been absent from our galleries. Although we had made concerted efforts to give voice to a range of sexual orientations, ethnic groups and sexual proclivities, *Intimate Encounters* appeared to be an exhibition with the potential to empower members of the disabled community while simultaneously addressing issues surrounding body image, desirability and prejudice.

Funding and freedom

Denied not-for-profit status at the time of its founding, the Museum of Sex sustains itself with the proceeds from admission tickets and special events, supplemented by sales at the museum store. Although a lack of public funding is rarely (if ever) regarded in positive terms, the Museum of Sex – as a for-profit institution – undoubtedly benefits from the absence of political constraints which generally accompany funding from governmental sources (although it is fair to say that being a self-sufficient institution is a mixed blessing).

The relationship between audience interests and those which curators might wish to pursue is complex, at times reviving debates regarding the boundary between education and entertainment. Although there was an institutional desire to bring *Intimate Encounters* to the Museum of Sex, we also needed to discuss how the installation would be received and be prepared to counter questions which inevitably arose during our early discussions such as, 'Is the subject engaging or popular enough to attract (paying) visitors?'

Organization and presentation

In planning the installation, the first concern involved the physical space itself and the need to address issues of accessibility. The Museum of Sex was created by adjoining two buildings originally constructed in the late 1800s. Navigating through the museum, which consists of three galleries spanning two floors, can be an awkward experience for any visitor. Although the museum adheres to accessibility standards established by the Americans with Disabilities Act (ADA) of 1990, the constraints presented by the historical fabric of the buildings undoubtedly complicate issues of access. For example, although a lift is available, most patrons reach the second-floor galleries by using the staircase. To access the lift, it is necessary to exit the museum and re-enter through an alternative door. Because the lift services the entire building, and also leads to the museum's offices and storage area, it is kept locked and thus patrons wishing to use it must be escorted by a member of staff.

After careful consideration, part of the Spotlight gallery located on the second floor, which hosts small rotating exhibitions, was chosen as the venue for *Intimate Encounters*. The exhibition consisted of 14 photographs and their accompanying stories, selected from the original group of 40. Four were selected to be displayed as large prints based on their exceptionally striking visual qualities, and the remaining ten pieces were mounted as smaller prints. Where possible, the text remained in its original form. When editing was necessary for length, all parties reviewed it before it was finalized. Since the original project was completed several years earlier, participant biographies were updated as necessary to reflect their most recent work.

A few objects from the museum's permanent collection were added to the display, including several issues of *Playboy* printed in Braille and an auto-biographical documentary on Ellen Stohl, the first woman with a disability to pose nude for *Playboy* magazine. Ellen Stohl's life was changed for ever by a car crash at the age of 18. Since that time, she has dedicated much of her life and work to explorations of female sexuality and how it is affected by the experience of disability. Stohl was a virgin at the time of her accident and recalls her second question upon learning that she was paralysed as, 'Can I have sex?'[3] As a result of the accident and before fully coming to terms with her sexuality, she was in the position of having to re-frame it to incorporate both bodily changes and the way that others related to her. Stohl sought to express herself in the form that epitomized heterosexual male desire – the *Playboy* centrefold. Through an appeal to Hugh Hefner, she got her wish and was featured in the July 1987 issue.[4]

The Braille *Playboy* was offered as a tactile experience and provided a springboard for a discussion on law and equal rights. In 1985, the Republican Representative from Ohio, Chalmers P. Wylie, introduced an amendment that would cut funding to the Library of Congress, forcing them to cease production of Braille editions of *Playboy*. The amendment was approved by the House of Representatives, sparking outrage over allegations of censorship and the enforced de-sexualization of persons with disabilities. It should be noted that the Braille editions included neither images nor advertisements, and was the library's sixth most popular publication at the time. The Blinded Veterans Association, the American Library Association and Playboy Enterprises, Inc. challenged the decision in court, citing a violation of First Amendment rights. A Federal District judge ruled in their favour and production resumed, continuing through to the present day. This discussion was used as a case study in the regulation of disabled sexuality and the struggle for equal social rights. By including a sample that could be touched, people with vision impairments were able to have a tactile experience and sighted visitors had the opportunity to experience a familiar object in a new way. Alongside the original *Playboy* photographs was a recent documentary consisting of Stohl's experiences in finding love, getting married and having a daughter. With nearly two decades passing between posing for *Playboy* and being interviewed on film, she was again coming to terms with changes to her body – this time as a result of pregnancy, childbirth and aging. The Braille copies of *Playboy* and material on Ellen Stohl served as a supplement to the main discussion of disability and sexuality presented via the installation of *Intimate Encounters*.

In the time leading up to the exhibition opening, we felt secure in the quality of images that would be displayed since we viewed *Intimate Encounters* as a 'self-vetted' project in which the disabled subjects had actively participated. Additionally, we made every attempt to conform to established standards in accessibility for the design of displays which included guidelines for everything from the size and font of label text, to the hang height for artworks. We knew the exhibition would be viewed and judged within the context of the entire museum, which consisted of displays that did not always conform to these standards. However, the design improvements incorporated into *Intimate Encounters* were done with the intention of making these a part of all subsequent exhibitions.

Controversy

The first indication of complications followed the distribution of the initial press release, several weeks before the exhibition even opened. An invitation to the opening reception and a copy of the press release were emailed to local leaders in the disability community as an effort to reach out to and involve the New York-based constituencies. Unfortunately, the response it generated was intensely negative. Criticisms focused on the terminology used in the press release, the lack of local community involvement during the planning process, and the lack of clarity in how the museum would accommodate the needs of patrons with disabilities.

In the museum's press release the layout of the museum building was described as 'handicapped accessible', a phrase which, with hindsight, we know was ill-informed and inappropriate. Despite the many variations in preferred terms which can be found both within and between communities and through time (Linton 1998), there are nevertheless certain terms that are nearly universally frowned upon today – 'handicapped' being one of them. The inclusion of such language further underscored a concern voiced by community leaders that qualified disabled individuals had not been adequately involved in the museum's planning process. As a result, we not only risked losing the support of the local community but were also facing a possible boycott.

Due to our financial constraints, we had been unable to hire any external paid advisers on this project. We hesitated to approach individuals from disability organizations to work free of charge since consultancy is the way that many advisors make their living and we did not want to risk being insulting. So, while preliminary contact with disability groups had been made during the planning stages (largely via email), this had dropped off as the exhibition approached, despite both sides asserting the need for more in-depth conversations. When email communication slowed, we had merely assumed that there was no desire on the part of individuals to work for free and we did not wish to push further for an in-person visit. Again, with hindsight, this situation was regrettable. We had rather naïvely believed the local community would support the project since the disabled subjects of the portraits had been so active in shaping the way they were represented. What we had assumed was a lack of interest in our project was, in fact, the result of a perception amongst disability organizations that, in our reliance on email, we had made only a token effort to engage with the community. As it turned out, there were miscommunications and misunderstandings on both sides.

Following contrite explanations, messages, and ultimately a face-to-face meeting, many members of the community decided that it would be best to attend the exhibition opening reception and assess the merits of the project for themselves. It was our hope that these influential leaders in the community would support the project and distribute the exhibition announcement to their network. However, by not including them in all aspects of the planning process we vastly under-estimated issues that were close to the local community as well as differences in political perspective between disability rights activists in different countries. The opening reception provided an opportunity to bridge this divide. Belinda Mason was in attendance as well as Denise Beckwith, one of the participants in the project. Both travelled to New York from Australia, specifically to discuss their perspectives and experiences working on *Intimate Encounters*. Denise Beckwith's portrait – The Little Mermaid (Plate 11.1) – was accompanied by the following text:

The Little Mermaid
Denise Beckwith

In my eyes I am not disabled ... My disability is a label given to me by society though invisible to myself. I see pride, passion and power as the elements of a successful being. People say there is no such thing as an equalizer, but I disagree as sex is something everyone yearns for – it is a social freedom. Everything is possible and nothing is normal!

The title for the photograph is so appropriate because like the Little Mermaid, I am searching for freedom and things unknown. Like the Little Mermaid wanted love, I too yearn for that. I have been so close on numerous occasions, but as I have to stand up at some point (and use my crutches to walk) once I have met a man and they are forced to realize I am disabled, they seem to become somewhat scared. I don't often allow myself to become intimately involved for fear that one day my partner may feel obligated to take care of my personal requirements.

Denise is a Sydney 2000 Paralympian Swimmer. She is currently studying when she doesn't have speaking engagements.

Denise has Cerebral Palsy.

One feature of the project that proved particularly problematic for some was the inclusion, in the biographical labels accompanying each image, of a statement identifying the individual's impairment (for example, 'Denise has Cerebral Palsy' or 'Dominic has scoliosis and chronic pain').

Disability studies researcher and activist Simi Linton attended the opening and later discussed this issue in her blog.[5] In her view, the decision to include the line referring to the individual's impairment was regrettable, since 'it re-inscribes a medical perspective on this culturally important moment' (Linton 2007). Linton's discomfort was shared by other visitors who interpreted the reference to the subject's impairment as part of a strategy to aim the exhibition at a non-disabled audience.

In seeking to clarify the intent of the statements and the perspective of the participant subjects, Linton contacted two of the other participants in the project, Mat Fraser (Plate 11.2), and Tom Shakespeare. An extract of the text accompanying Fraser's image reads:

Entwined
Mat Fraser with partner Patou Soult

Disabled people's sexuality has been denied throughout history, especially in the media imaging of our Society. This is a glorious chance to celebrate my own disabled sexuality with my partner Patou, and so we all say, 'fuck your denial, here we are!'

Mat is a disabled actor/musician/writer, does Live Art, TV presenting, Cabaret, and even some modeling ... he is multidisciplinary, though it was never intended. He is both a disabled artist and a disability artist, in that he simultaneously seeks a mainstream acting career as a non-disabled actor might do, but all of his self-produced works deal with the social construct that is disability in one way or another.

Mat has short arms as a result of Thalidomide.

Mat Fraser replied to Simi Linton confirming that he did not object to the identification of his impairment, stating 'It was an honor and privilege to be part of this great exhibition, and I welcomed a non disabled person for a change, dealing with this subject so sensitively and with such innate understanding of her subjects.'

Tom Shakespeare, academic, performer, and co-author of *The Sexual Politics of Disability: Untold Desires* (1997), replied with similar views to Fraser on these issues:

I don't have a problem with the inclusion of my impairment on anything ... I wrote the basic descriptive statement about my own image. I really like the show. One of the things it demonstrates is that you don't have to be disabled yourself to make strong and progressive images – you just have to work respectfully with disabled people ... I think some folks find some images quite challenging. Good.

Clearly, the statements of impairment held different meanings and led to different interpretations in the New York activist community than they had abroad. If we had hired advisors prior to installation, would these statements have been removed in response to local political concerns? If so, would this have altered the interpretation of the work, and in what ways?

How might we have sought to reconcile local concerns with the intentions and preferences of the original participants?

Conclusion

As our first foray into the topic of disability and sexuality, the project was limited in size and scope. In this respect, one of the main criticisms from the New York disability community was that the exhibition was too basic in its treatment of an important subject. For these sophisticated and politically active visitors, the premise of the exhibition – that being disabled does not preclude sexuality – was supremely obvious and they wanted to see the topic taken to the next level. Not exploring the boundaries further was, in some instances, interpreted as catering to the needs of a non-disabled audience.

Reconciling the needs and interests of different kinds of visitor is something which all museums can find challenging. From our perspective, we knew (from previous visitors' feedback) that people walk through our doors with highly variable levels of experience and subject familiarity. Catering to visitors with such diversity of background and knowledge is a challenge as we must provide introductions and baseline information along with enough detail to satisfy our more knowledgeable visitors.

Of course many who visited the exhibition were indeed non-disabled and their reactions, captured on visitor response forms, suggest that *Intimate Encounters* played an important role in challenging their preconceptions and expanding their understanding of disability. Several listed the exhibition as their favourite in the museum and many wrote comments referring to the fact that they had never seriously thought about the subject of disability and sexuality and went on to examine their own previously held assumptions. For the museum, these were important outcomes and reflected the absence of representations of disabled people with their own sexual identities, in the broader media.

Although criticisms of the museum were sometimes difficult to deal with at the time, they resulted in lessons learned which continue to inform our discussions both in relation to how representations of disability might be developed in future programmes and in terms of how we build relationships with a range of communities.

Notes

1 Indeed, while the revealing of hidden histories has become an important feature of museological practice over the past 30 years, representations of disability in museums have remained relatively rare, an absence which echoes the broader social marginalization historically experienced by persons with disabilities (Delin 2002).

2 There is great variation in preferred terminology. The 'people-first' perspective, developed in the 1970s, advocates the use of 'people with disabilities' as a way of privileging the individual over their impairment. Since the 1990s, the term 'disabled people' has become

increasingly used in the politically active field of disability studies and in disability rights groups where it functions as a unifying marker of identity. Both styles of terminology will be used in this text, acknowledging the validity of each perspective.

3 Her first question was 'Will I live?'. See 'Meet Ellen Stohl', *Playboy*, July 1987.

4 For a detailed critique of the photographs, see Garland-Thomson (2002).

5 See Linton (2007) for the full posting.

References

Delin, A. (2002) 'Buried in the footnotes: The absence of disabled people in the collective imagery of our past' in R. Sandell (ed.), *Museums, Society, Inequality*, London and New York: Routledge, pp. 84–97.

Finger, A. (1992) 'Forbidden fruit: why shouldn't disabled people have sex or become parents?', *The New Internationalist*, July, 233. Online. Available http://www.newint.org/issue233/fruit.htm (accessed 6 June 2009).

Garland-Thomson, R. (2002) 'Integrating disability, transforming feminist theory', *NWSA Journal*, 14(3): 1–32.

Hevey, D. (1992) 'The enfreakment of photography' in L. J. Davis (ed.), (2006) *The Disability Studies Reader,* 2nd edition, New York and London: Routledge, pp. 367–78.

Linton, S. (1998) 'Reassigning meaning' in L. J. Davis (ed.), (2006) *The Disability Studies Reader,* 2nd edition, New York and London: Routledge, pp. 161–72.

—— (2007) *Museum O' Sex, Disability Display*, Online. Available http://similinton.com/blog/?p=51 (accessed 20 October 2008).

Mason, B. (2002) *Intimate Encounters*. Online. Available http://www.belindamason.com/art/ie_07_05.html (accessed 27 March 2009).

Sandell, R. (2007) *Museums, Prejudice and the Reframing of Difference*, London and New York: Routledge.

Sandell, R., Delin, A., Dodd, J. and Gay, J. (2005) 'In the shadow of the freakshow: The impact of freakshow tradition on the display and understanding of disability history in museums', *Disability Studies Quarterly,* 25(4). Available http://www.dsq-sds.org/article/view/614/791.

12

THE RED WHEELCHAIR IN THE WHITE SNOWDRIFT

Geraldine Chimirri-Russell

> In spite of living all my life in poverty, of numerous deaths of loved ones, of all the rotten luck in my gamblings on horses, bingo, provincial and express lotteries, of the unkindness and hate of others, of ill health and the fact that I'm so miserable that no woman would dare marry me, I could never say that my life was an unhappy one nor could I ever say that it wasn't rich and full in experience. Above all, I always felt blessed to be keenly aware of life totally.
>
> (Soop 1979: 15).

Behind a modest house on the Blood Reserve in southern Alberta lay a wheelchair, abandoned in a snowdrift. Its owner, Everett Soop – Aboriginal journalist, cartoonist and disability activist – had died in 2001 at the age of 58, having lived much longer than he or the medical fraternity had expected. His fame as a cartoonist and journalist was primarily limited to the Aboriginal community, where his newspaper contributions to the *Kainai News* had been read and enjoyed (Figure 12.1). Towards the end of his life, his body crippled by muscular dystrophy and no longer able to produce his cartoons and to earn a living, he was thrown into poverty; however, his indomitable spirit emerged and he became an outspoken advocate for disabled people.

His work on behalf of the Aboriginal disabled community brought him national recognition, and a posthumous award of the Meritorious Service Medal (Civil Division), Canada. Soop had a notable life but, as history shows, many notable lives are soon forgotten. In 2003, Dr Heather Devine, Curator of Indigenous Heritage at The Nickle Arts Museum, University of Calgary, after seeing a sample of Soop's cartoons, put forward a proposal to feature a selection of his work in an exhibition. This chapter reflects upon the exhibition[1] and also charts the curatorial journey undertaken as the interpretive focus developed from being a retrospective of Soop's cartoons to an opportunity to explore the diverse but interrelated aspects of Soop's life – as an artist, journalist, politician and activist – in ways which could potentially impact visitors' thinking on a range of issues.

Figure 12.1 Everett Soop, 'What you mean I'm a federal property???', *Kainai News*, January 1982, # 1, p. 2. India ink, pencil crayon on paper, 17.5 x 13.4 cm (Collection of Glenbow Museum, Calgary, Alberta, Glenbow Archives M-9028-1545).

A shift in focus

Initially Devine intended the focus of the exhibition to be on Everett Soop's political cartoons, seeing his early work as an exemplar of the use of news media for aboriginal political activism in Canada from the late 1960s. One of the earliest publications set up to serve the needs of Aboriginal people was the *Kainai News* produced by the Indian News Media Inc. on the Blood[2] Reserve at Standoff, near Cardston, Alberta. In 1968, when plans were made to publish the newspaper, Everett Soop had recently returned to the Reserve after being awarded an Indian Affairs scholarship to allow him to take courses in journalism and art studies in Calgary.[3] It was quickly realized that his talents as a writer, artist and illustrator, and journalist could be put to good use in the nascent publication. These artistic and creative talents, together with a biting wit and his political motivation, made his work hugely successful.[4] He was prepared to follow his own understanding of how political change could be achieved and was willing to be brutally honest when he presented the world he witnessed to his reading public. As Soop himself later commented; 'Self-determination requires healing, and healing means no longer pushing unpleasant realities under the carpet' (Soop quoted in Greer 2001: 7).

There is a very large corpus of Soop's work, both cartoons and editorials. Some of the pieces are too fragile to display, and some pieces are inevitably more visually compelling than others. Museum curators are well aware that the presentation of too much information and too many visual images can confuse an audience in the brief time they have available for visiting an exhibition. The development of an exhibition entails selection of both material for display and also a clear message, or story line, that will place the material in a comprehensible framework. In the process of selection, the focus of the exhibition can change. As more material becomes available, the potential for a richer and more meaningful message can be revealed. This occurred during the preparation of *Everett Soop, Journalist, Cartoonist, Activist*. As research got underway, we became acutely aware that this exhibition had the potential to have an important impact upon our audiences. There is power in the written word, there is power in images, and there was power in Everett Soop – his story and experiences. It seemed necessary to portray the man and his work in a meaningful manner, by showing the interrelatedness of all aspects of his life and, perhaps most importantly, by allowing his voice to be heard. In developing this exhibition, wherever possible, quotations from Soop's work were used in preference to an interpretive curatorial text. Similarly, I have drawn heavily on Soop's own words in this discussion of the exhibition process. His own strong views were often forcefully and powerfully expressed:

> To be handicapped and to be Native means to be doubly pitted against the whole Canadian establishment. One has only to glance at the struggling Native population in nearby towns and cities to realize that Native people do not have the skills and the natural 'know-how-ness' for coping in an urban environment. Compound this plight with a disability, physical or mental, and the result is awesome – human misery and hopelessness that takes more than a welfare cheque to alleviate ...
>
> As the government bureaucrat would say, 'There are many words to address the purpose, the objectives, the principles, beliefs and values of the handicapped.' For once, instead of talking and writing about the native handicapped, how about talking to him directly, so that he may feel that he still has some dignity in life.
>
> (Soop 1988: 13)

Although The Nickle Arts Museum had, through its history, shown the work of a number of Aboriginal artists, this was the first exhibition that attempted to celebrate both the artist and his work, and the artist as a disabled individual. In addition to this unfamiliar territory we were also faced with the desires of Everett Soop's family to avoid eulogizing him as a suffering hero, but rather to depict him as he was – a brilliant, many-faceted and flawed human being, who happened to have a disability. By following the family's wishes the exhibition became multi-layered and much stronger, and opportunities emerged to present and discuss issues related to the lives of disabled people in the past and today. This approach would also allow us to respond to a recent Canadian Government report, highlighting the biases commonly found in the media, which stated:

> With respect to news and information programming, [...] in addition to perpetuating general stereotypes, the language used in dealing with disability issues and people with disabilities often serves to feed the myth that people with disabilities are suffering, or are afflicted with conditions that victimize and 'medicalize' their status.
>
> (Human Resources and Social Development Canada 2006: 32)

Widening our horizons

Like many other museums, the extent of our awareness of the needs of disabled people had been primarily limited to facilitating ease of access to the museum building, installing automatic doors and providing for the basic comforts of patrons in wheelchairs through accessible washroom facilities. Our perspective mirrored that described by Abbas, Church, Frazee and Panitch in their observation of the relationship many cultural organizations have with disabled constituencies:

> ... many discussions around access have focused on making arts venues physically (and to a lesser extent financially) accessible for disabled patrons, rather than to disabled artists. Implicit in this mainstream discourse on arts and accessibility is the idea that disabled people's place in the art world (if they have a place at all) is as consumers, rather than producers of artistic work.
>
> (Abbas *et al.* 2004: 45)

Our horizons were widened when we prepared to display the work of a disabled artist who had been outspoken concerning the conditions that people with disabilities faced and who also portrayed their experiences and perspectives in his cartoons.

It is possible to divide Soop's life into two stages: his early life and career as a journalist and cartoonist, and his work as a disabled activist and political satirist. These two interdependent stages drove the development of the exhibition, its construction and message. To assist the exhibition's visitors in understanding the concept of two aspects of his life, we physically divided the gallery area into two sections.

Soop had developed an interest in art from an early age. It was also at an early age, about 11 years old, that his family had noticed that he had problems with mobility. It was not until he was 16 that the family received the diagnosis that both he and his younger brother Clement (Shorty) had muscular dystrophy. In the first part of the exhibition we presented material related to his early life. With personal family photographs and stories, we were able to present Everett Soop within the context of his immediate family and the broader context of his Aboriginal community. To understand the man as an advocate of the native disabled community, it was necessary to show how strong his ties were to his family and Aboriginal heritage. We designed a wall of family photographs and a seating corner with chairs and a table that was used for perusing an album of family photographs. Aboriginal visitors to the exhibition were anxious to locate people they knew and distant family relations. As well as photographs and pictures on the wall we also incorporated, within the family album, quotes from Soop's writings and pieces of his published and unpublished poetry. Although we had made the seating arrangement flexible enough to accommodate people in wheelchairs, it was only later that we realized that the photograph album was too heavy for some of our disabled visitors to lift. It was a significant realization that making museums accessible for visitors with disabilities is an ongoing process, and dialogue with the disabled community is always necessary.

Not all impairments are physical. Emotional traumas can also have debilitating mental effects. Many Aboriginal people who, as children, were taken from their families to be educated in centrally located Residential Schools, have been emotionally scarred by this experience.[5] Born in 1943, Soop attended St Paul's Indian Residential School until Grade 5. He then numbered among the first generation of Blood Indians to attend school off the reserve, and in 1964 completed high school in Cardston, Alberta (Greer 2001). In the general area of the family photographs we featured an unpublished video interview of Everett Soop, recorded by his friend Rick Tailfeathers, discussing his experience of St Paul's Residential School. The unedited video showed Soop's humour and humanity in discussing the school, but excerpts from his earlier journalistic writings show a lingering bitterness at the treatment he received as a child:

> My mind often dwells for hours on those days that are still so vivid in my mind. Running away, getting a strapping, breathing, getting a strapping, expressing my sense of humour, getting a strapping. It didn't matter what I did; somehow I always ended up getting a strapping, whipping, lashing, or my hairline pulled up. Ears twisted. Slapped in the head, or maybe a full nelson by supervisors, teachers, principal, or whatever. If you behaved and did as you were told you didn't fare any better because your peers nearly always administered the licking.
>
> (Soop 1976: 7)

Soop's mother worked for 27 years at this school and so, unlike many of his fellow students, he had not experienced the trauma of being separated from his family. The school building to all intents was his family home for that period of his life.

We limited representations of Soop's artistic work to his cartoons, and these were straightforward to display, grouped into a variety of themes. The Glenbow Museum in Calgary now holds the bulk of Soop's cartoons, preserved by his friend Hugh Dempsy and later given to the museum by Everett Soop's heir, his great-niece Quindy. Other examples of his work are held by Libraries and Archives Canada and by the Soop family. We were fortunate in being able to borrow examples from all these sources. Many of the cartoons are very funny and endeared him to his reading public: even now they do not seem dated. The absurdities he saw in his fellow man, whether Aboriginal or not, are timeless and required no explanations. His observations relating to the clash of cultures are some of the most amusing. In one cartoon, published in the *Kainai News* in 1970, he shows two boys sitting on the floor watching a western on television. One turns to say to the other: 'Do you think us Indians will ever get to be the good guys?'

There were two entrances to the gallery spaced about two and a half metres apart. On the wall separating these two entrances a desk was located. Visitors could examine this desk either on entering the gallery, during the exploration of the theme of Soop's early life, or before leaving the exhibition. The desk was placed to represent Soop's career as a staff member of the *Kainai News*. Above it were displayed a number of his cartoons that referred to his time working as a journalist – mainly caricatures of fellow workers, or comments on the problems he had meeting deadlines. On the desk surface were placed a jumble of personal possessions: partially completed cartoons, his sketchbook, a sheet of his unpublished poetry, sketches of friends, a book of Jewish humour, a braid of sweet grass, family photographs, his personal business cards while he was a member of the Premier's Council, a Bible tract, a tie and a shabby cap.

The desk provided a simple tool for revealing and examining the many layers of Soop's life and character. We used the drawers to feature aspects of his character and interests. In the upper drawer were displayed a collection of his paintbrushes, still encrusted with paint. In another drawer we showed a selection of his cassette tapes that indicated his eclectic delight in such varied music as Country and Western, Elvis Presley, opera, sacred and native music. We displayed his book, *My Tribe is Right Behind Me*, as well as a personalized licence plate that featured some of his cartoon characters. There was a page from the *Kainai News* discussing his feelings about his people, together with an eagle feather and sweet grass. In one of the lower drawers we displayed an empty bottle of booze, a cartoon about journalists being alcoholics and his comments about drinking. In another drawer we included his Bible, his mother's prayer book, and his diary with his final entries that noted Bible readings, topics for prayer, notes on the pains that he was suffering and the people who had been to visit him.

On the top of the desk was a cap that belonged to his father and this provided a link to the hat case that was placed centrally in the gallery. Like all Everett's hats, this cap had a name – the 'contestant's cap'. The family knew well the story of how this hat got its name. Everett's father, Arthur, had attended a rodeo where, dressed in normal work clothes including his cloth cap, he had been drinking quite heavily. Arthur decided to go into the restricted area reserved for those participating in the rodeo events. The security people, having seized the intoxicated Arthur, stated that the area was reserved for contestants only. Arthur replied with slurred speech that he was a contestant and amazingly was allowed into the restricted area. The family loved the story and Everett kept the cap as a memento. However, in one of his cartoons (published in the *Kainai News* in March 1979), featured in the area of the exhibition devoted to social issues, a man is depicted wearing a similar cap. Here the cap wearer is seated on a broken-down sofa with another man, both of them looking very drunk and holding bottles. The caption reads: 'Drinking is inherited if you keep passing the bottle.' Both Everett and his father were alcoholics.

In this part of the gallery we used other tools to introduce Soop the man. From childhood Soop loved to dress up and, as his brother Louis remembered, Halloween was his favourite time of the year. His usual day-to-day expression of this love of dressing up was to wear different hats. Louis allowed us to borrow three more of Everett's special hats and by displaying them, together with images of Soop wearing them, we were able to show him in different guises and also, metaphorically, to show the varied aspects of his character and the careers that he had embraced. There were three hats: one was his 'derby' that he wore for the photograph that accompanied his image in the *Kainai News*. This represented Soop the journalist. Another was his 'missionary' hat. Soop was a profoundly religious man, especially in the later period of his life. The photograph that depicts him wearing this hat shows him clasping a bottle of alcohol. Alcoholism was a recurring problem in Soop's life and added to the physical problems he faced from muscular dystrophy. This hat represented the complexities of the man himself. The last hat was his 'Will Sampson' hat. Will Sampson was a Muscogee Creek Aboriginal actor and painter who played Indians as real people and not as some hackneyed collection of Hollywood clichés. Everett and Will Sampson were different in many ways but shared a desire to portray the Aboriginal people of North America with as much accuracy as possible using their individual talents. Both men spoke to groups about the injustices facing Aboriginal people. Sampson also dealt with issues associated with alcoholism and substance abuse. This hat represented Soop the advocate.

Soop was keenly aware of the social issues that disrupted life for the Aboriginal people of Canada, and for disabled Aboriginal people in particular, and he spoke forcefully on these issues in his role as chair of the Premier's Council on the Status of Persons with Disabilities:

> It is difficult to isolate the housing problems faced by people with dis-abilities from those faced by many able-bodied Aboriginal people living in First Nations communities or Metis settlements. Over-crowded, sub-standard housing conditions are commonplace for Aboriginal people living outside major centres. An estimated one half of all Indian housing lacks such basic facilities as adequate insulation, indoor plumbing and electricity ...
>
> People with disabilities have virtually no public transportation, even within their communities. They must rely on friends or family for even the basic necessities like shopping. Other activities, such as recreation or employment are impossible.
>
> (Soop *et al.*1993: Section 11)

Interpreting disability

A thematic display of sports cartoons flanked one side of the opening to the second part of the gallery while cartoons depicting social issues – often bru-tally honest in their treatment of family violence, vandalism, suicide and alcoholism – flanked the other side. The next section of the gallery dealt with Soop's political advocacy and addressed disability issues most directly. The central exhibition in the latter section was Soop's wheelchair which was placed on a low plinth. In the initial period of the development of the exhibition, Devine had established vital links with the Aboriginal commu-nity, Soop's family, and particularly Everett's elder brother, Louis. It was on one of her visits to the Kainai (Blood) Reserve at Standoff that she discovered Everett Soop's wheelchair abandoned in a snowdrift. The red fabric con-trasted strongly with the white snow leaving a vivid impression. She recog-nized that the wheelchair would have great visual appeal within a gallery despite the ripped fabric, rust and wear: it would be an iconic object.[6] She asked Louis if she might borrow it and was pleased to receive permission. The wheelchair became a silent, but significant, component of the exhibition. We also featured Soop's walking stick which he used extensively before being confined to a wheelchair. Within the case that contained the walking stick we included factual information on muscular dystrophy and, most importantly, Soop's own perspective on disability:

> I never did really see myself as a cartoonist, I saw myself as a humorist. So the way I viewed muscular dystrophy was almost incidental to what I wanted to do. I guess it stopped me from doing a lot of things I wanted to do, some things I wanted to be ... To

175

me, life is all about people and the world around you, not what you
become.

(Soop quoted in Greer 2001: 7)

Soop was blessed, or possibly cursed, with a character that demanded honesty
of expression. This trait brought him a level of notoriety and also created
many enemies. The unpleasant realities that he lampooned were not just to
be found in the homes of family and friends, in the federal and provincial
governments, but also in local Band politics. In many cartoons he depicts
chiefs, elders and councillors looking affluent while other native people look
poor and in need. There were many people on the reserve who felt that his
satire should only be levelled at white society, and when Soop attacked what
he saw as local corruption there were people who threatened him. His tena-
city in clinging to his ideals despite violent opposition honed his strengths
as an advocate.

After years of attacking Band politics he decided that the way to make
change was to actively participate in local governance to address the wrongs
that his pen and brush could not alter. He decided, therefore, that he should
run for office as a councillor. He participated for two terms but found the
experience very difficult:

> There is so much decadence and immorality that it is hard to over-
> look them. It is fine to expose corruption and evil, but not at the
> sacrifice of missing completely the good in the world.
>
> Seeing what is wrong is easy, but it is being blind to the perversion
> of good that is hard to detect.
>
> My wish is that every Indian should become a councillor for at
> least one term. Then they'll have an idea of what hell is like. It
> looks great on the surface but when you get through you are left all
> alone, because you did what was right. All alone because you did
> worry. All alone because you helped a friend. All alone because you
> were fair to an enemy. Alone because you turned to the devil. Alone
> because you turned to God. In other words you lose regardless of
> what you do.
>
> (Soop 1990b: 4)

Although difficult, the experience made him far more politically aware and
astute, and it was after this time that Soop began in earnest his work as an
advocate for disabled people and for the Aboriginal disabled community in
particular. Soop's work in his position as Chair of the Premier's Council for
the Status of People with Disabilities was instrumental in his being awarded
the Meritorious Service Medal.[7] This important achievement was depicted in
the exhibition by a video of his brother Louis accepting the medal from Her
Excellency the Right Honorable Michaëlle Jean, Governor General of

Canada. We were also able to display the medal and some of the other documents recognizing his achievements.

Conclusion

Once the exhibition was opened it became very evident that reading about the issues and talking hypothetically about the exhibition were not the same as real involvement. The exhibition was a first step in what should be an ongoing discourse on disability issues within the museum, artistic and academic communities. Everett Soop – writing and protesting the injustices that he saw around him – made progress, but the continuation of this process has been painfully slow. It was with profound regret that we realized that, in the past, the museum had only paid lip service to the needs of the disabled community. Satisfied with some minor changes to the building designed to facilitate access to people in wheelchairs, it initially seemed that we were doing our part. Like the many able-bodied Calgarians who think nothing of parking in spaces reserved for disabled people merely to save a few moments extra to walk from their cars to the stores, we had been oblivious to the real issues facing disabled Canadians and our role in presenting these to the broader community.

No matter how hard we try to change situations there is always opposition. Museum exhibitions join the ranks of reports, books, articles and impassioned eloquence: all of which can change some perceptions. However, perseverance is necessary and breaking conventional stereotypes is part of the process. Perhaps the last words should go to Soop, never conventional, who continued to fight for social justice despite the obstacles faced by the metaphorical snowdrifts he encountered:

> My hands shake at the thoughts of so many stacks of paper and proposals that sit in politicians' offices ... I am growing weary of plodding through the snowdrifts piled up by bureaucrats.
>
> (Soop 1988: 14)

Notes

1 The exhibition *Everett Soop: Activist, Journalist, Cartoonist*, was made possible by financial support from Canadian Heritage, Museums Assistance Program, and by support from the University of Calgary. It was also made possible by the incredible generosity of Louis Soop who provided a wealth of family stories and mementoes that enriched the exhibition.

2 The Blood Tribe are also known as the Kainai, and are part of the Blackfoot speaking First Nations people.

3 In the early 1960s, only 4 per cent of Indian students on Reserves in Canada remained in school through Grade 12. Soop was one of the first generation of Aboriginal people who had attended high school off the reserve, and one of the few to receive further education.

4 For discussion of the importance of Soop's political satire see Robertson (2008).

5 The issue of treatment of native children in Canadian Residential Schools continues to be unresolved despite apologies from the Churches, and despite financial compensation. Everett Soop can be seen discussing this issue in a CBC video: *For survivors, the hurt comes back.* Broadcast Date: 15 March 1991. This can be accessed as number five on the website http://archives.cbc.ca/society/education/topics/692/ (Accessed March 2009).

6 Louis Soop continued this generosity and loaned many of his brother's personal belongings that gave the exhibition a vital richness.

7 The citation for the award reads: 'An advocate for Aboriginal people and physically challenged persons, the late Everett Soop, who personally suffered from muscular dystrophy, worked unselfishly for the cause of First Nations peoples living with disabilities. His efforts during his tenure with the Alberta Premier's Council on the Status of Persons with Disabilities culminated in 1993 with the publication of a major report entitled Removing Barriers: An Action Plan for Aboriginal People With Disabilities. Mr. Soop, who passed away in 2001, is remembered for his relentless quest for social justice for his people, as well as for his unique contributions to his province and his country.'

References

Abbas, J., Church, K., Frazee, C. and Panitch, M. (2004) *Lights ... Camera ... Attitude! Introducing disability arts and culture*, Toronto: Ryerson RBC Institute for Disability Studies Research Education.

Greer, S. (2001) 'The pitbull of native journalism', *The Globe and Mail*, Toronto, p. 7.

Human Resources and Social Development Canada (2006) *Advancing the Inclusion of People with Disabilities: A Government of Canada Report*, Ottawa: Government of Canada.

Soop, E. (1976) Gitskenip Column, *Kainai News*, 31 August, p. 7, reprinted as 'School Days' in E. Soop (1990) *I See My Tribe is Still Behind Me!*, Calgary: Glenbow Museum, p. 39.

—— (1979) 'Creative Boredom'. Gitskenip Column, *Kainai News*, June number 2, p. 15, reprinted in E. Soop (1990) *I See My Tribe is Still Behind Me!*, Calgary: Glenbow Museum, p. 42.

—— (1988) 'Being Indian and Handicapped', *Saskatchewan Indian*, April 1988, pp. 13–15.

—— (1990a) *I See My Tribe is Still Behind Me!*, Calgary: Glenbow Museum.

—— (1990b) 'Kahm-Stahn!' *Kainai News*, January 18, p. 4, reprinted as 'Look to Ourselves' in E. Soop (1990), *I See My Tribe is Still Behind Me!*, Calgary: Glenbow Museum, p. 154.

Soop, E. *et al.* (1993) *Removing Barriers: An Action Plan for Aboriginal People with Disabilities*, Government of Alberta: Premier's Council on the Status of Persons with Disabilities, Online. Available *http://www.seniors.gov.ab.ca/css/premiers_council/publications/Barriers.asp* (accessed 29 April 2009).

Robertson, C. (2008) 'Trickster in the press: Kainai editorial cartoonist Everett Soop's framing of Canada's 1969 White Paper events', *Media History*, 14(1): 73–93.

13

FACE TO FACE

Representing facial disfigurement in a museum context

Emma Chambers

In 1995, surgeon Iain Hutchison decided to use the legacy of his mother (Dr Martha Redlich) to fund an artist-in-residence project at the oral and maxillofacial surgery department of St Bartholomew's and the Royal London hospitals. Hutchison had six aims for this *Saving Faces* project: to illustrate for the public in an acceptable, non-clinical way what is, and also isn't, possible with modern facial surgery; to illustrate that people with facial disfigurement lead normal and fulfilled lives; to allow a portrait artist access to people with extraordinary faces; to capture the emotional journey undertaken by the patient in a way that simple clinical photography cannot; to illustrate the physical surgical process necessary to treat the patients for those members of the public who might be interested in this more anatomical aspect; finally, he believed that the process of sitting for a facial portrait after surgery when the artist is totally focused on their face might be cathartic for the patients and assist in their recovery.

The recent theft of body parts from the Royal College of Surgeons and their use in art projects had made the medical world nervous about any artistic venture involving patients. Hutchison struggled to persuade the hospital hierarchy, who initially opposed the project, that *Saving Faces* would not harm the patients or cause adverse publicity for the hospitals. This process took six months before he was able to commission Mark Gilbert, who had already painted his niece and mother-in-law, to paint portraits of patients before, during and after facial surgery. Gilbert then worked between 1998 and 2000 producing nearly 100 works.

The complex images that resulted from this period operate at the interface between the medical record and the portrait and raise uncomfortable questions about the relationship between appearance and subjectivity and the ethics of viewing. How does facial disfigurement affect the way that we construct identity? How should these works be displayed, viewed and discussed? In what way does their exhibition in a museum or art gallery context challenge or reinforce prejudices against facially disfigured people?

The portraits were intended for an exhibition, *Saving Faces,* to inform the public about the possibilities and limitations of facial surgery, and the original brief for Gilbert was simply to record the progress of the surgical operations. This remit developed as the project progressed and the interactions between surgeon, artist and sitters gave the portraits an overt role in assisting in the patients' recovery and social reintegration. Drawing on theories of the 'illness narrative' which mediates between medical discourse and the patient's experience of chronic illness and disability (Kleinman 1988; Garro and Mattingly 2000), I will analyse the conditions of portrayal and spectatorship that developed in the medical portrait sitting and the ways in which these allowed the patients to create their own illness narratives.[1]

The portraits were exhibited at the National Portrait Gallery, London, and regional art galleries in England between 2000 and 2002, accompanied by a publication explaining the artist-in-residence project and a folder of case histories describing the surgical procedures the sitters had undergone, and generated extensive and largely positive press coverage. In considering responses to the exhibition I analyse press reviews and visitor comment books from the National Portrait Gallery, Victoria Art Gallery, Bath and the Djanogly Art Gallery, Nottingham. These represent a rich resource which both responds to and augments the exhibition content. As Sharon Macdonald has argued, the visitor book can be seen as an 'interactive exhibit' and an integral part of the exhibition, and the act of writing in visitor books constitutes part of the ritual of exhibition-visiting (Macdonald 2005: 119). Contributors to the visitor books were self-selected, and it is not possible to assess retrospectively how representative a sample of the exhibition visitors they constituted. However, it is still possible to identify patterns of response which can tell us much about the impact of the exhibition.[2] I will analyse these responses to the exhibition in relation to wider debates about facial disfigurement and representation of disabled people in museum displays. I will then consider the ways in which the *Saving Faces* exhibition constructed meaning both through the display of paintings and texts within the exhibition itself, and through the varied perspectives added to this by responses from the press and comments from the general public, which themselves became integrated into the exhibition experience (Sandell 2007: 78).

Mark Gilbert already had a successful track record as a portrait painter, having won three prizes in the BP Portrait Awards in 1994, 1995 and 1996. The initial remit that Hutchison set for Gilbert was to make portraits of patients, in a head-and-shoulders format, both full face and in profile. The portraits were to be representational and avoid abstraction, or overtly formalistic artistic styles such as cubism (Grove 2002). The selection of patients as subjects was made by the surgeon, primarily to illustrate particular medical conditions for the public (Thomas 2002). Although the prescribed format for the portraits conformed to the conventions of medical photography, the choice of painting as medium was intended to differentiate the works from the photographs routinely used to plan and record surgery (Irving 2002). Hutchison also believed that the process of portraiture would produce something that could not be achieved with photographs through the way that the portrait painter would interact with the patients over a period of time (Hutchison 2007).

Gilbert had to work quickly to keep pace with the surgery, using a mixture of portrait sittings and photographs that had been taken by the surgeons when the patient was admitted. This contributed towards his decision to avoid extraneous detail by using plain coloured backgrounds and head and shoulders format (Gilbert 2007). The uniform head-and-shoulders format of the portraits of the sitters before surgery, and the pairing of 'before and after' images place the portraits within a regime of medical classification and comparison, corresponding to the dynamics of the early nineteenth-century institutional photographic archive, used to classify the criminal, poor, sick and insane described by John Tagg:

> A vast and repetitive archive of images is accumulated in which the smallest deviations may be noted, classified and filed. ... The bodies ... are taken one by one: isolated in a shallow, contained space; turned full face and subjected to an unreturnable gaze.
>
> (1988: 64)

Yet even as the compositions of Gilbert's portraits evoke the conventions of the medical archive, the oil paint medium and the process of making the image over time through the portrait sitting exceed the boundaries of archival documentation, and set up a different set of expectations.

Gilbert was acutely aware of the different conditions under which he would be working and the constraints that this might place on his usual painting practice (both in relation to his subjects' approval of their portraits as an acceptable likeness, and in terms of the ethical implications of using them as subject matter to explore purely formal artistic concerns, as he had previously done in his uncommissioned portraits). An obvious comparison for portraiture using medical subject matter is the work of Francis Bacon, but despite his admiration for Bacon's work, Gilbert rejected Bacon's interpretative distortions for an approach that didn't 'sanitise or flatter' and which he described as 'absolutely straight' (Gilbert 2007).

Ernst van Alphen has argued that it is the visible signs of the artist's interpretation, such as Bacon's distortions of facial features, that demonstrate that he has produced the essence of the sitter through a creative visualization of inner emotional states, rather than solely representing external appearance (1997: 254). Gilbert's partly self-imposed constraints on creative visualization are illuminating about the ways that formal and aesthetic qualities in portraiture are influenced by the conditions of its production, and the problematic nature of the aesthetic in a medical setting. Indeed, Alan Radley has argued that an aesthetic dimension or 'the ability to engage in fancies, to contemplate beauty and to create space and time for frivolous activity' is lost both from the life of the patient and from an authorized discourse about illness, leading to a 'colonisation of the person' by medicine (Radley 1999: 782). Gilbert's rejection of experimentation with composition and form to convey inner emotional states as inappropriate, and his adoption instead of a painting style that was as 'straight' as possible highlights the constraints that ethical considerations place on the aesthetic in a medical setting.

Gilbert has described how the early head-and-shoulders portraits he made of sitters were often kept small and executed very quickly to keep pace with the surgery, but the painting of the final portrait after surgery was a more relaxed process where it was possible to develop the pose and setting and include objects and people who were significant to the sitter (Gilbert 2007). The first full-length portrait came about as a result of the sitter, a small child, being dressed by her parents in a green velvet dress for her portrait after surgery (Bond 2002: 46) (Plate 13.1). In these final portraits sitters are shown full-length in a more conventional portrait composition, which refers to their life outside the hospital through clothing, people and objects, such as the portraits of Henry de Lotbinière who was depicted in his barrister's wig and gown (Plate 13.2) and Henry Ekpe who was painted together with his young son.

Illness narratives and the medical portrait sitting

The charting of a medical and biographical journey, through a temporal series of 'before', 'during', and 'after' portraits, has parallels with verbal and text-based 'illness narratives'. The illness narrative told by the patient has become an important concept in sociology, psychology and medical anthropology, because of the way that it relates illness to the social world of an individual and to society and culture as a whole, as opposed to the emphasis on the disease in isolation in the narratives of medical professionals. The illness narrative, as Hydén has argued, also has an important function in reconstructing identity.

> Chronic illness alters the relationship between the patient's body, self and surrounding world. Thus, for the chronically ill, the reconstruction of one's own life story is of central importance. Narrativising the chronic illness within the framework of one's own life history makes it possible to give meaning to events that have disrupted and changed the course of one's life.
>
> (1997: 51)

Analysis of narrative structure has identified a distinction between 'story' (a sequence of actions and events), and 'discourse' (the discursive presentation of events) (Garro and Mattingly 2000: 12). In an illness narrative, 'discourse' enables the patients to take control over the presentation of their story, and to fashion a new identity that incorporates their medical condition into their social world. In a similar way, the distinction between story and discourse can also be usefully employed to understand the conventions that shape Gilbert's portrait series, and the interplay between the empirical representation of the sitters' appearance before and after surgery, and the compositional and aesthetic decisions that shape this representation into a portrait that constructs an identity and conveys a sense of self. Garro and Mattingly have emphasized the way that 'creating a narrative, as well as attending to one, is an active and constructive process' (2000: 1) which is 'grounded in a specific cultural setting, interaction and history' (2000: 22). Hunt (2000: 88–89) has emphasized the performative nature of the illness narrative, and the medical portrait sitting can also be understood as a performative space where the patients' social identities are reconfigured through the introduction of a visual narrative of recovery into the portrait and where the interaction with the portrait painter is crucial to creating meaning and re-engaging with the aesthetic.

Historians of portraiture have long contended that the formation of identity through portraiture is not simply conveyed by the finished work of art but is also actively constructed through the relationship between artist and sitter (West 2004: 37–41). This relationship is based on visual interaction and an exchange of looks. Rosemarie Garland-Thomson's analysis of the regime of vision to which disabled people are subjected sheds new light on the nature of this interaction:

> Staring at disability choreographs a visual relation between a spectator and a spectacle. A more intense form of looking than glancing, glimpsing, scanning, surveying, gazing and other forms of casual or uninterested looking, staring registers the perception of difference and gives meaning to impairment by marking it as aberrant. By intensely telescoping looking towards the physical signifier for disability, staring creates an awkward partnership that estranges and discomforts both viewer and viewed.
>
> (2002: 56–57)

Research on the visual interaction between facially disfigured people and the general public has established the way in which facial disfigurement denies a person anonymity and the 'civil inattention' usual between strangers in public spaces, instead subjecting them to overt visual and verbal reactions to their condition (Lister 2001: 3–4). However, in the portrait sitting the artist engages in a process of close looking and non-judgemental attention with the consent of the sitter, and this interaction of looks counteracts the disabled sitter's usual experience of inappropriate forms of looking, and informs the meaning of the portrait. The face-to-face interaction between portrait sitter and artist is one of respect and attention and results in the development of a relationship, and in a depiction of subjectivity rather than disfigurement.

Paul Farrand, the medical psychologist working on the *Saving Faces* project, concluded that the artist/sitter relationship was important in providing a safe environment 'similar to that derived from a therapeutic counselling relationship' where patients were able to talk 'initially about everyday things, but during later sittings also about issues related to their surgery or the effects of their disfigurement' (Farrand 2000). He also analysed the ways in which the post-operative portraits allowed patients to adjust psychologically to their new appearance and its relationship to their perceptions of inner identity:

> Often patients with facial disfigurement have difficulties reconciling differences they believe to exist between their appearance and their personality. Seeing their post-operative portraits however has provided these patients with an image of themselves which matches the image of the person they have always believed themselves to be. Interestingly, the view was often expressed that standard photographs did not serve the same function. Whilst these captured the physical characteristics of the patient they did not capture the patient's personality.
>
> (Farrand 2000)

This observation that photographs could not function in the same way as the paintings indicates the importance of the artist/sitter relationship, and the belief that identity is produced as much by the *process* of portraiture as by its *result*.

Although Hutchison did not originally want Gilbert to depict the patients' bodies, feeling that this would be a distraction from the subject of facial surgery (Bond 2002: 45), the fact that many of the final portraits are full length also allows them to subvert the conventional comparison of 'before' and 'after' images with identical compositions in medical records. This removes the sitter from the regime of hospital classification and comparison and places them back in the context of their everyday life, where they have contributed to the representation of their recovery from illness through the discussions between artist and sitter about how they should be portrayed. One patient's interaction with Gilbert particularly demonstrates this shaping of a personal narrative through portraiture. Roland S asked to be painted in his radiotherapy mask, as this was the most traumatic part of his treatment:

> I wanted Mark to paint me in the mask because I felt the mask was an important part of the process. When he did the painting I was standing up with the mask on and I could feel the tension rising

again. When I look at that picture I say to myself, yeah, that's how I used to feel, and it doesn't bother me at all to look at it. I've got the mask at home. I couldn't leave it at the hospital. My grandson plays with it. He thinks it's lovely.

(quoted in Bond 2002: 47)

An object that was once a focus of horror has been neutralized and rendered mundane by its inclusion in a portrait (Radley 1999), and as the sitter collaborated with the artist he recontextualised the mask within a visual and verbal narrative that ended in his recovery. This effect is heightened by the anecdote about the new function of the mask. As a significant symbol of his illness, given permanence in Gilbert's portrait, its meaning has been further transformed outside the hospital where it has become a symbol of the continuance of everyday family life.

Gilbert attended many of the patients' operations, and included paintings depicting these operations in his series of portraits of some patients. Although these are the most overtly medical of the paintings, and might be considered to objectify the patient, I would argue that the insertion of a 'during' into the sequence of 'before' and 'after' disrupts the familiar presentation of 'before' and 'after' surgical images for public consumption, and creates a new space for the subject, unrestricted by the conventions of traditional medical visual narratives. For the sitters these works represented a visualisation of their surgical ordeal, which made sense of the relationship between before and after and allowed them to explain it to others (Bond 2002: 47). Through these operation paintings patients were able to gain access to aspects of their illness history usually only available to medical professionals and incorporate it into their own narrative of their return to health. For Gilbert the move away from the portrait format also allowed a more purely formal approach, and the challenge of conveying a wider range of skin and flesh textures than those normally required by portrait painting (Mackenzie 2002).

The Saving Faces Exhibition: images, texts and voices

The exhibition *Saving Faces*, was unusual in including images of ordinary facially disfigured individuals in a museum context. Recent research has indicated that the representation of disability within museum displays is very limited, often reinforces stereotypes of disabled people as dependent invalids or exotic specimens, and there are very few representations of disabled people as 'ordinary active individuals'. This absence of disabled people from museum narratives is explained, at least in part, by curators' concerns about how to display material relating to disability without being exploitative or insensitive (Sandell *et al.* 2005). In fact, public and press responses to the *Saving Faces* exhibition were overwhelmingly positive, but a small

185

minority of visitors considered it was inappropriate subject matter for a fine art exhibition or exploitative or sensational in its presentation.[3] I will argue that the reason that public response was so positive was largely as a result of viewers' knowledge of the active participation of the patients throughout the process of making and exhibiting their portraits.

In the small publication accompanying the exhibition, Farrand described how the patients were involved in the decision to exhibit their portraits and were keen to do so, seeing the exhibition as an opportunity to educate the public about the nature of facial disfigurement and to allow them 'to see the person beyond the appearance' (Farrand 2000). Reviews of the exhibition, and comments by visitors, reveal that the paintings clearly succeeded as a public information project. However, these sources also reveal that the representation of medical imagery in fine art and the range of critical responses considered appropriate to it were still sensitive issues. The paintings were displayed alongside short labels with the patient's first name and surname initial (for example, Roland S) and the date of the work. Case histories of the patients were also available in a folder for visitors to browse through, and comments in the visitor books indicate that they were clearly an important factor in shaping visitor responses to the exhibition through the way that they contextualized the visual imagery of the portraits and allowed viewers to make a connection with the people portrayed. One visitor to the National Portrait Gallery, for example, wrote:

> So inspiring to see what people have to go through, the work the surgeons are able to do, people's stories, and how the artist has shown all this and the help this process has given the patients.

There were also several comments in the visitor books from people with personal experience of facial disfigurement and surgery and all of these responded positively to the exhibition. A visitor who saw the exhibition at the Victoria Art Gallery in 2001 wrote:

> I have had maxifacial [sic] surgery and as I have walked around this gallery I am exhilarated by what I see. I appreciate the courage and feelings of these people and if by seeing this exhibition it changes one person's view of 'disfigurement' then it is an amazing achievement.

But responses from disabled viewers were not unanimously positive and the presentation of the exhibition provoked some criticism from within the disability media. One reviewer, for *Disability Now*, wrote:

> The idea was to 'show that people with a facial disability are able to enjoy happy, successful and fulfilled lives' and to explore potential

186

benefits for the sitters. The paintings are arresting. Against the one-colour background with a series of seemingly loose, broad, brushstrokes, Gilbert conjures up a strong emotional presence. This suggests a high degree of mutual respect between artist and sitter on which the exhibition's success rests. However, and sadly, the presentation was very medical, which I found to be old-fashioned, voyeuristic and patronising: simply inappropriate in this setting.

(Reynolds 2002: 34)

There is no specific discussion of this 'medical presentation', but it is likely that the reviewer is referring to the way that the case histories defined the sitters within a medical rather than a biographical or an artistic discourse. Indeed, the case history has been described as 'one of the most powerful tools of the Western medical profession'. Its impersonal language 'turned the disabled person into a medical narrative' and 'the doctor into an authority on such narratives' (Cassuto 2002: 119–20). The case history presents a medical rather than social account of disfigurement, and its inclusion in an exhibition context can be seen to reproduce the power relations between medical professionals and patients which exist in a hospital environment. A typical case history for *Saving Faces* was that of Roland S:

Roland is a 51 year-old owner of a transport company. He lives in London with his wife Iris. He has two sons and a daughter and five grandchildren. He likes to play golf. In 1999, Roland thought he had toothache and an abscess on his left upper jaw. It turned out that this swelling was in fact caused by a malignant cancer of his upper jaw and maxillary sinus (*squamous cell carcinoma*). The surgery involved removal of his left upper jaw, sinus, cheekbone, nose, palate, and the lower part of his eye socket. A large dental plate (*obturator*) was used to fill the defect. His cheek, which had been peeled back to facilitate removal of the cancer, was replaced at the end of the operation. After the surgery Roland was treated with six weeks of radiotherapy. The mask is worn during the treatment to ensure that the patient always receives the radiotherapy at exactly the correct site on their body. Roland found this claustrophobic.

Despite their presentation in a gallery context to a general audience, the case histories presented in the *Saving Faces* exhibition record a minimal amount of biographical information, devoting the majority of the text to a detailed account of the patient's disease and its treatment. Biographical and medical information are not interrelated to describe the disease as part of the sitter's life history, and the style of writing is technical rather than discursive.

Longer press features often included interviews with the sitters, focusing on their stories (Thomas 2002; Falconer 2002). Roland S, whose case history is quoted above, described his experience in *New Scientist*:

> It started as toothache, but when they took the tooth out and took a biopsy on the abscess it turned out to be cancerous. It was rather urgent because it was spreading across the roof of my mouth. The surgeon cut around the nose and up right underneath the eye. He pulled all that skin back and cut out the whole upper part of my left jaw and right back to my ear and up to my eye. He had to put a brace in under the eye so I wouldn't lose it. Obviously I lost my left nostril.
>
> When they asked me if I minded being painted I thought it would be good for me, and I thought it would be good for other people, to make them aware of what can be done. During the painting I used Mark like a doctor, he was getting all my little troubles. I'd tell him things about things that weren't right, then I'd get a phone call from one of the surgeons and it would all be sorted out.
>
> It was especially helpful with the radiotherapy. I had major problems with that and with the mask I had to wear. I would tell Mark about the mask, how I could hardly breathe out of it and how it came right down my throat. You're lying on your back and the machine starts up and you can feel a noise humming in your ears and you can taste burning flesh and then you get the smell. It was horrible. They gave me some tablets to calm me down. That happened every day for twenty minutes for six weeks. I dreaded it.
>
> (quoted in Bond 2002: 47)

The journalists' texts which accompanied these interviews conformed, in some ways, to common stereotypes for representing disability by describing the interviewees primarily in medical terms and characterizing them as brave survivors (Barnes 1992). However, these interviews also gave the sitters a voice that was not present in the exhibition displays and which told of the same experiences in very different language from the case histories.

The ethics and aesthetics of viewing: visitor comments and press reviews

Richard Sandell's work on museums as institutions with the capacity to counter prejudice has noted the ways in which visitor comments books allow visitors to 'perform their own tolerance' and to participate in 'conversations and debates in which individuals either endorsed or challenged the expressed opinions of others' (Sandell 2007: 124–25). A significant number of visitors described the exhibition as 'thought-provoking', 'moving', 'inspiring' or 'humbling',[4] and many comments focused on the way that the exhibition content was perceived to educate the public, by asserting the importance of a common humanity and inner virtue over surface appearance.[5] One visitor to the Victoria Art Gallery, for example, wrote:

> Remarkable and moving – a tribute to the invincibility of the human spirit and a necessary corrective in our image-conscious society.

At the National Portrait Gallery, the exhibition coincided with an exhibition of celebrity portraits by photographer Mario Testino, and both visitors and press reviewers frequently compared the two shows to make a moral comparison between frivolity and virtue. A review in the left-wing magazine *Tribune* is representative of the main preoccupations of the press reviews:

> Two exhibitions installed at either end of the main corridor at the National Portrait Gallery could hardly be more different in intention or effect. Fashion photographer Mario Testino shows large-scale, lushly coloured photographs of celebrities from Naomi Campbell to Princess Diana. ... By contrast Mark Gilbert's exhibition *Saving Faces*, of paintings of people whose faces have been distorted by surgery or disease sombrely documents an aspect of real life that is far from the artifice of Testino's world. During a year as artist in residence at the facial surgical department at the Royal London Hospital, Gilbert focused on the incredibly powerful surgical process and the resulting changes in the facial appearance of the sitters. His portraits convey not only the intensity of faces damaged by trauma but also the changing emotions, character and confidence of the patient. By not setting out to produce mere medical illustrations or objectively to record change, his portraits evoke the courage and spirit of the subject. Gilbert forces us to examine our own attitude to deformity and disfiguration.
>
> (Cooper 2002: 21)

This review exemplifies a common distinction in the press between the aesthetic criticism applied to Testino's work and the focus on profound and morally uplifting subject matter for Gilbert's. Other reviews reveal a deep discomfort with the idea of applying superficial aesthetic judgements to the work. One reviewer wrote: 'it is very difficult, possibly even crass, to talk about aesthetics, presentation, artistic expression – the usual critical speak – when what you see in front of you are pictures that look like massacres' (Irving 2002: 7).

The visitor books show much greater engagement with the aesthetic impact of the works and comments often focused on composition, colour and handling of paint.[6] Some viewers also noted the way that expectations of medical subject matter and the viewer's engagement with it were transformed by the aesthetic qualities of painting:

> We seem so used to before and after photographs and expect to see people always made beautiful. Some here have been, but for many it has been an ordeal to be left safe or to look ordinary. I also wonder whether the painting rather than the photograph adds to [the] way we need to know or see here. I think it stops us from glancing and moving on.
>
> Visitor comment, National Portrait Gallery 2002

A significant number of visitors described the paintings or their sitters as 'beautiful'.[7] However, one of the few press reviews to discuss the works in aesthetic terms was one that also strongly objected to the exhibition:

> The portraits provide a freak show that is both distasteful and uninformative. ... Mazeeda appears twice – in close-up as a monster with a grossly enlarged cheek and, after the tumour has been removed, as a cute three-year-old in a green dress. Intense green grounds create a carnival mood that enhances the freak show aspect of the first painting and the sentimentality of the follow-up. Over a nine-year period Henry de L underwent 12 operations to remove tumours from his salivary glands. Three paintings show his face sliced open and the flesh folded back; these Bosch-like horrors are bordered with bright red, presumably to enhance the gore. ... The portraits were used to help patients come to terms with their appalling experiences. I hope they succeeded as therapy; as an exhibition, they are deeply offensive.
>
> (Kent 2002: 46)

This view was shared by a small minority of viewers to the exhibition who felt that the exhibition was exploitative or that the subject matter was inappropriate for the setting, or had questionable value as art.

> Obviously everyone is very brave or are they – what choices do they have? How far removed is this from the Freak Show? Would you still stare if the pictures were the real people here instead?
>
> Visitor comment, National Portrait Gallery 2002

However, some viewers felt that the exhibition allowed them to look at disfigured faces in a way that would normally be taboo, to engage with them emotionally and to consider them in aesthetic terms.

Amazing, overwhelming exhibition. It is great after all this 'art about art' shit to see something which is art about life and has the courage to face reality, cope with emotions and a really difficult part of human life, which normally no one wants to look at, but here is presented in such a 'beautiful' way that you cannot resist staring.

Visitor comment, National Portrait Gallery 2002

Others focused on the way that the paintings relied on the eye contact between viewer and sitter characteristic of conventional portraiture to create an emotional connection:

Found looking into *eyes* v. moving.

Visitor comment, Djanogly Art Gallery 2000

One comment from a facially disfigured viewer especially drew out the importance of eye contact and this face-to-face encounter:

I wish everyone living in Bath would try and spare the time to have a look, gain a little insight that the artist has managed to capture – into the real human being inside, beneath any disfigured, abnormal face and then next time they see me, or the first time they see me they are not so shocked, horrified and scared and look into my eyes at me ... very severely facially disfigured ...

Visitor comment, Victoria Art Gallery 2001

These responses to the exhibition highlight the emotional projection involved in visitor responses to the portraits, but the process of consensual looking that takes place in the portrait sitting and the licence to gaze in an exhibition is very different from the real life experiences of facially disfigured people (see Garland-Thomson, this volume).

Saving Faces and the representation of facial disfigurement in society

The *Saving Faces* exhibition was pioneering in its display of images relating to facial disfigurement in a museum context and its inclusion of the subjects in the decisions about making and exhibiting their portraits. However, the politics of the project still bear close examination in relation to wider debates about facial disfigurement and disability in society. Always envisaged as an educational project, these portraits have partly been used to demonstrate the ability of plastic surgery to transform lives by altering the appearance of an individual rather than altering society's response to facial disfigurement. While the positive impact of facial surgery on the individual patients' lives has clearly been considerable, and facial surgery was a life-saving rather than an elective option in the case of the cancer patients, the idea that facial surgery can change a person's life is controversial for disabled people and focuses on a medical rather than a social definition of disability, highlighting the way that assumptions and decisions made by health professionals are based on concepts of a normative body (Barnes 1992: 42).

Some facially disfigured people dispute the medical profession's right to present their faces as problems to be fixed and argue for greater tolerance of facial disfigurement in society. Vicky Lucas, who participated in the television programme *What Are You Staring At?* broadcast on 6 August 2003, succinctly stated her reasons for not undergoing surgery:

> I realised that the reason why I was so unhappy was not because of my face, but the way some people would react to it. I decided that it wasn't my face that I wanted to change, but social attitudes. I'm not against plastic surgery. It's just that my personal choice is to not have it. Now, at the age of 24, I'm used to seeing my face reflected back at me in the mirror and I'm okay with it. ... But my face is integral to who I am. The way people treat me and the way I've had to learn to live my life has created the person I am today.
>
> (Lucas 2003)

If, as Sandell (2007: 106) has argued, the museum is very often seen by the public as a uniquely unbiased and authoritative voice, Lucas's very different perspective on facial disfigurement and surgery demonstrates that museums must be alert to the politics of presenting the public with a single perspective on disability issues in an exhibition, and the importance of taking account of a range of voices and interests.

Whilst the texts included within the *Saving Faces* exhibition were didactic and medical in tone, texts such as press reviews and visitor comments discussed the issues in different language and from different perspectives. Incorporating texts of these types into the exhibition itself would have enabled the exhibition to communicate a range of messages to different audiences. While sitters and disabled visitors found the display empowering, the content could also be read by other disabled groups as presenting (even endorsing) a 'medical' model of facial disfigurement. The supplementary texts in the press and visitor books containing contributions from disabled visitors also demonstrate the importance of giving disabled people a role in contributing to exhibitions about themselves and a voice within the exhibition itself.

The exhibition clearly engaged the public and succeeded in its objective to raise awareness of facial disfigurement, but it also produced unexpected moral and aesthetic responses to the work and raised problematic issues about the 'appropriate' way to look at images of facial disfigurement. The encounter with the facially disfigured sitters depicted was mediated by biographical information which encouraged an engagement with the sitters as individuals, particularly in the final portraits where sitters had been reconnected with their everyday lives outside the hospital (Sandell 2007: 161–62). However, a presentation of the paintings in a manner that acknowledged their status as fine art would have fully integrated the sitters' images into the mainstream discourse of the art museum and re-engaged with the aesthetic dimension that is lost from medical discourse. While press and public responses reproduced a positive stereotype of disability to some extent by viewing the sitters as 'brave' survivors, they also recognised that they were ordinary people who had overcome adversity rather than victims in need of sympathy and provided a rare instance of ordinary disabled people being featured positively within a museum context.

Notes

1 Research and early drafts of this article were completed during a Leverhulme Fellowship in the History of Portraiture at the National Portrait Gallery in 2007, and I would like to thank the Leverhulme Trust and the National Portrait Gallery for their support. I would also like to thank Mark Gilbert and Iain Hutchison and the staff at The Facial Surgery Research Foundation (formerly Saving Faces).
2 I have analysed the comments quantitatively to establish numbers of positive, negative and ambivalent responses and the frequency with which certain adjectives are used. I have also used a qualitative approach, grouping the responses thematically to assess the aspects of the exhibition experience to which visitors responded most frequently.
3 Of 810 comments in the visitor books, 747 were coded 'positive', 23 'negative' and 40 'ambivalent'.
4 The adjective most frequently used to describe the exhibition was 'moving' (114 visitors), other commonly used adjectives were 'courageous' or 'brave' (75), 'inspiring' (70), 'wonderful' (63), 'amazing' (59), 'beautiful' (57), 'thought-provoking' (42), 'interesting' (41), 'powerful' (32), 'humbling' (31) and 'emotional' (23).
5 152 visitors noted a moral message in their comments.
6 152 visitors commented on the moral message whereas 111 commented on the aesthetic impact or skill of the paintings.
7 57 visitors used the word 'beautiful'.

References

van Alphen, E. (1997) 'The portrait's dispersal: concepts of representation and subjectivity in contemporary portraiture', in J. Woodall (ed.), *Portraiture: Facing the Subject,* Manchester and New York: Manchester University Press, pp. 239–56.

Barnes, C. (1992) *Disabling Imagery and the Media: An Exploration of the Principles for Media Representations of Disabled People,* Krumlin, Halifax: The British Council of Organisations of Disabled People and Ryburn Publishing.

Bond, M. (2002) 'About Face', *New Scientist* 16 February: 44–47.

Cassuto, L. (2002) 'Oliver Sacks and the medical case narrative' in S. L. Snyder, B. Brueggeman and R. Garland-Thomson (eds), *Disability Studies: Enabling the Humanities*, New York: The Modern Language Association of America, pp. 118–30.

Cooper, E. (2002) 'Face to face with deformity', *Tribune* 12 April: 21.

Falconer, M. (2002) 'Face exploration', *Hampstead and Highgate Express,* 1 March: 27–28.

Farrand, P. (2000) 'Portraiture as therapy', in I. Hutchison, M. Gilbert and P. Farrand (eds), *Saving Faces*, Nottingham: University of Nottingham Press.

Garland-Thomson, R. (2002) 'The politics of staring: visual rhetorics of disability in popular photography' in S. L. Snyder, B. Brueggeman and R. Garland-Thomson (eds), *Disability Studies: Enabling the Humanities*, New York: The Modern Language Association of America, pp. 56–75.

Garro, L. C. and Mattingly, C. (eds) (2000) *Narrative and the Cultural Construction of Illness and Healing*, Berkeley and Los Angeles: University of California Press.

Gilbert, M. (2007) Interview by Emma Chambers, 12 August (unpublished).

Grove, V. (2002) 'The scalpel and the easel', *The Times,* 27 February, *Times2:* 10.

Hutchison, I. (2000) 'The Saving Faces Project' in I. Hutchison, M. Gilbert and P. Farrand (eds), *Saving Faces,* Nottingham: University of Nottingham Press.

Hunt, L. (2000) 'Strategic suffering: illness narratives as social empowerment among Mexican cancer patients' in L. C. Garro and C. Mattingly (eds), *Narrative and the Cultural Construction of Illness and Healing,* Berkeley and Los Angeles: University of California Press, pp. 88–107.

Hutchison (2007) Interview by Emma Chambers, 20 July (unpublished).

Hydén, Lars-Christer (1997) 'Illness and narrative', *Sociology of Health and Illness,* 19(1): 1997: 48–69.

Irving, M. (2002) 'In the eye of the beholder', *Independent on Sunday*, 3 March, *Arts Etc.:* 7.

Kent, S. (2002) 'Mark Gilbert', *Time Out,* 1650, 3–10 April: 46.

Kleinman, A. (1988) *The Illness Narratives: Suffering, Healing and the Human Condition*, New York: Basic Books.

Lister, I. (2001) *The Psychology of Facial Disfigurement: A Guide for Health and Social Care Professionals*, London: Changing Faces.

Lucas, V. (2003) 'Why I want you to look me in the face', BBC News, Online. Available http://news.bbc.co.uk/1/hi/magazine/3128203.stm (accessed 27 March 2009).

Macdonald, S. (2005) 'Accessing audiences: visiting visitor books', *Museum and Society*, November, 3(3): 119–216.

Mackenzie, M. (2002), *Saving Faces*, film, The Facial Surgery Research Foundation.

Radley, A. (1999) 'The aesthetics of illness: narrative, horror and the sublime', *Sociology of Health and Illness,* 21(6): 778–96.

Reynolds, A. (2002) 'Saving Faces', *Disability Now,* 4 April: 34.

Sandell, R., Delin, A., Dodd, J. and Gay, J. (2005) 'Beggars, freaks and heroes? Museum collections and the hidden history of disability', *Museum Management and Curatorship* 20(1): 5–19.

Sandell, R. (2007) *Museums, Prejudice and the Reframing of Difference*, London and New York: Routledge.

Tagg, J. (1988) *The Burden of Representation: Essays on Photographies and Histories*, London: Macmillan.

Thomas, D. (2002) 'Portraits at the cutting edge', *The Sunday Telegraph,* 3 February: 10.

West, S. (2004) *Portraiture,* Oxford: Oxford University Press.

Part 3

UNSETTLING PRACTICES

14

'OUT FROM UNDER'

A brief history of everything[1]

Kathryn Church, Melanie Panitch,
Catherine Frazee and Phaedra Livingstone

From September 2006 to July 2008, the School of Disability Studies at Ryerson University in Toronto produced an exhibit titled *Out from Under: Disability, History and Things to Remember*. Activist in its content and orientation alike, the exhibit both championed historical acts and moments of social transformation at the same time as it proceeded from an activist curatorial position – one intended to contribute to progressive understandings of disablement. The authors of this chapter were all involved; Catherine, Melanie and Kathryn as co-curators, Phaedra as one of fourteen exhibitors.[2] In this reflective account, we narrate our way from the invitation that sparked the School's engagement to the exhibit's initial installation in a disability arts festival, to its further installation in a premier Canadian cultural venue – the Royal Ontario Museum (ROM).

As we go, we imagine the disabled artists and performers who are creating disability arts and culture as an increasingly dynamic force for change in Canada and abroad (Abbas *et al.* 2004; Roman and Frazee 2009). We imagine disability activists whose stories, individually and collectively, gave *Out from Under* its energy and direction. And we imagine students of Disability Studies – our own students – who are learning and negotiating disability politics, as well as practices of activist and arts-informed inquiry. What have we learned that can assist these audiences in their various tasks? Having navigated our way into a major museum, what is revealed from a position of disability presence rather than absence? What are the complexities surrounding how a completed work – an exhibit already curated and produced for another setting – is received, supported and interpreted to the public by a host museum? Finally, what are the implications for practitioners, located in museums and other cultural organizations, of engaging with an activist approach to interpretation, one that challenges conventional modes of exhibit development?

Contemplating this writing, we were flooded with the enormity of attempting to convey the history we have lived with *Out from Under*. For two years, every action we took to move the exhibit ahead required us to negotiate the politics of disability representation that are tucked into a relentless progression of mundane tasks and decisions. For this reason, our chapter gives you a broad sweep of the whole process – forgoing for now the pleasures of probing its nooks and crannies. We glance back in time to the exhibit's origins, peer behind the scenes to reveal its key deliberations and turning points and highlight the ways in which exhibiting involved risk and discovery, celebration and remembrance, social inquiry and political action.

Origins (a curatorial narrative)

In 2006, organizers for the Abilities Arts Festival, an event celebrating Disability arts and culture, approached the School of Disability Studies[3] with a request that we contribute a Canadian disability history exhibit to their autumn 2007 programme. This invitation signifies the beginning of a broader process of community–university connection that is woven through the project. Who we are is one strand of that pattern. Arriving late to academic careers, each of us trails a long history of paid and volunteer work with community-based organizations, both local and national. Each of us lives in, fosters and/or draws from networks of relationship to disability worlds: physical, intellectual and/or psychiatric. Each of us, in different ways, chips away at an activist agenda. We are border-crossers; hybrid rather than 'pure' scholars, and this subjectivity was a key ingredient of our project. Neither historians nor museum specialists, our particularities remain central to the broader account of disability history that we mobilized together.

We begin by recounting the origins of *Out from Under* in a voice that could be called the 'curatorial we'. It conforms to the shape that we – Catherine, Melanie and Kathryn – have given to our labours in the ebb and flow of 'trialogue' at each stage of this project.

Invoking the classroom

In the winter of 2007, with the clock ticking on the Festival invitation, the School of Disability Studies introduced a Special Topics course titled 'Exhibiting Activist Disability History'. Working from critical questions such as 'what is history?' and 'who gets to make it?', we began to mobilize an exhibit that would profile resistance to discrimination and the marginalization of disabled people.

One of our innovations, then, was to jumpstart exhibit development through the reciprocal learning and teaching of the classroom. The strength of this move lay in adopting a forum in which disability representation is already on the agenda. As a School, we marinate continuously in the struggle

198

to address the invisibility of disabled people in and across a range of situations without reproducing or reinforcing 'that telling glance' (Davis 2002: 35) or 'the stare' that turns people with disabilities into objects of curiosity (Garland-Thomson 2006). Working with this dilemma is front and centre in everything we do. So, although exhibit development was new on our list, it made sense that we would favour our own expertise.

There were, however, limitations to this approach. Although we knew we would present the exhibit at least once in the disability community, we had no reassurance that our project would ever find an audience with the general public. Working without a museum partner, we had limited access to the display and production skills that abound in these institutions. Nor could we call upon their financial resources. At the same time, by containing the development process, we buffered museum personnel from exposure to the political sensitivities surrounding disability until after the exhibit was fully developed. Had they worked with us from the ground up, they would have confronted more 'harshly' situations and positions that we introduced 'softly' at a later stage in the process. Our relative isolationism prevented the direct transfer of representational expertise to the museum itself, and thus was less effective in altering taken-for-granted practices. On the other hand, it permitted our exhibitors to proceed boldly, without the censorial inhibitions of institutional oversight. The benefits and drawbacks of this situation would become more clear as our work progressed.

Engaging the students

Making exhibits more responsive to diverse communities is not just about choosing new or different artifacts – it is also about making new social relations. In the UK, for example, the Research Centre for Museums and Galleries recruited disabled individuals who were also experts in the cultural field to constitute a 'Think Tank' that would play a central role in shaping the interventions that eventually appeared in venues across England and Scotland (Dodd et al. 2008). Our 'think tank' was made up of people who assembled for the course, a group that assumed some unusual features. It included several students of Disability Studies who registered for credit. Active as undergraduates in our programme, these individuals are simultaneously workers with disability-related job histories. As word of the project spread, we acquired significant others: alumni yearning to return to our hothouse of activist scholarship, a researcher with a national independent living organization, and scholars from other universities. We enhanced and extended the group by inviting recognized leaders of the disability movement to join us.

Quite naturally, these people hooked us into disability as it is transacted and negotiated in the environments they inhabit: from large congregate care settings to community organizations and service agencies, from school systems to trade unions. The disability activists strengthened our grounding in the lived history of their work, while connecting us to representative organizations. They contributed decades of experience with education, career and advocacy initiatives as well as irreplaceable knowledge of human rights campaigns and public policy battles. To press the meaning of representation, then, it was not so much who each member represented that mattered as the fact that each one took on the task of representing what we were doing to the key groups and audiences in their networks. Our work radiated out from this human centre.

Thus we did not follow the more conventional practice of selecting participants in order to represent a particular range of disability experiences or organizations. Instead, we created an opportunity for collective work that expressed our actual circumstances and invited membership to form around it. By stretching the definition of 'student' in unusual ways, we built a group – primarily women – whose members extended and complicated the project's portrait of participation. Our task was to work across diverse locations and mixed embodiments in the creation of an exhibit. What we shared in common was a point of view as protagonists, participants and allies to progressive social movements in Canada.

Gleaning a collection

Out from Under started with a group of people rather than a collection. In order to establish a material base for exhibition, each participant in the course was asked to bring an object that they felt was significant to disability history. Trusting our decision to 'fall into' rather than to drive the project, we had no idea what things would turn up (Church 2008). However, we found that we had provoked a collection of 13 objects: a shovel, photos of three early residents of a psychiatric hospital, a poster, a sweat suit, an IQ test, a programme from the Shriners' Circus, a trunk, a portable respirator, a death certificate, a Braille watch, a bulletin board, a photo of a disability activist, and a Canadian flag.

Looking back, it is clear that we side-stepped two dilemmas: one of working with pre-established collections, and another of choosing some objects over others. We simply accepted all of the objects that participants brought to class. In this way, object selection became a social process rather than a curatorial task. In the course of searching something out, each person not only helped generate a collection but developed a stake in it as well. All of us were delighted to encounter the objects that other participants had serendipitously 'found'. By the time the class met, these objects carried tracings of their relation to the contributor as well as to the histories of disabled people. The 'how I found it' stories became, unexpectedly, an important genre that we later incorporated into exhibit materials. Retaining and honouring these relations is evidence of the feminist methodology that lay, implicitly, at the heart of our project. The narrative and reflexive 'turns'

(Kohler Riessman 2002) enabled us to savor the particularities of local stories while searching out their extra-local significance (Smith 1987).

Teaching for discovery

The course on exhibiting disability history was held over two weekends. Our approach was to excavate hidden disability histories through a process of presentation and amplification. During the first session, we orchestrated a 'go round' with all participants at the table, having them introduce their object, telling us why they thought it was important. Having dug deeper into their objects, participants arrived for the second 'go round' bearing not just the thing itself but a mock-up installation.

In both sessions, we relied on participant knowledge, impressions and associations to move explorations along. We worked from the particular object to the general context without erasing the links between them. We traced the connections between the objects and the people who owned or used them: past and present, individuals and groups. While we were pre-occupied with objects from start to finish, we worked towards a 'peopled' exhibit, one that would be alive with disabled characters, their families, friends and allies (Panitch 2008). Much creativity was at play here. In fact, we generated more ideas than we could use – as we were later to find out.

The process was not without risk. The exhibit might be too particular. Rooted in personal narratives, it might fail to communicate the broader patterns of disablement shaping the stories we told (Oliver 1990; Thomas 2007). The exhibit would not be comprehensive of all disability movements, visionaries and watersheds, and would almost certainly fail to communicate the breadth and fullness of Canadian disability history. Worse, it might be considered elitist or exclusionary.

What constitutes 'history' in this context? This question was an active piece of our problematic. On the one hand, we were familiar with inter-disciplinary scholarship, Canadian and international, that could inform class discussions and exhibit themes. On the other hand, we knew that the written record on disability history – especially the activist history to which we aspired – is missing, fragmented, or hugely compromised both by medical fixations on deviance and pathology and by the cultural tropes of tragedy and heroism (Shakespeare 2000; Rieser 2004). Given this circumstance, we could not use objects merely to reflect or illustrate a pre-existing and pre-authorized history. Instead, we drew what we could from scholarship that was aligned with our purposes even as we worked to fill scholarly silences by discovering and producing a fresh account (Panitch and Yoshida 2008).

Out from Under, then, arrived at a general history. Our almost random collection of objects opened into a much larger story of people with disabilities: generations of lives dominated by demeaning labels and life-altering categorization, by segregation and forced confinement, by the monotony and uniformity of institutional life, by unpaid labor and bodily harm, by the good intentions of charitable benefactors. Surfacing throughout are significant acts of individual achievement as well as the growth of national disability movements struggling to claim power, dignity and full citizenship rights.

That said, we have never viewed *Out from Under* as completely representative of disability history in Canada. Even when the exhibit was finally ready for installation, we understood it as a work-in-progress. Rather than being definitive or comprehensive, the project was invitational. We used the objects we collected and the stories we derived from them to invite visitors and other potential exhibitors into a process of discovery that had only just begun. Clearly stated on the final text panel of the exhibit and repeated in the exhibit catalogue, our message remains the same. Our project is intended to spark further discoveries and reflections that advance the ongoing work of making disability history *public* history.

Deliberations and turning points

In this next section, we tease out various strands of labor whereby the authors engaged with the making of *Out from Under*. In the following exchanges, we break the 'curatorial we', used in the chapter thus far, in favour of singular voices. While creating an exhibit required tremendous collaboration from all of its participants, each also has their own story.

Designing (Kathryn)

By July 2007, our project had reached a point where participants from the exhibiting course were ready to present their work to the student body at the School's annual Summer Institute. Each tableau occupied its own table; each told a complete and complex story; each had a unique visual style that expressed its presenter's flair for display. This pilot presentation – not yet titled – excited audience members with both its historical assemblage and its method of working from objects. Some still prefer the immediacy and vitality of this iteration to those more polished versions that came later. As people mingled and chatted after the event, someone new circulated amongst them: drifting from table to table with notebook in hand was a design consultant named Debbie Adams.

Debbie was present because, as curators, we had reached a crucial turning point with our work. The course was over; our participants were drifting away to embrace the brief glow of summer. With a scant three months remaining before our Abilities Arts opening, the exhibit was still uncomfortably reminiscent of a high school science fair. We knew that an amateur production would not be taken seriously. Given that disabled people have long been treated as second-class citizens, we firmly believed that nothing less than a top-quality production would suffice. From a design perspective, Debbie's major concern was to create a cohesive aesthetic for the exhibit, an instant signal to visitors that all of the installations belonged to the same storyline. She insisted that each installation revolve around a single object rather than the clusters that some had become. She pressed us to clarify the primary message that each would contribute to the whole. I bounced back and forth between designer and participants until we reached agreement over what to keep, what to remove and what might be added to each display.

It was a significant transition, and not always comfortable. On the one hand, participants lost a measure of control over their work; on the other, their installations were enhanced in useful and exciting ways. The process ended well for two reasons. While she sharpened the work done by participants, our design consultant respected and did not dislodge it. Participants retained the final say, even as they were pressed to find the critical essence of their installations.

The summer passed in a blur. My days were organized around email and telephone exchanges with Debbie and tasks arising from our formidable checklist, repeatedly revised as we inched towards the deadline. We plotted the exhibitors on a grid, charting everything that had to be assembled to complete each installation. Having 'de-cluttered' the project, Debbie now wanted to enhance its core objects by adding supporting materials: photos, archival documents, lists, letters, stickers and clippings, for example. These had to be collected afresh, or manufactured.

While crafting a design that was sophisticated and flexible, Debbie also researched a display system to suit our needs. Her choice was comprised of aluminum rods and connectors, magnetic joints and light-weight metal trays that would be easy to assemble: 'like giant tinker toys', she reassured. Indeed, we assembled it ourselves the first time out. Taken with its practicality, we did not expect the pedagogical 'lift' the system gave to our modest collection. The effervescence of the tubular structure – its bird-like bones – allowed viewers to perceive and absorb the weighty social chronicle that it carried.

Crystallizing (Catherine)

As the enthusiasms of our intensive sessions built, a mosaic of contributor voices and styles found expression in titles for each of the thematic installations that comprised the whole. Some titles were ironic, while others were bittersweet. 'It's a Miracle!' wryly chided the hucksters of cure. Another title, 'Great Expectations', spoke wistfully of engagement in reform campaigns that yielded only symbolic results. Some were evocative, while others were declaratory. 'They Fed and Clothed Each Other' summoned the spirit of solidarity among asylum inmate-labourers. 'A Billboard is a Site of Struggle' drew attention to activist utterings pinned to workplace corkboards. Some were polemic, while others were rhetorical. 'No Voices, No Choices' challenged the clothing practices of institutions where residents' individuality was stifled. 'What's in a Name?' traced the eugenic history of medical categories carried forward into today's language of taunt and insult.

But would the intended ironies bound up in these cleverly constructed titles translate beyond 'insider' circles to viewers unfamiliar with disability history (and politics)? Would these titles beckon audiences accustomed to histories spoken in 'neutral' tones? Would they soothe where they sought to unsettle? Were they adequately calibrated for a liberal reader, a militant reader, a literal reader, a bigot? Did they leave enough, or too much, of the interpretive work for audience members to do for themselves?

Our design consultant helped us to appreciate the complexity embedded in these titles and impressed upon us the need for a harmonious, unified approach. Ever-vigilant to the perils of too much creativity, especially with an exhibition of such diverse perspectives, emotions and eras, she urged a re-thinking, a higher-level curatorial venture in titling. On a conference call at summer's end, we brainstormed. It seemed an impossible task. Paring down the titles we had might well reduce the chaos factor, but at what cost? Bland or overly simplistic would be intolerable. We resisted sacrificing the singularity of these assembled histories, and the powerful agency of their origins. As we contemplated how to generate some sense of movement and purpose in our titles we stumbled upon the possibility of single action words. A list of present participles began to emerge: 'Fixing', 'Aspiring', 'Labouring', 'Struggling', 'Dressing', 'Naming'. One by one, we warmed to the idea. 'Breathing' cinched the deal. An installation featuring a cuirass (a 1950s innovation in portable ventilator technology) had presented a particular challenge of focus. Originally titled 'Maverick Minister on the Move', this installation profiled the intrepid volunteerism of a pastor-turned-repair-mechanic who determined that his own daughter – and the sons and daughters of every community visited by polio – should live securely at home. The contributors, one of whom was herself a ventilator-user with deep activist credentials, were clear on the need for a message of liberation. But we worried that the overlays of benevolent service that audiences would likely bring to this narrative could eclipse the disability perspective necessary to understand the installation in the way that we intended. 'Helping' was not the story here. The revolutionary act of *breathing* was the story, supported by threads of resistance, ingenuity, and alliance. 'Breathing' was everything we could wish for in a title: simplicity paired with sub-version, translating the everyday act of respiration as defiant and autonomous. The text crafted to accompany the installation would arc back to the title, leaving no room for misinterpretation:

> This installation honors the man, the movement he nurtured and each and every breath of freedom and flourishing in Independent Living.

Musing (Phaedra)

The 14 separate exhibitors involved in creating *Out from Under* brought a diverse range of identities, allegiances and interests to the project. I contributed as an exhibitor and offer here my reflections on the experience as a museologist and museum professional, with activist experience. For some time before learning about the project, I had been researching a collection of archival photographs documenting a 1924 exhibition on mental health and early psychiatry in Canada. The question of how one might interpret their staged and offensively labelled images to contemporary museum audiences stymied me. Ethical concerns raised by the photos included: How might they be thoughtfully used today to address our history of discrimination against disability? The standards of care have changed and the young patients depicted would not be similarly photographed today; can their right to privacy be balanced with the desire to show how their condition was framed and labelled in 1924? Does the opportunity to challenge discrimination, afforded by displaying the images, outweigh the risk of offending viewers?

This project was a fortuitous opportunity for my study. Neither collections-based research nor 'best practice' in museum representation could resolve my questions. Conducting exhibit development in this unique classroom setting, I was not limited by conventional museum interpretation expectations, such as a focus on authenticity and provenance. The approach of *Out from Under* liberated my interpretation, allowing me to experiment with a shift from a material history analysis to arts-informed inquiry. I was able to address the ethical dilemma by transforming the original artifact into an artifact-cum-artwork.

Setting out with an exhibit agenda – to present disability history as an activist intervention – rather than an interpretive plan facilitated my process. As a group conceptualizing art installations, we did not have to debate and come to consensus on a grand narrative of disability history to which we would each subscribe in our work; we could focus on the development of our own piece, independent of the others. Given the huge diversity of issues, moments and interpretations in Canadian disability history that could be presented, this avoided possible conflicts about priorities and privileging of some topics over others.

I took the photograph of a poster as my object, and selected the bottom right image as the detail I would use. The girl in this image returns your gaze and asserts her social being. Her anonymous portrait's inscription is now an inflammatory label that reads 'Moron (high grade feeble-minded)'. Drawing on my experience and research in museum learning, I knew that the sensational nature of the poster demanded purposeful engagement with the viewer in order to stimulate self-reflection. Reproducing the image of the girl onto a mirror, I decided, would inscribe the viewer in the presentation, causing (at least) a literal reflection and hopefully a deeper intellectual response. My concern for purposeful display through viewer engagement was addressed by the same measure that addressed concern for the girl's privacy: with a cut out, reminiscent of the 'black box' treatment in later medical photos. While simply covering her eyes would have dehumanized her, when seeing our own eyes in her face, we cannot help but identify with the girl's ghostly image overlaid on the mirror.

With the portrait now reframed and transformed, the poster's antique medical terms still required viewer reflection. How could I keep the viewer from turning away from the emotionally charged terms – idiocy, imbecility, moron – and instead prompt thinking about how medical labels and negative attitudes towards disability have colluded over time to become colloquial slurs, or 'bad names'? I attempted a flip-book layering of chronologically labelled images, envisioning time-lapsed projections, to demonstrate shifts over time in medical terminology related to intellectual disability. My display text read:

> What's in a Name?
>   Over the last century, the medical terms for intellectual dis-
> abilities have changed a lot.
>   How would you feel if you were called one of the names used in
> the pictures here?

The resulting prototype offered an interactive, but distracting, experience. Intent on a constructivist display (Hein 1998) employing experiential learning, I subsequently opted simply to use the mirror and add the list of 'names' under a re-draft of the above text. I submitted my mirror, label text and a supplementary artist's statement for the Abilities Arts Festival exhibition, assuming my art installation would remain as I had created it.

In the months leading to the Festival, a designer was hired and the decision made to unify the displays textually and visually. Being minimal, it was decided that my display needed more content, to blend in. Although I resisted it, the archival image I had drawn from was added to the display. I was told some text from my artist statement would also be added. Shortly before the opening I was emailed the revisions – the leading question had been replaced with a text focused on the poster and sarcastic in tone. While I understood the intention behind the changes, the use of irony and the overshadowing of the engagement I had tried to create were frustrating. Although production had begun, a last-minute addition of the text I had submitted was made, in small font under the mirror.

The display bears my name, but through design and curatorial choices, the final version is really a hybrid of two displays with different genres. In particular, the scale and prominence of the sensational poster competes visually and affectively with the mirror. The added text and image shift the display away from a history-informed art piece to artful social history; rather than experiencing ideas through a constructivist engagement, the display is shifted to achieve a didactic and expository mode of communication (Hein 1998). Showing the poster reintroduces ethical dilemmas I had chosen to avoid. This shift served the goals of exposing disability history and developing an overall aesthetic for the show, but I wonder if the compromise limits the transformative potential I had hoped to achieve in the 'Naming' installation?

Negotiating (Melanie)

In October 2007 *Out from Under* premiered at the Abilities Arts Festival where it was extraordinarily well received. By working our networks, we made sure that two highly placed members of the Royal Ontario Museum were in attendance: one was a senior manager with responsibility for exhibits, the other was a museum Trustee named Christine Karcza. A corporate champion for accessibility and a woman with a disability, Christine was already lobbying on our behalf. Our negotiations started right there on the exhibit floor. Reading the texts, the exhibit manager searched for balance in the presentation – her preferred style of museum interpretation – encountering, instead, an unequivocal point of view. She had misgivings. How might a residential worker react to the critique of her workplace depicted in 'Dressing'? Our response – that it had been written by someone who had worked in an institutional facility for many years – seemed only marginally reassuring. Yet, the exhibit manager was unable to resist the exhibit's striking design. If a balanced perspective was elusive, the high-quality presentation and visual appeal of *Out from Under* was seductive. Shortly after this key encounter, we were invited to mount a 12-week run at the ROM.

A number of intersecting dynamics kindled that invitation. It came at a transitional moment when the ROM was, in the words of its CEO William Thorsell, 'creating a radical re-imagination of architecture, function and public space'. He spoke of its role as 'the new Agora, the common space, the new city square' (Thorsell 2007). Daniel Libeskind's artful Crystal had opened a new front door to the ROM, provoking animated public conversation about the museum's engagement with the city. For Christine Karcza, the time was ripe for our exhibit. She recognized it as the perfect vehicle to drive her activist message home to the Board of Trustees. And she had in her corner the newly appointed President of the ROM's Board of Governors, a one-time provincial government minister on whose watch the landmark Accessibility for Ontarians with Disabilities Act (2005) became law; a woman who recognized that welcoming the exhibit and its point of view could also be part of her legacy. Such was the terrain from which the invitation arose to bring *Out from Under* inside. But there were material forces, too. Compelled by the expense of the ROM's reinvention in the face of declining government operating support, the museum was searching for bigger crowds and, of course, tickets at the door. In *Out from Under* they began to envision a new market.

Our adventure in search of history called upon negotiating skills at many turns: as teachers we invited our students to negotiate the politics of display; as an academic collective we negotiated the concept of history itself; and as disability studies scholars we negotiated the very use of the word 'activist'. However deftly we may have maneuvered the various twists and turns to this point, the negotiating skills required to carry out the next phase of work – to see the exhibit displayed in one of Canada's foremost cultural institutions – were by far the most complicated and taxing. I likened the relationship to planning a wedding – with the ROM as our prospective in-laws. 'How do WE stay in charge?' I demanded in a marginal note to myself after only our second meeting with museum staff.

At the root of this tension was an encounter between two very different cultures. On the one hand was the enduring, long-standing and permanent reality of Canada's oldest and most established museum; on the other were the elastic, dynamic and gritty worlds of disability. Negotiating the ground between them permeated every arrangement we made with the ROM. Indeed, the museum's well established practices set us up for marginalization, broken promises and inequities on a number of fronts – from exhibit space to opening ceremonies to communications strategies.

Our first adventure was a narrow escape from cramped quarters. Initially, we were offered a small room with three doors that attracted a steady traffic flow of ROM employees. Disappointed, we began the process of shrinking our layout, but voiced concerns about accessibility. Later on the ROM fully appreciated the implications of this potential downsizing. Eager to showcase their accessibility agenda, the critical question suddenly dawned on them: How would VIPs comfortably view the exhibit in that tiny space on opening night? Concerned they would be severely criticized for a lack of accessibility, they found an alternative – overnight. If we delayed the opening by two months we could have the more generous 'west wing'. We were grateful. We needed the time. And they saved themselves considerable embarrassment.

Having won that battle, we proceeded towards a grand opening. The invitation to bring the exhibit into the ROM had come with an explicit promise of an evening celebration. Deep into planning, however, we were confronted with a last-minute proposal to replace the much-anticipated evening gala with a scaled down mid-day coffee party. Was it because we were a community exhibit (not a blockbuster), a disability group (not prospective donors) that the promise of a gala could be so easily rescinded? If the word 'negotiate' is large enough to contain within it elements of protest, anger, disappointment and betrayal – all this we expressed to our ROM partners. A reversal of fortune was ultimately assisted by a successful approach to our University president who saw the strategic importance of the gala and offered to share the costs.

Designing the guest list was another contested arena. Both sides agreed to submit an equal number of names. But almost immediately this 50–50 split did not feel equitable. The museum's list included prominent citizens and members of boards and committees who frequently receive invitations to openings and decline a good many. On the community/university side, invitations of this sort were rare and eagerly sought after. We tried but failed to get a larger share. It was only when the electronic invitation was circulated that we saw our chance and seized it, forwarding it on in snowball fashion to swell our numbers and fill the gallery to capacity. RSVPs flooded into the Museum's central booking system from guests whose names appeared on no list at all – our allies and friends who were determined to be part of this historic moment.

On opening night, the gala welcomed 350 people, many from the disability community, who rolled up on the red carpet and took the Crystal elevator to the third floor where they were greeted like royalty. It was a ritzy event with a menu that boasted an 'upscale take' on some old classics, all passed around by servers. At our behest attention was paid to allergies and food ingredients, to café tables and bars at various heights and to hors d'oeuvres requiring minimal dexterity. As the celebration soared, only a handful of us knew that this extraordinary evening came perilously close to not happening.

Arriving (Catherine)

Linton (1998: 3) describes one effect of disabled people's arrival in the public commons as 'upping the ante on the demands for a truly inclusive society'. Linton's use of a betting metaphor captures the sense in which our own efforts represented a high-stakes gamble. Our very presence at the museum would mobilize the expectations of an astute and politicized disability community. We welcomed the leverage that such expectations afforded to a larger activist project – the project of 'making way' for disability in bastions of mainstream culture. But at the same time, we understood that falling short of an exemplary standard for accessibility would have dire consequences.

We attended to the details of the exhibit's features with ambition and fervour. All texts were produced in Braille, large print and audio formats. Supplementary verbal descriptions of the exhibit's visual elements were prepared precisely and evocatively, in a way that mirrored the tone and content of each installation.[4] Video and audio podcasts of American Sign Language (ASL) and visual descriptive components were produced for online distribution via social networking sites. Replica artifacts had been procured by contributors and would be available for tactile examination by audience members with visual impairments. Supplementary programming would include a major public lecture on 'Blindness at the Museum' by international author and scholar Georgina Kleege[5] – followed by a live staged reading of exhibit descriptions and texts. Our ASL translation represented a breakthrough in Deaf Cultural content: the interpreters were themselves culturally Deaf, their translation achieving a level of depth and fluency impossible in the signed English that is customary for such productions.[6]

209

But our ambitions were soon caught up in the slow grind of an enterprise less nimble than our small band of freewheeling, 'can-do' collaborators. Weeks passed before the museum could provide a mounted flat screen monitor for our ASL video in an ante-room adjacent to – but not inside – the exhibit. Wall-mounted boxes for Braille materials took a heartbreakingly long time to appear, and once installed, their contents were easily carried off and could not be promptly restocked. Touch table displays could not be secured and were therefore locked away, brought out only when volunteers were present to supervise their handling; the scheduling of these tactile opportunities remained sporadic and mostly inscrutable to potential users. Exhibit-specific training of volunteers was overlooked until a chance encounter with one of the exhibit curators made such training an urgent concern.[7] Although exhibit text and interpretation was made available via podcasts, many audience members were unaccustomed to downloading these onto their own digital audio players before visiting the museum, and of the two units available for loan at the museum information desk, one that disappeared early in the exhibit's run was never replaced. Many other visitors were unfamiliar with digital technologies altogether, and unable for various reasons to operate them successfully to access the exhibit text; many Deaf visitors did not own devices capable of playing the ASL and other video interpretation we had developed. Visitors with cognitive and learning impairments experienced the exhibit as 'textually dense' and 'too difficult to penetrate without significant support' (Ignagni and Abbas 2008: 90; Patterson *et al.* 2008: 98–100).

Despite these difficulties, the presentation of *Out from Under* at the Royal Ontario Museum offered us a brief moment at the summit of our ambitions for entry into public culture. As gala guests poured in to the foyer of the steel and glass ROM Crystal – an extraordinary and dramatic 10-storey structure – they encountered a panoramic and utterly arresting projection on a massive overhead wall. There, in the soundless eloquence of American Sign Language, the première screening of our translation video privileged Deaf visitors with a sneak preview of what was to come and signalled to all, in proportions equal to the moment, a clear triumph of upstart entry into public culture. Arriving, evidently, is merely where the journey begins.

Rising

To conclude, we return you to the exhibit's opening gala, a scene that Melanie set with her delicious back story. This was our finest hour. As the champagne flowed, in our finale for the formal ceremony, Christine and Catherine riffed through a kind of syncopated spoken-word anthem, free-associating from the phrases 'We remember', 'We celebrate' and 'We welcome'. With a sly grin, Catherine called out, 'Tonight, we remember that we belong, and that *belonging looks good on us.*'

Intended as radical incantation, the words affirmed the pride and place of an uppity rabble. We had arrived in significant number, and our presence was unmistakably consequential. There was much in this occasion to evoke Simi Linton's now-classic narration of a community having summoned 'the temerity to emerge':

> We have come out not with brown woolen lap robes over our withered legs or dark glasses over our pale eyes but in shorts and sandals, in overalls and business suits, dressed for play and work – straightforward, unmasked, and unapologetic. We are, as Crosby, Stills, and Nash told their Woodstock audience, letting our 'freak flag fly'. ... We may drool, hear voices, speak in staccato syllables, wear catheters to collect our urine, or live with a compromised immune system ... We have found one another and found a voice to express not despair at our fate but outrage at our social positioning.
> (Linton 1998: 3–4).

Together, we were celebrating not so much the opening of an exhibit, as the rise of a body politic.

Notes

1 Our acknowledgement to Julie Young (2008) for the inspiration provided by her chapter title.
2 *Out from Under* was created by 14 exhibitors working with 13 objects. They are: Terry Poirier, Ruth Ruth Stackhouse, Phaedra Livingstone, Sandra Phillips, Carrie Fyfe, Ryan Hutchins, Sarah May Glyn Williams, Audrey King, Karen Yoshida, Cindy Mitchell, Kim Wrigley Archer, Christine Brown, Jihan Abbas and Jim Derksen.
3 The organizational vehicle we used for this work is the Ryerson-RBC Institute for Disability Studies Research and Education. The Institute's contributions in cultivating both opportunity and audience for disability arts and culture are documented at www.ryerson.ca/ds/activism/perfomance.
4 Christine Brown, contributor of the installation titled 'Labouring', authored a complete visual description of the exhibit, after consultation with blind stakeholders and fellow contributors. David Reville, faculty member at the School of Disability Studies, subsequently performed an audio recording of these texts for CD and podcast distribution.
5 Presented at the Royal Ontario Museum, 24 May 2008.
6 ASL interpretation by Donovan Cooper and Giulio Schincariol; Project coordination by Penny Schincariol with Gus Mancini, consultant.
7 On a chance visit to the exhibit, Kathryn encountered a volunteer docent reinterpreting an installation that profiled asylum practices of unpaid patient labour. 'Notice that they lived to be quite old', he intoned. 'They had food and a roof over their heads ... They were probably happier in the asylum than they would have been on the street.' Alarmed by his insistence upon a narrative of protective benevolence that covered over the exploitation of these women's labours, we (successfully) urged his reassignment to another area of the museum.

References

Abbas, J., Church, K., Frazee, C. and Panitch, M. (2004) *Lights ... Camera ... Attitude! Introducing Disability Arts and Culture*, Occasional Paper, Ryerson-RBC Institute for Disability Studies Research and Education, Ryerson University. Online. Available www.ryerson.ca/ds/research (accessed 6 June 2009).

Church, K. (2008) 'Exhibiting as inquiry: Travels of an accidental curator', in A. Cole and J. G. Knowles (eds), *Handbook of the Arts in Qualitative Social Science Research,* Thousand Oaks, CA: Sage, pp. 55–70.

Davis, L. (2002) *Bending Over Backwards: Disability, Dismodernism & Other Difficult Positions*, New York: New York University Press.

Dodd, J., Sandell, R., Jolly, D. and Jones, C. (2008) *Rethinking Disability Representation in Museums and Galleries*, Research Centre for Museums and Galleries (RCMG), Leicester: University of Leicester.

Garland-Thomson, R. (2006) 'Ways of staring', *Journal of Visual Culture,* 5(2): 173–92.

Hein, G. (1998) *Learning in the Museum*, London: Routledge.

Ignagni, E. and Abbas, J. (2008) 'Media and messages: Exploring old and new worlds of developmental disability and the media', *Journal on Developmental Disabilities*, 14(3): 86-92. Available online: http://www.oadd.org/dics/JoDD 14-3 Ignagni.pdf.

Kohler Riessman, C. (2002) 'Analysis of personal narratives' in J. Gubrium and J. Holstein (eds), *Handbook of Interview Research: Context and Method,* Thousand Oaks, CA: Sage, pp. 695–710.

Linton, S. (1998) *Claiming Disability: Knowledge and Identity*, New York: SUNY Press.

Panitch, M. (2008) *Disability, Mothers and Organization: Accidental Activists*, New York: Routledge.

Panitch, M. and Yoshida, K. (2008) 'Out from Under: making disability history visible', Inaugural Conference on *Disability History: Theory and Practice*, San Francisco State University, California, August 2008.

Patterson, J., Vo, T. and The Compass Youth (2008) 'Out from Under: disability, history and things to remember', *Journal on Developmental Disabilities*, 14(3): 98–100.

Rieser, R. (2004) *Disabling Imagery*, London: British Film Institute, pp. 48–80.

Roman, L. and Frazee, C. (eds) (2009) 'The unruly salon', *Review of Disability Studies,* Special Forum Issue, 5(1).

Oliver, M. (1990) *The Politics of Disablement*, London: Macmillan.

Shakespeare, T. (2000) *Help*, Birmingham: Venture Press, pp. 1–20.

Smith, D. (1987) *The Everyday World as Problematic: A Feminist Sociology*, Toronto, ON: University of Toronto Press.

—— (2005) *Institutional Ethnography: A Sociology for People,* Lanham, MD: AltaMira.

Thorsell, W. (2007) 'The museum as the public agora', Address to the Empire Club, Toronto, 3 May 2007.

Thomas, C. (2007) *Sociologies of Disabilities and Illness: Contested Ideas in Disability Studies and Medical Sociology,* Basingstoke: Palgrave Macmillan.

Young, J. (2008) 'Looking back: A brief history of everything', in G. Hunt, G. Rayside and D. Rayside (eds), *Equity, Diversity, and Canadian Labour,* Toronto: University of Toronto Press.

15

TRANSFORMING PRACTICE

Disability perspectives and the museum

Shari Rosenstein Werb and Tari Hartman Squire

Our society and their [Nazi] society starts with the notion that people
like me are not the way people should be. We are not the kind of
people who are wanted and who are valued.[1]
(Harriet McBryde Johnson, disability rights activist and author)

The United States Holocaust Memorial Museum in Washington DC serves
to both educate the public about the Holocaust and honour the memory of
all of the victims. It strives to balance the enormous archive of historical
content that was primarily created and documented by the perpetrators with
the perspectives of the victims, survivors, rescuers, resistors and others whose
voices were silenced at the time.

When the museum opened in 1993, the Nazi persecution of people with
disabilities was not as widely known as it is today. The permanent exhibition
included a section about the 'Science of Race' that incorporated a brief discussion of eugenics and the sterilization of 'hereditarily defective' persons as
well as a section about the 'Murder of the Handicapped'. (The Museum used
the word 'handicapped' to reflect the policy and wording of the Nazi era,
rather than a term acceptable by contemporary standards.) As part of a series
of materials exploring the victims of Nazi persecution, the museum also
produced and distributed at the information desk, a booklet about the sterilization and murder of people with disabilities. In 2004, the museum further explored this history through the temporary exhibition, *Deadly Medicine:
Creating the Master Race*, which focused on the role of scientists and medical
professionals in legitimizing racial eugenics policies that led first to the
sterilization, then to the murder of German citizens with disabilities and
ultimately to the attempted destruction of all Jews.

This chapter explores the impact, on both staff and visitors, when the museum
invited author, attorney and disability rights activist, Harriet McBryde
Johnson, to share her unique observations and insights at a public event in

213

2006, presented in conjunction with the temporary exhibition, entitled *Legitimizing the Unthinkable: A Disability Rights Perspective on Nazi Medicine.*[2]

After outlining the structure and focus of *Deadly Medicine*, we relate how the exhibition provoked and informed contemporary discussions about public policy and bioethics. We next discuss the extensive preparations by the museum in anticipation of Ms Johnson's participation in the programme. These included a commitment to making the programme fully accessible to patrons with disabilities; hiring a disability strategic marketing, development and accessibility consultant; conducting an institution-wide audit of the museum's accessibility; renewing its relationship with national disability community leaders; and extending the event's reach through its website and online conversation board.

Highlighting Ms Johnson's important contribution to the programme, this chapter then relates how lessons learned and relationships developed for *Legitimizing the Unthinkable* were utilized in subsequent museum programmes and resources – including the travelling *Deadly Medicine* exhibition – and how museum staff continue to have productive conversations about inclusive and accessible programming and finding ways to incorporate Universal Design principles[3] into the museum's ongoing work and community outreach.

We dedicate this chapter to Harriet McBryde Johnson (Figure 15.1) who died unexpectedly on 4 June 2008. Her untimely death is a great loss. In

Figure 15.1 Harriet McBryde Johnson. (Photo by E. David Luria Photography)

this chapter we quote extensively from both her interviews and writings to reflect the profound importance of her thinking on the museum. Her legacy, her insights, humour and impact live on to empower all of us to keep fighting for social justice.

Exhibition as provocateur

The British scientist Francis Galton, who coined the term 'eugenics' in 1883, used it to promote the idea of improving the human race by eliminating 'undesirables' (people believed to have genetic defects or otherwise undesirable traits) and multiplying the 'desirables' by encouraging reproduction among those believed to have desirable, inheritable traits (Kevles 2004: 41).

In *Deadly Medicine: Creating the Master Race*, curator Susan Bachrach used 210 artifacts, 235 photographs, survivor testimonies and films, to show how Nazi scientists and medical professionals helped legitimize the racial eugenics policies that led to the mass sterilization and murder of people with disabilities, and ultimately the near annihilation of European Jewry. The exhibition included such items as a life-size transparent male figure produced in 1930 as an icon for the health of the 'national body', a wheelchair (c. 1920) from a German institution, and medical instruments of the type used in the Nazi sterilization programme. In the exhibition, 'Inspired and guided always by historical photographs and films, [designer, David] Layman, grouped objects, graphics, and audio-visual programs at strategic points along the visitor path into environments which evoked, variously, a laboratory, doctor's office, operating room, "euthanasia" facility, and concentration camp' (Bachrach 2007: 21).

The exhibition consisted of three sections: *Science as Salvation: Weimar Eugenics, 1919–1933*; *The Biological State: Nazi Racial Hygiene, 1933–1939*; and *Final Solutions: Murderous Racial Hygiene, 1939–1945*. The museum's website[4] provides an overview of the exhibition, with historical photographs, images of artifacts and explanations by the exhibition's curator. The first section of the exhibition provides the historical backdrop of the Nazi eugenics programme, highlighting the influence of racial hygiene or eugenics on public policy, on public health education and on government-funded research. During this time supporters of eugenics put forward the view that modern developments in medicine and costly welfare programmes were interfering with Charles Darwin's theory of natural selection, by keeping the 'unfit' alive and enabling them to reproduce and multiply (Kuntz and Bachrach 2004).

The next section of the exhibition describes the Nazi Racial Hygiene programme and how it was implemented in the earlier years. State policy was informed by a politically extreme, anti-Semitic variation of eugenics. In order to eliminate what were considered to be biologically threatening genes from the population and to strengthen the 'national body', public health measures were put into place to control reproduction and marriage (ibid.).

The last section reveals how the Nazis took the programme to murderous conclusions. The Nazis used the Second World War as both a cover and an excuse for killing 'undesirables' who were seen as 'burdens on national resources'. Hitler authorized 'mercy deaths' for people judged 'incurable'. Hundreds of asylum directors, paediatricians, psychiatrists, family doctors and nurses came to support the murders 'for the good of the Fatherland' (ibid.).

Between January 1940 and August 1941, more than 70,000 Germans institutionalized because of mental illness or other disabilities were brought to one of six centres in Germany and Austria and were asphyxiated in gas chambers by carbon monoxide. After growing awareness of the killings created public unease and a few individual church leaders spoke out, Hitler halted the gassing programme. However, euthanasia murders continued as part of medical practice. Doctors and nurses used starvation diets and overdoses of medication to kill patients in hospitals and mental institutions across the Reich. From 1939 to 1945, an estimated 200,000 people with disabilities and others were killed in the various euthanasia programmes (ibid.).

After the war, only a very few of the biomedical experts who helped to implement and legitimize Nazi racial hygiene policies were ever indicted or held accountable – legally or otherwise – for their actions. Many continued their professional careers with their integrity and reputations unscathed.

The *Deadly Medicine* exhibition was part of the museum's ongoing effort to explore the historical significance of how, during the Holocaust, professionals in a position of public trust – whose very job was to protect individuals and the broader society – instead collaborated in the implementation of the Nazis' discriminatory and murderous policies directed at vulnerable populations. For ten years prior to the exhibition, the museum had been exploring Holocaust history in workshops designed to highlight ethical responsibility with law enforcement professionals, judges and military service members. With this new exhibition, the museum now had the opportunity to engage the medical, scientific and disability communities in similar, and highly significant discussions.

Making connections

Since the main exhibitions at the museum are driven by historical narrative, the curators and historians focus the exhibition content on the historical record of the period leading up to, during and just following the Nazi era, without making any overt contemporary connections between past and present. This interpretive approach is designed to allow members of the public to draw their own meaning, conclusions and connections.

Deadly Medicine's provocative content provided many opportunities for visitors to make contemporary connections and explore their own sense of ethical responsibility. As part of the preparation for the museum's public programmes, bioethicists, medical professionals, and scientists were invited to preview the exhibition and share their perspectives. While walking through the first part of the exhibition, several of these guests found themselves sympathizing with some of the early choices and decisions made by professionals during the Nazi era. Sherwin Nuland, for example, Professor of Medicine at Yale University and the best-selling author of *How We Die*, visited the exhibition and, in his review for *The New Republic*, wrote:

> To my startled dismay, I found myself understanding why so much of the German medical establishment acted as it did. I realized that, given the circumstances, I might have done the same ... What we learn from history comes far less in studying the events than in the recognition of human motivation – and the eternal nature of human frailty.
>
> (2004: 32)

For the visiting public, the exhibition elicited a wide range of emotions, raised many questions and stimulated conversations, even between strangers. To capture these reactions, comment books were placed in the exhibition space, enabling visitors to share impressions, communicate links to contemporary issues, and identify questions the exhibition raised. Comment books revealed visitors were asking hard questions about ethics and values, and applying the new knowledge they had gleaned from the exhibition to their consideration of current public policy issues.

At the time the exhibition opened, media headlines focused on the highly politicized case of Terri Schiavo, a 41-year-old woman with brain damage who became the centrepiece of a national disability rights vs. right-to-life/death battle. One visitor wrote:

> There is a very gradual and evil progress toward the worst crimes ever committed. WE must always remember what happened and never, ever let this happen again. Is Terri Schiavo's situation an early sign?

Further visitor comments raised yet more questions about the relations between disability, science and medicine today.

> Disabled people in America today still often have a difficult time and are not always well treated by government programs and agencies which are supposed to be there to help, but often don't. Our country seems to be losing its grasp on ethics in the health care and medical fields.
>
> Modern debates such as stem cell research, genetic modification of plants, and cloning. Without proper control, where will all this 'modern' research lead? I think we need to take/learn lessons from what the Nazis did and what we are doing today.

It raises questions about separation of science and government in our separated state of religion and government.

A forum for debate

To complement the exhibition, the museum hosted discussions with professionals from the medical, science and disability communities and the public. Leading thinkers in medical ethics, social science and public policy were invited to tour the exhibition, and then participate in a public interview series, entitled *Insights*, to discuss the implications of the history portrayed in the exhibition for contemporary bioethics and public policy issues. *Insights* participants included the aforementioned Dr Sherwin Nuland; Dr Leon Kass, Chairman of The President's Council on Bioethics; bioethicists Arthur Caplan and Ruth Faden; cultural critic Leon Wieseltier; and disability rights activist, writer and attorney Harriet McBryde Johnson.

An activist's perspective

The social-science literature suggests that the public in general and physicians in particular, tend to underestimate the quality of life of disabled people, compared with our own assessment of our lives. The case for assisted suicide rests on stereotypes that our lives are inherently so bad that it is entirely rational if we want to die.

(McBryde Johnson 2003a: 50)

Harriet McBryde Johnson was born in 1957 with a congenital neuromuscular disability that later required her to use a wheelchair. She lived most of her life in Charleston, South Carolina and became a lawyer and civil rights advocate focusing on people with disabilities. Her picture on the cover of *The New York Times Magazine* on 16 February 2003, and its caption, 'Should I Have Been Put to Death at Birth? – The Case for My Life' was a media milestone for disability rights activists, and it set in motion a newly-reframed debate among leading thinkers with and without disabilities from coast to coast. The article itself, 'Unspeakable Conversations', described one in a series of confrontations with the ethicist Peter Singer, who argues in favour of euthanasia for people with disabilities such as Ms Johnson. In November 2003, Ms Johnson's second *New York Times Magazine* article, 'The Disability Gulag', described institutions where 'wheelchair people are lined up, obviously stuck where they're placed' while 'a TV blares, watched by no one' (2003b: 59). In the article, she called for a major public policy shift away from the institutionalization of people to publicly-financed home care provided by home and community-based supports.

Based on these articles, museum staff concluded Ms Johnson would complement the range of speakers identified for its *Insights* events series meant to present diverse opinions and perspectives on the contemporary relevance of the history portrayed in the *Deadly Medicine* exhibition. When Ms Johnson was contacted about participating in a programme in connection with the exhibition, she expressed her pleasure that the museum was tackling the experience of people with disabilities during the Holocaust and agreed to participate. She was unable to travel during the cold winter months and so the programme was scheduled for the following spring.

Shaping the programme

In 2004, co-author Werb, as part of her public programming research, visited Hartheim Castle in Linz, Austria. This was one of the Nazi euthanasia programme sites and 60 years later it was dedicated as a memorial to the victims who were murdered because of their disabilities. Between 1940 and 1944, some 30,000 people classified as 'unworthy' by the Nazis were murdered in Hartheim Castle. People with mental and physical disabilities were driven to Hartheim on buses, led to be murdered in gas chambers (disguised as showers) and then cremated.

Touring the memorial, Ms Werb was surprised and profoundly affected by a small exhibition entitled *5 Ways to Hartheim*. This exhibition featured the work of a videographer who had traced the routes of five contemporary individuals with different types of disabilities as each tried to get from the town of Linz to Hartheim Castle for a visit to this important museum and memorial. The ironic conclusion was that, for people with disabilities, it is nearly impossible to get to the site via public transport because of physical barriers and lack of public services for people who are deaf, blind, or even those who simply speak a different language.

This exhibition was one of the influences on the development of the Harriet McBryde Johnson programme in several ways. First, it was important to ensure that both museum and online visitors with disabilities could fully participate in the discussion. In addition, it was necessary to bring a human perspective to the history presented in *Deadly Medicine: Creating the Master Race* and challenge the public's perceptions about the 'quality of life' of people with disabilities. Finally, it needed to be provocative, insightful and dynamic so that the conversation would extend beyond the event.

Getting the house in order

With Harriet McBryde Johnson scheduled for the *Insights* programme, museum staff members recognized that they had an opportunity to reach out to all people within the disability community – those with physical, sensory, hidden and intellectual disabilities. In order to ensure that the visit would be as accessible as possible for Harriet McBryde Johnson and other guests, staff members conducted a detailed accessibility inventory of the museum. The process began with an internal audit of services, resources and accessible spaces within which to present the programme and continued with the hiring of a strategic marketing audience expert, Tari Hartman Squire, this chapter's co-author.

The museum facility itself is compliant with the Americans with Disabilities Act (ADA) guidelines in terms of architectural and programmatic accessibility and strives to practise and achieve Universal Design principles. All videos within the museum that contain sound also contain captioning. Trained staff members offer 'guided highlights' tours for visitors who have low vision or who are blind. Vision aids (flashlights, magnifying lenses, monoculars and magnifying glasses) as well as large print and Braille versions of the museum's victim identification cards – companions to the permanent exhibition – are available. Video monitors containing highly graphic visual material are positioned behind 'privacy walls' that are made accessible to wheelchair users for their independent use. There are assistive listening devices for theater programmes, as well as standard and large-print brochures. The museum's Equal Employment Opportunity Office recognizes National Disability Employment Awareness Month in October with staff awareness programmes. However, it became clear during the inventory that some accessibility issues would need to be addressed before the event.

Where to present the programme?

The first major challenge was to find programme space to accommodate the many wheelchair users who might attend the event. The museum's two formal theatre spaces have fixed seating. The larger theatre cannot accommodate more than 12 wheelchair users (assuming they are not seated with a companion or guest) and the smaller theatre accommodates even fewer. The museum's four classrooms, while fully accessible, were not large enough for this event. Because the museum welcomed any number of wheelchair users, staff members considered either creating accommodations in the theatre or identifying an alternative space within the museum to present this programme.

To address this question, the museum developed an internal task force that included its architect, ADA officer, facility manager, special events coordinator, Webmaster, programme developers and accessibility consultant. The task force decided to create a new programme space in a large open passageway, construct a stage with a ramp (with a 12-to-1 ratio on the incline), and simultaneously broadcast the programme in the classrooms and theatre spaces. In addition, large monitors placed throughout the theatre spaces would present live captioning, sign language interpreters and Communication Access Realtime Translation (CART) services to make the event fully accessible to those with disabilities and functional limitations. CART also provided a verbatim transcript that was later added to the museum's website to serve as captions for deaf and hard of hearing online visitors witnessing the programme.

What's in a name?

Finding the right title for the event was an important part of the programme development process and involved a delicate negotiation between Ms Johnson's personal, provocative and direct style and the museum's institutional, historical and reverent approach. Ms Johnson's initial title suggestion was *Kill It! Don't Let It Suffer: A Disability Rights Critique*. For the museum, which also serves as a memorial, this title was deemed too confrontational. The discussion surrounding the programme title went back and forth via email, with several other titles proposed and rejected. In the end, all involved agreed on the title that was eventually used: *Legitimizing the Unthinkable: A Disability Rights Perspective on Nazi Medicine*.

Outreach strategy

In advance of the event, with strategic guidance from the accessibility consultant, the museum organized an 'open house' for national disability leaders from public and private sector entities, foundations and grassroots stakeholder groups. Curators gave participants a private advance tour of the exhibition that later generated a dynamic public policy discussion about how the Nazi eugenics movement had planted the negative attitudinal seeds for contemporary political challenges. The group met museum staff, discussed the exhibition's accessibility features (suggesting that the museum clear paths of travel, tilt artifacts forward in lower glass cases, and add audio components to the visual aspects), gave recommendations to develop outreach and strategic public relations plans and offered to help disseminate invitations to the *Insights* event.

The leaders who attended the 'open house' expressed their understanding of how each of their individual and collective efforts for human rights and equality were shaped and influenced by the events of the Nazi period. They wondered aloud what might have happened to them and each other if they had lived during that era. The event took on the climate of a 'think tank' with disability leaders in the middle of the room, surrounded by staff members along the perimeter, representing nearly every aspect of the museum's activity – education, special events, external affairs, exhibitions (including the curator of *Deadly Medicine*), engineers, donor relations, oral history, volunteers, public relations, advertising, outreach technology staff, and the museum director. The dialogue that took place that day and the insights that were shared had a profound impact on staff. The disability rights leaders were generous with their expertise, recommendations and guidance; they acted both as ambassadors *for*, and counsellors *to*, the museum.

Following the open house day, preparations continued. One-on-one training was conducted for key staff, including Dr Joan Ringelheim, the museum's then Director of Oral History, who would conduct the interview with Ms Johnson. Customized disability awareness training was presented the day before the programme to volunteers and event staff. Training covered topics such as appropriate language, etiquette and general information about types of disabilities.

9 March 2006

On the evening of 9 March 2006, more than 200 people with and without disabilities, many of whom were disability community leaders, arrived at the museum to tour *Deadly Medicine*. Dr Joan Ringelheim subsequently conducted the 60-minute interview, and began by sharing a personal reflection from her visit to Auschwitz in 1989:

> The room that surprised me the most was the room with the prostheses. In spite of all my studying, in spite of knowing about euthanasia, I had never thought about all of the people who came to labor camps and killing centers who had prostheses. I don't remember seeing a wheelchair, but I suspect there were wheelchairs there ...

Ms Johnson responded to Dr. Ringelheim's reflections by describing her own initial reactions to the *Deadly Medicine* exhibition:

> There is a wheelchair there that was from a facility for people with epilepsy and I suspect that facility had a lot of people with other brain conditions, probably cerebral palsy, strokes, that often accompany epilepsy, and so this wheelchair may have been used by one of the folks with cerebral palsy, the crowd I run with. And when I saw this chair, my first surprising reaction was, 'what a cool chair!' My friends know that I love vintage wheelchairs. I am sitting in one now.
>
> ... This chair in the exhibit was one of the old pre-war wooden chairs and I actually had sat in chairs like that as a child. I had a loaner that had the recliner feature. And so I looked it over and it had a really unusual suspension system. I couldn't tell whether it had a tilt mechanism or whether they were shock absorbers, but there was something going on in the frame that was different, and it was like, you know, some of that cool German engineering. And that was the thing I wanted to touch.
>
> And then, of course, we have these bonds with our wheelchairs. They are very personal and many of us love our chairs. And I started thinking ... I wonder whose chair it was. And then I thought, wait a minute, it's an institutional chair. It may have bonded with a person for a while. But it probably didn't belong to one owner. And certainly not over its entire history. It would have been many users and it would have been owned by the institution. And then I just desperately wanted to know about all the people who had sat in that

chair and how it came to survive. And, you know, the chair seemed a strange kind of survivor that I wanted to know more about and I had a real hard time not touching it.

Over the course of the interview, Ms Johnson responded to a wide range of topics: her impressions of the exhibition; connections she made between the Nazi era and today's world; disability activism; perspectives on 'curing' disease and the institutionalization of people with disabilities. Throughout the programme, Ms Johnson offered serious, informative and thoughtful responses and communicated with her typical open, friendly, humorous, and engaging style. One particular part of the discussion focused on the attitudes people hold toward those with disabilities and helped explain why Ms Johnson consistently protested the Jerry Lewis Telethon:

> Jerry Lewis once called the disabled children or children with muscular dystrophies 'mistakes who came out wrong'. And that, I think, is pretty exactly the attitude behind *Deadly Medicine* – 'mistakes who came out wrong.' And he would raise a truckload of money to do research, to cure. A lot of their research does also go to genetic counseling and various ways of preventing births of people like me. So that part of it's alive and well. But this whole notion that we are mistakes, that we are not what is wanted, is there. And even if people refrain from rounding you up and gassing you or forcibly sterilizing you, it's a very uncomfortable world to live in, knowing that you're not what people want.

The programme, *Legitimizing the Unthinkable: A Disability Rights Perspective on Nazi Medicine,* had an important impact on the museum staff, the audience, the public, and on Ms Johnson herself. Several days after the event she wrote a letter thanking Ms Werb. In it she wrote, 'How wonderful to find everything done just right, not only for me, but for a beautifully inclusive audience. Beyond that, the Museum deserves lots of praise for linking disability issues to the most fundamental questions for humanity, and for linking the past with today.' A month later, she published an essay which chronicled the programme's impact on her, entitled 'Wheelchair Unbound', which appeared in the *Lives* section of *The New York Times Magazine* on 23 April 2006;

> I'm at the United States Holocaust Memorial Museum in Washington, touring an exhibition: *Deadly Medicine: Creating the Master Race.* Tomorrow evening I will be interviewed onstage by a museum official. In a sense, that will make me a temporary display, an object of interpretation, a body in a wheelchair, a body so pared down and twisted up by a genetic neuromuscular disability that it doesn't need a nearby Nazi to get a reaction. In another sense, I will be an interpreter, talking from experience as a disability rights lawyer and activist.

The exhibit tells of a eugenics movement that sought to apply principles from Darwin and animal husbandry to humans. In Germany, it proceeded step by step from voluntary 'healthy baby' campaigns to forced sterilization and the murder of some 200,000 disabled children and adults.

Looking at the photos of doomed children, I see my old crowd. They could be us. In 'special' schools and camps for children with physical and mental disabilities, we grew up knowing we were a category of person that the world did not want. Most of us had a story of some doctor advising our parents to put us away or to let us die. We owed our survival to parents who had irrationally bonded with us, who held old-fashioned notions of right and wrong. We knew we were lucky and hoped our luck would hold. To increase the odds, we tended to be charming. We developed thick skins. [...]

By the time I roll onto the stage the next night, I've thought a lot about there and here, then and now. When the first question comes, I tell them about my fascination with the wheelchair, and somehow it sounds funny, and laughter fills the room. We shuttle between the tragedy of Germany then to the comedy of here now, from the horror of bureaucratic killing to a funny confession that I, too, tend to stare at disabled people on the street. Before I know it, I'm giving them a real show. [...]

What has come over me? Part of it is surely the tendency to compartmentalize. But there's more. In this room, people with disabilities in thrilling variety make me feel at home. It's like the disability ghetto of my childhood, but so much better. That was a community of exclusion, created by nondisabled people who considered us unfit. This is a community of inclusion. Here people, disabled and not, are gathered by choice.

So many staff members were involved in the development of this programme and afterwards shared their feelings about what they had experienced. The day after the event, one administrative professional stated she 'felt proud of working at an organization that would take the time to create a program such as this one'. Other museum staff members talked about how the programme made them confront their own prejudices about people with disabilities and how Ms Johnson expanded their thinking about 'the value of life.'

Continuing conversations

To extend the reach of this programme, the museum created an online presence, posting the transcribed video on its website, and hosting a public discussion board. An email notice about this online component was sent to all who attended the programme and was advertised on the museum's website. Staff developed questions for the discussion board based on the museum interview with Ms Johnson. The discussion continued from April 2006 to February 2008 and the public used these forums as an opportunity to continue the conversations started at the museum event.

Visitor engagement often revealed that, while the issues were capable of eliciting powerful responses, for most visitors they were rarely straightforward. Responding to one of the questions posed on the discussion board – 'Who should decide what needs a cure?' – one of the respondents, Andrea, wrote:

> I think that it is important for medicine to keep striving to find cures for ALL diseases and disabilities, but not for the traditionally accepted reason. Rather than a desire to see ALL disability cured, I have a desire to see all PEOPLE with disabilities have the opportunity to be cured. I myself would probably not accept a cure for my disability were one to be offered, because I believe it has played a large part in making me who I am, and I am proud of that, but that is no reason why someone else in my situation should not be given that same opportunity; not everyone has my disability or has the acceptance of it that I am fortunate enough to be raised to have. The very IDEA of eugenics makes me sick, and thinking about the Holocaust scares me because I surely would have died for several reasons. I do not condone eugenics, but I certainly support legitimate medical research. In short, every DISEASE or DISABILITY needs a cure, but not every PERSON with these diseases or disabilities needs a cure.

Program offshoots

After the event, the newfound and refreshed inclusion of people with disabilities stimulated the creation of additional accessible programmes including one event in a series called *We Honor and Remember*, focusing on the non-Jewish victims of Nazi persecution. During the month of October, designated as National Disability Employment Awareness Month, the museum presented a full day of programming to honour *Nazi Victims with Disabilities*. This included captioned films and testimonials, speakers and discussions. Subsequently, Museum Historian Dr Patricia Heberer was invited to speak at several national disability gatherings, such as the National Disability Rights Network and American Council of the Blind where she discussed eugenics and the current-day disability rights movement.

When the museum's exhibition department was ready to upgrade video monitors for guests using wheelchairs, staff members who had worked on the Harriet McBryde Johnson programme became involved. Local disability leaders were brought back in to provide counsel on use of language, design, access and other issues. Members of the exhibitions department listened carefully to the voices of people who would be using the video monitors, ultimately strengthening the quality of the product that was offered.

A modified version of the *Deadly Medicine* exhibition was developed to tour, beginning in December 2006. The first destination was Pittsburgh. Building on the success of the museum's 'open house', FISA Foundation (a member of the Disability Funders Network) provided support to conduct outreach to local students with disabilities. The University of Pittsburgh's Associate Dean for Disability Programs, Dr Katherine D. Seelman, presented a public lecture around the social, political and cultural implications of the exhibition in terms of public policy, media images and negative attitudes toward people with disabilities.

The beginning, not the end

The United States Holocaust Memorial Museum's engagement with the world of disability rights proved to be a powerful force for change. Individual and institutional practices were, in many instances, questioned, rethought and ultimately transformed in ways which strengthened the museum's capacity to engage visitors in often challenging, contemporary debates relating to disability. The *Deadly Medicine* exhibition stimulated public conversations about the role of Nazi medical and science professionals in the persecution and murder of people with disabilities. These conversations were explored further when Harriet McBryde Johnson provoked people to think about the value of human life and to confront their pre-conceived ideas about people with disabilities. The museum built an accessible environment that enabled a diverse public to confront these important issues. In doing so, it paid tribute to the memory of a largely neglected Nazi victim group, people with disabilities; and at the same time honoured the lives of people with disabilities today.

Notes

1 Extract from the interview with Harriet McBryde Johnson at the event – *Legitimizing the Unthinkable: A Disability Rights Perspective on Nazi Medicine* – held at the United States Holocaust Memorial Museum on 9 March 2006. See http://www.ushmm.org/museum/publicprograms/programs/insights/2006/.

2 Ms Werb was working at the US Holocaust Memorial Museum during the time the exhibition was on display and the programmes described in this chapter were presented. The views reflected here represent her perspective.

3 Universal Design principles aim to create accessible integrated design solutions for the greatest number of users, in contrast to those which are aimed specifically at people with disabilities or functional limitations, and which can segregate and stigmatize.

4 See http://www.ushmm.org/museum/exhibit/online/deadlymedicine/ for an online version of the exhibition.

References

Bachrach, S. (2007) 'Deadly medicine', *The Public Historian*, 29 (3): 19–32.

Kevles, D. J. (2004) 'International eugenics' in D. Kuntz and S. Bachrach (eds), *Deadly Medicine: Creating the Master Race,* Washington, DC: United States Holocaust Memorial Museum, 41–60.

Kuntz, D. and Bachrach, S. (eds) (2004) *Deadly Medicine: Creating the Master Race*, Washington, DC: United States Holocaust Memorial Museum.

McBryde Johnson, H. (2003a) 'Unspeakable conversations', *The New York Times Magazine,* February 16, p. 50.

—— (2003b) 'The disability gulag', *The New York Times Magazine,* November 23, p. 59.

—— (2006) 'Wheelchair unbound', *The New York Times Magazine,* April 23, p. 160.

Nuland, S. (2004) 'The death of Hippocrates: when medicine turns evil', *The New Republic*, September, 13–20, 31–39.

16

RECIPROCITY, ACCOUNTABILITY, EMPOWERMENT

Emancipatory principles and practices
in the museum

Heather Hollins

In the 1980s, as the disability movement gathered momentum in the UK, a powerful conceptual tool emerged in the form of what became known as the social model of disability. The social model, widely debated but nevertheless still influential today, rejects an individualist, medicalized conception of disability and instead draws attention to the multiple barriers which exclude disabled people from fully participating in society. Building on these ideas in the early 1990s, disability studies academics began to examine the ways that disabled people had also been excluded from the research process. Challenging the way that disabled people had historically been used and exploited as 'research subjects', a new research paradigm emerged which came to be known as emancipatory disability research.

This new paradigm aims to give disabled people control over the research agenda, seeks to benefit those involved in the research process and ensure that outputs are accountable to disabled people, in the way their views and experiences are represented. This research philosophy marks a significant shift in thinking and aims to tackle fundamental power inequalities within the research process itself. In this new model, the role of the researcher as expert is challenged as disabled people's embodied knowledge about their impairments is given an equal footing to the researcher's knowledge. One of the central aims of emancipatory research is that the process should be used as a tool to change society.

This chapter will explore the implications emancipatory research principles and practice might hold for museums. I shall argue that emancipatory methods can usefully inform the ways in which museums establish relationships with disabled communities; relationships that move beyond short-term consultation and a narrow focus on creating physical access to ones which are genuinely collaborative, holistic in outlook, equitable and inclusive. I briefly review the museum context and the ways in which the sector has responded to disability issues to date before unpacking the concept of emancipatory research practice to identify the principles and characteristics that underpin this approach. I conclude by reviewing recent work at the Holocaust Centre, in north Nottinghamshire, England, and a project which used an emancipatory approach to support a group of young disabled people to work collaboratively with staff at the Centre's Memorial Museum, challenging both issues of access and the representation of the disability history of the Holocaust. This grassroots approach aimed to enable the young disabled people to gain access to power and decision making 'behind the scenes' with the project acting as a catalyst for change within the museum.

Museums and disability

In his influential book, *The Politics of Disablement* (1990) disability activist and academic Mike Oliver argued that disabled people have been denied access to the key political, educational and cultural institutions which could enable them to participate fully in society. Although 20 years have passed since Oliver highlighted the exclusion of disabled people from cultural institutions and despite museums' increasing concern over that period with issues of access, audience development and inclusion, it can be argued that provision for disabled people as museum visitors remains patchy; few institutions take an inclusive, holistic approach to the planning and delivery of their services, and histories of disability continue to be under-represented in most organizations' collections and displays (Solon 2001; Kaushik 1999; Candlin 2003). Although recent legislative drivers have played an important part in focusing attention on disability issues (Lang *et al.* 2006), improvements in accessibility continue to be small in scale, incremental and fragmented.

What then might a holistically inclusive museum experience look and feel like? This vision would include accessibility at every step along a visiting journey from the point a disabled person inquired about the museum through to the satisfactory conclusion of their visit. It would involve the provision of an inclusive website, accessible marketing targeted at the disability press and accessible media, clear signage and exhibitions which supported the needs of people with physical and sensory impairments, people with learning disabilities and those with mental health issues. Accessibility would extend across the whole museum site to include the building, visitor services, café and toilets, and disabled visitors would recognize the excellent customer service as all staff would understand the needs of this audience. From start to finish disabled people would know that this was a place for them, as the museum would clearly demonstrate this through its environment, content, the actions of staff and the ease of the visit. Disabled people would not feel separated or segregated from their companions and would not need to engage in awkward conversations about access difficulties. Importantly, they would also see disability histories, topics which affect their

229

contemporary lives and the lives of disabled people past and present represented within the museum's displays and learning programmes.

How might this vision of the inclusive museum be realized? More particularly, what principles and protocols might be borrowed and adapted from
emancipatory research practice to inform the way in which museums represent and interpret disability and disabled peoples' lives in a thoughtful and
respectful manner?

The emergence of emancipatory research

In the early 1990s, the field of disability studies began to critically analyse
the traditions and protocols of the research process. Leading researchers –
notably Oliver (1990, 1992), Morris (1992), Abberley (1992), Rioux and
Bach (1994) and Zarb (1992) – argued that the process of research into disability had operated to exclude, marginalize and oppress disabled people.
Oliver (1992), Barnes (1992) and Zarb (1992) looked at the methodologies
that had developed from the scientific and social science research traditions
and concluded that their use and application were contributing to the
exclusion of disabled people. Frequently cited within this literature was a
critique of the research process by Paul Hunt (1981). Hunt described the
disempowering experience of being a disabled subject of research undertaken
in a care home setting. At the end of the research, when the findings were
published, the disabled people involved in the study had felt offended by the
way their lives and views had been represented. When analysing the way in
which their experiences had been scrutinized and interpreted, they felt that
they had not been listened to nor had they been consulted over the direction
of the research. This left them feeling disempowered and with a sense that
they had been treated with a lack of respect. Indeed Hunt (1981) went as far
as to say that they had felt victimized by the process. The main beneficiary
in the research, he argued, had been the researcher who had advanced their
career by 'using' the disabled people's views to answer their own research
agenda. As Oliver (1992) and Barnes (1996) later highlighted, the experience which Hunt brought to light is not exclusive to research which focuses
on disabled people and is, in fact, prevalent across research projects in the
social sciences. 'To put it bluntly', Oliver stated, 'research has been and
essentially still is, an activity carried out by those who have power upon
those who do not' (1992: 110). Research concerned with disability, it was
argued, tended to be researcher-oriented; that is, based around the agendas
and priorities of non-disabled researchers (Hunt 1981; Barnes 1992; Oliver
1992; Zarb 1992). At the centre of this type of research is a power inequality
which maintains the researcher as the 'expert' and a gatekeeper to knowledge; the disabled people's life experiences and knowledge of their impairments are 'mined' to answer the researcher's question and agenda. The flow
of knowledge about the topic under investigation is in one direction

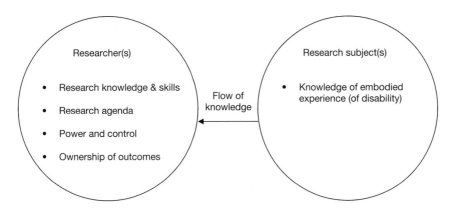

Figure 16.1 'Traditional' social sciences research practice.

(towards the researcher) as the aim of the investigation is not to enrich disabled people's lives or challenge the exclusion of disabled people within society but rather to address a set of questions devised by the researcher. In mainstream social sciences practice the researcher is in control of what is asked, how the research is conducted, how it is interpreted and the outcomes; both in terms of how the study is published and how it is presented to the wider academic community (Figure 16.1).

Here the disabled subjects of research receive no tangible benefits from participation; their life opportunities are not improved by their involvement. As Kitchen asserts, this type of research compounds 'the oppression of disabled respondents through exploitation for academic gain' (2000: 45).

This analysis of the power relationships that are at play in the process of academic research also resonates with more recent debates in museum studies. Peers and Brown (2003), for example, discuss the changing nature of relationships between museums and source communities. During the 'great age of museum collecting' museums acted as the principal authority on their collections; 'objects and information about them went from people all over the world into museums, which then consolidated knowledge as the basis of curatorial and institutional authority' (ibid.: 1). During this time museums retained control of the collection of objects and the knowledge, ideas and values that were attached to them. This control was subsequently reinforced through the process of interpretation and display of those objects in ways which reproduced oppressive hierarchical understandings of different cultures (Sandell 2007). New relationships between museums and source communities based on more democratic, empowering and egalitarian principles and practices have been established in recent years. However, it can be argued that many museums continue to establish and maintain one-sided relationships with communities through which research (for curatorial purposes or to inform education or audience development initiatives) is undertaken to address topics and questions decided upon by the museum. Thus, when consulting or conducting research with disabled people, questions might be framed primarily around museum-oriented concerns (what do you know about this object in our collections?) rather than through a more open and equitable agenda which begins with the priorities, interests and concerns of the disabled person.

Emancipatory disability research principles

Exploring ways of addressing the inequities they identified in traditional social science practices, researchers within disability studies, notably Barnes (1992), Oliver (1992) and Zarb (1992), began to develop a new research paradigm. Emancipatory disability research, as it became known, placed the social model of disability at its core. Just as the social model aimed to place the onus on society to remove disabling barriers, emancipatory research aimed to remove disabling barriers from the research process. Although this new model marked an important departure in research principles, the same research tools as seen within established social sciences research approaches – such as interviews, focus groups and oral history techniques – were retained. What distinguishes emancipatory research is the set of underlying principles which shape the way that the research is planned, implemented, analysed and disseminated to remove disabling barriers and which place disabled people's voices at the centre of the process (Stone and Priestley 1996; Zarb 1992; Kitchen 2000).

From the works of Oliver (1992), Morris (1992), Zarb (1992) and Chappell (2000) five key principles of emancipatory research practice can be summarized. First, research should be used as a tool for improving the lives of disabled people and they should directly benefit from their involvement. Second, there should be greater opportunities for disabled people to be researchers, either as the primary researcher or as collaborative researchers in the study. Third, researchers must adopt a more reflexive approach to their work. They should be responsive to the needs and issues that arise during the research process, and be willing to improve or modify their approach, to ensure that the disabled people are able to fully participate. Fourth, the democratic organizations[1] of disabled people should act as commissioners and funders of research and, finally, researchers should be accountable to the disabled people involved in the research in terms of how it is conducted, interpreted and published.

Oliver (1992) highlights empowerment and reciprocity as the fundamental principles on which emancipatory research is based. Disabled people are empowered by being directly involved in the research process and, moreover, they receive reciprocal benefit from their participation in ways which should lead to positive changes for the wider disability community. In this model there is a shift in the power relationship between the researcher and the disabled participants with mutually beneficial outcomes being negotiated for both parties (Figure 16.2).

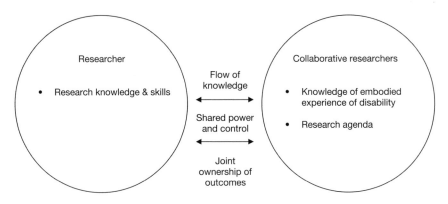

Figure 16.2 Emancipatory disability research model.

In research which follows emancipatory principles, the topics under investigation are important to disabled people because they have decided upon the research agenda themselves, either as commissioners of the project or by holding decision-making power within the research process (Barnes 2003). In this model the role of the expert researcher is also challenged as both parties have knowledge which is useful to the research process. The researcher supports the disabled participants to gain new knowledge and skills around research practices so that they can become actively involved in the research process, and the disabled people share their knowledge about the embodied experience of living as a disabled person. Similarly, the researcher and the disabled collaborators equally own the outcomes of the research.

As Barnes comments, 'accountability is a major consideration for all those striving to do emancipatory disability research' (ibid.: 7) and, by involving disabled people throughout the process, the researcher can stay accountable for the way that they conduct the study. Examining how this accountability might operate in practice, Kitchen (2000: 38) describes the empathetic feedback loop through which participants have 'the opportunity to correct misinterpretations and influence the direction of the research'. This ensures that the experiences of disempowerment that disabled people have felt during research – such as those described by Hunt (1981) – are not replicated as disabled people's views are placed at the heart of the research.

The new vision of research practice offered by the emancipatory model shares some common ground with newly emerging models of the museum. Eilean Hooper-Greenhill, for example, posits a conception of the post-museum which, 'rather than upholding values of objectivity, rationality, order and distance' will instead 'negotiate responsiveness, encourage mutually nurturing partnerships, and celebrate diversity' (Hooper-Greenhill 2000: 153). Emancipatory research practices, I suggest, offer museum leaders and practitioners a set of principles and ways of working that might usefully guide their institutions towards this radical new form. However, this application of principles from one context to another throws into relief an issue that has proved to be contentious in the field of disability studies – the role of non-disabled professionals.

The role of non-disabled professionals

Emancipatory principles were developed to support and advance disabled people's rights, address power inequalities and ensure that they could fully participate in the research process. However, there has been some debate about how achievable these principles are with the predominantly non-disabled research community (see, for example, Branfield 1998; Barnes 1992, 2003; Chappell 2000 and Shakespeare 1996). Academics such as Branfield (1998) have argued that only disabled people can conduct emancipatory disability research as, he asserts, only they can truly understand the needs of disabled people. Other writers within disability studies such as Barnes (1992, 2003) and Shakespeare (1996) have strongly refuted this idea, drawing on the counter argument that disabled researchers with a particular impairment cannot understand the needs of people with impairments that are different to their own. This issue is pertinent to our discussion of the museum context since recent research has confirmed that disabled and deaf people are under-represented within the sector (Museums Association 2008). While more needs to be done to address this under-representation and related inequities in opportunity, I would support Barnes and Shakespeare who argue that the emancipatory aims behind a study can be achieved as long as disabled people are fully engaged within the research process.

How then might this research methodology be of use to museums when thinking about their approach to access and the representation of disability issues within the museum space? In the next part of this chapter I will explore how emancipatory disability research principles can be applied to the museum context to support museums to become more holistically inclusive. It will focus on how the principles described can go beyond the realms of research to influence the way that museums as institutions involve disabled people in shaping services and developing approaches to the representation of disabled people's lives within the museum space.

Emancipatory practice in the museum

Recent years have seen a growing body of practical guidance available to museum practitioners to support efforts to make museum buildings, exhibitions and programmes accessible to visitors with physical and sensory impairments, people with learning disabilities and those with mental health issues.[2] Moreover, recent action research exploring the challenges behind the interpretation of disability histories in exhibitions has been disseminated in ways designed to stimulate and support more developments in this relatively uncharted territory.[3] Why then, does practice remain patchy with initiatives fragmented and often narrow in scope?

Factors such as the need for staff training and the limited availability of resources for the implementation of access improvements might frequently be cited as barriers which continue to prevent museums from moving forward, but a more fundamental issue lies behind the slow progress most museums have made. The development of a holistically inclusive museum requires that thinking 'behind the scenes' gives priority to disability access and representation through a fundamental rethink of organizational practice and behaviour – a process which results in ensuring access not simply to museum buildings but to the process of decision making which shapes the museum's services and facilities.

Focusing on exhibition development, Majewski and Bunch (1998) usefully identify three tiers of access. The first concerns access to the physical spaces of the exhibition; the second tier considers intellectual and sensory access to the exhibition's content; and the third level is concerned with the representation of disabled people and disability-themed issues within the display narratives. Building on this notion of differential levels of access, but approaching the issue from a broader perspective of access to opportunities to shape institutional policy and practice, I suggest that there are four stages through which museums might progress in developing genuinely collaborative, empowering and reciprocal relationships with disabled people; relationships which reflect the egalitarian qualities embodied in emancipatory research practice (Figure 16.3).

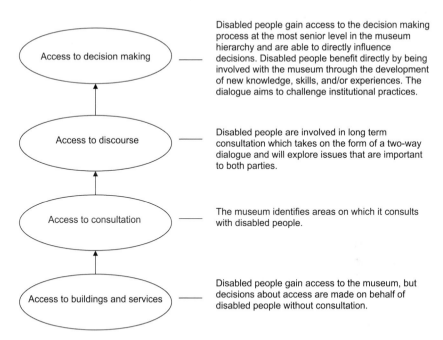

Figure 16.3 Towards emancipatory practice: evolving relationships between disabled people and the museum

Each level in this model represents a shift in the balance of power between the museum and the disabled people with whom they aim to collaborate. The lowest level of access that museums can afford disabled people is access in through the door. In this scenario, museum staff and management will make decisions about access issues (either consciously or unconsciously) without direct consultation with disabled people. This mirrors the approach discussed earlier by Peers and Brown (2003) with the museum still viewing itself as 'the expert', the gatekeeper to knowledge and the primary source of authority. This level of access is likely to result in presumptions being made about disabled people's needs. Through lack of thought and good intentions, the museum space, exhibitions and programme will fail to be fully inclusive. It is very unlikely that attempts to represent disability-themed histories will be considered at this stage of development.

At the next level – access to consultation – museums will begin to think about asking disabled people for their views and opinions. This stage again resonates with the evolving character of relations between museums and other kinds of community:

> In the initial stages of realising that their relationships with and representations of source communities were no longer adequate, museums began to consult with members of those communities ... However, consultation is often structured to provide outside support for the maintenance of institutional practices, and source community members are wary of contributing to museum-led consultation exercises which do not lead to change within museums or benefits to their people.
>
> (Peers and Brown 2003: 2)

Although, Peers and Brown are describing relations between museums and the culturally diverse and often geographically dispersed communities from which many collections have originated, their analysis might equally be applied to contemporary engagement with disabled people. In relationships typical of this second tier of access, the consultation will be museum-oriented and undertaken in response to an issue that the museum will want to resolve. Disabled people's opinions will be sought, but the relationship may be short term and dissolve once the issue has been addressed. This type of consultation has its place, but will not enable the institution to move towards a more holistically inclusive way of working.

At the third level – which I term access to discourse – the museum will endeavour to establish a longer-term mode of consultation where they work with disabled people in a more sustainable way. Again Peers and Brown (2003: 1) describe a similar change in relations between museums and source communities:

> In some parts of the world this shift has occurred ... so that source community members have come to be defined as authorities on their

own culture and material heritage. These changes have been given impetus by new forms of research and relationships which involve the sharing of knowledge and power to meet the needs of both parties.

Relationships operating at this level will be more dialogic, the needs of both the museum and disabled people are considered and a mutually beneficial relationship begins to develop. Although disabled individuals may benefit from participation in the research project (for example, through gaining skills and experiences that might be put to use in other settings) this will be incidental rather than a planned and purposeful outcome. As there is no commitment to power sharing, the disabled people will not gain full access to decision making at the highest level. It is likely that the museum staff facilitating the consultation will occupy relatively junior levels within the organization and will have to advocate the views of the disabled people to senior staff. This may create difficulties as the staff involved will not have direct decision-making power within the museum hierarchy, and therefore it may be difficult to implement any suggestions put forward in the consultation process.

The fourth level in this model – access to decision making – provides an opportunity to create a framework within which the power to make changes in policy and practice is shared between the museum and the community. This level most fully reflects the motivations, goals and values enshrined in emancipatory research practice. Here museum and disabled people collaborate to create a dialogue where both parties have shared authority and a mandate to dismantle barriers which contribute to the cultural exclusion of disabled people from society. The relationship will aim to empower disabled people by giving them access to decision making at the most senior level in the museum management hierarchy. It will also aim to improve the life opportunities of the disabled participants by creating a reciprocal relationship which directly benefits both parties. For the disabled partners this may include opportunities to gain knowledge, skills or experiences which support life or career aspirations. At this level of dialogue the relationship will enable the disabled people to challenge issues of institutional discrimination and support the development of holistically inclusive practices. The disabled people may act as 'critical friends', enabling museum staff to increase their capacity to represent disability histories in their displays and the confidence to tackle interpretation of disability-related issues. The museum will accrue increased awareness and understanding of access issues of all kinds and the process of power sharing will provide a catalyst for organizational change.

Emancipatory disability research at the Holocaust Centre

In this last part of the chapter I reflect on attempts to move a single institution – the Holocaust Centre in North Nottinghamshire, England – towards a more holistically inclusive way of working, through the application of emancipatory principles to a project carried out in collaboration with the Pioneers Youth Forum, a group which aims to support young disabled people between the ages of 15 and 25.

The Holocaust Centre was established in 1995 by the Smith family in response to a visit to the museum at Yad Vashem, the Holocaust Martyrs' and Heroes' Remembrance Authority, during a family holiday to Jerusalem. Their visit provoked much reflection and prompted them to wonder why there was nowhere in the UK for survivors to go and remember the loved ones who had been killed during the Holocaust, or to talk to their families about the terrible events they had witnessed. The family decided to create a memorial garden with roses and plaques dedicated to the memories of Jewish people who were killed in the Holocaust. Their plans evolved and in 1995 they launched an education centre with memorial gardens, a memorial hall, a Holocaust exhibition and visitor facilities (Figure 16.4). Currently around 180 primary and secondary school children visit daily, along with the general public, to explore the Holocaust and how the underlying issues of prejudice, racism and intolerance are relevant to our contemporary society. In 2006, when the project with the Pioneers Youth Forum began, the Centre was highly inaccessible for disabled people with physical, sensory and intellectual barriers across the whole site, a problem compounded by the near-total absence of the disability history of the Holocaust from the site's exhibition spaces and education programmes.

The Holocaust and disability history

Around 11 million people were killed during the Holocaust, with the largest grouping being 6 million Jews. Of the 5 million non-Jewish victims, an estimated 275,000 were disabled people. A further approximately 700,000 disabled people were sterilized under the Nazi eugenics programme (Disability Rights Advocates 2001). Despite the significance of disability to understanding the Holocaust, it has been argued that disabled people's narratives have become subsumed within mainstream, post-war public and academic representations. As Mitchell and Snyder state:

> [t]he murder of disabled people, unlike the killing of ethnic and sexual others, has continued to go unrecognised as a crime against humanity by anyone other than a handful of intellectuals and activists.
>
> (2003: 859)

This elision is reflected in limited public awareness. Recent research commissioned by the UK's Holocaust Memorial Trust identified that '55 per cent of people were not aware that disabled people were victims of Nazi persecution' (Shakespeare 2007: 40).

Figure 16.4 Banners in the 'Rise of Nazism' section of the main Holocaust exhibition at The Holocaust Centre, Nottinghamshire.

The Holocaust Centre's limited acknowledgement of disabled people's experiences conveys a powerful message to disabled visitors – that their histories are not important enough to be addressed, even when the narrative focus is a history of racial and cultural exclusion. Moreover, problems with physical access on site, which require wheelchair users to take a different route to the non-disabled majority, do little to offset feelings of separation for disabled visitors.

As part of a larger project to address these issues, and as a member of staff at the Holocaust Centre, I approached the Pioneers Forum, part of Nottinghamshire County Council's Youth Disability Services which aims to give young disabled people a voice with which to challenge access issues they will encounter in their lives and therefore improve their life chances by empowering participants to make changes. Drawing on the principles that underpin emancipatory disability research, I worked with members of the Forum through an extended form of consultation, designed to enable the young people to gain access to power and decision making at the Holocaust Centre. Through supporting participants to develop their knowledge about the Centre and the disability history of the Holocaust and to develop their skills in relation to museum practice it also aimed to challenge exclusionary practices within the institution through the process of collaborative working. These project aims were developed by the young people themselves.

Based on the work of Oliver (1992), Morris (1992), Zarb (1992) and Chappell (2000), the principles behind emancipatory disability research provided a framework for working with the young disabled people to achieve the highest level of access to power. The principles of emancipatory disability research were used as a framework to design the way that consultation sessions were developed with the Pioneers group. The principles were approached as follows:

Reciprocity – a reciprocal arrangement between the Forum and the Centre was developed. The museum benefited from the relationship as staff had an improved knowledge of the needs of disabled people and were able to access solutions to build into current and future planning. The young disabled people benefited as they gained skills in team working, advocacy, negotiation and communication along with new confidence in their abilities. This was particularly important for this group as many of the young people were affected by low self esteem and were not always able to voice their opinions.

Empowerment – the Pioneers were empowered by the process as the ideas they put forward were discussed with the museum and acted upon. Inevitably, it was not possible for the museum to implement all of the young people's ideas due to resource constraints but Forum members learned to challenge the museum on the issues that were most important to them and to negotiate solutions. They therefore felt that they were able to influence key decisions which were made within the organization and felt empowered by this process. The advocacy and negotiation skills they learned during the research could then be transferred to other areas of their life and support them to get their opinions heard by friends, family and authority figures in their life.

Sharing of expertise – all parties involved in the collaboration brought a unique perspective, knowledge and set of skills to the relationship. The aim was to share this knowledge to support each other in moving forward. Museum staff shared their expertise about the Holocaust Centre, the history of the Holocaust and the Centre's plans. The Pioneers shared their experiences of disability and potential access solutions which would support their needs.

Control – as their skills and confidence grew, the agenda for the consultation process was handed over to the Pioneers. They decided upon the issues that they wanted to work on with the Holocaust Centre. In the initial stages of the project they were given the opportunity to select which areas of the Centre's operations – including access to collections, exhibitions, facilities, programmes and so on – they wished to focus on. The group chose to work on the Centre's new Holocaust exhibition and on improving the Centre's approach to representing the disability history of the Holocaust.

Accountability – the Centre was accountable to the Pioneers for the decisions that it made in response to their suggestions through regular meetings and feedback on progress.

Reflexivity – the needs of the young disabled people and the museum were reviewed regularly to ensure that the project was benefiting and supporting all parties involved. Improvements or modifications were made to the working practices and plans as they developed to ensure that the Pioneers could fully participate in the collaboration.

Not surprisingly this experiment in the application of emancipatory principles to museum–community collaborations was not always easy as this was a new experience for both the Pioneers and the Centre. However, preliminary findings from the project suggest that the young disabled people involved felt empowered by their participation and, at the same time, developed new knowledge and skills. As importantly, the project had a significant impact on the development of inclusive practices at the Centre. Over time, the young people came to operate as a group of 'critical friends' to challenge the discriminatory practices and oversights which had created a situation of poor access and a lack of engagement with the significance of the Holocaust for disabled people. The young people are currently working on a project to create a sculpture for the Centre's gardens which explores the disability history of the Holocaust and its implications for contemporary prejudice.

For many museums, the creation of a genuinely inclusive experience, described earlier in the chapter, is likely to be challenging and fraught with complexity. However, the principles behind the emancipatory research process offer one way through which a framework for equitable dialogue between disabled people and museums can be created. Nothing less than this wholesale rethinking of institutional practice and behaviour is needed if museums are to move beyond piecemeal conversations about access solutions to support a wider political agenda focused on challenging the way that museums can act as discriminatory institutions that contribute to disabled people's cultural exclusion from society.

Notes

1 Some disability organizations are not led or governed by disabled people. The phrasing 'democratic organizations of disabled people' is intended to refer to disability organizations which are managed by disabled people.
2 See, for example, Re:source (2001), MLA (2003) and Deafworks (2001).
3 See, for example, Research Centre for Museums and Galleries (2004), Sandell *et al.* (2005) and Dodd *et al.* (2007).

References

Abberley, P. (1992) 'Counting us out: a discussion of the OPCS disability surveys', *Disability, Handicap & Society*, 7(2): 139–55.

Barnes, C. (1992) 'Qualitative Research: valuable or irrelevant?', *Disability, Handicap & Society*, 7(2): 139–55.

—— (1996) 'Disability and the myth of the independent researcher', *Disability & Society*, 11 (1): 107–10.

—— (2003) 'What a difference a decade makes: reflections on doing "emancipatory" disability research', *Disability & Society*, 18(1): 3–17.

Branfield, F. (1998) 'What are you doing here? "Non-disabled" people and the disability movement: a response to Robert F. Drake', Disability & *Society*, 13(1): 143–44.

Candlin, F. (2003) 'Blindness, art and exclusion in museums and galleries', *International Journal of Art and Design Education*, 22(1): 100–110.

Chappell, A. L. (2000) 'Emergence of participatory methodology in learning difficulty tesearch: understanding the context', *British Journal of Learning Disabilities*, 28, 38–43.

Deafworks (2001) *Access for Deaf People to Museums and Galleries: A Review of Good Practice*, London: Deafworks.

Disability Rights Advocates (2001) *Forgotten Crimes: The Holocaust and People with Disabilities*, Oakland, CA: Disability Rights Advocates.

Dodd, J., Sandell, R., Jolly, D. and Jones, C. (2008) *Rethinking Disability Representation in Museums and Galleries*, Leicester: Research Centre for Museums and Galleries.

Hooper-Greenhill, E. (2000) *Museums and the Interpretation of Visual Culture*, London and New York: Routledge.

Hunt, P. (1981) 'Settling accounts with parasite people', *Disability Challenge*, 2: 37–50.

Kaushik, R. (1999) 'Access denied: can we overcome disabling attitudes?', *Museums International*, 51(3): 48–52.

Kitchen, R. (2000) 'The researched opinions on research: disabled people and disability research', *Disability & Society*, 15(1): 25–47.

Lang, C., Reeve, J. and Woollard, V. (2006) *The Responsive Museum: Working with Audiences in the Twenty-First Century*, Aldershot: Ashgate.

Majewski, J. and Bunch, L. (1998) 'The expanding definition of diversity: accessibility and disability culture issues for museum exhibitions', *Curator*, 41(3): 153–61.

Mitchell, D. and Snyder, S. (2003) 'The eugenic Atlantic: race, disability, and the making of an international eugenic science, 1800–1945', *Disability & Society* 18(7): 843–64.

Morris, J. (1992) 'Personal and political: a feminist perspective on researching physical disability', *Disability, Handicap & Society*, 7(2): 157–67.

Museums Association (2008) 'Diversify', Online. Available http://www.museumsassociation.org/diversify (accessed 4 April 2009).

Oliver, M. (1990) *The Politics of Disablement*, London: Macmillan.

—— (1992) 'Changing the social relations of research production', *Disability, Handicap & Society*, 7(2): 101–14.

Peers, L. and Brown, A. K. (2003) *Museums and Source Communities: A Routledge Reader*, London and New York: Routledge.

Research Centre for Museums and Galleries (2004) *Buried in the Footnotes: The Representation of Disabled People in Museum and Gallery Collections*, Leicester: RCMG.

Re:source (2001) *Disability Directory for Museum and Galleries*, London: Re:source.

Rioux, M. and Bach, M. (1994) *'Disability is not measles'*, Toronto, ON: L'Institut Roeher.

Sandell, R. (2007) *Museums, Prejudice and the Reframing of Difference*, London and New York: Routledge.

Sandell, R., Delin, A., Dodd, J. and Gay, J. (2005) 'Beggars, freaks and heroes? Museum collections and the hidden history of disability', *Museum Management and Curatorship*, 20 (1): 5–19.

Shakespeare, T. (1996) 'Rules of engagement: doing disability research', *Disability & Society*, 11(1): 115–19.

—— (2007) 'World view', *Disability Now Magazine*, February: 40.

SOLON (2001). *'Survey of provision for disabled users of museums, archives, and libraries'*, London: Museums, Libraries and Archives Council.

Stone, E. and Priestley, M. (1996) 'Parasites, pawns and partners: disability research and the role of non-disabled tesearchers', *British Journal of Sociology*, 47, 696–716.

Zarb, G. (1992) 'On the road to Damascus: first steps towards changing the relations of disability research production', *Disability, Handicap and Society*, 7(2): 125–38.

17

DISABILITY, HUMAN RIGHTS AND THE PUBLIC GAZE

The Losheng Story Museum

Chia-Li Chen

In 1930, the Losheng Sanatorium was established in Taipei County, Taiwan by the Japanese colonial regime to confine and treat patients with leprosy. More than a thousand people were eventually segregated there, stigmatized and deprived of basic human rights. During these decades of segregation, patients formed supportive networks and relationships and many of them made the sanatorium their home. In the 1950s, when a new treatment for leprosy (Hansen's disease) was discovered, patients were allowed to leave but many who had faced years of isolation and discrimination elected to stay.

In 2002 however, the sanatorium was chosen as the location for the construction of a new maintenance depot for the Taipei metro, a decision which led to calls for the site to be preserved and sparked what became a high profile battle for the current residents' human rights. In 2007, the Losheng Story Museum was opened in the sanatorium and functions as a site of critical pedagogy – as a place through which residents are empowered to share their experiences in ways which facilitate visitors' reflection on how different authorities have marginalized disabled people and other disadvantaged communities.

This chapter considers the factors and motivations that shaped the emergence of the Losheng Story Museum and, more particularly, explores how these operate to construct a public gaze – a particular way of viewing and understanding disability. The museum's approach to interpretation – one that draws on and contextualizes residents' perspectives on their own experiences – is compared to that employed in an earlier photographic exhibition that documented life at the institution and which was displayed in a fine art museum setting, to explore the ethical issues bound up in attempts to represent disability in the public sphere. The chapter concludes by highlighting the potential challenges that may arise as the museum makes the transition into a new phase of development.

Human rights in Taiwan

To better understand the Losheng Story Museum's embroilment in the very public battle for residents' rights, it is helpful to review the background to human rights development in Taiwan. Before the lifting of martial law in 1987 people in Taiwan had limited rights. During the Japanese colonial period (1895–1945), Taiwanese people were considered inferior to their colonizers and their rights of education and employment were restricted. They went to different schools from their colonizers and had limited opportunities to take up positions of influence in the government. This social division is what Fanon described as 'a world cut in two' (1968: 38). In Fanon's analysis, it is through the division of the colonizer (the superior) and the colonized (the inferior) that colonial powers established and managed their empires.

In 1943, at the Cairo Conference, it was decided that Taiwan should return to mainland China once the Allied Forces won the Second World War. The reunion with mainland China, however, only lasted for four years. Even that short period of reunion during which Taiwan was ruled by the Kuomintang (KMT) – the ruling political party in China led by Chiang Kai-shek – was a turbulent time. The greatest massacre in Taiwanese history, known as the 228 Incident, occurred on 28 February 1947. During the Incident, the KMT massacred more than 20,000 Taiwanese people. In 1949 the KMT were defeated by the Chinese Communist Party and established their own government in exile. To legitimate and consolidate his regime, Chiang Kai-shek declared martial law in 1949 and two decades of what became known as 'white terror' ensued. During this time, more dissidents were either executed or sent to prison. Under martial law, people's political rights and freedom of speech were restricted.

Discontent subsequently grew in the 1980s and the first opposition party, the Democratic Progressive Party (DPP), was formed in 1986. In 1987, martial law was finally lifted. It was the first time that citizens in Taiwan got their full political freedom and democratic rights, enabling people to express their own opinions freely, form political parties and select their own political representatives (Chen 2003). This period of social transformation saw the emergence of rights movements for minority groups as well as demands for a formal apology by the KMT ruling government and compensation for the families of those executed in the 228 Incident. As a result, laws were passed to provide for compensation and several museums and monuments were established in remembrance (Chen 2007). In general, political rights and democratic reform have been largely improved since the 1990s, while more sensitive and complex issues – notably the rights of minority groups, the employment of new immigrants and the welfare of women, children and disabled people – remain to be improved. It is within this context that the battle to preserve the Losheng Sanatorium becomes one of the most controversial issues in contemporary Taiwanese society.

Leprosy and its metaphors

The Losheng Sanatorium was established to confine and treat patients infected with leprosy (today referred to as Hansen's disease), a chronic disease that, historically, has inspired abhorrence, distaste and fear throughout the world (Edmond 2006) and has often been viewed as a metaphor for personal or social corruption. As Marcia Gaudet argues:

> Hansen's disease is a real illness, but leprosy is a term that historically has maintained metaphorical meanings inspired by medieval beliefs, which cause emotional responses far out of proportion to any threat or danger.
>
> (Gaudet 2004: 90)

Indeed, Susan Sontag, in *Aids and its Metaphors*, describes leprosy as 'one of the most meaning-laden of diseases' (Sontag 1989: 92). Affecting humanity in different societies for centuries, leprosy has been an emblem of corruption and decay. Before Dr Hansen found the *mycobacterium leprae* in 1873, in China, the causes of leprosy were attributed to different factors, such as flu, venereal diseases and the sins of ancestors. In Japan, leprosy is called 'Disease from Heaven', meaning that it comes as a punishment from the gods (Liu 2004).

Similarly, in medieval Europe, people with leprosy were segregated not only because of fears of infection but also to keep those afflicted with the disease, and believed to be 'repulsive in appearance and immoral of action' out of public view (Manchester and Roberts 1989: 268).

> Segregation of sufferers was of paramount importance during the height of leprosy in the medieval period; this was not solely because it was believed that it would control the spread of the disease but that the abhorrent sufferers would be collected together and prevented from mixing with the rest of society.
>
> (ibid.: 268)

Many thousands of leprosariums were established across Europe and, when a cure for leprosy was later discovered, the institutions remained and later re-emerged to function once again as sites of social exclusion. As Foucault states: 'Leprosy disappeared, the leper vanished, or almost, from memory; these structures remained. Often in the same places, the formulas of exclusion would be repeated, strangely similar two or three centuries later' (1989: 5).

In contemporary Taiwan, it is the institution's history of exclusion and segregation that becomes a potent force for reconfiguring and reinterpreting Losheng as a site for preservation and a battleground for disability rights.

The establishment of the Losheng Sanatorium

Following immigration from China in the sixteenth and seventeenth centuries, more and more people in Taiwan became infected with leprosy and most of them received treatment in private care centres. It was not until the Japanese colonial period that the first public sanatorium was built to systematically seg-regate patients. Influenced by concepts of modern medical science and statistics (Yao 2001), the Japanese colonial government conducted a series of censuses in Taiwan to estimate the population infected with leprosy between 1900 and 1939. It showed that the number of lepers was relatively small compared to that of Japan, but that the number was rising. Many were receiving treatment from a Canadian missionary, Dr. George Gushue-Taylor (1883–1954), who planned to build a leper colony in Taipei County. Within this context, the colonial gov-ernment determined to take control of the health of the Taiwanese rather than put them in the hands of foreign missionaries (Fann 2005).

Under a humanist guise and the rhetoric of modernization, the Losheng Sanatorium – Losheng means 'happy life' in Chinese – was established in 1930 on a hillside in the area known today as Hsinchuang City in Taipei County. The sanatorium functioned as a place for both confinement and medical treatment. To prevent the spread of the disease, the sanatorium was divided into two areas: a contagious area for the patients and non-contagious area for doctors and nurses. An infrastructure grew around the sanatorium including the hospital, sewerage system, a shop, asylum and crematorium in ways which came to resemble a micro-society (Pan 2004). Here, residents' rights were restricted in the name of public interest; they had no freedom of movement, no opportunities for employment and were not allowed to bear children. If residents wished to get married, they were first forced to undergo surgical sterilization (Chang 2007). Apart from short periods of leave for family cere-monies or funerals, residents were not allowed to leave the sanatorium for their entire life. Wire fencing was set up around the sanatorium and guards patrolled to ensure segregation and to prevent patients from escaping.

As a result of these measures, the Losheng Sanatorium became an institution of compulsory quarantine as well as life-long imprisonment. The KMT regime inherited the policies of segregation from the colonial government in its early years. It was not until the introduction of multi-drug therapy (MDT) in the early 1980s that a policy of strict segregation was completely abandoned. However, at this time, most residents chose to spend the rest of their lives in the sanatorium, a decision influenced by three main factors. First, after decades of isolation, many residents had made the sanatorium their home, with a close network of friends to sustain them. Second, many residents had acquired impairments from the leprosy which made it very difficult for them to earn their own living in society. Last and most importantly, many residents felt intimidated by their experiences of discrimination and prejudice, making a return to society an uncertain and frightening prospect.

The residents' experience of segregation and stigma reflects the character of prejudice directed towards disabled people in other contexts. Sandell, for example, has argued that prejudice is 'not simply a fixed characteristic of a few disagreeable or deviant individuals but rather a pervasive feature of all societies and one in which, in varied and dynamic ways, we are all implicated' (2007: 27). Indeed, Fann's research into the history of medicine in colonial Taiwan (2005) suggests that, in order to efficiently manage the segregation of people infected with leprosy, the colonial government mobilized both official and social resources by stigmatizing Hansen's patients. Chang (2007) also argues that the laws enacted to confine Hansen's patients operated to deepen and strengthen the social discrimination they experienced.

How then might the museum – as an institution that very often reinforces dominant cultures and ideologies; that reflects but also shapes the perspectives and prejudices of the society in which it functions (Sandell 2007) – tackle the ethical and rights-related issues bound up in the site of the sanatorium? What interpretive approaches might be deployed to frame the public gaze in ways which counter the experiences of stigma and discrimination experienced by residents of Losheng?

'A Moment in Time'

Before the establishment of the Losheng Story Museum, several reports on the histories and lives of the residents of the Losheng Sanatorium appeared in newspapers and on television. In 1995 there was also a photographic exhibition, shown at the Taipei Fine Arts Museum, entitled 'A Moment in Time: Chronology of the Leper Village'. The exhibition comprised images by Qing-Hui Zhou, who had tired of being a press reporter and decided to rent a house near the sanatorium during the early 1990s. Zhou spent three years photographing and documenting the everyday lives of residents in the Losheng Sanatorium. The resulting exhibition featured photographs of buildings and a number of close-up images of residents. Zhou stated that his motivation for the exhibition was simply to be a storyteller. He explained: 'I would like to express the air of leprosy from every aspect, such as religion, peoples' lives, medical care and how patients face death.' He was also explicit in his criticism of historical Chinese attitudes towards people with leprosy, which view them as 'apathetic and immoral' but, in comparison, he argued that it was people who lived *outside* of the sanatorium who were insensitive and indifferent (Zhou 1996). Through the exhibition, Zhou intended to evoke in visitors empathy and understanding. However, 'A Moment in Time' unintentionally caused distress and hurt to the exhibition's subjects.

In order to display every aspect of residents' lives in the sanatorium and to show that many of them also have families living very normal lives outside of the institution, a wedding picture of one resident's son was included in the exhibition.[1] However, the display of the image in a public gallery caused unease and protest amongst residents and members of their families. The young couple in the image worried: 'What will happen if our colleagues visit the museum and see our picture here?' Moreover, residents themselves did not know that close-up photographs, showing the effects of leprosy on their features, and detailed images of aspects of their everyday lives, would be displayed and examined under the public gaze. According to a report by Lu in the *United Evening News* (1995), many residents would rather conceal their identities to protect the reputations of their families, although a few believed that the exhibition was acceptable if it could gain the public's attention and generate concern for their wellbeing.

According to the newspaper report, the photographer Zhou conceded that it was regrettable that the images were displayed without prior agreement from those being photographed. However, he defended the medium of documentary photography as a means of telling the residents' stories and he resisted calls to cancel the exhibition. He agreed to negotiate with residents and to take off display some of the most controversial photographs, including the detailed close-up images of individuals' features (Lu 1995). Despite Zhou's intentions the exhibition proved to be problematic by transforming residents, ordinarily hidden from public view, into objects of public scrutiny. The challenging issues surrounding the public display of disabled people and the interpretation of disability-related narratives within the setting of a public gallery had ethical implications that were far beyond the expectations and original intentions of the photographer.

Public interests vs. individual human rights

In 2002, when it was declared that the Losheng Sanatorium would be demolished for the construction of the Mass Rapid Transport (MRT) maintenance depot, students, urban planners and non-governmental organizations came together to form the Losheng Preservation Association to initiate a battle to save the site. As one of the last functioning sanatoriums in the world, Losheng not only bears witness to an important history of public health, but is also home for residents who were forced to leave their own families decades ago. Although the Taiwanese government built a new tower hospital nearby to accommodate the residents, many preferred to stay at Losheng for the rest of their lives. In 2005, with the support of volunteer lawyers, the Losheng Preservation Association won a lawsuit in Japan and 25 patients who were segregated by the Japanese colonial government received compensation. In December 2005, at the request of the Losheng Preservation Association, the Council for Culture Affairs applied the newly amended Cultural Heritage Preservation Act and designated the Losheng area a 'temporary historic site' which required the county government to assess the historical value of the location (Tsai 2007).

Meanwhile, there were more and more demonstrations in support of the preservation of the site and heated debates in the media surrounding the issue of the current residents' rights. According to local media reports, 'county government officials and local representatives expressed their support for the demolition, saying that any delay in construction would cause a tremendous loss of money and compromise the rights of over one million citizens who lived along the new metro line' (Tsai 2007). Thus, as the designation of the 'temporary historical site' expired, the Taipei County Government and the Taipei Rapid Transit Corporation refused to change the construction plans, citing economic arguments and the interests of the public as reasons for pressing ahead. Once again, public interest was being invoked as a reason to force residents to leave their home against their own will.

As Chang (2007) highlights, the discourse of 'public interest' is one of the primary causes for the violation of contemporary individual human rights and therefore deserves close examination. In the case of Losheng, public interest was cited as justification for the demolition of approximately 90 per cent of the site. Realizing the importance of collecting and documenting the significant histories and artifacts associated with the site, several students volunteered to organize the Making Museum group in the summer of 2007 and, just a few months later, the Losheng Story Museum opened on 12 December, 77 years after the sanatorium was first established.

Objects and trauma

Unlike most public or privately financed museums, the Losheng Story Museum was founded by student volunteers and residents with very limited resources. At the beginning, residents had a very limited understanding of the concept or value of a museum, nor did they think its establishment was as urgent and significant as the broader preservation movement. For them, the founding of the museum could be seen to signify the setback of the preservation movement since, from their perspective, it seemed that only a dying culture would be preserved in a museum. Some of the volunteer students also shared residents' doubts about the use of the term 'museum', which they associated with a place for things of the past not present. After much debate, they jointly decided on the name – the Losheng Story Museum – meaning a place of the stories of Hansen's patients and residents.

The Making Museum group encountered many challenges, aside from the task of naming, including the need to collect and document objects. In order to understand the relationship between objects and their owners, they designed and organized a treasure hunting and oral history workshop. Visitors were invited to assist in the task of collecting and to spend weekends visiting residents' homes to help identify potential objects and to find out more about their personal significance and their potential to tell a story. During the process, they found that some objects had lost their owners and were piled in a quiet corner; some others continued to be used in residents' everyday lives. Many of the objects – such as a knife, a towel or a pile of gauze – were neither precious nor beautiful but nevertheless played a vital role in many residents' lives and became symbols of their trauma and social exclusion.

Exhibitions in the Losheng Story Museum

Despite their initial wariness about the idea of a museum, many residents became increasingly interested in the processes of collecting and exhibiting objects. One resident in particular, Mr. Mao, came to play a critical role in the establishment of the museum. The Making Museum group was initially surprised to find that Mr. Mao, who had quietly supported the preservation movement from the outset, had been collecting historical objects and recycling them for many years and it was decided to create a separate room – Uncle Mao's Second Hand Shop – in which he could display them to visitors.

In this special exhibition room, Mr. Mao is free to display his collections as he wishes. In addition to old furniture, pictures and household objects, there are drawings by Mr. Mao on the wall. Since many of the historical buildings on the site have been destroyed by the metro development, he drew sketches of them prior to demolition in order to explain to visitors what the sanatorium used to be like. In addition to this special exhibition room, there are four main themes in the permanent exhibition: ancient Losheng (which displays fossils and material from nearby archaeological excavations); The Losheng Sanatorium of the Japanese Colonial Period (which shows objects and historical documents from this period); The Road to Emancipation (which documents how patients have fought to destigmatize Hansen's disease and charts the preservation movement through music, images and documents); and lastly, a section which explores the everyday lives of the Losheng Patients.

Since there is no external funding for the museum the exhibition has been created by the volunteers and residents themselves. Without professional design input, the atmosphere of the museum is fairly primitive; all labels are hand written and household lamps are used to light objects. When the museum was first opened, objects and documents were mainly displayed in cases borrowed from a private museum. Later on, displays were improved through the donation of spare cases from the Graduate School of Museum Studies at the Taipei National University of the Arts. Located in a corner of a surviving historical building on the site of the original sanatorium, the Losheng Story Museum displays powerful objects in a simple environment, telling difficult stories of residents' lifelong experiences of marginalization, exclusion and discrimination.

Directing the visitor's gaze

Sandell argues that the history of disabled people has largely been hidden since objects which attest to disabled people's lives are rarely displayed in museums and galleries. '[B]y neglecting to depict bodily difference in their exhibition narratives,' he states, 'museums not only reify the idealized human form but, in doing so, present a historically inaccurate view of the past' (2007: 147). Even where disabled people do appear in museum narratives, he continues, the ways in which they are represented very often rely on a 'limited range of negative stereotypes found in other media forms' (ibid.: 148). How then are visitors invited to view and understand the people and experiences they encounter in the Losheng Story Museum? What interpretive processes and devices are used to promote respectful ways of seeing and modes of engagement that resist the kinds of problematic responses that arose from the earlier 'Moment in Time' exhibition?

As Eilean Hooper-Greenhill has powerfully argued:

> The ways in which objects are selected, put together, and written or spoken about have political effects. These effects are not those of objects per se; it is the use made of these objects and their interpretive frameworks that can open up or close down historical, social and cultural possibilities. By making marginal cultures visible, and by legitimating differences, museum pedagogy can become a critical pedagogy.
>
> (2000: 148)

This analysis suggests that it is not only the objects themselves but the ways in which they are interpreted, presented and contextualized that play an important part in framing visitors' engagement with exhibitions. The photography exhibition 'A Moment in Time', which presented its subjects to the art museum visitor within an aesthetic framework through a series of close-up images that emphasized physical differences, successfully prompted visitors' curiosity but risked making people's traumatic experiences the object of the public gaze.

In contrast, the Losheng Story Museum seeks to juxtapose historical objects, images, and oral histories to depict not only the history of the sanatorium and the preservation movement but, importantly, the residents' lives and experiences. Images of residents are not the only exhibits in the museum, nor do they focus on physical differences. Moreover, the location of the exhibition and the atmosphere created by the simple display techniques utilized help to shape the ways in which visitors experience the stories. Where 'A Moment in Time' was displayed in one of the most high profile public museums in Taiwan – the Taipei Fine Art Museum – before the embroilment of the site of the sanatorium in debates around residents' rights, the Losheng Story Museum largely attracts visitors who share a concern with the museum, for the rights and respect of Losheng residents. Most importantly of all, the exhibition narrative is told from the perspectives of the residents themselves.

Empowerment (and agency)

What part then have the disabled residents themselves played in shaping the museum and how will their involvement develop? Though more and more residents have come to identify with the museum and to support its work, some have also expressed concerns about the emphasis on the preservation of historical buildings and objects rather than on residents' experiences. 'Do they only value the historical buildings rather than the people who lived here?' some have asked. 'Does the museum only assist in transforming the sanatorium into a historical site?' These questions raise important issues about the process through which the elderly residents of the sanatorium are empowered to share their memories and experiences with visitors and, through doing so, to challenge social prejudices.

Sharon Snyder and David Mitchell's analysis of what they term the 'cultural locations of disability' (Snyder and Mitchell 2006) is especially helpful here. They distinguish between

> cultural spaces that have been set out exclusively on behalf of disabled citizens such as nineteenth century charity systems; institutions for the feebleminded during the eugenics period; the international disability research industry; sheltered workshops for the 'multihandicapped'; medically based and documentary film representations of disability; and academic research trends on disability [and] more authenticating cultural modes of disability knowledge, such as the disability rights movement, disability culture, the independent living movement, and other experientially based organizations of disabled people.
>
> (ibid.: 3–4)

The former, they point out, can sometimes be shrouded in rhetoric which appears to foreground disabled people's interests but instead 'these locations exist largely at odds with the collective and individual well-being of disabled people' (ibid.: 4).

Snyder and Mitchell's analysis highlights the importance of personal narratives and a privileging of disability experience as prerequisites for developing alternative ways of seeing and knowing disability (ibid.: 5). Indeed, throughout the preservation movement, residents' rights and experiences have been at the heart of the campaign. Residents have been empowered throughout to take an active role in workshops, forums, art festivals and performances held in the sanatorium. By giving primacy to residents' experiences and personal narratives the aim has been to challenge dominant medicalized stereotypes, which present residents as passive recipients of treatment, and instead to highlight individuals' active productivity and creativity (Zhuang and Lu 2006).

Similarly, the development of the Losheng Story Museum has been shaped by a desire not only to document and interpret the histories of residents but, crucially, to create a public space for unmediated exchange and communication between the residents and the public. Drawing on and sharing their own personal experiences and memories, residents *themselves* provide visitors with knowledge and understanding related to the site – an 'authenticating' mode of disability knowledge to which Snyder and Mitchell refer.

Future challenges for the Losheng Story Museum

Histories and memories inscribed within the Losheng Story Museum encourage visitors not only to understand the history of the site but also to reflect upon how different authorities have suppressed and discriminated against a minority and how society continues to neglect the rights of disabled people. The museum's interpretive approach, which places residents' own experiences at the core, is designed to resist the creation of an aesthetic spectacle for public consumption and instead to counter stereotypes and encourage respectful ways of seeing (Sandell 2007).

While undertaking research for this chapter, a law was finally passed by the Legislative Yuan on 18 July 2008 providing compensation for Hansen's patients and also requiring that the Council for Cultural Affairs establish the Hansen Human Rights Park and a Museum of Medicine in the remaining area of the sanatorium after its demolition. This involvement of the government might seem, on the one hand, to offer increased support for the museum with the possibility of financial and other resources. However, it also poses potential challenges and threats. With the proposed demolition plans, the original historical building that currently houses the museum will be taken apart and reconstructed elsewhere. At present there are no detailed plans or associated funding to ensure that the museum can be re-established in a new location. Even more significantly, funding and direct involvement from governmental sectors will undoubtedly influence the museum's mission, interpretive philosophy and the style and content of exhibitions. The planned 'official version' of the museum, which places emphasis on the history of medicine, is very different from the current one that places residents' perspectives at its heart.

Consideration of the factors which shaped the establishment of the Losheng Story Museum and its subsequent development holds significance for understanding, more broadly, the museum's social role in representing disability and its complex relationship to human rights. The original museum is not simply a site for telling visitors about the complex and traumatic history of leprosy, public health and medical practice in Taiwan; it provides a locus for the exchange of ideas between residents, visitors, students and scholars of different generations and from various fields. Most significantly, it functions as a site of social education in which visitors are prompted, through encounters and engagement with residents' own personal experiences, to reflect deeply on the ways in which society stigmatizes difference (Pan 2004). The challenge that must now be faced is how to negotiate the development of a new museum, to ensure resources are channelled in ways which continue to make residents' voices heard, their marginal cultures visible and to ensure the continuing function of the museum as a site of critical pedagogy.

Acknowledgements

I would like to thank Ms. Zu Ching Wang for her helpful comments on this paper and Mr. Friday Wu and Uncle Mao for their continuing support for this research. Also special gratitude and wishes for all the residents of the Losheng Sanatorium.

Note

1 Although patients were required to be sterilized before getting married, some had children before entering the sanatorium and others had children secretly without getting married.

References

Chen, C-L. (2003) 'Learning, Recollection and Connection: A Study of Cultural Identities amongst Visitors to Local Museums in Taiwan', Unpublished Doctoral Thesis, Leicester: University of Leicester.

—— (2007) *Wound on Exhibition: Notes on Memory and Trauma of Museums*, Taipei: Artouch Publisher.

Chang, H-L. (2007) 'The violation and compensation of basic human rights of Hansen's patients', *Taipei Bar Journal*, 329: 67–85.

Fann, Y-C. (2005) *Disease, Medicine and Colonial Modernization: The History of Medicine in Colonial Taiwan*, Taipei: Daw Shiang Publishing Co.

Edmond, R. (2006) *Leprosy and Empire: A Medieval and Cultural History*, Cambridge and New York: Cambridge University Press.

Fanon, F. (1968) *The Wretched of the Earth*, New York: Grove Weidenfeld.

Foucault, M. (1989) *Madness and Civilization*, R. Howard (trans.), London: Routledge.

Gaudet, M. G. (2004) *Carville: Remembering Leprosy in America*, Jackson: University Press of Mississippi.

Gussow, Z. (1989) *Leprosy, Racism, and Public Health: Social Policy in Chronic Disease Control*, London: Westview Press.

Hooper-Greenhill, E. (2000) *Museums and the Interpretation of Visual Culture*, London: Routledge.

Lu, L-L. (1995) 'The controversy and protest of chronology of leper village exhibition: artist promised to remedy', *United Evening News*, 22 November.

Liu, J-C. (2004) *The History of Losheng Sanatorium*, Taipei County: Cultural Affairs Bureau.

Manchester, K. and Roberts, C. (1989) 'The palaeopathology of leprosy in Britain: a review', *World Archaeology*, 21(2): 265–72.

Pan, P-C. (2004) 'Heritage of medical culture – the Losheng Sanatorium', *Windows of Culture*, 70: 92–95.

Sandell, R. (2007) *Museums, Prejudice and the Reframing of Difference*, London: Routledge.

Sontag, S. (1989) *Aids and its metaphors*, New York: Farrar Straus Giroux.

Snyder, S. L. and Mitchell, D. T. (2006) *Cultural Locations of Disability*, Chicago: University of Chicago Press.

Tsai, J. (2007) 'Battle to save Losheng Sanatorium continues', *Taiwan Journal*, 20 March 2007. Online. Available http://taiwanjournal.nat.gov.tw/ct.asp?xItem=24051& CtNode= 122 (accessed 24 November 2008).

Yao, J-T. (2001) 'Knowing Taiwan: knowledge, power and the Japanese colonial govern-mentality of Taiwan', *Taiwan: A Radical Quarterly in Social Studies*, 42: 119–82.

Zhou, Q-H. (1996) 'To be a storyteller', Hsinchu: Tsing Hua University Arts Center. Online. Available http://arts.nthu.edu.tw/programs_show.php?fdkind2=238 time=2 fdsn=76 (accessed 27 June 2008).

Zhuang, Y. and Lu, C.Y. (2006) 'The forgotten national treasures: the sounds and images of Losheng fighters', *Humanistic Education Journal*, 208: 110–11.

18

A MUSEUM FOR ALL?

The Norwegian Museum of Deaf History and Culture

Hanna Mellemsether

The 100-year-old Trøndelag Folk Museum – an open-air museum of cultural history in Trondheim – has recently developed a new museum branch: the Norwegian Museum of Deaf History and Culture (NDM), which opened in March 2009 after a rather long and troubled planning period. This chapter focuses on the problems and challenges encountered by seasoned museum workers when confronted with disability issues, challenges around the uses of sign language and the dilemmas thrown up by politicized distinctions between an understanding of deafness (as disability) versus Deafness as culture.

Through an examination of this single case study, an account of how the museum evolved from private collection to public institution, and the ideology and values underpinning and driving this project, I aim to shed some light upon a series of difficult questions which will resonate in other countries and contexts. What is Deaf history and culture and should it be a part of our common (shared) cultural history? What factors might justify a new museum dedicated to this particular group? How do we make this place a museum for everybody, not only for those with a particular (often personal) interest in the Deaf community and Deaf history?

A visit to the museum

A small group of people visited Trøndelag Folk Museum in Trondheim on a fine summer Sunday a few years ago. I watched as they wandered through the labyrinths in our permanent exhibition, *Images of Life*, which portrays life in the Trøndelag region during the last 150 years. The group consists of elderly men and women, like so many of the museum's visitors who spend the weekend doing memory work. But unlike other groups, they do not talk loudly together, or whisper and point, putting their heads together. This group uses hands and eyes, fluently signing their shared experiences and personal histories as they take the tour. Watching from a distance, I notice that they walk rather fast, do not stop often to discuss the elegantly displayed and artistically lit objects behind the glass, nor do they read the text on the walls.

At first I am confused. The group comprises people with an interest in history, from a national organization for Deaf history that had specifically asked to see the exhibitions. Then I notice that, as they walk between the lighted objects and blocks of written information, their faces and hands are in shadow. Black walls surround the lighted showcases and blocks of texts, creating a dark, cave-like atmosphere in the exhibition gallery. The function of the artistic lighting is to direct visitors' attention towards the objects, the history, the message that the curators themselves want to tell. But the message is lost to this group of deaf men and women. They hurry politely through the exhibition, finding spots of lights outside of the intended pathway where they can see each other's hands and faces and communicate the way they do – in Sign Language.

All of a sudden they come to a halt in front of a poster depicting a magician performing in a local vaudeville hall in the 1940s. Hands move, laughter flows. One man takes centre stage and holds the attention of all the others for a long time. Questions are answered, anecdotes told and memories shared. The reason for this sudden activity was the fact that the magician in the poster was deaf; even more, he was the father of one of the visitors in the group. To the group of deaf people, he was 'one of us'; he represented their culture, in contrast to all the other stories, pictures and objects in the exhibition. None of the museum workers who had made the exhibition knew that the person in the poster was deaf; to them he simply represented the entertainment industry at a certain time in a particular place. With tremendous clarity, this episode gave us – practitioners in the folk museum – a powerful message about the importance and value of different parts of our community being visible within the stories we told. And it also suggested to us the possibilities inherent in alternative approaches to interpretation and the opportunities that might accrue through the re-presentation of histories.

From private collection to public museum

NDM started as a private collection in rented locations in the now abandoned School for the Deaf, in Trondheim (Figure 18.1). Two rooms were filled with hearing-aids, books, photographs and other artifacts mainly from the old school that was shut down in 1991. The exhibition at that time was of interest to those who had been pupils at deaf schools, or those who knew someone who had been – but not to many outside this narrow group. The primary motivation behind that early phase of the museum was the need to collect and preserve the histories of deaf people from a period that will be forgotten when the last generation, those who lived their formative years in Norway's segregated deaf schools, dies out. In the 1990s, these schools were closed down and deaf children in Norway are now, more or less, integrated

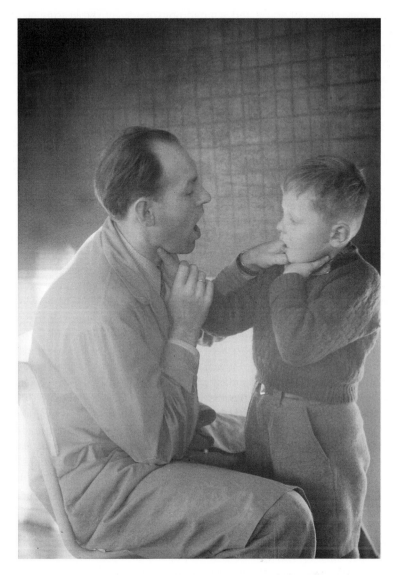

Figure 18.1 Speech training at Trondheim School for the Deaf, 1949. (Photographer: Foto Schrøder. Copyright: Norsk Døvemuseum/Trøndelag Folkemuseum)

in the public schools near their homes. The early exhibition, then, aimed to make visible a group of people who are not often represented in ordinary history museums. This process of recording how deaf people lived their lives is part of the construction of a common past for the Deaf as a cultural group. The narrative presented in the exhibition was that of a linear progression from bad to good, segregation to integration, discrimination to equality.

There were stories of abuse and wrongdoings made by the hearing world in the past, and about the struggle for self-respect and group rights for deaf people. Stories about deaf heroes, exceptional individuals within the deaf community, strengthened the narrative of the common past and helped to present a strong, vital community today.

The enthusiastic and dedicated people who had started the collections soon realized that the cost of the rent and of maintaining the collection was beyond their financial means. In 2001 the Norwegian Ministry of Culture and Church Affairs assigned the task of developing a national museum of deaf history and culture to Trøndelag Folk Museum. Thus started not only a new museum project, but also – as importantly – a subtle but significant change in the way the traditional folk museum worked.

The politicians who, in 2001, decided that the collection should be transferred to Trøndelag Folk Museum, might have intended us to create a small exhibition about the deaf community and the history of the deaf schools in Norway, within the confines of the existing folk museum. We soon realized, however, that if the Museum of Deaf History and Culture was to become more than an exhibition for a small group of people with specialized interests and experiences, we had to create a much larger project and, at the same time, secure the old school as a site for this development. The school for the deaf started in Trondheim in 1825 in a rented site, as the first Norwegian school for children with special needs. The building that now holds the museum was opened in 1855. It is a monumental building in a neo-gothic style, built for the purpose of the education of the deaf. And it is therefore also an important part of Norway's national educational history. It took us five years to convince the Ministry of Culture, but in 2007 we had secured financing for both the capital investment and the operating costs. A group of professional museum workers were put together, consisting of an exhibition architect, educational staff, historians and curators, none of us deaf, but experienced in making exhibitions and educational museum programmes.

It is always a risky project when a collection, built by the enthusiasm of a community passionate about the history towards which they feel a sense of ownership, is transferred to a professional museum. Those who had begun the private collection years earlier feared losing control and being misrepresented by the museum. These concerns had to be met with dialogue and involvement in decision making but questions remained. Who represented the deaf community? And how could the museum combine open dialogue with this community with the wish to communicate with visitors from all parts of society?

We decided to create a reference group comprising individuals from different groups within the deaf community. We sought to put together people of different ages and gender, people who are born deaf, people who had acquired deafness later in life, and also hearing children of deaf adults as well as hearing parents with deaf children. These people would have differentiated views of deafness; some would see themselves as members of the Deaf World, some would have a self-identity as members of a shared Norwegian culture. Some would see deafness as a handicap, others would see it as a sign of belonging in a unique and strong global Deaf culture. Common to all the people in our reference group is that they are fluent Sign Language users, which none of the museum workers are.

The history and culture connected to the use and development of Sign Language is the thread that connects the dots of factual history. We found that deaf people's practices and the experiences they have had through history and even have today, provide valuable material on which to draw when we want to make people discuss and reflect upon dilemmas concerning disability and culture, normality and abnormality and inclusion and exclusion. Our plans for the museum were discussed with this reference group, both with individual members and with the group as a whole. Ideas for the content of the exhibition, the museum's purpose, ideologies and goals have generally been well received although it is fair to say that concessions have been made on both sides. Throughout these lively discussions, however, the main focus has been preserved; the new museum will be an inclusive museum, not for deaf only and not for hearing people only.

Who are the 'Deaf'?

Defining people into categories is a difficult and often unnecessary practice. The search for clear and unambiguous definitions can be an indication of a 'curatorial need for definite knowledge' that can make museum workers (and academics) uncomfortable with open, fluid definitions and with unresolved questions (Dodd *et al.* 2004: 22).

Nevertheless, one of the first questions we had to ask ourselves when we started work on the new Museum of Deaf History and Culture was: who constitutes membership of the Deaf community? – a community whose experiences would lie at the heart of the museum. It is a paradox that we know more about the development of hearing aids and technological equipment than about the people who use them.

Deafness and Deaf culture are not necessarily neatly aligned with each other. Within the deaf community there are different factions with different approaches to deafness – notably 'Deaf' and 'deaf'; the capital D makes a difference (Lane 2005). Deaf mute, deaf and dumb, hearing impaired – the choices are many and not without consequences. Words have many meanings, they convey attitudes and prejudices and may hurt, even when used in a well-intended context. The words used in the discourse on deafness are just as important as those within other minority discourses concerned with homosexuality, ethnicity, gender, class and so on. During the time we have worked with the Museum of Deaf Culture and History, we have found it necessary to revisit definitions and terms we used at the outset and to change our use of certain words. We do not, of course, use the ill-famed 'deaf and dumb', which went out of use decades ago, at least amongst the well-informed, but which lingers on in the media. Deaf people are not dumb, in any sense of the word; neither are they 'mute'. Some deaf and hard of hearing people use the common denominator 'hearing impaired', although this is not accepted by all. In a Norwegian study, Haualand *et al.* (2003) found:

> Thirty nine per cent of the respondents said they identified them-selves as 'Deaf' and 60% said they identified themselves as 'hard of hearing' or 'hearing impaired'. Language competence appeared to be strongly connected with self identification. Of those identifying as hard of hearing/hearing impaired, 91% said they had Norwegian as their best language, while 80% of those saying they were Deaf had NTS (Norwegian Sign Language) as their best language. Approxi-mately 80% of all respondents know both NTS and both-either written and spoken Norwegian.

There are distinctions, both practical and cultural, between people who are born deaf, those who have acquired deafness after they have learnt a lan-guage, and people who are hard of hearing. In the museum we have a need for definitions that is either intended to create discussions and reflections, or can be used in specific contexts to help clarify and explain different elements in the museum exhibition or educational programme. Also deaf people themselves have different views on 'deafness' as disability versus 'Deafness' as culture, and some feel caught between the expectations to be integrated into the main society and the demands from their own culture.

We have not tried to find a neutral word, but will use the available vocabulary to highlight the ongoing debate about language, meaning and power in a gen-eral way. We use both Deaf and deaf, hard of hearing and hearing impaired, depending on the message we want to convey. 'Deaf' (with the capital D) will generally denote people who belong to the Deaf culture, who define themselves by their use of a common language – Sign Language. The use of 'deaf' (with a lower-case d) might be taken as a technical term to refer to the group whose hearing loss is more than a certain decibel level, people who have a spoken or written language as their first language, often people who are late-deafened. Hard of hearing generally refers to those who have a hearing loss less than a certain decibel level. But these definitions are not used to demarcate parts of the museum, or tell visitors who the museum is for or about. We find that by using the different terms in different contexts in the exhibition, the words *themselves* are exhibited and may create reflection on the power of naming and may also prompt connections with other discourses of difference.

Culture or disability?

We have elected not to focus on what deaf people lack but on what they have; a cultural identity expressed through Sign Language, an identity with a set of values and positive qualities attached to it. Their lack of hearing is not a problem when they are within the deaf community. Together with deaf people who use Sign Language, deafness is the norm and hearing is the abnormality. At a conference on deaf history in Paris in 2003, where all papers and presentations were delivered in Sign Language, the hearing museum curator became just as disabled as the deaf are when they attend an ordinary history conference: we both need an interpreter. The experience of being different was a useful introduction to the dilemmas and experiences of deafness when we, as hearing, started working on the Museum of Deaf History and Culture.

Deaf people are most often thought of as disabled and, historically, deafness has been defined as a medical problem, different and abnormal compared to the hearing population. The medical profession is constantly looking for ways of curing deafness. Together with the development of new forms of 'aid', from digital hearing aids to cochlear implants that all aim to reduce the effects of hearing loss, this medicalization of deafness places deaf individuals within the broad category of disabled people. It is clear that in the context of the hearing society, where communication through sound dominates, people who cannot hear are disabled. And within the Norwegian welfare system, you have to accept the categorization as disabled in order to access economic and social benefits and rights. But many deaf people would not identify themselves as disabled. Deaf people's self-identity and their relation to the hearing community have changed during the last decades. Identity is created. You are not born with a set of identity markers that you carry with you from womb to grave. Identity is made and re-made, in a dialogue with one's surroundings, with other people, family and friends that we interact with. Education systems, laws and regulations, norms and practices all play a part in forming our identities. For deaf people, the environment and networks that contribute to the shaping of their identities are not necessarily to be found in the neighbourhood, but might just as well consist of persons in Deaf organizations, in Internet chat-rooms or in the infrastructures that support international sports participation (Breivik 2007). If you grow up as the only deaf child in your family and in your school, if you are the only one using Sign Language, then the level of interaction might not be as deep and meaningful in your home environment as it is in a Sign Language community like the one you find in schools and organizations for the deaf.

The term 'Deaf World' is often used to refer to this Deaf culture that consists of Sign Language users – including people who are deaf, hard of hearing, their closest family, the interpreters, teachers and others who use Sign Language in their communication. As a cultural group, the Deaf World therefore includes more than the deaf and, as a minority culture, it is partly inside and partly outside the mainstream national culture. In Norway, Sign Language was recognized as a first language for deaf children in the education system in 1997 and, in 2009, Norwegian Sign Language was given the status of an official language. A new generation of deaf people will then have more opportunities to take part in different arenas, even in the traditional 'hearing' arenas, than did earlier generations. Better interpreter services, technological and cultural development function both as a means of including deaf in the hearing world and, at the same time, strengthening Deaf culture.

While the hearing community is built around institutions like family, relations, local or national society, deaf individuals often see themselves as belonging to a trans-local culture and history, and the deaf world as trans-national and global (Haualand *et al.* 2003; Breivik 2007). Deaf history tradition consists of both national and international narrations; it tells about deaf in many countries, about the deaf's relations to hearing communities; it is about their own educational institutions and deaf heroes and heroines. Contrary to the hearing community, Deaf culture and traditions are not transferred from grandparents and parents to children, but the culture carriers are more likely to be other deaf people or organizations for the deaf. The exception to this is where deafness is inherited and where deaf children grow up with deaf parents, grandparents and other deaf relations. NDM therefore becomes important as a carrier of Deaf history and culture. Indeed, preliminary studies suggest that the museum is an important part of Deaf identity building and has played a central role in the struggle of Deaf people to be recognized as a cultural group (Midtdal 2006).

Influenced by this understanding of deafness, and in line with our traditions as a museum of cultural history, we have taken a cultural approach to Deaf history. The museum will collect, maintain, interpret and promote the material and intangible history of the deaf community according to the norms and regulations contained in the International Council of Museums' (ICOM) codes of ethics, in the same way as the 'mother museum' – Trøndelag Folk Museum – does for the majority cultures. In addition, we also have a responsibility to show relations between deaf and hearing and to promote tolerance and acceptance between these communities.

Making history – dilemmas and controversies in deaf history

An important narrative in the Norwegian Museum of Deaf History and Culture is how a cultural group has emerged and changed its position and identity within Norwegian society. The museum shows methods, materials and individuals that, in different ways, have contributed to this process. This does not mean that the factual history of how deaf people have lived their lives, how schools and organizations functioned, is unimportant. In the new exhibition the material history of past life will still be presented as an important part of the memory work of the deaf community. After all, making the deaf community visible is one of our main goals as a museum. But we also want to address an audience beyond the deaf community, and to raise questions and highlight dilemmas that are relevant to other parts of modern society. Therefore we have chosen to let facts and stories in deaf history throw a critical light on aspects of our shared modern society.

We could have focused the museum on issues of deaf education and the origins of the School. To many in the community, this would have been welcomed. The single common institution that all deaf people in Norway experienced up until the 1990s is the deaf school. Most deaf and hard of hearing children were sent to one of the central schools for the deaf. For many it meant that they were sent away from their homes and families for a long period, and therefore formed strong and enduring bonds with the other deaf children at the school. Many deaf people want this to be what the museum is all about: the walk down memory lane, the nostalgia surrounding their formative years. These schools are central to deaf experience in many ways. Here, Sign Language was formed and reformed and, in the school communities, the first interest in organizations for and with deaf people emerged. In the beginning, the leaders of these organizations were hearing clerics or teachers, but it did not take long before the deaf themselves got involved and also took up positions of leadership. If Deaf culture has a cradle, the schools would be it. So, it would clearly be a logical and entirely valid solution if we had elected to make NDM a museum of the deaf schools.

Or, we could easily have made exhibitions based on the medical and technological history connected to deafness and hearing impairment. The development of hearing aids is, in itself, an interesting story that could warrant an exhibition. History has many examples of how medical professionals have tried to heal deafness, from hearing aids, amplifiers and computers to gene technology. For many in the Deaf community, there is a fear that Sign Language, and thereby the Deaf culture, will become extinct in the future and these concerns are reflected in the museum. The controversy surrounding cochlear implants is, to most hearing people, incomprehensible. How can some deaf parents deny their children the operation that would enable them to hear? The argument that they want to maintain the right to be deaf does not have many advocates in the medical professions. But who decides what is accepted and what are unwanted variations of humanity? While biological diversity is important in nature, it is not wanted in human society. How different are we allowed to be and how are the limits of differentness set? Is it individually experienced quality of life that decides, or is it simply the cost of 'adjusting' the individual to society? These questions are made all the more relevant with new developments in medicine and technology. In 1992 the so-called 'genetic error' responsible for a common type of inherited deafness was identified by researchers at Boston University in the USA. The finding was seen by many as a 'major breakthrough that will improve diagnosis and genetic counselling and ultimately lead to substitution therapy or gene transfer therapy'. The goal of such efforts as gene transfer therapy is to reduce and ultimately to eliminate Deaf births altogether. Thus, as Harlan Lane has argued, 'a new form of medical eugenics applied to Deaf people is envisioned' (2005: 303).

At NDM we have elected to present different (and often sharply conflicting) views and standpoints, not as dogmas, but as something to be reflected upon and discussed with and by the visitors. Our aim is therefore not to tell a true and uncontested story, but to provoke reflection and afterthoughts that may challenge prejudice. By focusing on Deaf culture, and its relation to mainstream culture, we aim to challenge prejudices towards differences in general, whether on the basis of race, class, gender, sexuality or disability. The ways in which 'we' interact with and treat otherness in our society have changed through time and across space. The new exhibition aims to challenge people's attitudes and prejudices and hopefully create greater respect for diversity by exposing the narrowness of the concept of normality.

Activism in museums

Working with the history of deaf people and Deaf culture, we were also drawn into the fight for deaf people's rights. Recognition of Sign Language as an official language is a demand from the Deaf community and the museum encountered expectations to support these demands. Likewise, other local campaigners occasionally approach us in order to have us sign petitions and letters to editors of newspapers with demands made on behalf of the Deaf community. Difficult questions, like the controversies surrounding cochlear implants or the question of gene transplant therapy in order to reduce or cure deafness, are also issues with both political and cultural implications that we confront in our museum.

But should we as a public museum get involved and seek to change things or should we instead aim to serve a 'neutral truth' as some forces in society seem to want and expect? Interestingly, the work on the NDM started at a time when the social role and responsibility of museums was increasingly open to debate, both nationally and internationally (Sandell 2007: 3). The Norwegian Archive, Library and Museum Authority (ABM), for example, started a project a few years ago called 'Brudd', meaning 'breaking away' (from traditions) – its purpose to create dialogue around the potential for museums to engage with unconventional stories and controversial exhibitions and to support professionals in addressing the difficult stories in our history (ABM 2007).

In a long-established institution such as Trøndelag Folk Museum, the notion that museums might be involved in activism and perhaps align themselves with political pressure groups was not without problems, and some museum workers saw this work as outside of the role and function of a museum *per se*. In many ways, this opposition to the idea of the museum as an agent for social change seems strange, since the Folk museum movement in the nineteenth century was, in itself, political: it sought to foster and perpetuate the political and cultural nationalism and regionalism of its time. Museums, as Sandell (2007: 5) has argued, 'have functioned to engender feelings of belonging and worth in some and, in others, a sense of inferiority and exclusion'. Why then should it be more controversial for a museum to get involved in working towards progressive social change today than in earlier times? The notion that museums offer neutral presentations of an objective, true past is no longer tenable and most practitioners acknowledge the subjectivity of the museum's collections and displays. The museum's role as a social agent is also confirmed in ICOM's code of ethics:

> Museum usage of collections from contemporary communities requires respect for human dignity and the traditions and cultures that use such material. Such collections should be used to promote human well-being, social development, tolerance, and respect by advocating multisocial, multicultural and multilingual expression.
>
> (2006: 10)

This paragraph might be meant to apply primarily to collections of sensitive material (such as human remains or ritual artifacts), but it might just as well apply to all collections from all contemporary communities.

Encountering disability: what difference does it make?

Trøndelag Folk Museum dates back to 1909 when a group of Trondheim residents started to collect characteristic examples of the way houses were built in earlier times. The area surrounding the ruins of King Sverre's medieval castle was appropriated for the site of the new open-air museum. The museum has more than 60 vintage buildings which show building traditions in Trøndelag, from town and countryside, from mountain to coast and from Sámi huts to city mansions. The majority of the houses are from the eighteenth and nineteenth centuries. In short – a typical Norwegian open-air museum, established in a period of strong national and regional identity-building in a young, independent Norwegian state. As for most folk museums at the time, the aim was to construct a history of a community of strong, independent and proud people, to show achievements and accomplishments in the past to confirm the newborn national identity.[1] The museum portrayed a homogenous community – with indigenous Sámi history only included as a tribute to 'the quaint others' or perhaps to make a contribution to the Norwegian tourist industry. A hundred years ago, nobody wanted to show disability and disabled people, if not in connection with histories of medical advancement or in the tradition of the curiosity cabinet. However, our encounter with Deaf culture a few years ago played a part in bringing about a broader shift in thinking and practice within the Trøndelag Folk Museum.

In recent years we have had projects for young refugees and asylum seekers in cooperation with another museum, library and schools. We have made extensive use of museum theatre to involve our visitors in engaging with a variety of difficult contemporary topics. In 2005 we developed a project which focused on friendship and war: what happens when neighbours all of a sudden become national enemies? The case we used was the factual history, from 1905, when Norway broke away from the union with Sweden. While our independence came about without actual war, the recent struggle for self-determination in the Balkan states had a different result. Here, neighbourhoods and even families found themselves fighting against each other. Through a storyline method, the visitors were forced to take sides, to reflect on dilemmas and difficult decisions people in similar situations today have to make. In 2008 we ran a museum project dealing with sexual abuse. Again, we used museum theatre as a means of interacting with the visitors who had to take up the role of judges in a modern-time court case, but where the evidence, witness statements and all the facts were taken from an actual court case concerning a case of sexual abuse or rape in Trondheim in 1889.

Trøndelag Folk Museum is an institution which was founded to conserve and represent the history of a homogenous (although imagined) Norwegian culture. And yet, even within a large and, in many ways, traditional organization such as this, the museum's encounter with Deaf culture contributed to profound changes and a process, still underway, which challenges our own understanding of what a museum is today, our role in society and our obligations towards more diverse audiences than those we had previously engaged or even recognized.

Note

1 Much has been written about the role of museums in constructing and promoting national identity. A descriptive history of the background and development of open air museums from a Scandinavian perspective can be found in Rentzhog 2007.

References

ABM (2007) *Brudd: Om det ubehagelige, tabubelagte, marginale, usynlige, kontroversielle*, Skrift 26, Oslo: ABM Utvikling.

Breivik, J. K. (2007) *Døv identitet i endring. Lokale liv – globale bevegelser*, Oslo: Universitetsforlaget.

Dodd, J., Sandell, R., Delin, A. and Gay, J. (2004) *Buried in the Footnotes: the representation of disabled people in museum and gallery collections*, Phase 1 report, Leicester: RCMG. Online. Available http://www.le.ac.uk/ms/research/Reports/BITF2.pdf (accessed 12 March 2009).

Haualand, H., Grønningsæter, A. and Skog Hansen, I. L. (2003) 'Uniting divided worlds: identity, family and education in the life projects of deaf and hard of hearing young people', *Disability Studies Quarterly*, 23(2): 75–88. Online. Available http://www.dsq-sds-archives.org/_articles_html/2003/Spring/dsq_2003_Spring_08.asp (accessed 12 March 2009).

International Council of Museums (2006) *ICOM Code of Ethics for Museums*, Paris: ICOM.

Lane, H. (2005) 'Ethnicity, ethics, and the Deaf-World', *Journal of Deaf Studies and Deaf Education*, 10(3): 291–310.

Midtdal, Å. (2006) 'En uhørt historie. Norsk Døvemuseum som del av døves identitetskonstruksjon', unpublished thesis, University of Oslo.

Rentzhog, S. (2007) *Open air museums: the history and future of a visionary idea*, Stockholm, Østersund: Carlssons Jamtli förlag.

Sandell, R. (2007) *Museums, Prejudice and the Reframing of Difference*, London and New York: Routledge.

19

COLLECTIVE BODIES

What museums do for disability studies

Katherine Ott

Desire is a complicated thing. It can lead those whom it ensnares into wild and unfamiliar places, as they attempt to arrest the ache issuing from it. Scholars and curators alike often must bear up under continually unfulfilled desires. Curators, especially those who come from an academic background, long to demonstrate their expertise through labels that are way too long and specialized for their public to appreciate. Despite significant advances in the art of museum communication in recent decades, many curators still have hard lessons about brevity and language to learn, if they want their work to be noticed. Academics, on their part, sometimes regret that their books, articles, and conference panels attract comparatively small audiences. When they open themselves up to the sensory world of artifacts, they encounter thousands of curious and attentive gallery visitors.

Both groups share an educational focus but not a common vocabulary. Curators deal more immediately with the ethics and effectiveness of their work than do most university faculty. Museums generally interact with a cross-section of people and get feedback on their product through attendance, public reviews, and letters. Their work product is public and they are accountable to artifact donors, visitors, funders, colleagues and museum management. If their output is boring, irrelevant or inaccurate, their workplace collapses – visitors stop coming. Academic scholars have captive audiences in the form of students who pay large fees to hear what they have to say. Students pay attention in order to get grades and diplomas. They do not browse for items of interest, as gallery-goers do. A professor's output can be uneven across the semesters and she or he may never feel pressure to consider the ethics of how they work or what they produce.

This chapter is a move towards common ground by suggesting ways that disability studies scholars might use museum principles and practices to reach into cognitive areas of students' brains that are untapped through typical classroom teaching. It explores ethical and historical dynamics related to the process of exhibiting the history of people with disabilities, including how objects are collected, selected and interpreted. Taking an American perspective on scholarly practice and drawing upon examples from American museums, the chapter addresses contemporary exhibition practice and places it within both the history of exhibiting anomalous bodies and the modulating influence of the disability rights movement. The collecting and exhibition of disability artifacts have much in common with other areas of museum practice that embody ethical challenges, such as the display of culturally sensitive materials, human remains, and the mission of the recent museums of conscience movement; topics which have received much more attention in the museum studies literature. It is also material and visual culture-grounded rather than prose dependent and therefore guided by different conventions of explication. What makes an artifact authentic or worthy of documentation and preservation may have little to do with what was written about it and everything to do with how it was made and used – data that may only be available from a close reading of the artifact. To draw the example out further, in studying or displaying artifacts, curators have no trouble in citing other objects rather than books, to support their argument.

Museum authority

Museums of history, art, and culture can contribute several kinds of important work to the growing body of knowledge related to disability and disability studies. The most obvious contribution is the modelling of inclusion through examples of how to welcome all visitors. They can also do the important heritage work of historical validation, demonstrating that people with disabilities have always been a part of events, as agents of change, and subject to the same forces and circumstances as everyone else. This often includes special redemptive recognition of the disabled side of famous people, such as Franklin Roosevelt, Mary Todd Lincoln, Mark Twain and others. The heritage phase of reclaiming and valorizing disability is necessary but not nearly as interesting as the content that comes after it, when disability can be explored as complicated and contentious. A parallel in this is that of the early years of African American history, when scholars recovered and celebrated inventions, discoveries and works of art that were made by people of African heritage. It was not until much later that those same inventors and discoverers were explored as complex human beings, who might have owned slaves themselves, committed unsavoury acts, or been flawed in some way.

Surveys and studies document and continually confirm that museums are trusted and respected sites for the conveyance of knowledge. In a typical study, 80 per cent of visitors reported that museums are more authoritative than films or books when it comes to imparting information (American Association of Museums 2001).[1] This is so despite popular scepticism and caution about the heavy influence of nationalism and the state on the interpretation of the information imparted. Museums are embraced with an expectation of learning supported by expertise (Dodd *et al.*, this volume).

Internationally, museums compete within the tourist market for dollars and attendance.[2] Travellers have numerous choices for leisure activities, from arcades, parks or dining out, to trekking and extreme sports. Museums historically have operated under two powerful agencies: the state and the market. These modulating forces necessitate that museums be both cultural barometers and gate-keepers, in order to stay viable. What gets in and displayed is what the public will tolerate and the state will support. This makes museums significant locations for the intellectual work of modern citizenry. Visitors grant museums the authority to shape them, challenge them and affirm them.[3] State and public entities such as community mores and laws, media reporting, and philanthropy and funding often serve as dampers to intellectual freedom in ways that those teaching a university class do not often experience. Museums have become prime forces in the creation of citizenry and public life. They are open classrooms where strangers rub shoulders and learn what they and their fellow citizens value.

In this way, museums are an ideal location where visitors can be prodded to re-frame what they know, using a disability consciousness. Objects are one of the most powerful tools for understanding 'Why?' Almost any object can be shown to be part of the documentation and explication of disability, depending upon who used it and under what circumstances. Objects are polysemic and vibrate with those who animated them, across the decades. The core of each object is alive with its particular history, waiting for an interpreter to release its narrative.

Toppling the 'word', reading objects

Museums document and preserve parts of the historical record that universities do not. Museums collect artifacts and stories otherwise lost. The existing records in archives and libraries are most often those of people with resources, access to words, or identified as worthy of study. Poor people, women, children, and the disenfranchised leave few written records and documents and easily slip away out of history's grasp. The material culture of marginal people and their communities is usually undervalued and discarded unless museums gather and preserve it. Although museums have not been proactive in this kind of collecting, besides the objects still in the custody of families, they are the only place where such materials exist. The lives of everyday people with disabilities can be retrieved through the material and visual culture they have left behind. It is the archaeology of the disappeared and hidden.

Working with objects such as these requires an orientation to evidence that diverges from that of traditional documentary sources. It does not emphasize words and text. Objects are particular and unique in several important ways, each with repercussions for disability theory. The material record provides tangible evidence of things that disability studies students can only imagine or

271

read about. It gives tactility, flesh and animation to people with disabilities from the past, through their corsets, crutches, IQ tests, school yearbooks, invalid feeders, peg legs, knuckle boards, Braille writers, begging cups and tinted lenses, as well as objects unrelated to their disability.

Museums bridge the gaps between words, things, people and ideas.[4] Studying an object such as a wicker wheelchair is like taking out a thin slice of historical experience and freezing it in time. It gives evidence about mobility, travel surfaces, the size, strength and activity level of the user, the user's relationship with the pusher, expectations about where the user would travel (not far and not on public roads), and furniture design. A back-brace or a truss creates a past of three dimensions, with size, shape and weight. A shoulder harness and a split-hook hand give a tactile, sensory dimension to the past and lead to questions about what one would commonly want to pick up or touch and why.

A traditional, text-based historian, without hesitation, will say that 'History is change over time'. An historian trained in material culture might say that 'History is about our ability to fashion things of ever greater complexity in increasing numbers' (Csikszentmihalyi and Rochberg-Halton 1985: ix). The transactions between people and the things they create are central to the human condition. And the first rule of studying material culture is that you must see it, touch it and visit it to comprehend it. Sensory experience is essential to knowledge because words are limited. Words are general, while experience is particular and individual. When you have studied one person with a disability, you have studied one person. Words, because they refer to general things, like autism or cerebral palsy, are imprecise and misleading. Temple Grandin, one person with autism who lives in Colorado and is an inventor and professor and created a squeeze box for herself in which to relax, is specific. Words create a unity that does not really exist. Temple Grandin's autism is unlike anyone else's. In addition, words do not embody meaning but merely facilitate it. They convey meaning. Words are removed from the thing – they describe things. When you touch the words 'leper's bell' on the page, you have not touched the bell itself. Likewise, 'lobotomy knife' refers to a class of instruments. But holding a lobotomy knife that was used in procedures on people that destroyed their frontal lobe provides direct experience of those people. Touching the thing itself is a sensory experience. Sensory thinking – thinking through your senses – does not follow the same syntax or logic as thinking through words.[5]

There are pitfalls with objects, of course. Objects can be misleading. Consequently, when working with objects, it is essential to find similar examples for comparison. This is often difficult because the candidates for comparison are scattered: in museums, homes, private collections, on eBay. Locating them is further complicated because they can be classified in any number of ways. An orthotic shoe might be a shoe, crippled apparel, an orthotic, a club-foot device, or a cobbler's craft piece. It is also tempting to interpret the object in hand as representative of all others. A willow wood articulated lower limb could become what everyone used without corroborative evidence of its typicality. And because the wooden leg looks crude and feels heavy to us today, in our plastic and carbon fibre world, it is tempting to judge the object in terms of the present and assume that the long-ago user found it heavy, too. But perhaps the user was so pleased with the mobility it allowed that its weight was immaterial. The task of a museum worker is to figure out how to link objects to objects instead of objects to words.

Disability, perhaps more than any other subject, is relational. Even the authority to define one's disability is dispersed across family, community, the state and healthcare providers. Needs and accommodation are met through interdependent negotiations. People with disabilities live in a web of relationships, in family configurations composed of biological members and paid attendants, in institutions where they interact with staff and peers, in schools, on playgrounds with other kids and their care-givers and with all manner of connections to power and resources. Disability is grounded in relationships. The relationships are obvious in the material culture, such as clothing, medical maintenance accessories, and the aids for daily activities that require assistance. A sippy cup, designed to prevent spills, implies that the person filling it is not the same as the person using it. A flexible straw is suggestive but not confirmatory of assistance. Ownership of clothing with Velcro very likely accompanies other objects designed for ease of use, such as grabbers, vegetable peelers or quick-top pill bottles.

Subversion

The display of objects in a museum setting has a meta-context, as well. Museums are a form of knowledge performance that originated in the west as an off-shoot of colonialism, in the eighteenth century. By the twentieth century, museums had spread over the globe, taking with them the complicated issues of representation, plunder, power, authority, legitimacy and memory. The ethical struggles around collecting and displaying exotic others are particularly vital to disability content. If the curators are not people with disabilities, authority to represent the experience of others and authenticity of interpretation are areas of contention. Who is imagining the context and writing the interpretive label is both an ethical and professional matter. With historical evidence, imagination is always a factor in its analysis. The cultural authority of museums includes an additional dimension when the curator does not share direct embodied experience with the people interpreted. In addition, having one particular experience with a disability does not give a curator or scholar expertise in other experiences. Artifacts vividly capture this divide. For example, whether or not a cane collapses has instrumental meaning for a person who is blind. Someone who uses a scooter for mobility might not find that design feature to be notable.

Museums also share an intellectual heritage with early hospitals, creating an unfortunate intellectual hurdle for interpreting the lives of people with disabilities. Modern museums and hospitals emerged during the same era of scientific curiosity when exploration of the planet, other cultures and the human body were filled with low hanging fruit that could be rotely picked, uncomplicated by concerns for social justice or ethics. Physicians found early hospitals to be a fecund site for comparison and study of bodies and pathologies not previously possible. Sick people became 'cases' as effortlessly as foreigners became 'specimens'. Museums gathered and displayed artifacts in ways that encouraged new observations, insights and avenues of inquiry. The resulting wealth of knowledge confirmed the importance of 'objective', scientific analysis of humans through the aegis of experts, whether they were physicians and scientists, or curators and keepers.

Although their origins may be suspect, grounded as they are in pillage, privilege and exploitation of the notorious 'Other', the museum form has an important and redeemable role for modern culture. Artifacts, and the exhibitions that display them, operationalize and make concrete human experiences so that others can imagine, learn from, and connect with them. One of the core functions of exhibitions is to hold topics up for examination and discussion. Museums give visitors things to think about and are forums for conversation. Docents in the 2005 exhibition 'Whatever happened to polio?' at the Smithsonian's National Museum of American History reported that visitors stayed two to three times longer in the hall than expected and engaged them in discussions about their memories of polio. As curator, I received emails about photographs in the exhibition, usually from younger visitors convinced that a family member whom they had heard stories about was shown. So powerful was their experience of history within the exhibition, that they projected themselves into the stories through the photographs, willing themselves into a shared past. On several occasions, I observed visitors moved to tears and overcome with emotion when looking at artifacts. Many of them wrote comment cards, to keep the conversation going or to punctuate their private experience with testimonial. The surrounding wall of one gallery had a running panel of casual photographs, framed like a family photo album. Visitors spent long minutes staring, pointing and examining the images. The museum context gave them licence to stare at the people which polite etiquette would otherwise forbid.

Museum exhibitions that focus upon or integrate the history of people with disabilities carry a double burden. They must educate visitors away from their prejudices and negative assumptions about people as well as provide appealing content that can engage those not otherwise inclined to attend. Encouraging visitors to relinquish their stereotypes while presenting new frameworks, concepts and even language for understanding people with disabilities is especially complicated because many aspects of past oppression and discriminatory behaviour are still acceptable (Sandell and Dodd, this volume; Dodd *et al.*, this volume). This is all the more difficult because of the nature of the marketplace and competition for tourists' bodies. A clever curator and designer can turn stereotypes and assumptions on their head, propelling the visitor inside the experience of someone they might otherwise pity or ignore. For example, the disgust some visitors feel about artificial eyes might lead to curiosity and understanding when the acrylic eye has the logo of a football team laminated on it. In a willing museum, aversion can be turned into subversion.[6]

Activism and conscience

Museums are one of the few places where large and diverse audiences encounter the variety and complexity of human experience. Because the basis of museums is sensual learning – all the senses are enlisted – what is learned is visceral and often non-verbal, as well as pedagogical in the traditional, textual method. Museum education is learning of a different sort. It is not guided by books or a classroom setting with an instructor, which is the strength of schools and universities. Gallery learning is unguided and capricious. Because the senses are so active in a museum, the immediacy of museum learning carries the possibility of creating disability awareness and consciousness with more lasting effect than simply reading about or hearing a lecture on the subject. Museums can bring disability studies to life and plant the seeds of understanding that support social change.

Museums, in this sense, have more in common with social activists than classroom professors. In a museum, visitors encounter the unexpected first hand and 'in the flesh'. People can keep a distance when things are found only in prose – mere shadows of what they are in the wild. When found face-to-face, sensual components of learning are activated and information is non-verbally absorbed. This immediacy gives museums cognitive and emotional affinity with street activists. The personal and unexpected encounter with a real object, or a passionate activist, instructs along a different dendritic path than the cooler verbal one. This difference is easily apparent after an hour of observing visitors in a museum gallery.

Exhibiting the history of disability also has much in common with museums of conscience. Both entities address human behaviours that can be controversial, painful and fraught. Both kinds of exhibition dwell on the boundary between advocacy and scholarship. And both display knowledge about the world that is essential for the wellbeing of marginalized groups.

In the United States, few museums have included disability content in exhibitions. Even sites that might properly have an affinity with disability because of their missions to expose discrimination and hatred, such as museums of tolerance and conscience, generally have little or nothing related to disability. For example, the Museum of Tolerance in Los Angeles has two permanent exhibitions; one devoted to global civil rights and the other to the Holocaust. Neither one includes the struggles of people with disabilities for rights and social justice. The museum's film on crimes against humanity, entitled 'In Our Time', includes abuses in Sudan, Armenia, the Soviet Gulag, Cambodia, by the Nazis, and the murder of journalist Daniel Pearl but nothing on sterilization of and experimentation on people with disabilities or involuntary commitment to asylums, violence and discrimination against people or Nazi atrocities committed on them. The Lower East Side Tenement Museum in New York is similarly silent on disability. The Holocaust Memorial Museum in Washington DC mounted an excellent although temporary exhibition in 2005, *Deadly Medicine*, that chronicled the history of Nazi eugenics related to extermination of Jewish people and people with disabilities.

In 1999, the International Coalition of Historic Site Museums of Conscience[7] formed to promote understanding and awareness of past atrocities and intolerance. There are currently seventeen members. One member site is related to the history of disability. The Hadamar memorial in Germany commemorates the thousands of people with disabilities put to death under Nazism.[8] The Coalition pushes for confronting difficult and contentious issues, often those of the relatively recent past, such as Apartheid in South Africa and the 'disappeared' in Argentina, and emphasizes the need for interpretive participation by people with competing viewpoints. Members also strive to prepare visitors to deal with the sensitive, often politically charged issues depicted. All of the members share an interest in broadening civic engagement around human rights. These are the same concerns of those who teach and interpret the history of disability. There is much work to be done so that institutions promoting tolerance come to understand disability as fundamental to their missions.

One of the pervasive traumatic contemporary issues where this is taking place is that of cemetery reclamation. In the nineteenth century and for most of the twentieth, state institutions typically buried asylum and hospital inmates in graves marked by numbers, rather than names and dates (Plate 19.1). People were warehoused under generally poor conditions and the grave-markers, intended to facilitate record keeping, reflect the status of people living within the institutions. Their status was similar to other displaced, stateless persons such as illegal immigrants or homeless people, without legal standing and socially dead. Elsewhere, similar mass and anonymous gravesites have been designated as locations of conscience, such as the northern sector of Santiago's General Cemetery, where Pinochet's victims were buried. The quest to repatriate P.O.W. remains from Viet Nam and North Korea is another expression of the pervasive drive to affirm the identity of fellow humans who have suffered at the hands of other humans. In the 1990s, activist groups in the United States began reclaiming the unmarked graves in hospital cemeteries and placing markers on them that included names and dates.[9]

As is true with exhibitions on issues of human rights and conscience, the visitor's emotional response to disability is key. Visitors may already know most of the content or be aware of the important issues interpreted but seeing artifacts and images often brings an unexpected emotional intensity for them. The emotions may range from depression and aversion to inspiration and joy. Most visitors hope for and expect an emotional impact from exhibitions, in addition to learning something. But when is depression a good thing? When is inspiration counter-productive? What role does advocacy play in the content of exhibitions about historically discriminated-against groups? In the classroom, guided discussion, assigned readings, and guest speakers lead students to deeper understanding and provide space for emotional responses to ebb and flow through ongoing examination. A gallery impersonally engages a visitor for a few minutes. They then take their emotional state to the next floor, into the elevator, or the gift shop. In the process, they digest what they have encountered and begin to make sense of it. They also may have replaced disturbing information with the more amenable by the time they re-board the bus. The educational impact of an exhibition cannot be measured by an exam.[10]

The exhibition of disability also relates to the anthropological dilemmas of interpreting culturally sensitive materials. The Smithsonian's Natural History Museum has the heads of five Maori clans people. They are sequestered in a vault and special permission is required from the clan for viewing them. The spiritual significance of the heads and their careful tattooing gives them unique power and value. Human remains, such as bones, shrunken heads, skin and artifacts that contain them carry ritual and sacred power.[11] The potential for powerful emotional and spiritual response resides in artifacts related to disability, as well. Leg braces, for example, have been described by wearers as intensely personal artifacts, imbued with the owner's sweat and other body fluids, dinged and damaged from use. One person compared the display of her leg braces to putting her underwear into a public showcase. Similar sensitivities arise in the display of lobotomy knives, straitjackets and corsets. In 2004, a member of a medical sciences storage room tour at the National Museum of American History declined to participate because he was terrified of encountering an iron lung, so horrific were his childhood memories of polio epidemics.

The nature of their use and the potentially painful consequences of encountering artifacts in an exhibition raise ongoing questions about how to collect such artifacts, how to document and contextualize them, and how to display them. This is especially difficult when the curator has little or no life experience with disability or is not familiar with basic concepts in disability studies. Educating others is one of the primary tasks of a curator as well as a classroom teacher. Perhaps common desire will lead to common purpose and vocabulary between both groups.

Notes

1 See also Thelen and Rosenzweig (1998).
2 For an account of some of the recent marketplace ins and outs, see Sturken (2007).
3 For more on the role of museums in public life, see Harrison (2007); Hudson (1987); Bennett (1995).

4 For more on approaches to understanding material culture see, for example, Alberti (2005); Csikszentmihalyi and Rochberg-Halton (1985); Tilley (1991); Appadurai (1986); Kouwenhoven (1982); Douglas and Isherwood (1996); Hoskins (1998); Belk (1988); Lubar and Kingery (1993).

5 The non-verbal power of objects is discussed in McCracken (1990: 104–17).

6 For more on representing disability in museums, see Sandell (2007) and Dodd *et al.* (2008).

7 The organization has since been renamed The International Coalition of Sites of Conscience. See http://www.sitesofconscience.org.

8 A report on Nazi extermination of people with disabilities was produced as part of the Disability Holocaust Project. The report serves as an activist call to include the history of people with disabilities whenever the Jewish Holocaust is interpreted. See Disability Rights Advocates 1999.

9 See, for example, Shapiro 2000: 62.

10 For more on visitor reactions to emotionally difficult material see Doering and Pekarik 1996 and Sandell 2007.

11 For more on collecting culturally sensitive objects see Gulliford 1996; Kirshenblatt-Gimblett 1991 and Messenger 1989.

References

Alberti, S. (2005) 'Objects and the museum', *Isis,* 96: 559–71.

American Association of Museums (2001) *Trust and Education, Americans' Perceptions of Museums: Key Findings of the Lake, Snell, Perry February 2001 Survey*, Washington, DC: American Association of Museums.

Appadurai, A. (1986) *The Social Life of Things: Commodities in Cultural Perspective*, Cambridge: Cambridge University Press.

Belk, R. (1988) 'Possessions and the extended self', *Journal of Consumer Research,* 15: 139–68.

Bennett, T. (1995) *The Birth of the Museum: History, Theory, Politics*, London: Routledge.

Csikszentmihalyi, M. and Rochberg-Halton, E. (1985) *The Meaning of Things: Domestic Symbols and the Self*, Cambridge: Cambridge University Press.

Disability Rights Advocates (1999) *Forgotten Crimes: The Holocaust and People with Disabilities*, Oakland, CA: Disability Rights Activists.

Dodd, J., Sandell, R., Jolly, D. and Jones, C. (eds) (2008) *Rethinking Disability Representation in Museums and Galleries*, Leicester: University of Leicester.

Doering, Z. and Pekarik, A. (1996) *Assessment of Informal Education in Holocaust Museums*, Washington, DC: Institutional Studies Office, Smithsonian Institution.

Douglas, M. and Isherwood, B. (1996) *The World of Goods: Towards an Anthropology of Consumption*, London: Routledge.

Gulliford, A. (1996) 'Bones of contention: the repatriation of Native American human remains', *The Public Historian,* 18: 119–43.

Harrison, L. (2007) *The Temple and the Forum: The American Museum and Cultural Authority*, Tuscaloosa: Alabama University Press.

Hoskins, J. (1998) *Biographical Objects: How Things Tell the Stories of People's Lives*, New York: Routledge.

Hudson, K. (1987) *Museums of Influence*, Cambridge: Cambridge University Press.

Kirshenblatt-Gimblett, B. (1991) 'Objects of ethnography' in I. Karp and S. Levine (eds), *Exhibiting Cultures: The Poetics and Politics of Museum Display*, Washington, DC: Smithsonian Institution Press, pp. 386–443.

Kouwenhoven, J. (1982) 'American Studies: words or things?' in T. Schlereth (ed.), *Material Culture Studies in America*, Nashville, TN: AASLH Press, pp. 79–92.

Lubar, S. and Kingery, W. D. (eds) (1993) *History From Things: Essays on Material Culture*, Washington DC: Smithsonian Institution Press.

McCracken, G. T. (1990) 'The evocative power of things' in G. McCracken (ed.), *Culture and Consumption,* Bloomington: Indiana University Press, pp. 104–17.

Messenger, P. (1989) *The Ethics of Collecting Cultural Property*, Albuquerque: University of New Mexico Press.

Sandell, R. (2007) *Museums, Prejudice and the Reframing of Difference*, London and New York: Routledge.

Shapiro, J. (2000) 'Marking forgotten lives: old mental institution graves are named at last', *U.S. News and World Report*, October 9: 62.

Sturken, M. (2007) *Tourists of History: Memory, Kitsch, and Consumerism from Oklahoma City to Ground Zero*, Durham, NC: Duke University Press.

Thelen, D. and Rosenzweig, R. (1998) *The Presence of the Past: Popular Uses of History in America*, New York: Columbia University Press.

Tilley, C. (1991) *Material Culture and Text: The Art of Ambiguity*, London: Routledge.

INDEX

280